The Force of Obedience

The Force of Obedience

The Political Economy of Repression in Tunisia

BÉATRICE HIBOU

Translated by Andrew Brown

polity

First published in French as *La force de l'obéissance* © Editions La Découverte, Paris, France, 2006

This English edition © Polity Press, 2011

The translation of this work was supported by funding from the Centre d'Etudes et de Recherches Internationales (CERI) de SciencesPo and Fonds d'Analyse des Sociétés Politiques (FASOPO)

Polity Press
65 Bridge Street
Cambridge CB2 1UR, UK

Polity Press
350 Main Street
Malden, MA 02148, USA

ISBN-13: 978-0-7456-5179-8 (hardback)
ISBN-13: 978-0-7456-5180-4 (paperback)

A catalogue record for this book is available from the British Library.

Typeset in 10 on 12 pt Stempel Garamond
by Toppan Best-set Premedia Limited
Printed and bound in Great Britain by MPG Books Group Limited, Bodmin, Cornwall

The publisher has used its best endeavours to ensure that the URLs for external websites referred to in this book are correct and active at the time of going to press. However, the publisher has no responsibility for the websites and can make no guarantee that a site will remain live or that the content is or will remain appropriate.

Every effort has been made to trace all copyright holders, but if any have been inadvertently overlooked the publisher will be pleased to include any necessary credits in any subsequent reprint or edition.

For further information on Polity, visit our website:
www.politybooks.com

Contents

Full Contents

Preface to the English Edition

On 14 January 2011, Ben Ali fled Tunisia. For nearly a month, since 17 December, a huge protest movement had shaken the country, initially among young people and in peripheral regions, starting in Sidi Bouzid and gradually affecting all generations, all social classes and all parts of the country. Everyone knows how the humiliation suffered by the young Mohamed Bouazizi, a street seller who became a martyr and national hero, had led him to set himself alight: this sparked daily demonstrations in support of him, which were brutally suppressed. As a result, the capital was engulfed by revolt, and the sovereign was forced to leave. The palace revolution which sounded the death knell for the reign of Ben Ali was orchestrated by the general staff of the army and a section of the elite in power for over twenty years; it aimed at pre-empting this social upheaval so as to prevent it from being transformed into a revolution.

The present book was written between 2004 and 2005 and published in French in 2006. It gives some indication of how an extraordinary social movement was able to develop despite tight control by police and Party, leading to a profound political change in Tunisia itself, and also dragging Egypt and perhaps other countries in the region along in its wake. My book also brings out the real challenges that now face Tunisians. For it is not in itself the departure of Ben Ali and the 'clans' that has radically altered the modes of government and the exercise of power in Tunisia. Nothing has been definitively decided, and this is why I prefer to speak neither of revolution nor of democratic transition. It is too early for that, even though the possibility is still open. The real transformation, which is without any doubt a fundamental one, resides in the disappearance of fear. In the public space, and not only in the secret space of their private lives, people are talking, defying the police, expressing their joys, their fears, their expectations and their demands. But as far as everything else is concerned, the essential aspects of the 'Ben Ali regime' are still largely in place.

What is happening in Tunisia is important, over and above what this country in North Africa actually represents, with its small population, lacking any income derived from the economy, energy sources or geopolitical clout, or any dominant position in the region. These days, it benefits from the impact of the Tunisian 'revolution' on the rest of the region, in Egypt of course, but also elsewhere in the Arab world and sub-Saharan Africa. But history had already shown how this 'little country' could serve as an example. On independence, the model of the single party as established by Bourguiba, justified by the desire to build the nation and consolidate an interventionist state, inspired the regimes set up in many other recently independent countries; likewise, the Supreme Commander, Bourguiba himself, took over for his own ends the nationalist, secularist reformism of Kemal Atatürk, transmitting this theme to the Arab world. The medical coup d'état of Ben Ali on 7 November 1987, when Bourguiba was summarily declared too ill to rule, was at the time presented as a break with the latter's authoritarian tendencies, and inspired the wave of democratic demands in several African countries two years later. Now we know what the result was, in Tunisia and in the rest of the continent: the restoration or indeed consolidation of authoritarian rule generally triumphed. And even if we can wax ironic at this 'exemplary' role and the race to be 'first' claimed by many Tunisians, the fact remains that the analysis of the modes of government and the exercise of power in this country helps us to grasp what is happening in many other situations.

The Tunisian revolt: a demand for inclusion, justice and dignity

In fact, contrary to the analysis widespread among political commentators, in the media, or among former members of the opposition, political domination was not embodied mainly in the absolute power of Ben Ali, in the rapacity of those in the President's family, or in the way that violence and police control made all political life impossible. Opponents were very few in number. Even if their repression (or even their elimination) had important effects, by spreading fear and persuading people that their example was not to be copied, we need more than this potential violence to explain the obedience shown by Tunisians for decades. This obedience was, much more profoundly, the result of a link forged between, on the one hand, the latent violence relayed by the police and the tight supervision of the single party, and, on the other, various powerful mechanisms of inclusion. It is the political economy of domination which this book dissects – a political economy that mainly operates by means of the insertion of disciplinary and coercive techniques of power into the most everyday economic and social structures and practices. Most often, these measures are neither violently introduced nor imposed from on high, but they ensue from the dynamic interplay of arrangements, negotiations and compromises at the basis of what I have called 'a security pact'. By means of this, the state attempts to forestall any kind of uncertainty, risk, or danger, and it is in this respect legitimate, being the response to a desire for the state, a desire for protection, a desire for consumption and modernity among the population. Two significant qualifications need to be made, if we are to understand recent developments. On the one hand, accepting this pact as a functional device is not the same as accepting the modes of government and submission that go with it. There could still be discontent, criticism, even exasperation. But these were always expressed in the private sphere. These constraints and this coercion were, however, considered as acceptable since they were inseparable from other elements considered as positive, like standards of living and lifestyles, access to the consumer society, and a certain emphasis placed on national unity. On the other hand, the pact set out to bring the whole population within its scope, but of course it could not achieve this objective; there were fault lines at its heart, opened up by inequality and exclusion.

The protest movement which developed in December 2010 and ended up in a widespread popular revolt, followed by the departure of Ben Ali, was made possible, in fact, by a weakening in the mechanisms of social integration and the decline of the security pact. It is no coincidence that it was young people in marginalized regions who comprised the spearhead of opposition. Since the end of the 1990s, hidden by quite decent growth rates, the economic landscape had been worsening in terms of job creation, and the situation grew even bleaker after 2008. Unemployment figures were not open to discussion, even though official data (the figure remained stable at around 14–15%) aimed to conceal the problem. Every year there were some 140,000 new job-seekers, as against just 60,000 to 65,000 jobs being created, mainly localized in the greater Tunis area and along the coast.[1] There is no doubt that, every year, the security pact found it more and more difficult to integrate young people, especially those in the interior of the country. In Sidi Bouzid, Gafsa, and Benguerdane, and at all the demonstrations, slogans systematically voiced the demand for work, calling for jobs or quite simply for the possibility of gaining access to the labour market. This quest for inclusion – necessary if you were to live, increase your well-being, or at least lead a decent life – was expressed in terms of *khobza* ('bread' in Arabic) as Hamza Meddeb pointed out in a remarkable analysis long before the events of December 2010 and January 2011:[2] young people expressed their desire to satisfy their vital needs just like other sectors of the population. Bread is the pre-eminent example of a normality that must be accessible to all, or which should legitimately be so. And this is especially true since official speeches for over a decade had been constantly vaunting the Tunisian 'economic miracle'.[3] These speeches had an effect that was not paradoxical (it was perfectly logical), but was certainly quite odd and unforeseen by the rulers: they aroused expectations, created hopes, and fuelled frustrations.[4] As Michel de Certeau showed in a quite different context, the discourse that makes people believe is the one that takes away what it urges them to believe in, or never delivers what it promises.[5]

However, the security pact should not be understood in purely material terms, and the break-up of the mechanisms of social insertion does not explain everything. The protest movement, with its broad extent and its deep rootedness in society, was also and perhaps above all born of the sense of injustice and humiliation. Here too there was no denying the slogans: they emphasized the sought-after dignity and respect. The generational effect was fundamental, and not just in economic terms: the demand for inclusion was also a demand for recognition on the part of a generation subjected more than any other category of the population to police violence, suffering from the censorship of the media, with a keener sense of the injustice of unequal division of wealth and the victim of corruption on a daily basis.[6] In other words, exclusion was also felt in terms of morality and citizenship, with young people experiencing all these practices as a lack of recognition and respect. These feelings went a long way back, and did not spring to life in Sidi Bouzid, on 17 December 2010, when Mohamed Bouazizi was once again the victim of extortion on the part of the authorities and was slapped on the face by a policewoman. For several months, protest movements had been developing, even though they had been contained up until then: wild and illegal strikes in textile factories and the tourist sector; more isolated demonstrations against crooked bosses; or more structured protest movements, some of them quite significant, as was the case in the mining area of Gafsa between January and July 2008,[7] or those in Benguerdane in July and August 2010.[8] This also highlights the importance of contingency in any political event. If Ben Ali's departure was made possible by protests occurring in Sidi Bouzid (and not by those in Gafsa or Benguerdane), this was simultaneously because there was an effect of accumulated bitterness and frustration, because certain gestures appeared indecent (such as the visit paid by Ben Ali to the sick bed of Mohamed Bouazizi) and because police violence at peaceful demonstrations and even at funeral processions for the victims of the repression was fierce. Public authorities did not understand the full measure of the revolt; they could not interpret it or give any meaning to it. In fact, domination is not a controlled exercise of power, strategies, or certain decisions; it is a process that is at once uncertain, unfinished and partial, involving many different actions, and varying and concomitant understandings of reality. The revolt that was transformed into a political change was a perfect example of the 'singular randomness of events':[9] the crack in the wall that all these untimely gestures and actions opened up was less the result of a decision properly speaking – police repression – than of the unexpected and non-programmed action of human beings, of the life of conflicts and the reversal of relations of force, of the unforeseen, of the indefinite nature of things, of the 'insolence' of daily life, and of the ambiguity of words and deeds.[10]

But if the protest did assume such significance, this is also because the despair and sense of humiliation felt by young people in the interior regions joined forces with other frustrations, other discontents, and other demands: the business community suffered from the rapacity of the 'clans' and the ups and downs of an administration and a judicial system that took orders from on high; some found it difficult to live under the tight supervision of their country by the police and the single party, others suffered from the total absence of press freedom and freedom of information and public expression; broad sectors of the middle class deeply resented the way the process of upward social mobility had been brought to a halt for them or their children, when it was still a vaunted feature of Tunisian life (some had indeed suffered from a drop in social standing) . . . For behind the sense of unanimity, the obligatory consensus, the rituals of the single party and the personalization of power, many other things lay concealed.

Even if the silence was massive and allowed this unanimity to exist, the acquiescence of the population could mean anything except acceptance.[11] Ben Ali's photo could be seen everywhere; in public spaces, the streetlamps, shutters and other objects were painted purple, the President's favourite colour; certificates of payment into the presidential charity (especially the notorious National Solidarity Fund, or '26.26') were put in pretty frames and hung on the walls; people went to demonstrations and applauded on cue. But these signs did not express any belief in the benefits of the President's 'solicitude', they did not praise his 'progressiveness', they did not declare the 'faith' of the citizens in a protective regime. They were merely a way of participating in a formalized ritual, thereby showing that people knew the system and that they recognized its mechanisms: such behaviour showed that they knew (full well) how to behave in a ritualized context so as to maintain or even improve their social status without thereby accepting or rejecting the rules of the political game.[12] The coexistence of entirely ritualized formalities and rules with the meanings which the populace gave to these rituals thus provided the dominated with significant room for manoeuvre by allowing the flourishing of new and original practices different from the dominant official norms, opening the way to often invisible transformations which nonetheless widened the field of possibility and left room for the unpredictable . . . right up until the 'revolution'. These slippages of meaning and this room for manoeuvre became more visible as the conditions enabling the acceptance of compromise broke up, and as obedience, not previously experienced as submission, became intolerable. Modes of government, concrete measures and, in particular, practices of power did indeed often make repression a painless, or even invisible and insidious process, precisely because they also rested on the positive elements embodied in responses to popular demands. For instance, social policies enabled inequalities to be reduced, solidarities to be expressed, and social integration to be achieved – but at the same time they brought about control, disciplining, punishment, and reward. Those who benefited from these policies did not necessarily register this coercive dimension; they did not necessarily interpret aid as a possibility of surveillance, though this does not mean that it was any the less present. But the 'force of obedience' can weaken or even vanish when these positive elements (inclusion, a response to demands for respect, protection, and economic and social security) fade or vanish, allowing the coercive or even violent dimension of these measures and practices to become apparent. It is in these terms, too, that the extraordinary social movement that led to the departure of President Ben Ali needs to be understood.

The challenges of the future: emerging from the 'miracle' and the political economy of repression

The effects of the demonstrations, the protests, and more generally the social upheaval that followed Mohamed Bouazizi's desperate act are enormous. They are best seen in the lifting of a taboo: that of fear and imposed silence. But to speak of revolution is certainly premature, quite simply because, as regards the modes of government, there is, as I write, not (as yet) any break. Even less can one speak of 'democratic transition', because the latter needs time and radical transformation, especially of the direction of the political economy and the exercise of domination analysed by this book. I would like to sketch out the challenges which the new political era needs to confront, in particular the knots which this political economy needs to undo for any real process of democratization to be successful.

The place of the RCD (Rassemblement Constitutionnel Démocratique) is probably one of the biggest issues, since the single party lies at the heart of the security pact. The RCD has indisputably deep roots in society. The single party has not only played a police and surveillance function, but via its cells, the district committees and associations, it has acted as a social mediator. Its different levels have simultaneously transmitted central power, relayed modes of government and political regulation, and been places of redistribution, clientelism, enrichment, and upward mobility – a space for mediation and a vehicle for grievances. This is why the population has placed such high hopes in the single party: even if we cast doubt on the figure of two million members (i.e. a fifth of the population, or one out of two active members), there is no doubt that the RCD is deeply implanted in society. Many people have taken advantage of this system thanks to social programmes, sanitary caravans, gifts for Eid, and the obtaining of various kinds of authorization (taxi permits, building permits, opening a shop, a restaurant or a bar, in short all activity whether legal or illegal), the acquisition of approval and the facilitation of access to the administration, and the granting of statutes clearing the way for aid. The RCD thus appears as a network of interests and clients, providing jobs, bursaries, administrative facilities, aid of every kind, lodging, banking facilities, and free health and transport passes … Furthermore, the RCD's active members have been able to enrich themselves directly and embark on a process of upward social mobility. Thus, in six or seven years, the president of a district cell could become a town worthy and build himself a prestigious house or open a profitable business. As one can see, material and symbolic interests are too powerful and historically constituted for them to vanish without any tensions arising. It is known that the RCD members were mainly passive, supporting the party not as active members but so as not to appear on the side of the opposition. But the minority of active members have everything to lose. It is likely that, with certain members of the police forces, they were part of the militia that terrified Tunisians during the first days after the downfall of Ben Ali. It is indeed disturbing to see that the feared violence and chaos almost disappeared on the formation of a Government of National Unity dominated by the RCD. The single party still represents something positive for whole swathes of the population. The instrumentalization by politicians of questions of security, violence, stability and chaos is highly likely, especially since former members of the RCD are not the only ones to be playing this game, as is suggested by the positions adopted by the army and especially by the opposition parties that have agreed to enter the first provisional government. This theme – the rejection of violence and adventurism – is of great potential significance within Tunisian society as a whole. The reformist tradition, which all political tendencies claim to represent, does indeed emphasize the values of temperance, the rejection of violence and the maturity of the Tunisian people. It is clear that the scarecrow of disorder can easily be brandished, to the advantage of the RCD or its eventual successor. The dismantling of the single party, and even more the disappearance of the symbiosis between this, the administration and the state, thus constitutes one of the major issues of the current period. And this raises social problems – problems of political economy, as we have just seen, but also political problems. How, in concrete terms, and with what can the RCD be replaced in remote regions, at the local level, in situations where the administration and even the police were not present but were represented by Party members? How can real estate, goods, civil servants, and financial resources that had to some extent been privatized to the profit of the RCD be returned to the state without any due accounting? What is to be done with the party networks that structured the whole public space? It is not a change of name or the dissolution of the central committee (or even the formal dissolution of the party itself) that will create a new state of affairs, but rather the whole restructuring of the political field. Likewise, the political economy of mediation and inclusion needs to be re-thought. These two processes are not simple, and inevitably require time.

A second issue is corruption. In the media-inspired frenzy of events, and in a simplistic vision of Tunisian despotism, the rapacity of the 'clans', i.e. the families linked to President Ben Ali, has been stigmatized as one of the mainsprings of the old regime. But the analysis of the mechanisms of inclusion that I put forward in the following pages suggests that they are far more complex. In particular, however significant it may have been, the question of rapacity in high places cannot be either overestimated or understood outside the wider processes that are commonly called corruption. The rapacity of the 'clans' was first and foremost a form of extortion imposed on pre-existing economic activities. The family members composing them (essentially the brothers, children, nephews and sons-in-law of Zine El Abidine Ben Ali and his wife Leïla Trabelsi) were never business people, and were never considered as such. They merely took advantage of their positions of power to build up a position where they could accumulate wealth, by monopolizing the role of intermediaries in privatization, in import-export operations, in access to public markets, and in access to information. They also proceeded by intimidation, forcibly obtaining percentages of capital in successful businesses, and they indulged in strategic marriages to broaden their field of intervention. At the time, this corruption merely involved the most important Tunisian businessmen (or businessmen operating in Tunisia). The latter must indeed be seen separately, and several of them had an ambiguous position vis-à-vis those in the President's close family; they were often the victims of the family's rapacity, but they quite commonly sought the latter's support, at least initially, in the hope of seeing their own businesses prosper.[13] The population as a whole, however, was not directly and materially concerned by this rapacity, even if the impudence of the 'family' and the immorality of its behaviour were felt by everyone to be a lack of respect, a conception unworthy of the state – witness the way that certain slogans were repeated at demonstrations. On the other hand, the question of daily corruption constitutes a real challenge for the populace as a whole. It was also central in the economy of negotiations, arrangements and compromises that constituted a golden age for the Tunisian 'miracle' and the country's security pact. It took the shape of various interventions: calling an acquaintance to help you form a judgment, activating a network of friends, locals or professionals to get round a rule, mobilizing the party to avoid having to pay off a debt or tax, and using family relations to obtain a favour. But it also assumed a financial form: you had to pay in order to land a job or obtain a bursary, get your ID papers in time, open a business, sell in the streets, participate in contraband networks . . . The stigmatization of the 'great' was carried out by former opponents and certain sectors of the UGTT (Union générale tunisienne du travail) who had long made a hobbyhorse of this; it also resulted from a facile and over-generalized reading of Tunisia in terms of dictatorship or absolute power. But it was not these practices which directly mortified the future demonstrators, and fuelled their sense of injustice. These young people faced this economy of 'making do' and inclusion by the margins – an economy kept going by the corruption of the police, the civil service and, especially, RCD members.[14] Like rapacity, but in another way, this 'small-scale' corruption was a mode of government that formed part of the 'insidious leniency' whose role and operation I examine in this book. Corruption protects and includes, it allows active people to get involved in business, to succeed, or quite simply to live or survive; but, simultaneously, it disciplines and controls, it normalizes things in the guise of participation in a system of exchange, of privilege, of special favours, which does not embrace merely the 'great' but the whole of the population. Not all of this disappeared with the flight of Ben Ali and his mafia of acolytes, even if exposure and criticism will now find a hearing more easily.

The 'economic miracle' constitutes the site of a third challenge. This discourse, as everyone knows, was the result of a spin put on economic data; associated with an absence of debate, it comprised a fundamental mechanism of the exercise of domination. Not only did this discourse conceal the real state of the Tunisian economy, but it was aimed at normalizing behaviour and thought by constructing a fiction: that of a stable, financially secure, macroeconomically efficient, and socially just Tunisia. If a basis for democracy is to be laid, this fiction of unanimity needs to disappear. To a certain degree, this is already the case, since the protests and the popular movement have largely been fuelled by an exposure of the prevalent inequalities, injustice, unemployment, and more generally of the difficulties that faced people in their ordinary lives. But one thing is still a cause for disquiet: nothing has been said, up until now, even by former opponents, of the very limits of the Tunisian economic system. For the latter was set up in the 1970s and for decades produced perfectly decent results; it has indisputably been running out of steam since the end of the 1990s.[15] The dualist organization of the economy and international specialization do not make it possible to create enough jobs, nor to encourage diversification in wealth creation; the niches in the job market (mainly the textile industry and tourism) remain low-qualified and unsophisticated, aimed at the lowest segments in the hierarchy of these sectors; attempts to renew offshore activities have been marked by the same characteristics, generally taking the form of new call centres, which are undemanding in terms of the labour force they employ; redistribution policies reach their limit in a period of budgetary equilibrium, when there is a neoliberal norm in public action. Migrations, which, until the first years of the twenty-first century, constituted a real safety valve for the Tunisian economy, were largely slowed down by Tunisia's European commitments. But the perpetuation of this model was the aim of the technocrats of the Ben Ali regime who now constitute the very framework of the provisional government, beginning with the Prime Minister, Mohamed Ghannouchi. And this raises two significant problems. On the one hand, it is unlikely that these same actors, who have been in power for over a decade, or even in the case of some of them for two or three decades, are capable of changing their minds. On the other hand, and much more important, it is impossible to separate the economic from the political spheres. The pages of this book suggest, indeed, that the economy is political, and that the shape of the Tunisian economy also defines that of the exercise of domination. To follow not only political commentators and foreign partners but also the vast majority of former opponents in drawing a distinction between 'wicked' and 'filthy' law-enforcement officers and 'nice', 'clean' technocrats betrays a particularly impoverished vision of the political sphere. We here encounter a myth that is widely shared – that which envisages technocracy as an apolitical structure, able to bring about, in complete independence, an economic miracle in spite of repression, police violence, and violations of public freedoms.[16] It goes without saying that the involvement of technocrats is not in the slightest politically neutral, and that it finally leads to their participating in the economy of domination and even repression. It is also these same technocrats who set up economic, financial and social measures and mechanisms authorizing the exercise of power.

Several other changes necessary to the coming of a revolution in Tunisia, and a real democratization of the country, can be mentioned. First and foremost, of course, is the disappearance of potential police violence and the surveillance of the single party, but also the disappearance of the latent violence represented by the enforced consensus, by arbitrary measures, and by a formalist conception of a rule of law riddled by states of exception, in which the law appears less as the guarantor of a certain justice, of fundamental freedoms and humanity, than as playing a role in social engineering and facilitating economic development. We might also refer to the necessary transformation of one fundamental actor in Tunisia, namely the UGTT, whose political role has always been fundamental but ambiguous, the development of a critique of history and the reformist myth, or indeed the restructuring of the political field to enable real parties to deploy their networks throughout society and fuel a pluralism which Tunisia has practically never known. This preface is not the place for such debates. It suggests that the current situation is still entirely open and that further developments will depend on the outcome of the various tensions, conflicts, and relations of force on the ground, which not only set the former beneficiaries of the 'Ben Ali regime' against the opponents of the latter, but are also structured around faultlines defined in much more complex social, generational, geographic, political and ideological terms. By setting out some of the current issues at stake, this preface has also in particular aimed to underline how important it is, if we are to gain a better understanding of domination and repression, to take into account the political economy in which they operate rather than focusing merely on the leader and his close family.

8 February 2011

Introduction

Relations of domination, and the way domination is exercised, definitely constitute one of the most classical questions of political sociology, and one of the questions which, these days, are the object of an indisputable renewal in the very terms of analysis. And so, why should I tackle such a hackneyed theme, thereby running the risk of having my research seen as naive, pretentious, superficial, or pointless? The reason is simple: in my view, within the extremely rich range of analyses that focus on the question of domination from different angles and different fields, there is little material that considers the political economy of domination to be central. The ambition of the present work is thus to take a first step in that direction. With Tunisia as a case study, my work aims to investigate in greater depth the question of domination – and repression – on the basis of an analysis of daily life in its properly economic dynamics, taking the economic as a place of power, a non-autonomous field, and one of several sites within which the relations of force and the interplay of power can be analysed. It is not, thus, a question of analysing the economy of a political regime – of whatever type or status – but of carrying out a political analysis of the economic that will show how the most commonplace economic apparatuses [*dispositifs*] and everyday economic operations also, at the same time, play a role in the mechanisms of domination.

From this point of view, the processes at work are much more subtle than investigations couched in terms of the 'political' manipulating and instrumentalizing the 'economic', the 'politicization of the economy', the 'economy' in the service of the 'political' (or its quite widespread variant – illustrated in grossly simplistic form by the case of Tunisia – of an 'economic miracle' enabling 'political stability'), the 'political use' of the economy, or an exchange between 'political obedience' and access to 'economic advantages'. These notions all imply a separation between distinct 'spheres', the economic and the political – not to mention the social. They suggest that the relations between these 'spheres' are all one way, and they transmit a mechanistic and utilitarian vision of social relations and their dynamic interplay. The political economy which I propose is quite different: it sets out to understand the economy politically, in terms of its own techniques and mechanisms. It aims at restoring the ambiguity and incompleteness of the mechanisms and apparatuses of control and discipline, taking full account of the complexity of social relations, the plurality of practices, and the multiplicity and ambiguity of meanings that different actors attribute to these. If we are to investigate the field of analysis of the disciplinary, indeed repressive exercise of power, we thus need to delve deep into the very mechanism of the economic cogs and carry out, following Foucault's example, a 'political anatomy of the detail'[1] – while also, following Weber (an equally central inspiration) producing a political anatomy of the economic detail.

The intellectual significance of our case study, Tunisia

Going into detail means choosing a specific 'field'. This is where contemporary Tunisia struck me as an obvious choice, not merely because of my own research trajectory, but also because of the way public authorities as well as everyday actors in Tunisia emphasize the role played by the 'economic miracle' in the 'stability' of the 'regime'. I have tried to go beyond the simplistic explanations mentioned above, but have taken seriously this relation – a highly significant one, as I emphasize – between the economy and the exercise of domination. My work thus enables us, in my view, to make an advance on two important fronts in the general analysis of domination.

The first concerns the question of legitimacy. An analysis of the debates, demands, expectations, tensions, and small-scale confrontations that occur on a daily basis will evince clear points of friction that highlight – often as a kind of photographic negative – issues linked to the legitimacy and credibility of power. It will also bring out types of behaviour or ways of thinking that have been sifted out by the legitimate exercise of domination. Over and above the mere problematic of accepting a regime that seems the only possible one, the question which arises is less that of the legitimacy (or not) of a certain government than that of the nature of legitimacy – in particular, that of the criteria and mechanisms that govern the complex and heterogeneous processes of legitimization. If we pay attention to economic mechanisms and processes, we find that the latter transmit highly specific types of legitimization which operate by criteria based as much on mechanisms of inclusion as on the effectiveness of power in terms such as: success; economic well-being or a decent standard of living; stability and enhancement of living conditions; the protection or restoration of the state and its sovereignty; and the principles of national grandeur and influence. The case of Tunisia shows that a detailed analysis of the mechanisms of legitimacy and its criteria brings out the existence of certain practices that enable us better to grasp the dynamics involved in the exercise of domination, the interplay between different actors, the transformations of power relations and modes of government, and the representations, *imaginaires*, and subjectivities of the political sphere.

The Tunisian example that I put forward in this book brings out a second major theme, that of a systematic critique of intentionality. The banality of explanations in terms of conspiracy or secrecy is an illustration of the significance of intentionalist understandings of the political on the part of the actors within a given society. The same applies to analyses centred on the responsibility of the 'Head of State', the 'ruling class', the police, the single party, or this or that category of the population when it comes to repression. It is equally true of ideas about the role of an economic policy or measure in the exercise of domination. Although it is rarely appealed to as such, the intentionalist hypothesis underlies those analyses which 'politicize' the interplay of actors, arguing in terms of exchange and compensation, and highlighting the instrumentalizations and the capacity for anticipation and adaptation which we find in existing regimes. If we focus on the concrete detail of economic apparatuses, on the small print of the effective procedures of domination and the practices of the relevant actors, we reach a much more ambiguous conclusion. On the one hand, it is impossible to deny the fundamental role played by the 'Head of State' and the 'upper tier of leaders', the often extreme centralization of the political and administrative organization, the arbitrary nature of decisions handed down 'from on high', the intensive use of police techniques, and the urge to control and intrude into private life. On the other hand, however, an analysis of everyday economic life highlights the tangible nature of compromises and negotiations – and hence of the intentions of other actors, following their own proper and indeed autonomous logics, as well as the element of contingency and inevitable improvisation, and the possibility of escaping from the grip of the political, if only by aloofness and indifference. We thus become aware of the additional existence of margins for manoeuvre, for a potential exercise of freedom, despite all the constraints, the shows of force and even the use of violence.

The political economy of the exercise of domination and repression in Tunisia set out in the following pages does not thus appear 'interesting in itself', but as an 'experimental field' that enables us better to understand domination and the infinite different modes of its exercise – in other words, as a 'way of producing a general anatomy' of domination.[2]

An undeniable repression

My Tunisia-based analysis is above all an attempt to understand the economic apparatuses, the mechanisms and the techniques that, in the final analysis, lead to the acceptance of a regime that is commonly called an authoritarian regime, or even a dictatorship. It focuses on the economic cogs of the exercise of power and domination that have made it possible to lead a normal life in the Tunisia of the 'Change' (which is the way the new regime designates itself), the Tunisia that, since 7 November 1987, after the 'medical coup d'état' against Bourguiba, has been presided over by General Ben Ali. It aims to detail the concrete forms assumed by the relations of force that simultaneously authorize both control and economic security, surveillance and wealth creation, 'economic miracle' and 'repression'.

All the same, the repression that can be attributed purely to the police must not be forgotten, and a quick overview of the ways it operates will also enable us to understand the interest of an analysis centred on the economic. The facts are overwhelming, and the Islamists were the first victims of this police repression, as witness the cowardly sense of relief that was felt by many 'democrats' on both sides of the Mediterranean, more attentive to defending the 'secular state' – or the idea they have of it – than the universality of human rights.

Certain documents have revealed the inhuman conditions experienced during the 1990s by the militants of the Mouvement de la Tendance Islamiste (MTI), which later became Nahda (Rebirth), and which some of them continue to suffer:[3] mistreatment and torture that have sometimes led to the death of the victims or their suicide; solitary confinement that sometimes lasts for years on end; overcrowded prisons; the absence of any bed or space to lie down; sleep deprivation; poor food and malnourishment; lack of sufficient water; the difficulty or impossibility of maintaining any contact with the outside world; poor hygiene and the spread of diseases; negligence or laxity in medical monitoring and sometimes even the complete absence of this or any medical care; development of drug addiction, the use of psychotropic and neuroleptic drugs; forced labour in conditions of near-slavery; the banning of prayer; systematic and humiliating body searches; promiscuity, sexual aggression and rape; a ban on studying or receiving letters or parcels; isolation, restriction of visiting rights and 'basket' rights (food and clothes brought by one's family), and so on. Everything is done to grind people down and dehumanize them. Political prisoners first and foremost, but also common-law prisoners who also suffer these practices in gaol, in police stations and on the premises of the Sûreté nationale and the Garde nationale, or in barracks. Prison, and the police treatment of social problems, constitute entirely independent modes of government, just like the attempt to impose public order by attacking private life and the most intimate aspects of a human being.

Things do not stop at the prison gates. On their release, ex-detainees are faced with discriminatory practices that they find even more difficult to cope with than those in gaol.[4] Three sentences excerpted from my interviews with former political prisoners express the many different dimensions of this 'very gentle' repression, which is in fact a mode of the 'state of exception [. . .] when naked life – which normally appears rejoined to the multifarious forms of social life – is explicitly put into question and revoked as the ultimate foundation of political power'.[5]

They steal our lives from us, they refuse to let us play any part in social life; this is even more serious than refusing to let us take part in political life.

We are denied any right to social life, to life full stop.

There's a constant attack on private life. When the police come into a house, when they seize your passports, ID, diplomas and medical cards [*carte de soins*]. And at any moment, even if you've been sentenced, even if you've done time in gaol, even if your case is theoretically closed, you can be summonsed, questioned, detained, re-sentenced.

On being released from gaol, a former detainee finds all his papers withdrawn, sometimes for several years: ID, social security card, passport, school and college certificates, war veteran's card. According to former political prisoners, however, the most humiliating part comes just after that. It is what is called, in Tunisia, 'administrative control': depending on the available manpower, and at the discretion of the police, with the greatest degree of arbitrariness, the former detainee has to present himself once, twice, four times a day, or even every two hours, just to show his presence and 'sign on', at a police station allotted to him – one which may be five minutes away from his home or several miles away, as is often the case.[6] In a very concrete way, these practices prevent him from finding a new job and leading a minimum social life; in other cases, he is purely and simply subject to banishment, far from his family and from his whole web of social relations. Administrative control apparently affects almost all political opponents – 90 per cent of them, according to humanitarian organizations. In juridical terms, this is a punishment which complements the main punishment. Following article 23 of the Penal Code, administrative control merely enables the authorities to designate a place of residence for a maximum period of five years; however, in practice, the police apply it on a day-to-day basis. In any case, administrative control is often doubly illegal because it is not rare to see the police applying it even without any sentence having been passed.

Everything resides in the fine detail of the mechanics of this coercive procedure, in the way it controls movement and temporality. It is, for example, the responsibility of the former detainee to buy the notebook in which he has to sign his name, even if it is the police who scrupulously look after it – or less scrupulously, at times, since it sometimes happens that the said notebook is 'lost'. Punctuality is essential: otherwise, back before the court you go. The ritual of signing is sometimes doubled, and the individual being checked has to sign not only in the local police station but also at the gendarmerie or the regional offices [*direction régionale*]. Sometimes, the office to which he is assigned may be changed without his being warned of the fact, and from then on he is obliged to make an additional trip so as not to be penalized for being late (which counts as a refusal to sign) and prosecuted. From the year 2000, certain former detainees refused to sign and were sometimes punished for this act of rebellion by being sentenced to six months in gaol.

However, this grim picture needs to be qualified somewhat. Admittedly, administrative control is one of the many and varied techniques of what is called, in French, the *stratégie du pourtour* – the 'strategy of the periphery' or 'fringe strategy' whose purpose it is to intimidate, to make an example of someone, to shape people's minds and define the outlines of the social norm.[7] In this sense, exemplarity requires a rigorous and systematic approach. But this strategy is deployed in a strongly extraverted society and within a context where the pugnacity of 'international civil society' means that a certain discretion in repression is obligatory. The public powers do not seek any publicity in this domain – and those people who are psychologically the 'strongest', those who have the means, the knowledge and the courage to protest, by their words, by mobilizing humanitarian feeling, or by engaging on hunger strikes, see the intensity of the control diminishing or even disappearing.

Social death and internal exile

Once administrative control has been removed, a return to normal life in society is still not assured. Police surveillance is systematic, including rather unorthodox measures such as police visits at any time of the day or night: they are able to search, without a warrant, every corner of your house, take away papers or demand circumstantial details about the origin of your income and any sums of money found. Or there may even be 'gratuitous' violence, such as police harassment, beatings, attacks or burglary. But these police activities are not the ones that weigh most heavily on former opponents and sympathizers with the Islamist movement. Having come into close contact with physical death, they experience, outside prison, what they themselves call a 'social death' that is often even less bearable: the extreme difficulty, or even the near-impossibility, of having a social or even a private life.

Work often lies far beyond their grasp. Former civil servants are sacked. The private bosses who used to employ ex-prisoners, or might now be willing to do so, are subjected to pressures and threats (intimidations, police 'warnings', blackmailing of the fiscal authorities) which definitively dissuade them from employing them. Ex-prisoners who attempt to launch out into an independent activity (pedlars, salesmen in the *souk*, craftsmen or specialists in various kinds of service work) are harassed by the internal revenue, by the public health services, and by the municipal authorities. They find that the papers necessary for them to sign leases are taken away from them, so they cannot have any offices to work in; they are bothered by the police who extort money from them, damage or destroy their working tools and make it difficult for people to visit them. They are excluded from certain professions. They come across every kind of obstacle in their attempts to be reintegrated into society, starting with the difficulty, or even the impossibility, of getting their administrative papers back, in particular their ID cards and the notorious 'bulletin no. 3',[8] the attestation of a clean record and a veritable 'open sesame' for them to find a place in society.

When, by hook or by crook, they manage to find work, ex-prisoners are prevented from having any additional source of revenue – which is sometimes indispensable to the survival of their families. Their social security cards may be destroyed, which makes it impossible for them to have any access to medical health and *de facto* suppresses their affiliation to social security, even though the latter is compulsory. In these conditions, it is not unusual for Tunisian doctors to refuse to treat them, which is all the more drastic a measure in that many of them suffer from the consequences of their life in prison and need continual care. The result is that some of them are obliged to flee abroad in order to obtain treatment – to Italy in particular, where the Red Cross looks after Islamists free of charge – or to embark on hunger strikes to recover their medical cards. Students are forbidden to register at Tunisian universities or schools, even private ones. If they do manage to gain access to universities, they are not allowed to receive any bursaries or allowances or to have rooms on campus. All of them are frequently obliged to resort to illegal activities, since they are prevented – by aberrant administrative procedures or the withdrawal of papers – from paying taxes, paying off contributions into the *Caisse nationale de sécurité sociale* (CNSS – social security) or bank debts, renting offices legally, or performing any activity in accordance with the rules.

Interference in the private lives of these opponents who are reluctant to undergo political normalization goes even further, since it affects the people around them, who are often not politicized.[9] These people may be affected by the same administrative and economic measures, but as often as not the collective punishment consists in influencing the very essence of social relations and 'naked life'. Every step is taken to ensure that the pariah is shunned by his friends and relatives – shunned physically, socially and emotionally. Their ID is taken away so that they cannot visit him in prison. Administrative control or house searches may be extended to members of the family who have never been charged, arrested, or sentenced. The wives of detainees or ex-detainees may be forced to take off their headscarves and even divorce. I could go through a whole list of these practices, but their function is clear: they set a person apart, ostracize him and exclude him, subject him to trials and tribulations, and increase the sense of vanity associated with political commitment, while also turning it into a guilty activity. The case of that father of the family who was so driven to the edge that he staged the sale of his children in the *souk* is one of the best-known (because most revealing) stories of this intolerable attack on private life, but also of an irreparable despair and guilt.[10]

All these procedures are applied in a random but discretionary way. The intensity of administrative control, of extortion, of economic exclusion or police harassment varies in accordance with the agents of the authorities, with the nature of the opponents, and with the political moments and circumstances; no fixed rule emerges. The effect of uncertainty and variability is closely associated with the *stratégie du pourtour*, and it has a disciplinary function. But it also needs to be grasped as an expression of the diffuse exercise of power. Unlike what analyses in terms of 'repressive system' or 'authoritarian regime' suggest, these procedures are neither a result of clear orders from above, that is, from the presidential palace in Carthage or from the *Dakhilia*, the seat of the Ministry of the Interior, nor from an implacable logic relayed by an institutionalized security apparatus; they do not follow any definite, fixed, uniform and foreseeable rules.

The rhetoric and the discourse of the authorities have obvious effects of power. But the understanding of, and concrete reckoning with, the 'Islamist problem', of its violent and dangerous character for society, of the possibilities of division it entails, are not integrated in the same way by different groups of people. Room is left for individual actions that are more or less pernickety, aggressive, systematic or intrusive, on the part of the agents of authority who concretely exercise their power on opponents. Certain mechanisms are more pernicious and efficacious than others, certain procedures more systematic than others, certain members of the police or police auxiliaries more conscientious than others, and their sensibilities are inevitably all different. The behaviour of members of the police is also a response to other expectations and other rationalities than those of their hierarchy: over and above the repressive and disciplinary logic, the policeman acts in accordance with his own professional interests (the desire to create a good image of himself, to have a successful career), with his psychology, with contexts and events (the effect of zeal, the snowball effect of practices of control and repression – or, on the contrary, a lax and nonchalant attitude) and personal interests (the need for extra income, petty social vengeance, or the settling of accounts).

The treatment of Islamists does suggest that domination is not confined to the most obviously coercive repression, but also passes through economic and social mechanisms that are instrumentalized by police institutions and practices. The ambition here is an effect of normalization and not any quest for definitive exclusion: if they accept the norms of the dominant political system, these Islamist ex-prisoners are reintegrated into economic and social life.

While I was interviewing Islamists, former political detainees or people close to the prisoners, I was made especially aware of the necessity of a 'political anatomy of the detail' as mentioned by Michel Foucault in connection with domination and discipline, and more particularly of such an anatomy of the economic detail. I also realized how impossible it was to distinguish the economic from the political realm given the existence of a continuum, an inextricable interweaving between repression and social control on the one hand and, on the other, the most banal economic and social practices. While the analyses of authoritarian systems focus on institutions, organizations and political and social forms of behaviour, the economic dimension struck me as fundamental if I was to understand everyday domination. All of my work on the political economy of repression in Tunisia has been guided by this desire to apprehend concretely the way the economic mechanisms and technologies of power operate, and thereby to bring out their effects, their rationalities and even their 'benefits'.

Beyond repression, a political economy of subjection

In comparison with the Tunisian population, the number of Islamists who are victims of such breaches of human rights is really low. According to the organizations whose aim is to alert international public opinion to the issue, there seem to be a few thousand who are still trying to reintegrate themselves.[11] Other political opponents, those generally known in Tunis as 'democrats' and the militants of the extreme left, have been confronted – and some of them still are – by the same techniques of repression, albeit frequently of a lesser intensity. But the vast majority of the population – not to say almost the whole of it – leads a 'normal' life. While people may suffer from the absence of freedom of expression, from the weight of a single, often unrealistic rhetoric and sometimes from a somewhat over-massive police presence, they still appreciate the solicitude of the state and its economic voluntarism.

The aim of this book is precisely to understand, over and beyond the most brutal repression, the modes of government and the concrete economic apparatuses [*dispositifs*] of power that render constraint painless and even invisible, and render the 'servitude' 'voluntary' (in Étienne de La Boétie's expression). These apparatuses sometimes even mean that the mechanisms of submission and enslavement are actively sought out. With that in mind, I have tried to describe and bring out the rationalities of the mechanisms of subjection, submission and consent *starting from the economic dimension*. My aim was to penetrate the 'political economy' which Michel Foucault discussed so frequently, though he never really went into the concrete operation of the economic machinery. This perspective, inspired above all by my own intellectual itinerary, seemed to me particularly legitimate in that the rhetoric of the Tunisian authorities rests almost exclusively on the construction of one narrative: that of the economic miracle.

Works of classical political economy devoted to Tunisia, which echo the contemporary commentaries on the situation, highlight the dilemma between economic success on the one hand and, on the other, political closure and the systematic violation of human rights. Some of them develop functionalist arguments on the role of the economy in an authoritarian regime, presenting Tunisia as an example of sultanism[12] or as a 'bully praetorian regime'.[13] These studies emphasize the high degree of personalization of power, the extent of arbitrary decisions that disturb the normal working of the administration, a system of loyalty based on fear and gratification by the boss [*chef*], the weak degree of penetration of power into society, associated with the passivity of the latter, and – in the economic realm – the confusion between public and private, as well as the instrumentalization of positions of power for economic ends. Other specialists in political economy investigate in greater detail the apparent contradiction between political repression and 'economic miracle'. However, they more often than not see the political field as exogenous, and only rarely go into the dynamics of the play of power, offering a separate analysis of the economic and political logics, or analysing the political sphere on the basis of an economic argument.[14] Through the parallel between financial repression and political repression, Clement Henry Moore sets out to investigate the nature of the relations between the economic and the political and to provide us with a fundamentally political understanding of the financial system. But his work is a little disappointing in the way it reduces the political to mere politicking, and relations of power to an instrumentalization applied from on high.[15]

Juan Linz and Alfred Stepan do not discuss Tunisia, but they certainly do provide us with one of the analyses that best takes into account the political dimension of the economic field, with their notion of 'economic society', in other words the set of norms, institutions and regulations accepted by the whole of society – mediators, as it were, between state and market.[16] They underline the importance of economic machinery in relations of power and in the way this or that political form works. But, just like other work on 'transitology' or political economy, these two authors convey a mechanistic vision of power and share the implicit hypothesis of a definite link between democracy and economic form. While they reject the idea of any positive relation between political liberalization and economic liberalization, and offer an in-depth critique of the relation between democracy and development, Juan Linz and Alfred Stepan intimate that democracy is compatible neither with a controlled economy, nor with a 'pure' market economy. They thereby maintain a functionalist and teleological approach. In particular, none of these authors go into the concrete detail of the methods and the economic apparatus of power. Their analyses are still macroeconomic, mentioning percentages, growths and rates of inflation, formal definitions of economic policies.

In the following pages, I have tried to avoid these pitfalls by focusing my analysis on the apparent contradiction between economic situation, the normality of life in society and the reality of control and repression. I have made no attempt to draw up an inventory of the errors, naiveties, prejudices or moral positions of the works cited above. Instead, adopting a method derived from Foucault, I have tried, via localized concrete situations, to lay bare the mechanisms of the exercise of power and the socio-economic bases on which it rests. In the Weberian tradition, I have been attentive to the plasticity of social forms – which debars one from prejudging the connections between variables – as well as the diversity and multiplicity of arrangements and combinations [*agencements*].

It has long been known that no government is exclusively based on violence and repression, not even the most accomplished forms of totalitarianism.[17] The authoritarian, indeed totalitarian system, functions far beyond the mechanics of the police apparatus, as the latest book by Götz Aly shows, *Hitler's Beneficiaries: Plunder, Racial War, and the Nazi Welfare State*. In it, he analyses the Nazi regime as a 'dictatorship in the service of the people'[18] and shows how, as good demagogues, the Nazis had in particular tried to make the Reich popular and to foster an awareness of the regime's solicitude. In order to do this, they built up a consensus in the population on the basis of a 'fair' distribution of provisions, especially for the less well off, together with a stabilization of the *Reichsmark*, a particularly low rate of taxation, and benefits for the families of soldiers.

On the basis of this humdrum vision of the authoritarian or even totalitarian exercise of power, but also starting from the same observations on the apparent contradiction between 'economy' and 'politics', my research into Tunisia has led to another interpretation. These are mechanisms highlighted by the 'regime' or foreign donors in order to praise the capacity for adaptation and reform in Tunisian society, as well as the 'economic and social intelligence of the regime', which constitute, at one and the same time, the fundamental machinery of the system of domination. Practices of repression are inseparable from other practices, especially those meant to include the whole population, to satisfy its needs to the greatest possible extent, and to guarantee its security. The following pages thus show that the mechanisms of control of the Tunisian population as a whole are anchored in the most banal relations of power. Surveillance and normalization happen mainly via economic and social activities and types of behaviour that are themselves inscribed within relations of force internal to society, within the struggles spread throughout that society. But these practices can serve coercion or even repression just as well as they can enable the 'economic miracle' to take place. They authorize the exercise of punishment and gratification, but also ensure economic and social security. They are partly paternalistic, an aspect of social control, while at the same time they make control and social ascension, surveillance and wealth creation possible. This is also the reason why repression alone does not exhaust the practice of power, and why, if there *is* domination, it is often accepted.

Beyond authoritarianism, a 'secular' analysis of a political situation

My research has led me to reject certain approaches. So it has nothing to do with the substantivist analyses of the 1960s which aimed to define an intermediate position between democracy and totalitarianism and presented authoritarianism as a pathological political formula. It is also to be distinguished from neo-Weberian analyses of sultanism, an extreme form of patrimonialism in which personal domination and discretionary power prevail, and more generally from clientelism or populism. In all these kinds of analysis, the general problematic comprises classification, definition and lexical questions: power is considered as a thing, to be possessed and used; these regimes rest, in the final analysis, on a narrow social basis and exercise their domination through fear and the granting of rewards. Nor does my research have any affinity with transitology, the normative analysis of the passage from authoritarianism and socialism to democracy and the market economy. It is also far removed from its historicist and teleological conception of historical trajectories, of its positivist vision of democracy, of its institutionalist and formal perception of economic transformations, and of its one-sided understanding of the relations between capitalism and democratization. My work is different, finally, from 'Islamological' analyses that tend to turn religion into the key factor for understanding authoritarianism in the Arab world.

Instead, my approach falls explicitly within the purview of the historical sociology of the political, which constitutes an important part of the research developed in the CERI (Centre d'études et de recherches internationales) since the 1970s.[19] The affinities between my research and the work that has emerged from this tradition have placed particular emphasis on this method: leave totalitarian, or authoritarian, phenomena undefined; emphasize the plurality of situations; take it as a methodological *a priori* not to fix in advance the characteristics that you seek to validate or rule out by empirical research.[20] To this end, working at the margins has seemed to me to be of particular interest. So I have tried to work, not on the authoritarian exercise of power, if only because all power is authoritarian, but on the basis of concrete situations, very specific practices or particular geographical areas, to understand its exercise on the basis of localized social relations. I have sought to analyse less the institutions that set themselves up, in essence or by function, as repressive, disciplinary or policing, than the types of behaviour, rationalities, ways of life and understandings of being in society.

Thus, I have not analysed the party or the police as such, but I have attempted to describe their different points of insertion into society, via the most anodyne practices of recognition, the quest for material advantages, administrative routine, or conception of order and security. More than that, I have tried to find what, within the most banal kinds of economic and social behaviour, transmitted, unconsciously and involuntarily, the slightest desire for control and surveillance. So the reader will not find here any analysis of the political life, of the architecture and rationalities of Tunisian authoritarianism, but rather an analysis of little things and little reasons, practical (and often minor) modes of obedience and support, much more complex than the Machiavellianism of all-powerful central powers. I have tried to provide a 'secular history'[21] of a given authoritarian situation – in other words, a history as far removed as possible from dogmas and catechism, the catechism of the Tunisian authorities as much as of that of the 'international community' or the 'scientific community'. In order to achieve this, I have avoided studying 'authoritarianism' or 'reformism', 'liberalism' or *'dirigisme'*, as general, abstract categories – but I have followed, as much as my fieldwork allowed me, the day-to-day work of individuals, starting with common situations, with the way they understand power, authority, hierarchy and obedience, but also freedom and rebelliousness, acceptance and support. This last point is fundamental. The actors I have studied do not generally conceive of their situation, or that of their fellow-citizens, in terms of political constraint, of repression, coercion, or submission. Their evaluation was simultaneously more subtle and less explicit, and not merely because of fear and the absence of freedom of expression. Often, mechanisms felt as constraining are sought out, being as they are both protecting, enriching, and security-enhancing. What can be presented as a form of listening may also turn out to be an instrument of control; conversely, what can be perceived as a form of submission can also result from a convergence of different logics and interests. Domination is ambivalent, and negotiated accommodation is the rule. What outside observers may present as a constraint, or even a coercion, a power of normalization and discipline, is in fact most often experienced as a mode of normal life – in other words as rules that are, if not interiorized, at least negotiable, rules with which you can play. The painless and, so to speak, invisible character of constraint and even coercion may, in other situations, be made possible by the process of the routinization of the interventions and exercise of power; in other cases, support is partial and may arise from the quest for concrete and material advantages, or from modes of behaviour and lifestyles. In short, perceptions of reality are profoundly heterogeneous and this swarm of different views always – or almost always – makes it possible to find points of acceptance, utilization or convergence that make disciplinary power tolerable, acceptable, or even desirable.

So while I do not discuss authoritarianism, I obviously do talk about authoritarian situations or powers, usually with an adjective: disciplinary, normalizing, violent, coercive, or indeed continuous or discontinuous, centralized or delegated, and so on. Likewise, I do not talk of totalitarianism in relation to the current Tunisian regime, but I sometimes describe its regime as totalitarian. This distinction appears fundamental to me. All those '-isms', being abstract (and thus general and normative) categories, have not helped me to understand empirical situations. Instead, I have felt the need to designate, by this strong and connotation-laden term, certain visions of power, certain ways of thinking and conceiving of it. It is important to point out that, in Tunisia, the impossibility of public debate, the rejection of opposition, the absence of any political alternative, the equating of antagonism or objection with chaos, disorder and disunion, all considered as absolute evils – this all means that we need to talk of a 'totalitarian' vision of power, or of 'totalitarian thought'. Criticism is unthinkable in the world of one-dimensional thought.[22] This is not to say that the exercise of power is in itself totalitarian. Quite the contrary – all my work highlights the incompleteness of control and discipline, the proportion of support and acceptance (sometimes passive, sometimes altogether consenting and active): the, so to speak, utopian dimension of absolute control.

Fiction and the authoritarian exercise of power

The imaginary and fictive dimensions of the exercise of power, and of its interpretation, appear fundamental within this frame of analysis. In the course of my demonstration, fiction is often referred to, lying as it does at the intersection of three traditions which obviously overlap. First there is a legal tradition, with the figure of the *persona ficta* and the intensive use of 'as if'.[23] Resorting to legal fictions enables certain facts to be concealed, so as to consolidate a status quo (for example the efficient and rational working of a banking system), to foster a development (the maintaining of optimal relations with international donors) and to assert certain truths ('Tunisia is advancing towards democracy'; 'the economic consensus is a reality'). In this sense, the fiction is not a pure and simple illusion without any historical effect; it is a fabrication with significant effects on institutions and behaviour.

Then there is the literary tradition around this last theme and which was introduced into the social sciences by the work of Roland Barthes, Michel Foucault and Herbert Marcuse. The fiction here belongs properly to personal experience, the experience which you make for yourself, which creates something that did not exist before but exists afterwards, which names things. Fiction is the object of which you are 'completely master and which no shadow can hide from your gaze'. It is language which is, by definition, distance. It is the aspect of a fable.[24] It is in this vein that we need to understand discussions of the imaginary as reality, a grey zone between real and unreal, which needs to be taken into account if the complexity and plurality of ways of being is to be grasped, and if we are to act and to understand the society into which every individual is inserted, and thereby the processes of subjection which he or she experiences.[25]

Finally there is the functionalist tradition, emphasized in particular by historians of the economic sphere. The fiction of figures and refined statistics operates like a kind of magic, producing effects of authority. The fiction of the omnipotence of the state or of this or that actor (for example, in the Ancien Régime, of the foreign banker or the tax farmer) serves as a 'social lightning rod'[26] for the populace, since the fictive being enables popular wrath to be turned away. In the use I have made of it, fiction does not appear as so instrumental, but it is certain that the creation, often involuntary and unconscious, of fictions leads to clouding the issue of responsibility and diluting the exercise of power. It is this, too, which makes fictions something to be reckoned with.

This book focuses on the economic techniques and non-discursive practices of domination. So I will not be discussing the fiction of the 'miracle' as such, the construction and spread of the discourse on Tunisia's economic success, nor the many different modes of expression it has assumed; I will just refer the reader to another of my works on this subject.[27] But everything that I have to say on the economic apparatuses [*dispositifs*] of power cannot be understood without this discursive background. I will rapidly summarize this discourse. It is relatively simple in content: the Tunisian model, on this view, is characterized by social liberalism, that is, a *'juste milieu'* or golden mean between the market and social preoccupations, by a 'balance between political liberalism and economic liberalism', and by a 'pragmatism that is essentially progressive'. Economic success, attention to the social sphere, a specific path towards democracy and a multi-party system thanks to economic development, stability, security and moderation, a judicious balance between a decision in favour of modernity and progress, on the one hand, and respect for Tunisian values on the other, a harmonious relation between openness and national sovereignty – these are all recurrent themes in the discourses that monopolize the public space.

The legitimacy of the 'Ben Ali regime' stems essentially from this image, constructed on the basis of economic and social success. The latter is the result of highly specific techniques of formation of the economic discourse – for instance, the skilful choice of comparisons, the modification of techniques of accountancy or statistics and semantic slippage, the forgetting of past performances, the appropriation of social phenomena and re-interpretations of history, the concealment of divergent data, the negotiation of facts and figures, and the absence of any concrete actualization. It stems, too, from more general procedures that enclose discourse within a one-dimensional (and thus totalitarian) style of thinking – like the use of secrets and rumours, the rejection of any external scrutiny, the absence of any public space of debate, unanimity of opinion and enforced consensus, and formalism, or procedures that make choices seem natural and deliberately deny certain realities. The economic discourse that is thus constructed produces a world in which failures do not exist, and where only successes are recorded.

The fiction is written into a world of one-dimensional thinking; it thus becomes more and more real; it partly circumscribes economic behaviour and draws the outlines of its meaning. The spread of the validated discourse is made systematic by the authorities' obsession with control, intent as they are on preserving their image. The administration, the party and its satellites, a press and media that are totally subordinate – these are the instruments of a transmission of the official discourse into society. Manipulations are real practices. The construction of a radiant future, however, is the fruit of a much more complex and unforeseen process that often involves – without them knowing it – an infinite number of actors. This fiction, indeed, rests on a substrate, on perceptions, on the reproduction of prior analyses or interpretations and re-writings of history – in other words on an ethos that is broadly shared by Tunisian society as a whole. The staging of economic information and interpretation results mainly from the way mechanisms of power are inserted into the detail of everyday life. Economic fiction then appears as another instrument of subjection. As a mode of government whose terms are broadly shared by the population, its utterances are simultaneously part of the exercise of domination.

Return to Max Weber

The need to pay close attention to the concrete nature of economic apparatuses [*dispositifs*] and to the detail of the effective procedures of domination has made it necessary for me to choose several areas of fieldwork in Tunisia in which to carry out research on very precise themes. The interviews I have conducted there over the past nine years were not conceived as replies to hypotheses that I had formulated previously; on the contrary, they were decisive in the redefinition of my research and the refining of the questions I needed to ask. As much as I could, I repeated the interviews with the same people over several different stays, so as to build up a relationship of trust with them, and to understand the dynamics and the fluidity of the economic mechanisms of power.

I systematically sought to localize my empirical research, focusing on banks, industrial policy (what is called, in Tunisia, 'upgrading' [*mise à niveau*]), the privatization of public enterprises, organized solidarity (the notorious 26.26, that presidential account into which flow 'voluntary' gifts, or the *Banque tunisienne de solidarité*), tax authorities, and the forms of economic interventionism and liberalization, in particular external liberalization. Because 'the devil's in the detail', my method consists, in any given situation, of going into the actual workings of institutions, and, even more, of behaviours.[28] There are two types of theoretical influence here: on the one hand, the 'hymn to small things' and the 'political anatomy of the detail' of Michel Foucault; on the other hand, the 'complexity of the real' and the always highly empirical analysis of Max Weber.[29] This relatively precise localization of the analyses leads one not to seek any *one* cause for voluntary servitude or for the authoritarian exercise of power, but, on the contrary, to remain sensitive to the unfinished nature of practices, to causal plurality and what Max Weber called 'the composition of effects'. However, I must not exaggerate the precision of my analysis of real mechanisms. This work aims first and foremost to put forward a way of problematizing the exercise of domination – I hope it is a new way, and I could have gone into much greater detail about certain examples, certain procedures, and certain techniques.

The political economy I am carrying out is a non-quantitative economy, and it stands by this rejection. By definition, statistics is political – this has long been known and analysed.[30] Statistics is state knowledge; the state's knowledge about itself. The reason behind it is practical – more precisely, prescriptive. Since it is impossible to dissociate statistics as a conception of the state and as a way of thinking about society, statistics is the reflection of a state-controlled knowledge, and even more of the link between power and knowledge. Indeed, statistics are inseparable from mechanisms of control. So I have not used statistics as objective data that allow us to advance in taking the measure of phenomena and understanding causal relations. They interest me insofar as they are materials to be analysed and deconstructed if we are to understand the logics of the state, political preoccupations, the mechanisms of power and the techniques of knowledge. The material, the physical and the concrete – which constitute the privileged terrain of quantitative methods – also form my main area of analysis. But, starting with this same raw material, I am trying to do something that is not essentially a matter of measurement.

Rejecting the quantitative does not mean rejecting the technical – quite the opposite. As those working on the border between the hard sciences and the social sciences have shown,[31] the detailed and inevitably technical understanding of economic behaviour or institutions is indispensable for a grasp of their political significance. Technicity itself is political, and only by going into the real mechanisms of these calculations (such as bad debts as a percentage of the banks' commitment) or these procedures (the recovering of credit or the auditing of bank accounts) can we understand the construction of a fiction (that of a solid and efficient banking system), its modes of working (the creation of perpetual dependencies), its social and political functions (the execution of a pact of social and, in particular, economic security).

I perceive political economy as an analysis that seeks to understand the political and social significance of economic behaviour.[32] In opposition to the dominant political economy, in particular the way it apprehends power as a right which you possess, as a transferable good, alienable by a legal act (in other words as an exchange), the Weberian conception of political economy that I am seeking to develop – and which it would be more precise to call the historical sociology of economics – defends an non-economics-based analysis of power, including economic power. It aims to turn dysfunctions, uncertainties, and reversibilities into the common lot of economic functioning, and to turn the plurality of types of behaviour into a systematic rule. There is no coherence, simply because behaviours and institutions are human activities and creations. This approach is aware of the plurality and heterogeneity, as of the contingency and uniqueness of situations, and it also hopes to counter facile explanations and ready-made analyses, such as reference to the '*dirigiste* tradition' or the 'authoritarian liberalism inherent in the Tunisian government'. What do authoritarian liberalism or *dirigisme* actually mean? What are the modes and effective realizations of these slogans or these general accusations? What do they really cover?

Interpreting work in the field

I feel I need to give some more detail about the ways in which I conducted my fieldwork in Tunisia, firstly in order to explain the extremely fluid and general nature of the sources or interviews that I mention throughout the book, and secondly because the field itself was a concrete and personal experience of the repressive apparatuses [*dispositifs*] of the exercise of power that enabled me better to grasp the reality of the situation in Tunisia and to give material shape to it.

In my second period of fieldwork, in April 1998, at a time when I had simply been questioning my interviewees on the opening up of Tunisia to Europe, on the conditions of economic liberalization and the way they understood the Euro-Mediterranean Partnership, I was cordially invited to hear the 'right' version of 'Ben Ali's Tunisia' and to relativize my 'normative' and 'biased' judgements which had failed to take into account the 'specific forms' of the political sphere in this 'exemplary country in the Maghreb'. From that date onwards, I was regularly followed in my fieldwork, including when I was conducting anodyne interviews or interrupting my work because of Eid and 'enforced' holidays with non-Tunisian friends. This tailing of me became more intense once I started more systematically to meet opponents, human rights workers, lawyers and in particular Islamists, former political prisoners, and also strikers and actors in social movements not controlled by the central tradeunion organization. This 'heavy' policing took various intense forms: I was systematically followed, from my arrival at the airport where two or three police officers in civilian dress 'greeted me', and during my trips by taxi, in Tunis and environs, or by *louages* (i.e. collective taxis) between the main towns in the country. From the moment when I was put up, for obvious reasons, in a hotel rather than at a friend's house, 'my' room awaited me faithfully while, in the lobby, two or three men lounging on the sofa observed my comings and goings, alerted by the hotel employees. At the airport, I was subjected to measures of intimidation that were more symbolic than really alarming. When I dined out, I was obviously the focus of renewed attention, even, or particularly, when I met diplomat friends. My meetings with lawyers defending Islamists, former political prisoners or their friends and relatives, were followed up more closely, with police men in civvies, straight out of bad cop films, with leather jackets, dark glasses and faces like gangsters, hurrying to keep up with me. But this treatment was not reserved for my stays in Tunisia. In France too, my office at the CERI was 'visited' three times, and my computer hacked.

In all these cases, I was never in danger. These were just intimidations, and (as it turned out) ineffectual ones when it came to dissuading me from carrying out my research, but very effective when it came to convincing me of the need to understand the working of such a widespread and yet such an apparently limited police 'system'. But these measures were not fundamentally addressed to me. They concerned, first and foremost, the people I was speaking to; and in this sense their effectiveness was hit-and-miss. Some of the people I regularly saw became, from one day to the next, unavailable, being 'on sick leave' or 'away travelling'. Others tried to preach to me, telling me that I was not giving an account of the 'good' things that existed in Tunisia or, more subtly, trying to fill my schedule with sterile meetings or to convince me yet again of the reasons for this or that policy, of the existing dangers and the advantages of the measures taken. Other interviewees, on the contrary, never stopped agreeing to see me, speaking more and more openly, mocking the police and the way they tailed me as soon as they realized this was happening. On this last point, my strategy was to say nothing to the people I interviewed from the business world: I asked them purely economic and financial questions even if, at the end of the interview, my questions might be understood, by those who so wished, in more political terms. The reason for this position was that my interviews were focused on technical points and these people were integrated tightly enough into power relations to be able, themselves, to evaluate the risks they were taking in talking to me; they definitely knew what they could and could not tell me. Instead, when my interviews were more directly political, I mainly questioned individuals 'who had nothing to lose' because they themselves were being followed by the police, more intensely than I was myself, and they had long since more or less learned how to handle this surveillance. When I spoke to 'average Tunisians', I made sure I passed through intermediaries who were used to this kind of risk, so as not to put my interviewees in a potentially dangerous position. Unfortunately, on two or three occasions, in spite of my precautions, I did compromise employees and workers on strike; as a result of our encounters, they were subsequently harassed and questioned.

Generally speaking, during the interviews, my interviewees were obviously 'constrained' by the society they lived in. Entrepreneurs, bankers, workers, strikers, trades unionists, members of associations, lawyers and even certain donors and foreign partners quite legitimately did not wish to disturb their daily relations with the 'authorities'. Thus, as soon as my questions started to seem a bit 'dodgy' to them, they grew tense, fell silent, evaded my questions or concluded by saying '*that*'s political, we can't talk about it' or, even more explicitly, 'it would be an obvious step to take this measure but it would be political and we can't argue about that. Tunisia isn't like France'. This too was an integral part of my fieldwork, of the way I understood how the political works in Tunisia. In this context, clichéd political slogans are powerful, but the force of interviews is equally powerful: intonations, silences, 'irrelevant' answers, reasons that do not stand up or are partial, hints and veiled allusions, jokes and anecdotes served up without any comment, things that 'people say' and rumours, apparent contradictions, moments of awkwardness and short-circuits – all allowed more information to get through than my interviewees themselves realized. Sometimes the situation was the other way round: asking questions on highly technical subjects, my interviewees would 'let themselves go', in their own words, and talk about more general subjects, ruminations that were vague but no less revealing of the political significance they themselves gave to the technical measures I was asking them about. They expressed a need to generalize, to 'launch out' into large-scale political rationalizations, into a discussion and even a confrontation, with this remark that I heard so frequently: 'no, you're not being a nuisance, you're helping me to think'; 'we need to stop being so blinkered', or, even more explicitly, 'people should be able to criticize, to look at things from a certain distance, and in our society that's not easy – you're giving me a chance to do so'.

Thus, an important part of the way I pursued my work consisted in treating what my interviewees told me as subtly as possible. I did not try to consider their words as justifications to be taken at face value, as defining elements of the configuration of behaviour. Paul Veyne's analysis of 'things and the veil of words'[33] was of particular help to me, since it echoes the situation I found out in the field: if people indisputably do say things, you still cannot take their word for it; but their words nonetheless need to be taken seriously insofar as the practices they mention 'are still definitely live issues'.[34] So I have tried to work out what was being said even when those saying it were unaware of its meaning. Sometimes the actors were mistaken, sometimes they were not, sometimes they came out with a 'true' reason, sometimes one that was 'false'. Often they would put forward arguments linked to a given result, but they would without any doubt have referred to others if the result had been different, in a classic process of *post hoc* rationalization. I have tried to treat their utterances as revelatory of values, of ideas, of disparate and contradictory justifications, attempting to pinpoint the greatest number of possibilities, and motivations as diverse and heterogeneous as possible.

I have not tried to construct a definitive analysis of the 'Ben Ali regime' and its machinery of domination, or of the causes behind Tunisian authoritarianism. Rather, I have tried to shed light on fragments of the disciplinary exercise of power, of the piecemeal, incomplete and unfinished reasons for accepting – and even supporting – practices of domination. The explanations I give throughout the book, for instance in terms of 'economic fiction', of 'social pact', of 'construction of the consensus', of the 'police state' or 'the random rule of law' are unable – even when combined – to grasp the exercise of subjection. It is in this sense that my repeated references to Étienne de La Boétie need to be understood. The author of the *Contr'un* [*Anti-Dictator*] is less interested, after all, in showing the various mechanisms of what he calls 'voluntary servitude' than in showing the incomplete nature of the processes of domination, their indeterminate shape and even their contingent character. While I do not offer my readers an exhaustive analysis of the machinery of discipline and consent in Tunisia, I hope that this book will more generally have enriched the understanding of the exercise of an authoritarian power by taking systematic account of economic practices and their ambivalence in the analysis of domination and subjection.

Part I

Power by Credit

The banking sector, the real keystone of the political economy of Tunisia, allows us to get right to the heart of 'the political anatomy of the detail', as Michel Foucault called it. Bankers are, above all, brokers, financial intermediaries. And yet they are more than that: involved as they are in national and international political life, they gather, provide and even create economic, political and diplomatic information. They depend on the central power, and yet they also prop it up. They share identical values and perceptions. They are members of the same community of interests and often of ideas. They sustain the relations between individuals and groups, link together the whole – or almost the whole – set of individuals involved. They act as a 'transmission belt' between the central power and the population. There is thus a close bond between economic ethos, social structuring, political organization, power relations, state formation, and the system of extraction and financing.

An analysis of the banking system turns out to be all the more relevant in Tunisia in that debt constitutes one of its main underpinnings and one of the most profitable resources of its political economy. Financiers are 'intermediaries' of the state – and they are all the more indispensable in that fiscal pressures are weak and, to an even greater extent, the collection of taxes is inefficient. This is just as much the case now as it was before. Mohamed Lazhar Gharbi has emphasized the extent to which, in the colonial period, banks – more than taxes – were a means by which the state could maintain its ascendancy and an instrument of its financial and political control: public capital offered it a way of monitoring the finances of the Protectorate, and private capital endorsed the domination of local wealth by colonial capital.[1] Other historians have shown that, in the pre-colonial period, during the eighteenth and in particular the nineteenth centuries, the *lazzams*, a sort of tax farmers, and the big tradesmen continued to finance the power of the bey with their credit, together with the European banks.[2] Today, the economy of Tunisia still finds it difficult to gain access to currency and finance its imports. Obtaining finance from the banks thus turns out to be of fundamental importance.

It may seem rather arid to approach Tunisian political economy by way of the banking system; I hope readers will forgive this austere technical introduction. However, this chapter contains a financial analysis, not of the banking system, but of its political economy. A critique of financial practices sheds particular light on the exercise of power in Tunisia, especially the ways in which political domination is deployed in the economic and social machinery.

1

Bad Debts

An examination of the stages in the life of a credit makes it possible to grasp in detail all the possible points at which power is anchored in the financial world: an analysis of the request for credit and the kind of person making the request, an analysis of the extent to which the bank is sound and its risks divided up, the drawing up of guarantees, the granting and follow-up of credit, repayment, funding, and recovery. My research suggests that at every stage of the existence of a credit and debt, the regulations, behaviour, practices, and interpretations of debt shift away from a harmonious cycle of credit towards the creation and perpetuation of bad debts. The extent of these appears to be considerable, and it is a politically sensitive matter. International donors have seen this clearly. For the past few years they have been basing their interventions on these notorious debts.

Book-keeping and the treatment of bad debts

In all countries undergoing adjustment, only when the situation has been stabilized do international organizations tackle the 'structural' aspect of the reforms. Finance is often one of the last sectors to be affected by modernization: public authorities and bankers are better able than other sectors to resist periods of disequilibrium, thanks to their privileged access to resources (currency, debt, information) that in their case never dry up, or at least do so to a far lesser degree.

In Tunisia, the structural reforms began in the 1990s. International organizations continued to exert pressure on the Tunisian authorities to review their banking system and, more generally, their financial system. Originally, their aim was to find a way round the obstacles that lay in the path of privatization and of the development of the private sector. The main points of concern were the extent of the bad debts, the closure and protectionism of the finance system, the importance of the public sector, and the archaic nature of the way the banks and, even more, the insurance system worked, as well as the lack of any financial instruments worthy of the name.

Bad debts had first comprised restructuring programmes in adjustment facilities, but then appeared as the keystone of the current system, certainly favoured by the public nature of the banks, but not only by this. If we analyse the concrete functioning of the debt economy, we will be able to understand the creation of bad debts not as a symptom of crisis, a deviation from a particular economic model, or an economic and financial pathology, but as a mechanism for fully financing the economy, and above all as a means whereby power is exercised.

A multiplicity of sources

Like other strategic and political data, quantitative information about bad debts is taboo and difficult to obtain officially. Figures 'circulate', but are difficult to verify, to tally, and to check – but also to analyse, since precise information on how a particular figure, a rate or a percentage are constructed is impossible to gather. The monetary and banking statistics cited by official bodies are not always made public, or are scattered and do not necessarily tally with the same facts. The data provided by international organizations – the IMF, the World Bank and the European Union – are often out of date and, in particular, suffer from the same defects, since they can only be provided from national data, at best reprocessed.[1] The lack of real information on their effective significance and the difficulty of establishing long series comparable across time are equally important considerations. In spite of all this, if we take the situation in other countries (and especially the international norm set at two per cent of banking commitments) as our reference points, there is no doubt that the phenomenon of bad debts is huge and central in Tunisia:[2] depending on the period and the source, the rate varies between 20 and 40 per cent.

The last figures available to me, from 2003, mention rates of bad debts of 23.9 per cent of banking commitments, representing 16.3 per cent of GDP for deposit banks alone, and 28 per cent for development banks. In December 2002, it appears that the total of these debts rose to 5.8 thousand million *dinars* (DT – some 3.5 thousand million euros), i.e. 23.1 per cent of banking commitments and some 21 per cent of GDP.[3] At the start of the same year, the amount appears to have been 'merely' 5 thousand million DT, i.e. 21 per cent of banking commitments, underlining the severe decline in 2002, due to the combined factors of the drought, the recession in Europe, the international political crisis and its dramatic impact on tourism (the attacks of 11 September 2001, the Djerba synagogue bombing). These figures are not all that far removed from those made public by the IMF in 2001 on the basis of data from 1999, though we do not really know how these figures were established. According to Article IV of the IMF, bad debts represented 3 thousand million DT, i.e. 22.4 per cent of the total credits and 20.3 per cent of GDP at the end of 1999:[4] the development banks at that date had over 65 per cent of their credits in bad debts or debts that could rapidly become bad – but this rate approached a 'mere' 20 per cent for the commercial banks (both public and private).[5] In 1996, payments outstanding owed by businesses to banks appear to have represented over 2.5 thousand million DT, to which we need to add individual debts.[6] According to the official position, these problematic data did, however, show an improvement in the banking system, since the rates of bad debts reached 35 per cent of the total of credits and 29 per cent of GDP in 1994, or even more before the budgetary and financial restrictions at the end of the 1980s and the structural adjustment.[7] These varying figures need to be viewed with circumspection and taken with more than a pinch of salt: even when these figures come from official sources, they say nothing about the changes, from one period to another, in the methods of evaluation and categorization (public, parapublic, private, formal, informal) of bad debts.[8] Now, the level at which it can be considered that an insolvent debt can be listed as a bad debt varies at different times and sometimes even from one establishment to another.

In the following pages, my aim is not to discuss the relevance of this policy. Some people propose one set of arguments (the method used to finance development, the characteristic shape of emerging markets, the legitimacy of social choice and developmentalism), others put forward a different set (the risk of a crisis in liquidity, unsustainable debt, growth without development, and so on), and both might well be right, in their different ways. My aim is, rather, to try to understand the mechanism at work, in its variations and its details, and especially in the complexity of the relations of power that it implies.

However reliable the quantitative data, one thing appears clear: the system of loans that are not repaid (or are 'non-repayable'), of written-off or bad debts, is a huge reality with a macroeconomic, macrosocial and macropolitical significance. The segments of the national economy most affected by this phenomenon are the hotel industry, the sector of small and medium-sized enterprises (SMEs) and significant business figures[9] – in other words, the very framework of the Tunisian economy. After all, tourism provides over half the currency earnings of the service sector (roughly one third of total currency earnings), employs 12 per cent of the active population and represents six per cent of the GDP and 15 per cent of the current receipts for goods and services. Also, SMEs form over 97 per cent of the fabric of Tunisian business.[10] And finally, the participation of 'big fortunes' (big business figures and speculators close to the President) can be measured by the concentration of credits. In 1986, 136 firms and individuals monopolized 50 per cent of credits.[11] Today, the lack of accessible information means that no comparison can be drawn, but my conversations with bankers and international donors suggest powerfully that the phenomenon has at best been maintained and probably reinforced.[12]

Contrary to rumour, the origin of these bad debts and the mechanisms that created them cannot be reduced to political interventions on behalf of 'well-connected' personalities, even if the latter are significant in quantitative terms and even more in terms of representation and legitimization.

In the world of SMEs, bad debts usually arise from two combined factors. From poor evaluation and unprofessional management of risk, on the part of the bankers; and, on the part of the entrepreneurs, from hit-and-miss management, from a lack of competence, especially in the financial domain, and from a confusion between private assets and business assets, all of this within a legal and social environment favourable to activity and employment rather than to creditors. Significant business figures can for their part draw on political connections. This relation may be direct, as for those who are 'close' to central power – to whom the banker can never refuse a loan, even if he already knows in advance that it will never be repaid. It can also be indirect, via figureheads: several credits are granted to totally insolvent persons who are nonetheless known to be qualified representatives or intermediaries of these same people close to power. Several public businesses have thus apparently been handed over to them, directly or via go-betweens, without the latter laying out the least sum of money, as the operation is financed by a 'non-repayable' loan provided by the banks. This claim has to be treated with caution, since information on operations of privatization is particularly scarce. The adoption, by the *Banque centrale de Tunisie* (BCT) of a circular dated 23 November 1997 authorizing the acquisition of privatizable businesses through bank loans does, however, suggest that this mechanism has played an important role.[13]

For the 'historic' business figures, if we can call them that – those whose positions in society and notoriety go back to the 1970s – the political connection is more subtle: the bank loans on the basis of a name and a reputation: it knows that, if there are any difficulties, it will be able to call on financial support. Big business figures are indeed 'heroes of the national economy', the 'spokesmen of the Change', where 'Change' is, we recall, the way Ben Ali's regime designates itself, sometimes in spite of themselves but, as often as not, with their consent and to their advantage.[14] These entrepreneurs generally pay back their loans, though often belatedly. In their case, bad debts may be the effect of difficulties in the overall financial situation, of a surplus of diversification and thus a sudden increase in the number of their activities, of dubious alliances, or of bad investments. They also result from a skilful handling of the flaws in the banking system: in the absence of a proper functioning of the Credit information bureau which consolidates the set of debts an economic operator owes to all the financial institutions, entrepreneurs currently exploit the plurality of bank accounts.[15] They can have one or more accounts in deficit, in the name of their businesses, with one or more banks, and keep one that is massively in credit, in their own names, with another bank. They thus earn money by making their personal holdings bear fruit, while at the same time they avoid being penalized either by the non-payment of interest due, or by delays in repayment. Because of their social role, they will not be punished (or only rarely).

The case of tourism is emblematic and thus merits particular investigation. The financial problems of this sector stem, in the final analysis, from the weakness of shareholders' equity and the extent of debt. The international norm sets the level of credit at 50 per cent (60 per cent maximum) of the cost of financing: anything higher means that the level of debt becomes unsustainable. Now, Tunisian firms on average contribute only 10–15 per cent of shareholders' equity, even today.[16] And this creates several problems, especially since few entrepreneurs started out professionally in the hotel industry. They are generally property developers or proprietors of groups undergoing diversification, and they choose the hotel sector for personal assets reasons.

In the 1970s, the way the 'non-repayable loan' typically worked in the tourist sector was hampered by *rentier* and unprofessional practices. A private developer would ask for, and obtain, credit for the construction and development of a hotel complex, for example. With this money, he would start by setting up a research consultancy to implement the planned complex, and designating himself CEO, drawing as such a comfortable salary, a company car, sometimes a house and various expenses.[17] In this way the credit was soon used up. Either the project was declared bankrupt, even before the hotel had been built, and the debt immediately was written off or the bank unblocked new credits to finish the construction of the hotel and finance its activity, delaying by several years the partial repayment of the credit. Another variant consisted in a request for credit that was, right from the start, inflated, with the bank simultaneously financing the hotel and the developer's related expenses.[18] These actors have become more numerous and have consolidated their institutional position; it was the official intention of the public authorities to support a new source of fresh foreign currency, by enjoining on the banking sector an 'unstinting support' for the tourist sector.

Recent years have been those of stagnation and purge. Some entrepreneurs have been eliminated, and a restructuring process started at the beginning of 2004, with the help of international donors – the African Development Bank, the Arab Fund for Economic and Social Development, and the World Bank.[19] The sector is saturated, and lax banking packages have become less common. However, apart from excessive debt, another characteristic problem is still encountered, one that is also at the origin of several difficulties in payment: the inadequacy of bank loans when it comes to the specific needs of the sector. Tourism in Tunisia is in medium-term debt (in general, seven years redeemable annually) whereas the rule is rather to lend on a long-term basis (some fifteen years) with three- to four-year periods of grace.[20] This explains, even apart from international events, the very delicate situation which the sector is going through at present and the necessity of restructuring it from top to bottom.

Continuous discharges of debt, real but purely formal

The relative stability of bad debts does not, however, result from any laissez-faire on the part of the financial authorities. At official gatherings between bankers and international organizations, the BCT reckons that the sums injected into the Tunisian banking system to recapitalize the public banks and help out the private banks between 1992 and 2000 amounted to 6 thousand million dollars. The various operations of bank restructuring have always taken place under the auspices of the donors – IMF, World Bank and European Union – who have given loans but only with several written conditionalities. The banks themselves partly finance these restructurings, by abandoning their claim to part of the capital or interests. In spite of these massive interventions, at the end of 2002, the bad debts had, so to speak, reconstituted themselves. *Pace* the Tunisian authorities, the production of bad debts is not a thing of the past, but seems to proceed from the current political economy of Tunisia.

Three methods for cleaning up the accounts and discharging bad debts have been retained. As far as public debts are concerned, large-scale operations undertaken with the help of international donors have made it possible for institutions with increasing liabilities to be rendered viable. In 1997, a first structural adjustment facility (SAF I) for the banking sector made it possible for the situation created by the arrears of the big agricultural offices (cereals and oils) to be stabilized. The European Union had at that time gifted 100 million dollars and the World Bank lent 75 million dollars, measures which accompanied the wiping out of 1 thousand million DT of bad debts run up by these offices and owed to the *Banque nationale agricole* (BNA).[21] This operation was made possible thanks to a 99-year loan from the Central Bank to the BNA – which took it to mean an increase in shareholders' equity and not a debt owed to the state.[22] Thanks to this creative accounting of bad debts, the rates of the latter fell sharply between 1995 and 1999.[23] In the absence of any effective improvement in its methods of management, the banking situation very rapidly found itself turning 'tense', and the donors again urged the Tunisian authorities to clean up the accounts. The second facility (SAF II) concerned public and parapublic enterprises and the banks as a whole. Thanks to the loan of 120 million dollars from the World Bank and to the gift of 80 million dollars from the European Union, international organizations contributed to the wiping out of 549 millions of dinars of bad debts; the latter were consolidated as a state debt, and the banks could thus no longer consider them as a problem, nor deposit funds into them. In return, the public authorities committed themselves to repay them in 25 years at a zero interest rate, that is a painless effort of some 32 million DT per year.[24]

The second cleaning-up procedure concerns the modification of the techniques for depositing funds. The banks were authorized in 1999 to write off a significant proportion of their bad debts by funding at 100 per cent those which had shown no movement for four years. The same year, the banks benefited from a state guarantee for the credits granted to public businesses, thus seeing a number of bad debts disappearing from their accounts. In 1998, the banks were enabled to deduct the sums corresponding to provision for losses up to 50 per cent of their profit. This rate was raised to 75 per cent from 1999.

The creation of societies for debt collection – the third streamlining technique – accompanies the growth of political awareness of the problem. But if two societies of this type existed before, it was only in February 1998 that the activity of debt collecting societies was organized and regulated. The finance law of 1999 allowed each public bank to create a debt collection society in order to try and recuperate a minimum of private debts pending. At the end of 2000, a law extended this technique to banks as a whole, authorizing them to resort to the technique of *defeasance*, that is to sell debts in the symbolic *dinar* to streamline their accounts.[25] It hardly matters, in the final analysis, that these debt collection societies were active and that the operations launched proved successful: the interest of the technique lies elsewhere, in the way the difficulties were shunted outside the banking sphere. Even in the opinion of the international organizations, it is unlikely that these institutions manage to extract any significant sums from these activities.

The methods of provisioning are themselves revelatory of the artificial character of financial adjustment from the predominantly accounting perspective. In spite of the self-congratulatory plaudits of the BCT, we may well doubt the efficiency of these procedures for at least two reasons. On the one hand, all observers doubt the realism of the provisioning rates of the banks:[26] the state arbitrates in favour of taxation, and favours the existence of profits, even if they are fictive, thanks to the systematic underestimation of the risks incurred by banking commitments. Thus, it is not uncommon to see debts being provisioned at 25 per cent when the real situation of the enterprise in debt and its financial capacity should rather lead to opting for provisioning at 50 per cent. The IMF considers that the provisioning shortfall rose in 2002 to 3.5 per cent of the GDP, which is considerable. On the other hand, the provisions are constituted once deductions have been made from the guarantees held by the banks. Now, the evaluation of these guarantees is not carried out independently.[27] The current economic deterioration may lead to a fall in the price of goods guaranteed on the market; in particular, the dominant tendency is towards an overestimation of the value of the goods guaranteeing the loan. As a result of bureaucratic and nationalist considerations, the administration will not underestimate the value of the national assets. Furthermore, the banks are often incapable of concretizing the sale of the goods in question, as entrepreneurs are protected by very favourable laws, or by instrumentalizing justice.[28] There is a consensus on any numerical data which present improvements, a favourable balance sheet and profits, whatever may be the economic and financial reality. This is a common procedure in Tunisia, and points to a golden rule of Tunisian political economy: a fiction, constructed and widely accepted, appears more important and even more efficient than the reality.

All these operations are techniques for keeping accounts, reclassifying debts, cleaning up bills, and 'making up the figures', even though nobody has actually changed their behaviour as a result. It is difficult to incriminate the inability of regulators to impose new measures of risk control. It is difficult to blame the inability of banks to adopt new criteria of credit allocation or new methods of assessment of financial constraints; difficult, too, to doubt the aptitude of economic actors to pay off their debts, and difficult to refer to the lax attitudes or incompetence of the international organizations. The discourse of the Tunisian authorities suggests another path – that of the conscious decision to massage the figures to the detriment of any real cleaning-up. Parliamentary debates show that the public powers intend to help the banks to throw off certain constraints and to concentrate on the granting of credit, but that, all the same, they are not questioning the ways in which the banks intervene, nor the role of the latter in society.[29]

This hypothesis is corroborated by the recent history of relations with international organizations. Actually, ever since the 1980s, the World Bank had been trying, without success, to force the banking sector to reform. So when the sector was in fact restructured in 1999, this happened mainly as a result of a new turn of events on the international stage. With the financial crises in Asia and Russia, and more recently with the financial repercussions of the 11 September 2001 attacks, the cost of borrowing on the international markets became, comparatively speaking, too high. Tunisia, being a skilful recipient, decided in part to bow to requests from donors to profit from certain of their funds.[30] But this turnaround can also be explained by the adoption of a subtle strategy whereby the external constraint was bypassed – a reform was adopted when the results expected from it had already been more or less realized. Thus it was that the 1999 reform was accepted with few worries, especially since the bad public and parapublic debts had already partly been liquidated by the creative accountancy described above. This is added proof – if added proof were needed – of this current economic situation and temporary decision: the Tunisian authorities merely adopted certain fragments of the financial reform, those that they could accommodate most easily and that fundamentally modified neither the way in which the banking sector was managed, nor the social relations underlying it. Any massive privatization of the banking sector has always been rejected for very clear reasons: the banks are considered as instruments at the disposal of the government; fewer direct interventions on the part of the Central Bank do not in the least imply any less vigilance on the part of the central power when it comes to banking activities and institutions.[31] Since then, this approach has never been abandoned and certain banks are destined to remain within the purview of the state for long years to come: the mission of the *Banque nationale agricole* (BNA) is to support agriculture, the *Banque de l'habitat* (BH) is for accommodation and tourism, and the *Société tunisienne de banques* (STB) supports SMEs.

International donors have in any case taken good note of this, accepting the 'progressive' and 'prudent' strategy of the Tunisian authorities. The latter, to be sure, accepted and realized, in November 2002, the privatization of 52 per cent of the UIB (*Union internationale de la banque*) to the benefit of the *Société Générale* and that 54 per cent of the *Banque du Sud* at the end of 2005 to the benefit of Andalumaghreb SA, an alliance between the Moroccan bank Attijariwafa Bank and the Spanish Bank Santander. But this disengagement does not, for the time being, represent any real break: foreign banks were, right from the start, constrained to compromise with certain rules of the Tunisian banking sector, especially the lack of transparency around the management of credits and the negotiation of the gross trading profit.[32] The change in status of these two banks should not have much effect if we hypothesize that they will behave like other Tunisian private banks, especially like the foreign banks, whose methods of management and risk assessment are not noticeably different from those of the public banks.

The ambiguities in the modernization of the banking sector

All the same, this permanent situation obviously does not prevent there being technical improvements and real transformations, which follow the philosophy of liberalization to the letter.

A real improvement and a real liberalization

For a decade now, the process of modernization of the banking sector has made some real advances, propelled by new regulations issued by the Central Bank, by the increased presence of foreign banks, by projects of technical aid financed by donors, and by the emergence, however timid, of a certain degree of competition or by the needs of external financing. Since the official launch of the clean-up of the financial sector in 1992, the banks have improved the management of their funds, cleaned up their portfolios, and increased their shareholders' equity.[33] They have diversified their offers and their financial instruments, even if much still remains to be done. They have proceeded to systematic computerization and have tried to recruit more highly qualified personnel.

The process of liberalization has been the subject of several analyses.[34] In short, the banks no longer need the prior agreement of the BCT to grant loans, and interest rates are now free, even if, in reality, there are several notable exceptions due to the interventionism of the supervising authority and the banks' cartel strategy. With the era of adjustment, the development banks have become ideologically obsolete and the process of liquidation of these entities has started; in 2001, a new law modernizing the banking sector consecrated the universal bank and is pursuing the organizational and legal modernization of the sector.

The most significant transformations are found in the domain of regulation, mainly around the role of regulator of the Central Bank. Observers unanimously regret the lack of competent, autonomous and responsible personnel able to take decisions; they also highlight the ubiquitous nature of the BCT in the economic and financial management of the country; but, at the same time, they insist on the extent of the transformations – over the past decade – in the role allotted to the Central Bank and the subtleties of its exchange-rate and monetary management. The convertibility of the *dinar* is not yet complete, but it now affects all current operations, and only capital operations are strictly supervised. The BCT has adopted international standards: to fight inflation and to stabilize the real effective exchange rate, it skilfully manipulates its currency mix, its rates of intervention, its reserves, and its relations with commercial banks. However inadequately, the interest rate is starting to play its role as a signal. Considering these disparities, we might put forward this hypothesis: in spite of the cost of such a strategy, might it be that the Tunisian authorities have adopted a behaviour in conformity with the norms of the IMF when it comes to currency management (flexibility of adjustment with the aim of stabilizing the rate) in exchange for the perpetuation of a sort of subsidizing of credit in national currency aimed at protecting the level of buying power of Tunisians as much as possible?

The classification of banking assets is one of the most important measures taken by the BCT to modernize the banking sector. Banks are now obliged to classify their assets into four categories: 1) assets that require a follow-up; 2) uncertain assets; 3) worrying assets and 4) compromised assets (including – but not exclusively – debts which are more than 360 days overdue). A law of 1994 increased the BCT's powers of regulation. It updated the rules whereby banks are managed, fixed prudential norms and the ratios of liquidity and obligatory reserve. To intensify its control, the BCT can henceforth keep a very close eye on banks, including on-the-spot monitoring. It can, in particular, oblige them to increase their capital, to establish provisions for bad debts or litigious debts, or to abstain from distributing dividends. The Central Bank could exercise this kind of control previously, but this law emphasizes the desire of the Tunisian authorities to align themselves with international norms and, to some extent, to respond at least formally to the demands of international donors. According to the inspections of the BCT, in 2002, the Cook ratio – which measures the level of commitments of a financial institution with respect to its shareholders' equity – was respected by all banks, apart from the *Banque du Sud,* which proved prickly on this point.[35] Over and above the slowness inevitable in the application of such measures, respect for these ratios nonetheless has something formal or even fictive about it, when we realize that the banks do not carry out any correct reporting, that there is no real punishment for those who go bankrupt, and that the classification of debts is often subject to negotiation.[36]

A system mired in the past?

In spite of these new norms, new criteria for assessment, and new rules of control, why has the banking system changed so little since the start of the 1990s? Why is the relative level of bad debts still so high? Why is there still such an urgent need for provisioning?

A *trompe-l'oeil* modernization: this would be one, brutal way of interpreting the situation. On this view, the supervisory authorities are adopting new norms and institutions based closely on international models so as 'to create a good impression of themselves', as it were – to show that the country is adapting; but they are doing so very gradually, without necessarily adopting the spirit of those models, selectively and without convincing the parties most concerned: the banks. The latter are, it would thus appear, tranquilly perpetuating their archaic modes of operation. Proof lies in the repetitive character of the reforms announced. Clement Moore Henry notes, for example, that the themes that came into prominence as early as 1981 can be found in identical form at the end of the 1990s,[37] and, we might add, at the start of this century too.

However hasty, this interpretation is supported by numerous examples. On the government side, delays and time-lags in the adopting of written stipulations and juridical decisions support this view. Nothing has been done to oblige enterprises to present consolidated accounts in spite of the increase in the number of groups resulting from the proliferating number of companies.[38] Ever since March 2000, the information held by the two credit bureaus already in operation, the one for risks and the other for unpaid cheques, had to be centralized. However, they have not always been used as warning signals, mainly because they do not take any account of the state of debts classified or eligible for refinancing by business; it is as if nothing were being done to dissuade debtors, or to encourage the banks to be prudent about future bankruptcies. The management of the public banks is still administrative and political: subject to ministerial supervision for the least little operation, they have no autonomy of internal management; they are not subject to the code of private companies, and are still run by politicians more than by technicians.

The 2001 bank law is another example of this *trompe-l'oeil* modernization. A Tunisian banker has called it a 'reflection of the real competences of the country: a surface gloss of modernity laid over archaic practices that still continue'.[39] This assessment – which some might consider sweeping – is, however, not entirely unrealistic: at a time of globalization and free exchange with the European Union, this law maintains the need for the authorization of the Finance Minister for various operations (article 11), makes no allowances for bank assurance (article 25), continues to require that the bank director must be of Tunisian nationality (article 27), does not cover off-shore banks even though these are financing an increasing number of on-shore activities, and has nothing to say about foreign banks. In any case, the 2001 bank law can well be considered as a typical example of those 'disbursement laws' that are aimed at fulfilling conditionality and undermining the constraints imposed by donors. Such laws, accepted by the latter, in the final analysis legitimate the strategies of all the actors in the politico-financial complex, and previous types of behaviour can perpetuate themselves since new laws have been voted in – and these are a guarantee of modernity.

The accusation of archaism concerns the banks, too. Even these days, credits are not granted on the basis of a risk analysis: who you know (relatives, friends, family, or political acquaintances) continues to be the prime factor. Banks still lend on the basis of a name they recognize rather than a project they wish to endorse. Their provisions remain for the most part inadequate. Training, personnel management, and labour reorganization are practically virgin territory. When the European Union wanted to allocate 10 million euros to training in the banking sector, the managers in the different institutions were incapable of formulating the requirements of their sector and of deciding what exactly they needed in terms of technical assistance.[40] It hardly matters whether this incapacity results from a certain incompetence, or is the expression of a lack of good will, or reveals the absence of determination to change management styles. The silence of bank managers shows what a gap there is between what liberalization requires of financial institutions and their often very limited capacities. These days, as before, it highlights in particular the role of banks in the regulation of a social order implicit in the Tunisian economy: bankers, constituting as they do a mechanism of conveyance, the symbol of modernity, an efficient machine for allocating resources, are 'disposers lending on deposit' rather than financers.[41]

The recurrent failure of the Tunis Stock Exchange also suggests that we look at another facet of the extent to which this modernization is merely superficial: the persistence of behaviour that undermines the efficiency of modern techniques. In 2002 – nearly ten years after the measures taken to boost the Stock Exchange – its significance in the economy is still marginal (9.6 per cent of GDP) and even more in investment funding (barely five per cent of private investment). At the end of 2003, only 45 companies were listed in Tunis, including scarcely twenty or so that were industrial and commercial enterprises, with the majority of them being offshoots of local banks.[42] This failure can be explained by the numerous dysfunctions of the institution: rigging, insider trading, lack of regulation, lack of transparency and absence of trust. But these characteristics are not specific to Tunisia and, in other places, they have never prevented a stock exchange from developing. In spite of a real modernization of the market, the introduction of electronic listing and technical cooperation with the Paris Stock Exchange, the fact remains that businesses nowadays show no interest in being listed. Actually, bank financing is in general very easy for Tunisian groups to obtain. And it is really very cheap – competition in this very restricted segment of the market is harsh. In particular, banks have a remarkable 'advantage' over the finance market: they do not require accounts to be transparent.[43] Most listed businesses, it is claimed, regret having 'gone in for it' and are rumoured to have 'taken the plunge' merely to 'please the government' and show signs of good will (as with Monoprix and the SFBT) or to concretize arrangements with it (as with El Mazra in the Poulina group: it is said that becoming listed was the price to pay for lessening the amount of back taxes it had to pay and the period of grace it was granted). In the current state of the banking system, businesses in a position to be listed can very easily finance their growth and their activities from debt.

Difficulties in financing affect several small businesses for which, in any case, the Stock Exchange is out of reach. In fact, the Stock Exchange is the exact reflection of the highly specific modes of government: a huge gap between written stipulations and concrete practices; the absence of any real safeguards and of even a minimum of control; the personalization and concentration of power; and such intense hierarchization that, in the organizational pyramid, the actors very rapidly find themselves paralysed and stripped of responsibility. The *Commission des marchés financiers* (CMF: Commission for Financial Markets),[a] which has the task of controlling the markets and stock exchange operations, had no credibility at all from around 1994 to 2003. Since that date, under the influence of a new president whose competence and integrity are recognized by all, and as a result of the panic provoked by the demise of one of the most dynamic businesses, BATAM (which specializes in selling domestic electrical appliances on credit), it is starting to do its work by giving a dressing-down to some of the listed companies who were suspected of cooking the books.[44] However, this new start is proceeding in typical Tunisian fashion – by negotiation, *ad hoc* arrangements, and above all, slowly and gently. After all, the important thing remains respect for this social order in which nods and winks, and personal

---

[a]This is the equivalent of the COB: *Commission des Opérations de Bourse* or Commission for supervision of stock exchange operations, roughly equivalent to Stockwatch in Britain or the SEC in America. (*Translator's note.*)

relations, count for more than orthodox financial techniques. The Commission could have intervened more brutally since, legally speaking, it holds regulatory powers, disciplinary powers, and police powers. But in practice, it has little independence from the political sphere.[45] Not that it receives direct orders from Carthage – rather, it fears arbitrary decisions from higher authorities and worries, above all, about being contradicted or even penalized for decisions taken without the prior agreement of the central power. As various professionals remarked, with lucid bitterness, the liberalization and opening of the financial markets 'doesn't mean more market, or a market allowed to get on with things by itself', but the 'involvement of those in power in the market' and 'the dominance of uncertainty'.[46] Here too, the specificity of Tunisia is not being questioned. A considerable amount of research has demonstrated as much for the other countries in the Middle East and North Africa, or even for China.[47]

The selective, partial and incomplete understanding of market mechanisms might constitute a second source of explanation for the continuing fragility of the banking sector. So a well-known Tunisian banker asserts that Tunisia is characterized by 'a certain failure to understand the essential cogs and wheels of a financial market. Indeed, it is as if we had finished the main framework of a fine building and were now finding it really difficult to take the various decisions necessary to provide it with the equipment and the final touches necessary for it to be able to play the role we have in mind for it'.[48] This lack of understanding thus modifies the meaning of the measures of modernization and changes its effects from top to bottom: increase in the capital of the listed companies has in fact been transformed into distribution of reserves, with the Stock Exchange no longer playing its essential role of channelling savings towards businesses; the OEICs have been seen as a deposit and transformation operation, and not as a market operation. Similarly, 'upgrading', in particular the obligation imposed on businesses to reinforce their shareholders' equity, has indirectly reinforced the measures of 'portage': instead of contributing to restructuring the debts incurred by businesses, the measures undertaken to support the latter have had an effect which is, if not entirely the opposite, at least quite perverse: they have encouraged their bosses to run up personal debts to increase the capital of their businesses rather than seek funds elsewhere. Indeed, this last solution would indirectly have had the disastrous inconvenience of diluting the founder's capital and opening the accounts to the scrutiny of strangers.[49]

Clement Moore Henry says practically the same thing when he emphasizes how the market, in Tunisia, was set up before the actors could grasp the mechanisms that govern it, trapped as they allegedly are by state control and the prying interventionism – 'socialist', to make it even worse! – of the administration. This situation, he claims, was reinforced by the dependence of entrepreneurs on the state, and the liberal rhetoric of the government, which in reality concealed the expression of administrative interests.[50] We should without the least doubt distance ourselves from these two interpretations: the first betrays an elitist vision of economic relations and thus of the reforms, in that economic actors are considered incapable of understanding the benefits of the market; the second is too hostile to statism, in that the public powers are perceived as incapable of taking their desire for modernization to its logical conclusion; they both adopt a mechanistic and normative vision of the reforms. But they both bring out, very relevantly, a fundamental element that Max Weber had underlined with regard to the spread of capitalism:[51] it is impossible to transform people's behaviour and economic mentalities by economic policies. In other words, this incomplete understanding of market mechanisms is particularly expressive of a very specific ethos and very specific practices of the exercise of power.

Preference for bad debts, endlessly renewed

Another interpretation is possible, however: one that foregrounds the way the *preference* for bad debts continues to play a part. My hypothesis is this: liberalization and modernization, instead of putting an end to the 'bad governance' of entrepreneurs, paradoxically offer bankers and entrepreneurs new mechanisms that enable them to perpetuate their practices. A few examples will show what I mean.

Before the reform of 1995, a bank could not wipe out a debt unless it had been demonstrated by lawyers that the money had not been paid back. So it had to wait for the outcome of its action at law to be able to wipe off its account, or hope that the business would go bankrupt or go into liquidation. The law of 17 April 1995, originally aimed at protecting businesses in difficulty, avoiding a rise in unemployment and fostering reconversion, was quickly interpreted by the entrepreneur as an extra opportunity to ward off the demands of his creditors.[52] Once the business is under the protection of this law, creditors no longer have the right to be in contact with the debtor, and no out-of-court settlement is possible. While waiting for a verdict, they cannot ask for the least repayment, and certainly not embark on its recovery. Now, more often than not, the law decides in favour of the debtor, which transforms the whole process of bankruptcy into a veritable loophole. According to the bankers in Tunis, some half of all bad debts resort to the law on bankruptcy. The phenomenon, indeed, seems to be growing. In this way, the law is being instrumentalized by unscrupulous entrepreneurs, in particular by those the Tunisian bourgeoisie and traditional business figures consider as '*mafiosi*', 'nouveaux riches', and 'clan members': this practice thus constitutes another mode of the non-repayable loans mentioned above. On the other hand, the law seems to represent a technique for protecting oneself from the wrath of the central power. Thus it is rumoured that the brother of Kamel El Taïef, a recently disgraced businessman, close to Ben Ali, immediately placed his businesses under the protection of this law the minute he found out that his brother had been imprisoned, so as to avoid being prosecuted by the tax authorities, the CNSS (*Caisse nationale de sécurité sociale*) or directly by Carthage. Thus, using the law for one's own ends sometimes has a political connotation and is then akin to a rampant privatization of public interests. Generally, however, the law is used to cope with real problems of financing, without any political connotation, playing its social and protective role. The fact remains that this law has still not been changed, in spite of repeated requests from bankers.

How are we to interpret this situation? Is it a political instrumentalization aimed at controlling the economy more tightly? This seems doubtful in view of the tangle of interests that do not always converge, and the great number of different actors involved. We might conclude that this law was conceived by the central power to keep the process of creation of bad debts going and thereby protect immoral figures in power, at the same time controlling entrepreneurs – but this would be to fall into a rather naive Machiavellianism. By drawing up the law on bankruptcies, the administration was pursuing a real objective, 'upgrading businesses', modernizing them in the legal and economic senses. In particular, it attempted to put into practice the social watchword of the public powers: the survival of businesses, the maintaining of employment, and the quest for stability. Economic and financial actors, public and private, judicial institutions and even administrations have, however, interpreted the words of this law in such a way as to update or even revivify previous kinds of behaviour. In the case of litigation between an insolvent business and a bank, for instance, the Court of Appeal in Tunis always favours recovery, in other words, business.[53] Except for big companies, the judge is of course given no political directive for these little disputes of which the central power is not even aware. But the judges, having come from the same society, and imbued with the same ethos, are conscious of social issues, and they fear the effects of economic liberalization. They cannot be totally immune from the official, endlessly repeated discourse of officialdom and, like all Tunisians, they are subject to a political situation where criticism is impossible, even of technical subjects. An interpretation that favours the debtor was made possible by the absence of any definition of insolvency, since the legislator, for the same reasons, prefers to defer to the judge. So, without any hidden motives, the Court of Appeal in Tunis can appeal to such notions as 'serious difficulties' and non-intentionality so as to pass judgement in favour of employment and economic activity. If, for the bank, bad debts constitute a refusal to pay, the Court of Appeal generally chooses to interpret the situation as an inability to pay off the debt, not a deliberate intention to evade one's obligations.

This last example thus suggests that the process which generates bad debts is kept going by interpretations and activities that lie outside all regulation. Whatever may be the text of the law, the assessment of the risk depends, in the final analysis, not on the viability or the quality of the project, nor even on the financial situation of the entrepreneur and his business, nor even on the possibilities for development, but plainly and simply on the quality of the signature and the (re)cognition of the debtor. Even apart from the law on bankruptcy, a banker will not be encouraged to turn to the law to obtain payoff, as he is dissuaded from doing so by his political and social environment: 'he is helping Tunisia, you need to understand him and help him'; 'you just can't do that to him', 'he employs heaps of people') ... these are all arguments that he has internalized even before having to face the problem.

Crises update this social interpretation of debt by giving official sanction to tolerance of its partial payoff. Thus, in 2002–3, the state expressly asked the banks to close their eyes to non-payoff from hotels, in view of the severe crisis affecting the sector.[54] If he perseveres, the banker will have great difficulty in finding a judge able to implement the guarantee. Even if the government's social preoccupations spread out across society as a whole, such behaviour cannot be interpreted simply in terms of political slogans, of instructions to avoid unemployment, impoverishment and economic downturn. Much more profoundly, in a little country like Tunisia, there is a consensus that payoff can be delayed, and one should not drive the debtor up against a wall or make him lose face – everyone's dignity should be respected. The sense of security, social stability and economic paternalism is shared by those big business figures who, thanks to the interplay of relations (family, friends, political and regional acquaintances), are forever running into each other in professional and private life. Here it is personal relations that prevail, as well as the notions of personal credit, honour and reputation.

Laws and conditionalities cannot overturn the way the politico-financial complex works. When the UIB was partially privatized, after the criticisms about lack of transparency and retention of information that had accompanied most prior privatizations, the Government, the Central Bank and the privatized bank did everything they could to ensure that the operation was carried out in due form. Everything ... except access to the portfolio of credits, which, in spite of pressure from diverse quarters, was never presented in an adequately documented way.[55] The candidates were not given access to the credits already classified: the reason given was that their situation had been settled previously and thus could not constitute an element of assessment of the assets they would inherit. The *Société Générale*, which won the invitation to tender, knows the truth of the matter: it now reckons that the handling of these bad debts was very partial. Only after a long trial of strength, in which it called on the intervention of the French authorities, did it – for once – manage to impose their provisioning on the Central Bank. But it also reckons it bought up a far from negligible part of the market at the price of a modest entry ticket for a multinational, and access to a national market that is, in spite of everything, lucrative.[56]

A multiform debt economy

The extent of bad debts is nothing new. But, after a certain date, they started to be perceived as problematic. This date was relatively recent: even at the end of the 1990s, international donors had not identified bad debts as the central point of reforms. The harmful character of these bad debts appeared only with a change in the view of what constituted a 'good' financial system. Transformations in the international environment, the dominance of liberal ideology, the deepening of liberalization, the modifications in international regulations and the rising power of international organizations in this area were all necessary before this new interpretation could gain credence.[57] The need for finance constrained Tunisia to adopt these international norms: the shock of liberalization and international pressures created tensions that were a condensation of the dilemmas and contradictions of Tunisian political economy. The process of creation of bad debts really constitutes just one aspect – the now 'scandalous' and heterodox aspect – of the debt economy. The Tunisian financial system sustains it by financing the budget and, more generally, public policies, and by contributing to the functioning of the national economy and the development of mass consumption.

Financing public action

As in many other debt economies, the banking system serves, first and foremost, to finance government action via the financing of its budget deficit. By an effect of the diffusion of norms, Tunisia must however present budgets that are close to equilibrium and more or less respect the Maastricht criteria. But the state budget does not necessarily take into account the exact extent of public expenditure. Indeed, several state, parastate or parapublic financings pass through other channels able to bypass budgetary constraints – first and foremost via the banking system.

Thus, bad debts stem partly from a delegating of economic policies: these debts are in reality concealed budgetary expenses or, more precisely, non-budgeted expenditures of the state. They correspond to the financing of subsidies to agricultural offices, aid to businesses pre-financed by the banks and never or only partially repaid by the state, or even by operations of recapitalization of public enterprises.[58] Of course, it is difficult to distinguish between, on the one hand, mismanagement of public entities and, on the other, non-payment of officially due subsidies by the central administration, a policy of tacit participation in mass consumption and revenue (farmers, SMEs) and the financing of works of public utility carried out by big companies. Be this it may, this mode of financing is still widely used these days, in spite of official statements claiming that it is now obsolete. The behaviour of the Tunisian authorities would lead us to suppose this: in spite of repeated pressure from donors, they have not always provided the consolidated state accounts. The strategy of diversification mentioned above with regard to private entrepreneurs also concerns state actors:[59] indeed, the loose grouping constituted by the participation of public companies allows them to multiply the sources of financing and thus to lighten the burden of financial and political constraints.

Furthermore, thanks to the interplay of a diffuse form of state control and the historical legitimacy of state *dirigisme*, 'whether they are public or private, banks have been transformed into virtual agencies for the payment of loans from the Central Bank'.[60] Liberalization has merely shifted the forms of intervention and made its modes of operation more subtle, as part of a process akin to a dilution or concealed privatization of debt in a network of power and sociability.[61] The restructuring of the productive public sector passes mainly through the banks, especially through a selective use of credits and respect for dates of payment. Thus, credit for businesses whose liquidation has already been decided on can be cut off, and support for businesses destined for restructuring or privatization continued – even if this leads to the creation of new bad debts. Industrial policies pass through direct subsidies but also through major financial support that finds concrete embodiment in the opening up of lines of credit, rebate programmes, and financial aid, such as the *Fonds de Promotion et de Décentralisation Industrielle* (FOPRODI: Fund for Industrial Promotion and Decentralisation) or the *Fonds national de garantie* (National Guarantee Fund).[62] The very official and media-savvy 'upgrading programme' meant to accompany the modernization of the industrial fabric, thanks to aid for investment, draws on the banks, which are co-represented within the pilot committee for upgrading (the COPIL) – a bureaucratic organization if ever there was one.[63] The banks are thus directly inserted into the negotiation and construction of the entrepreneurial 'consensus': the allocation of subsidies is decided on the basis of different criteria. Crucial among these is the banking situation of the entrepreneur, which itself emerges from the nature and quality of his personal relations with financers and sometimes politicians.

Agricultural policies also pass through the banking sector: even if credit here has remained relatively low in comparison with the banks' financing of the rest of the Tunisian economy and the overall financing of agriculture, it has allowed the modernization of agriculture from the 1970s onwards, the concentration of wealth, and the rise of a new oligarchy.[64] Now as before, state-controlled decisions influence banking activity in particular because only the public banks provide credit to the peasants. Their resources comprise only marginally shareholders' equity and their activities rest essentially on budgetary resources and exterior resources, themselves guided by the public authorities within the framework of bilateral or international agreements.[65] The involvement of the banking sector as an intermediary for the public authorities also takes the form of the financing of big offices (such as the Office of Cereals or the National Office of Oils) and the taking over by the state of non-repaid debts from the public banks whose origin in reality lies in subsidies that were never paid.[66] Furthermore, the banks participate fully in the process of concentration, political patronage and social display:[67] small and medium-sized farmers find it immensely difficult to gain access to credit; they are directed to NGOs or to programmes of assistance in accordance with clientelist and partisan logic, and also a logic of small allocations that prevents any effect of modernization or development and any substantial improvement in quality of life and lifestyle.

Even though it is the object of an interventionism that is often more direct thanks to specific programmes and funds, social policy also passes through the banking system. Even more than in industry or agriculture, this commitment on the part of the banks is, in reality, an act of mediation to the benefit of the state. The *Banque tunisienne de solidarité* (BTS) is, in fact, a 'socially oriented line of credit'[68] more than a bank: it lends without guarantee, after an interview with the beneficiary of the loan and the obtaining of information provided by party cells, *comités de quartier* (local district committees), the social worker or the *omda* – literally the 'head of sector', corresponding to the lowest grade in the territorial administration – or else directly by police reports.[69] Likewise, the public authorities impose on all banks a certain quota of aid, at favourable rates, towards the creation of businesses within the framework of the *Fonds national pour l'emploi* (FNE, National Fund for Employment). Generally speaking, banking criteria and professional norms would seem to require that all these dossiers be rejected; provisioning for bad debts is, in any case, made the moment the loan is granted.[70] This latter has, in fact, no economic basis, but it fits into the politics of insertion and social aid which the Tunisian banks cannot evade, on pain of losing the trust of the authorities and being unable, when circumstances turn difficult, of gaining a favourable hearing.

Financing private economy and consumption

The debt economy also finances the investments and operating of the private productive sector. The official language used of bad debts emphasizes this dimension: in the absence of Tunisian capitalism at the time of independence, a national economy had to be built up at the same time that the national state and the national society were being constructed. The Tunisian banking system, at that time almost completely public, made this aim possible during the 1970 and 1980s, and entire private Tunisian groups could be created. In order to achieve this, banks were transformed into machines for distributing credit, in accordance with the guidance of the Central Bank, without much autonomy.[71] If this interpretation needs to be treated with caution, insofar as it places great emphasis on voluntarism and state control and conceals the other logics at work, it is certain that, even these days, Tunisian groups, mainly family groups, have little shareholders' equity, and are more deeply in debt than their economic, technical and financial status should allow, and that they operate and develop almost exclusively with money from the banks.[72] This historically constructed process facilitates the creation of bad debts. From the 1960s onwards, right up to the 1980s, it was easy to create and destroy businesses with 'public' money, that is the money of public banks, money from public savings and money not paid into the Treasury in the form of tax. Indeed, the state had very officially adopted a policy of fiscal laxity as a counterpart to this strategy of investment and construction of the national economy.[73] With the crisis of the end of the 1980s and 1990s, this behaviour showed up in a new light: it was even easier to pull out, to face the difficulties of liberalization, competition, recession and budgetary restrictions, now that the banks were continuing to provide 'adequate' financing via the acceptance of bad debts, incomparably more competitive than non-banking financing. In the absence of any reaction on the part of the banks, regulatory entities, supervisory authorities and debtors, the bank sector remained the main actor in the debt economy. The relative comfort in which the banks find themselves has prevented the massive use of other financial instruments such as the Stock Exchange and its several finance mechanisms, venture capital companies or leasing companies.

However, during a recession, the banking sector is no longer in a position to follow the frantic rhythm of credit requests. This is what explains the recent aggravation of inter-company business and the appearance of outstanding payments and inter-company debts now considered as non-recoverable.[74] The conjunction of the slowdown in lending by the banks, economic and commercial results that are worse than expected, mismanagement, and even plain and simple embezzlement, has led businesses that were already heavily in debt to the banking system to turn to their suppliers, from whom they to some extent took forced loans. The tense situation of the years 2001 and, especially, 2002, brought this problem out into the open; in reality, it is a recurrent problem. As an observer wrote in 1996: 'it remains the case that one of the causes behind the difficulties of businesses in every sector of economic activity and, thus, one of the reasons hampering their development and growth, is the accumulation and considerable volume of their outstanding payments'.[75]

But the debt economy does not, of course, concern merely the productive economy. Consumers too are part and parcel of these relations of debt. With the rise in the standard of living of the 1970s and 1980s, and the slowdown in growth experienced in the 1990s, in a period when the market was opening up and the supply of goods increasing, they are becoming even more heavily involved. The stagnation in revenue made the consumer credit that developed in the 1990s and 2000s all the more popular.

The extent of the debt, or even overindebtedness, of households cannot be assessed, given the highly political nature of the information. In 2003, its dimensions were, nonetheless, 'disquieting' according to the public authorities. In the absence of specialized institutions, this debt came about through various channels that all converged on the banking system. Only the better-off were able to resort directly to the banks via 'personal credits'; this means of coping was, however, limited by the lack of an official policy of consumer credit.

The middle class benefited from advances from the most secure and best-organized employers,[76] and, for certain products with a social dimension such as popular cars, from funds with surplus budgets, mainly the CNSS (*Caisse nationale de sécurité sociale*). But it was mainly the shopkeepers, hypermarkets and specialists in domestic electrical appliances, starting with BATAM, which made possible the explosion of consumer credit. The banks played a major, if hidden, role, by refinancing shopkeepers' bills. Before the passing of the law on 'sale with payment facilities' – for such is the official description of consumer credit – there were no regulations in this area and companies were able to make 'unauthorized' offers, with exorbitant conditions: certain products were sold on credit, sometimes for up to three or four years, at usurious rates that sometimes rose to 30 per cent or even 40 per cent. The banks hastened to refinance the bills and letters of commerce of these companies, as the activity was so lucrative. The law of 2 June 1998 limited the number of deadlines and stipulated that the price above which interest rates were calculated should be strictly identical with that of the cash purchase of the goods.[77] It thus attempted to limit the observed drift without, however, providing itself with the means of any real mastery of that very perilous sector, short-term – or indeed very short-term – credit. On the one hand, officially speaking, the banks still cannot offer consumer credit and specialized companies are still not authorized to operate in Tunisia. On the other hand, consumers are in reality unable to prove that the base price of the credit purchase is not the same as the cash price of the purchase – which also reduces the effectiveness of the struggle against the abuses of hire purchase companies.

Over the last few years, the gathering crisis, the aggravation of inequalities and the impoverishment of part of the middle class explain the astonishing drift which consumer credit has experienced: households short of money were getting into debt by buying goods on credit so as to be able to resell them on the unofficial market and thus obtain liquid assets.[78] Realizing that this kind of misappropriation of funds was taking place, and under pressure from shopkeepers in difficulties, the BCT gradually regulated the sector by lowering the credit term to 18 months, then authorizing *de facto*, but not officially, the consumer credit activities undertaken by banks via short-term credit lines. This first move towards normalization immediately brought out the extent of the problem: the volume of bills seems to have increased automatically by 30 per cent in 1999, after the passing of the 1998 law.[79]

Consumer credit was not encouraged by the banking regulatory authorities. On the contrary, the latter blocked the creation of specialized companies precisely because they were worried that they might lose control of the money supply, household debt and the economy in general. Simultaneously, however, they were unable to stop a process that lay outside their grasp thanks to too great consumer pressure, on the one hand, and to the opportunities and response capacities of certain shopkeepers and bankers on the other. Once the process had been triggered, the regulatory authority could only come to terms with it – something it did really well: consumer credit is part of the discourse of modernization, of increase in the standard of living, and of the economic democratization of the regime; it is a major preoccupation, while having the advantage of not being entered in the books under the bad debts of the banking system . . . at least until the bankruptcy of the main firm producing domestic electrical appliances offering consumer credit, BATAM, and then of Electro Kallel. This very particular form of credit, costly and relatively unregulated, is absolutely not created by the central power; but it is well established, and this, together with its social importance, make of it a particularly attractive instrument for the deployment of state strategies, and notably the unpredictable impulses of control and supervision of economic operators.

Bad debts, a 'modern' mechanism

These examples suggest that, far from being exhausted, the model of the debt economy, in this form of permanent creation of bad debts, is perpetuating itself. This statement flies in the face of the official rhetoric on the outmoded nature of this system, said to be directly linked to the nationalist, interventionist and developmentalist objectives of the 1970s and 1980s. The IMF recognizes, besides, that the liberalization (however timid it may be) of the Tunisian economy has contributed to the perpetuation of this system.[80]

According to the received idea, bad debts arise mainly from public actors. Here we can recognize the effects of a liberal rhetoric spreading across society under the (populist) form of the implicit questioning of the state, and of its administration in particular. It is true that the major offices and certain public enterprises have mainly been sources of significant deficits, largely financed on bank credit; above all, the operations of recapitalization of the public banks have been made public by the financial participation of international donors, and made visible by the open intervention of the state.

However, the three current sources of bad debts are the hotel sector, these days largely private and rendered so fragile that certain analysts describe it as being a systemic risk, the very diffuse sector of SMEs and the highly concentrated sector of big fortunes and personalities who are politicians and/ or speculators. As a result, after the state's operation to clean up balance sheets and recapitalize, bad debts are indeed mainly of private origin. This is another facet of the rampant privatization of the economy. During the financial restructuring of 1999, the number of bad debts negotiated by the World Bank for that same year finally fell into the following categories: 700 MDT (millions of dinars) of parapublic origin, 300 MDT of public origin, and 2 thousand million DT of private origin. There is no doubt that the participation of the private sector in the production of bad debts is crucial.

Public banks are those which suffer the most from bad debts of private origin. But we need to qualify this statement in two ways. On the one hand, the difference between banks is much less closely linked to the nature of capital than to its status, since development banks have to cope with more bad debts than commercial banks,[81] whether public[82] or private[83]. On the other hand, this assessment is certainly out of date, a reflection of the previous financial structure, largely dominated by public banks. From the end of the 1980s, private banks were massively affected by the phenomenon. The fact that Tunisian groups divide up their deposits and their funds between banks without bothering whether the latter are public or private, in a strategy of diversification and optimization of their capacity for borrowing, is not without relevance to this diffusion. The rising power of private banks was accompanied by the growth of their share in the granting of credit and their possession of bad debts. Furthermore, since the middle of the 1990s, the nature of capital means it is no longer possible to distinguish between commercial banks; what we are seeing, rather, is an individualization of the banks – a result of the participation or non-participation of a foreign bank in their directorial institutions, a result of the quality of their staff, and a result of the type of commercial and financial strategy of the management team. The rampant privatization of the Tunisian economy has led to the privatization of its debt economy and of its bad debts. It is within this context that we need to understand what has been called the 'criminalization' of the Tunisian economy by those close to the central power, with 'families' and 'clans' united in obtaining non-repayable debts and in the establishment of new bad debts.[84] These changes suggest that it is not the public or private nature that conditions certain types of behaviour, but simply an economic, and – even more – political and social context.

The absence of any major differences between national banks and foreign banks also reinforces this situation. Another received idea about the Tunisian banking system – admittedly not equally shared by all parties – holds that foreign banks are more virtuous and less lax when it comes to managing and following up debts. This assertion too is not without foundation. There is no doubt that foreign banks are subject to constraints, in particular to the respect of norms defined by the head offices, generally much stricter than those of the BCT. The subsidiaries of foreign banks can benefit from the technical, commercial, IT and computer know-how of their group. But the facts remain: foreign banks also experience rates of bad debts that are much higher than those accepted by the head offices, and they suffer from the same blindness and the same weaknesses when it comes to the criteria of family and reputation.

Only one example is necessary: the two banks most involved in the financing of the group Ben Ayed-BATAM which went bankrupt in 2002 are the UBCI (*Union bancaire pour le commerce et l'industrie* – its foreign shareholder is the *Banque nationale de Paris*) and Citibank.[85] The UBCI was certainly influenced by the family connections of certain of its Tunisian directors, and a former chairman of the bank was related to the Ben Ayed family. As for Citibank, it carried out the same political analysis as all the other banks in Tunis, in spite of its offshore status and its international strategy. BATAM, a symbol of the democratization of consumption, with its crucial social and political dimensions, and, what is more, close to the circles of the central power, was indisputably a 'good' risk. Admittedly, the foreign banks were the first to ring the alarm bell to warn the BCT, but they were also the banks most committed to the company. It is much more certain that they can allow themselves to be more virtuous and, in appearance, more lax as well, since they can benefit from more guarantees than the Tunisian banks: currently, foreign banks require that an equivalent sum to that of the loan proposed in Tunisia be deposited in a foreign market, in London, Paris or Geneva, which removes a great deal of the risk incurred. . . .[86] Nonetheless, it is just as certain that this episode is these days instrumentalized by a Tunisian banking sector that is reluctant to open up and is nervous of possible international competition, made theoretically inevitable by the liberalization of services.

This general panorama of the banking system and its modes of operation has shown the centrality of bad debts in the debt economy, a space in which creditors, debtors and intermediaries can meet, as well as public actors and private actors, bankers, entrepreneurs and consumers, administrations and markets, and national, foreign and international administrations, and so on. It thereby suggests the importance of the relations and mutual dependencies that enable the mechanisms of power to insert themselves into the economic and financial cogs of the machine in order to control, supervise and sometimes repress. The following chapter analyses the political significance of these ever-renewed interdependencies.

2

Dependence through Debt

The debt economy appears, in the tendentious but illuminating words of a banker, to be 'a question of culture on both sides'.[1] There is a culture of notoriety and fame: bankers continue to lend on the basis of a name. There is also a protectionist culture, one of state control: the bank, even when private, appears to economic clients, individuals and traders, as an intermediary, a representative of power. Continuing in the terms of the banker interviewed, we might even say that it is a question of culture on three sides: the state is in fact not the last to perpetuate this system by cultivating an interventionist, voluntarist and, here too, strongly protectionist 'culture'.

These 'cultures' did not, of course, emerge *ex nihilo*; the types of behaviour that characterize them are the expression of many varied interests. A rapid reading of the Tunisian banking system might lead one to think that the banks are the first victims of bad debts. But this is not actually the case. In one way, they are satisfied with this system: they make profits; their economic and even financial performance is still perfectly decent; intermediation rates are very high, the short-term credits by which they finance investments and productive activities are much more profitable than hypothetical medium- and long-term credits; the current gap between input and output creates financial costs that are highly remunerative, such as premiums and the costs of non-payment; above all, the banks pass losses arising from bad debts onto interest rates which are thus increased, according to the professionals, by some four or five points for the majority of credits.[2] While the lack of provision makes the profits pretty fictive, they still exist, and shareholders do actually pick up their dividends. Foreign banks spotted this: the *Banque nationale de Paris* never questioned its historical participation in the UCBI, a remnant of the French colonial presence, including during the period when it was refocusing and rationalizing its interests abroad; the *Société Générale*, Attijariwafa Bank and Santander have just accepted the 'handicaps' of the system to benefit from a consistent presence on the Tunisian market.

This suits everyone, agreed. But how does the system hang together? How can this headlong increase in credit and debt have lasted for so many years?

Collective participation in a fictive world

The favourable economic circumstances provide us with a first answer: the continuous growth in the economy and, even more, in its financial activity have enabled the banking system gradually to absorb the weight of bad debts.

The current 'alarmist' breakdowns result from cumulative calculation of the debts that have not been fully paid off for years or even decades, and do not reflect the reality of the situation at any given moment. An *e contrario* demonstration was provided by the economic crisis of 2002: growth had fallen to less than two per cent, and all the fragility and weakness of the banking system were suddenly revealed. The consequences in terms of businesses going bankrupt were real enough. However, during a period of growth, new loans enable businesses in debt to pay off old bills. On the side of the banks, even the partial repayment of previous debts as well as the payment of bank charges and assorted other financial costs cover the new loans quite adequately; thus, the system carries on, with ever more loans, ever more debts, and ever more interests and financial costs.

So, in a period of growth, nobody is affected: the banks are partially repaid, and repaid at least enough to enable them to live thanks to their margins on financial operations, thanks also to their lax practices when it comes to the constitution of loan loss reserve and the valuation of guarantees. Businesses see the weight and cost of bad debts being passed on to them in interest rates and margins of financial operations higher than they would be in a financial system that was run to a lesser degree on bad debts; but this cost is really felt by only a minority of them – well-managed businesses that do indeed repay all their debts.

And yet a banking system is, first and foremost, a system of belief; and like any system of belief, it holds together because everyone believes in it.[3] In Tunisia, everyone believes that the system is solid and, even more, permanent and stable. All those involved (banks, Central Bank, financial companies, businesses, public authorities, political authorities, international entities in contact with Tunisia) are aware of the fragility of the banking system, its weak points, its inadequacies, its key points, and its potential sources of systemic risk. But they all know, too, that the state and the international donors will always intervene to make up for these deficiencies. In particular, they are aware that it is not the economic and financial reality that counts here, but an accountants' reality, an imagined reality. We thus find ourselves, so to speak, in a fictive world. The difficulties – for example the importance of arrears or the extent of bad debts – are, in the worst-case scenario, not recorded, and in the best-case scenario are largely minimized, as the inadequacy of the provisions shows. Any chinks in the system are not acknowledged, and, for example, the systematic over-evaluation of guarantees and mortgages or the non-recovery of bad debts by the juridical system are never taken into account. In order to continue existing, the reality that is thus constructed, the reality of 'false concretes',[4] depends on people respecting the rules of this fictive world.

Language seems to play a crucial role here, with 'its indefinite ability to make people believe or surmise certain things, its aptitude to gamble on "trust" and to intimate that this trust necessarily exists; and its ability, also, to lead people to accept that what is said really is so'.[5] We cannot violate language, nor infringe the rules of fiction, on pain of being ejected from the system. Everyone believes and behaves 'as if': as if there were no systemic risks, as if the extent of bad debts did not pose serious problems, as if the prudential ratios were respected, as if streamlining and restructuring had taken place, as if the juridical system actually worked. As a result, the dividends handed out to shareholders are largely fictive: according to the estimates of Tunisian professionals, a realistic devaluation of the total amount of their guarantees (some 15 per cent), and thus an equivalent overvaluation of the provisions, could lead to banks' capital disappearing.[6]

Likewise, the Cook ratios are respected, so we are told, by all banks, but nobody knows exactly what is included in this ratio, how reportings are made, or how risks are evaluated. The balance sheets are improving and the bad debts represent a smaller and smaller proportion of them, but this progress results mainly from creative accounting and technical sleight of hand: this is the case with the reschedulings that turn a 'debt 4' (total loss) into a 'debt 1' (risky debt), without the economic and financial situation changing.

Facets of state activism

By setting itself up, *urbi et orbi*, as a lender – and thus guarantor – of last resort, the state plays a decisive role in the construction of this fiction, in particular via the *Banque centrale de Tunisie*. The state regularly takes over the debts that 'fall within its purview', the debts of offices, of development agencies, and of state-controlled and quasi-state-controlled enterprises. In addition, the BCT has clearly let it be known that a bank will never be 'abandoned' and that state support can always be counted on. Even more than its words, its actions have given credibility to its commitment and contributed to consolidating the fiction described above. In 1991, the *Banque tuniso-qatari d'investissement* (BTQI) found itself bankrupt after suffering severe losses (over 30 million dollars) in currency transactions.[7] The Central Bank immediately intervened to prop it up, drawing on the whole banking profession to do so: the other banks present on the Tunisian market had to write off the costs of their participation in this salvage plan under the rubric 'loss on exchange operations'. This situation has lasted. Until its privatization in 2005, the *Banque du Sud* survived thanks to 'drip-feeding' from the BCT, which plays the role not so much of an umpire and regulator but rather that, closer and more interventionist, of 'the bank of banks' or 'the mother bank'.[8] We see here, very concretely, what it means when everyone participates in the fictive world, when everyone respects the rules of the fictive world: it was the other banks which intervened directly in the salvage plan on the orders of the Central Bank, and not the state. In the case of the national offices too, the state assumed only partial responsibility, and the banks were forced to abandon their claim to the interest due.

To some extent, there is nothing exceptional about this unconditional support. Ever since the major financial crises, especially since the crash of 1929, the role of lender of last resort has spread across all banking economies.[9] This role was recently reactivated once the negative consequences of the liberal drift of the 1980s had been acknowledged. When the survival of a major bank or a national business is at stake, and thus when the national economy and national interests are involved, the state's direct intervention is recognized as legitimate, even if the causes for the bankruptcy lie with the company leaders who have managed in an inappropriate or inadequate way, failing to calculate the risks realistically or even indulging in embezzlement. Just to focus on the case in France, and on the most recent events, the state did not hesitate to intervene to save Crédit Lyonnais,[10] admittedly a public interest bank, or the Alsthom company, which is completely private. However, in the case of Tunisia, this commitment goes further. We ought however to hypothesize that state intervention is, in this case, different in nature. The banking fiction fully assumes this role of lender of last resort: the Central Bank or the state intervene on principle, whatever the bank, its size, its economic importance, or its political significance. In particular, this interventionism extends to many other areas. Admittedly, the BCT has modernized the way it intervenes, following structural adjustments. Its intervention still remains just as direct, and is carried out on the same day-to-day basis, for one reason alone: the operation of this fictive world. The Central Bank, for instance, continues to intervene in problems of liquidity, more frequent than is usually acknowledged,[11] so as to avoid a bank's falling into too severe difficulties or even going bankrupt. This fictive world functions by protectionism and, simultaneously, by tolerating irresponsibility.

State interventions need to be understood within the framework of the global debt economy, of the fictive construction of a solid banking system, at the heart of the economic performance of the country and its political stability. They go beyond the rubrics of 'state intervention', or 'controlled liberalism', and even of interventionism. They are systemic. They are non-official, and stem not from the state or one of its representative organizations, but from the whole system. Its own rules do not emerge from laws, codes, texts or directives, but most usually from non-written norms that all protagonists are familiar with.

The virtuous circle of external funding

The main tensions that the Tunisian economy is experiencing come from currency financing: this is the explanation for the strategic character, as far as the Tunisian authorities are concerned, of their relation with donors and the fact that foreign partners must at all costs play a part in this fictive world. If the external financial situation of Tunisia has improved since the crisis of the years 1986–7, it has nonetheless remained 'tense' since the mid-1990s. In order to finance its needs, the Tunisian economy absolutely needs to obtain additional resources from outside, since income from tourism, remittances from emigrants and exports are all insufficient. Borrowings, public or private, allow this minimum level of reserves to be reached. So the Tunisian economy finds itself, financially speaking, in a situation of dependence, which is expressed less in relation to its GDP – the percentage remains within acceptable limits[12] – than in relation to its requirement for financial needs, especially at the end of the month, and its ambitions for development.[13]

In these conditions, Tunisia needs first and foremost to appear as a disciplined pupil, a peerless reformer, an exemplary debtor. And, up until now, it has managed to do so.[14] In its category, it is almost the first beneficiary, which also enables it to gain easy access to international markets. Tunisia is in the front rank of official French development assistance, with eligibility for all instruments of bilateral cooperation, as well as the interventions of the *Agence française de développement* (AFD) and the 'emerging countries reserve'. It receives 14 per cent of the total of European funds committed to countries in the southern Mediterranean (the MEDA funds), even though its population counts for only four per cent of the total population of the third-world countries in the Mediterranean. Thanks to its very high ability to repay, one that is indeed excellent when compared to other African countries, it now constitutes the first portfolio of the ADB, even though it ought to draw only marginally on the resources of this institution which is specialized, first and foremost, in the financing of basic infrastructures. It manages to benefit from all possible sources of finance provided by bilateral and multilateral donors, drawing simultaneously from the instruments meant for the least advanced countries and those meant for industrialized countries, while benefiting from significant participation in capital.

Tunisia benefits from aberrant financial and geographical chunkings that it is able to turn to its own advantage: it sometimes belongs to the 'Africa zone' and then benefits from the relative under-development of the vast majority of its competitors; in other cases, it is part of the 'Middle East and North Africa' and can then profit from the different problems of its neighbours – political problems (Algeria), diplomatic problems (Libya, Iraq, Syria) or problems of rent (almost all the countries in the area). On the other hand, Tunisia is 'lucky' never to belong to an 'emerging' group or a 'middle income group' in which it might encounter much more significant competition. An analysis of the criteria which foreign bankers, donors and international markets use to evaluate the financial situation of Tunisia enable us to lift one part of the veil that surrounds the enigma of the Tunisian 'model'. All these groups look first and foremost at the debtor's ability to repay the debt. And the debtor in question is essentially the Tunisian state, which, for economic and historical reasons, has always made it a point of honour – and its proudest nationalist boast – to repay a debt exactly when it falls due. In the absence of rent, the Tunisian economy has rested, ever since independence, on a privileged access to external financings, an access that has been made all the easier in that its relations with the dominant actors in global capitalism are good.

'Stability', evaluated in economic and political terms, also constitutes an advantage which the Tunisian authorities cultivate with great skill. This implicit political preoccupation goes some way to explaining the laxity of donors when faced with the strategies of resistance and evasion, and even the drifts of their favourite recipient. Rating agencies and financial markets are positively influenced by macroeconomic stabilization and the impression of good management. They also take account of purely technical arguments, such as the scarcity of Tunisian paper on international markets or, even more prosaically, the assured support of donors. For all these groups, there is no overall panoramic view, no analysis of the impact of 'heterodox' practices on the workings of the economy, no investigation of the means by which these results are obtained, and no critical reflection on the political economy of the country. So foreign partners finance the Tunisian economy without asking themselves any questions and thereby share in the creation of the fiction of a healthy debt economy and of an efficient banking system. They thus contribute to the consolidation of an economy that they may, in spite of everything, judge severely, which constitutes not the paradox – since the evaluation is completely rational and logical – but the strangeness of the situation. As in the past, foreign financers are dealing, so to speak, with a double system of rules: rules that they apply to themselves and to western institutions, and rules specific to the 'natives', in a somewhat paternalist way.[15]

Despite the relative importance of debt, this view is legitimate for international organizations, such as the IMF, the World Bank and the European Union, which are subjected to political pressure from their main shareholders or contributors. This behaviour is apparently much more surprising on the part of markets and big companies specialized in consultancy and risk assessment. Rating agencies, indeed, judge one risk to be a sovereign risk: Tunisia's ability to repay its external borrowings.[16] The national financial system is generally taken into account only if it has an influence on currency transfers to external creditors – which has indeed never happened in Tunisia. Still, this particularly permissive attitude may be a cause for surprise, insofar as the Tunisian financial system results largely from a highly specific mode of the debt economy – a mode which I analyse in political terms as a complex of socio-political arrangements but which, in the system of thought and the 'ideological kit' of the foreign financial partners, can be analysed only in terms of inadequate management, of interference from the political realm, and of 'bad governance'. There is no need to recall that these practices are frequently condemned in the severest terms by these very same institutions.

In the specific case of Tunisia, such practices could have been particularly criticized as the fragility of the banking sector proves that they were not – and are still not – marginal. But once the general worry within the sector has been voiced,[17] no sign of general scepticism appears, let alone any lessening of confidence. This much is attested by the success of the first bond issue in euros taken out by Tunisia in July 1999, and all those which followed.[18] There are several justifications put forward for this, all interlinked: since nobody wants to destabilize a country which is actually managing to ensure far from negligible rates of growth and whose state is the infallible guarantor of all the banks, international donors, both public and private, deem it important not to come down on dubious behaviour, in the hope of contributing to the restructuring of the financial system; and, in their evaluation, financial markets take this international support into account – especially insofar as all parties involved find this situation perfectly acceptable: once again, Tunisia pays back its debts scrupulously and foreign private banks have no hesitation in financing the Tunisian state. This flattering evaluation nourishes the virtuous circle of good relations maintained by Tunisia with external partners and thus contributes to the permanence of the Tunisian financial system.

A network of converging interests

We are thus in the presence of an intermeshing of interests that proves the solidity of the banking system. This fictive world is made up of a set of mutual relations and common arrangements, which seems to suit everybody: banks, various state entities, entrepreneurs, consumers, international markets, and international donors. This interdependence is ceaselessly being renewed. Even though they pay dear for it, businesses are essentially financed by credit, knowing as they do that banking institutions are not very demanding. Banks are impelled to agree to give limitless credit to coopted businesses, anticipating intervention on the part of the BCT should any difficulties ensue, and aware as they are of the advantages in the present system. The Central Bank is permanently intervening since the budgetary cost of these operations is low, because tax-payers and consumers accept it implicitly, and because it is easy to mobilize foreign actors. Admittedly, banks are subject to its permanent presence and sometimes feel the weight of its injunctions. But, apart from the fact that the banks are structurally indebted to the Central Bank, they also benefit from its laxness when it comes to interpreting their balance sheets and, on the international level, from the good image and the favourable rating enjoyed by the country as a whole. In spite of the Government's imprecations in favour of the Stock Exchange, the hegemony of banking credit and its ease of access are implicitly favoured by the state, which also benefits from a favourable market for its government bonds, and siphons off, at no great cost, a large proportion of private savings. This enables it to mask the reality of the public deficit whose origin lies in the fact that parapublic entities are in debt to the banking system. The chain of dependencies is so extended that nobody appears accountable. This is also the explanation for the way that everyone finds it a comfortable situation.[19]

A good example of this intermeshing of interests is provided by the cleaning up of banks. Contrary to appearances, it is not the state structures (the Central Bank, the budget) that bear the main brunt of the costs. Banks take on a large proportion of these, as do donors and consumers. Of course, we can interpret this sharing of the burden as an imposition on the part of the public authorities; and, to some extent, this interpretation, broadly shared by the bankers, is perfectly legitimate. But this should not make us forget why this sharing out of responsibilities has been made possible. The answer is social: it rests on practices that are accepted because they are part of the banking routine and the most humdrum relations of power. When large-scale operations are carried out, as in 1997 and 1999, the state takes over public debts. But it repays them over a 25-year period at a zero rate of interest, which greatly reduces the annual budgetary cost of the operation (1/25) and throws part of the cost onto the banks since they no longer receive the interests that are theoretically due. In addition, the state benefits financially from the support of the international community, which, in return for the state's adoption of reforms, offers loans at advantageous rates (the World Bank) or, better, simply gifts the money (European Union). So there really is a sharing of the financial burden of restructuring, a sharing whose terms are more or less imposed by the Tunisian authorities – and more rather than less – but which takes account of the interests and positions of the parties concerned. By limiting the extent of the provisions, the BCT enables the banks to post accounting profits, which is favourable to them in terms of image and helps the fiction to be maintained. But it is equally favourable to the shareholders of these institutions and to the state budget, since the latter benefits not only from dividends, but also from revenue from the tax on profits. The international community is not outdone, since it can thus point to the success of its reforms and its contribution to streamlining, increasing the volume of its activities and justifying its existence.

This interweaving of interests also justifies the popular perception that 'the bank is the administration'. This is not because of the importance of the public banks, but because of the way they work and even more because of their social role. The nature (public or private) of the bank is of little importance in this respect. Both types relay the government's desiderata (the privileged financing of this or that sector, such as tourism and, more recently, exports), the decisions made within the sphere of economy policy (specific credit lines, such as 'upgrading' or help for 'young entrepreneurs'), and macroeconomic preoccupations (limiting the commercial deficit and the shortage of currency). In the popular imagination – but not only there – banks are thus partly the administration, and 'that means security, too'. Unlike the Stock Exchange, savings are safe there and the risk is zero. In particular, social relations and the effect of fame are more important than any other evaluation, because economic society is, in the final analysis, pretty narrow.[20]

Insofar as it is a fictive world, the banking system illustrates another characteristic of the Tunisian political economy: consensual management. The notion of 'consensus' is central to the Government's general rhetoric. It is also central to the politico-financial complex, on its own initiative, of course – but the main actors in the system also share in this general perception. Everyone has an interest in this financial system, and their interests are all the more closely linked because the state is present to guarantee this consensus, or rather to foster it, thanks to its ability to 'listen' and to its social preoccupations. As a result, in a sort of harmonious linkage, everyone seems to take up part of the 'burden', the banks first and foremost, but also the state, businesses, and consumers.

Faultlines in the politico-financial complex

Can we take at face value this serenely unproblematic reading of financial relations? Are there no flaws in this consensus? Can we not read the stirrings of scepticism among foreign partners as a sign of shaken confidence? The latter, who had always largely financed the Tunisian economy, have been allowing certain doubts to show through over the last few years.

From 2000 onwards, new loans have indeed started to find themselves on exactly the same level as the repayments that have fallen due, unlike the facilities granted during the previous years. This slowing down in the flow of funds could be interpreted as a limitation, on the part of the Tunisian authorities, of external debt, as had previously been the case, so as to reduce the financial burden and the political costs of such a dependence. However, as a result of persistent tensions on currency reserves and permanent requests for help from donors, this slowdown should be interpreted, rather, as the mark of a certain scepticism on the part of the latter towards the Tunisian debt economy, as a limit to the commitment of foreign partners.[21]

Tensions between certain banks and the BCT constitute a second sign of the fragility of this consensus. The failure of the privatization of the *Banque du Sud* in 2004 was, in this regard, very eloquent: the call for bids was declared to be unproductive, since the problem of bad debts of private origin had not been sorted out – and this would have been in any case impossible within the framework of the banking fiction.[22] Foreign banks realized this clearly – and even those already active on the Tunisian market refused to join the dance. At the end of 2005, it was only once this problem had been 'sorted' at the highest political level that the Moroccan and Spanish partners took control of the bank. The struggle between the *Société Générale* and the Central Bank over the UIB is another example that reveals a franker expression of the divergences within the financial community. Ever since it entered the Tunisian market, the French bank has been trying to obtain the 'truth about the accounts' and a re-evaluation, in a restrictive sense, of the value of the goods guaranteeing these problem credits.[23] But the Central Bank is reluctant, preferring a softly softly approach, which alone can preserve this fictive world of which it is the principle guarantor: after all, its first job is to guarantee the image of Tunisia and look after its financial resources in the short term. The solution it found reflects these contradictions: in 2003 and 2004, the UIB was authorized not to present any profits, but no losses either; however, other banks were not able to benefit from the same treatment, which increased the tension between banks. In addition, despite the increase of its participation in the capital of the UIB, the shares of the *Société Générale* remained at 52 per cent: the BCT had issued instructions that the CNSS and the BNA, minority shareholders of the UIB, buy up all the papers on the market.

Failings in management constitute a third index of the weakness of the consensus and even of the fictional nature of the banking system. The bankruptcy of the electrical domestic appliances company BATAM, which specialized in consumer credit, suggests that the Central Bank seems rather to be trying desperately to keep up with events rather than getting ahead of the game. Despite a popular demand that turned out to be stronger than all the prohibitions, the BCT refused the opening of consumer credit activities on the part of banks and specialized institutions. There was a complete difference in viewpoints here, since financers continued to request authorization to develop this activity. Likewise, up until 2002, the BCT had never bothered itself with supplier credit; it has still not set up any credit bureau for individuals, and created one for businesses only in 2000 – and it is still not working, at least not efficiently. This inactivity may of course be interpreted as a classic case of the way regulatory institutions lag behind economic practices, and behind the rapidity with which the actors involved can adapt. However, this explanation does not go far enough. It does not take into account the way the Tunisian bank system works: if the system were indeed managed on the basis of a consensus as deep as official statements lead one to suppose, then why have state authorities never responded to the requests made by certain key actors of the system for consumer credit to be organized? Why did they not take into account, at the time, the various remarks made by bankers consulted on the banking law of 2001?

The interventionism of the BCT constitutes another argument against the idea of consensus. The interventions of the Central Bank are often skilfully presented in the guise of a readiness to consult and to listen; the fact remains that certain remarks make it easier to understand the paternalism involved, and the relations of domination that go with them. The Tunisian government, for example, openly explains to the IMF that interest rates cannot fully play their role because the commercial banks are 'not mature enough and not strong enough' to respond in an appropriate way to the signals from the market.[24] We here find a characteristic that several social scientists have highlighted in the case of Tunisia: a systematically condescending and authoritarian attitude on the part of the elites in power towards the people, even the notables, for whom they draw up policies.

But this elitism is shared by the very same people who suffer from it. 'Consensus' is obtained between the dominant actors of the system, by concealing the existence of those who do not derive any benefit from it. And yet there are many of these outcasts of the debt economy and the 'virtuous' circle of bad debts: the majority of farmers (over 80 per cent) have never had, or no longer have, access to the BNA, especially since the restructuring of 1997;[25] the majority of Tunisian SME and artisans do not manage to obtain loans; all individuals on very low salaries or out of work, many independents and workers in the informal sector, purely and simply have no access to banking services. Inversely, a great majority of the Tunisians who reside abroad, as well as informal businesses, which are largely in a majority in the fabric of Tunisian industry and craft, do not depend on banking finance in order to set up their businesses.[26]

Individuals who are pursued for unpaid bills and non-repayment of debts are also the outcasts of the banking fiction; there are many of them, as is shown by the law courts, full to overflowing with people on trial for financial fraud and the prisons crammed full of people jailed for bounced cheques.[27] This is because the consensus on debt economy through bad debts covers only one well-defined area of society and reveals the real lines of economic and social inequality in Tunisia. These individuals, who have merely been following 'normal' practice, have been excluded from this social order only as a result of their deviant status or behaviour. In its dominant form, a bad debt is an affirmation of the norm, a contribution to social order; but it can also express perfectly well the – sometimes violent – expulsion of a person from the circles of sociability.[28] The consensus appears first and foremost as the consensus of economic and political elites, from which the middle classes benefit.

This insistence on consensus, stability and security needs to be understood and measured by the yardstick of the banking fiction. This is constructed and perpetuated by being inserted within a 'universe of closed discourse',[29] a world from which any critique is absent, any critical distance is impossible, any alternative is excluded, and any scrutiny from outside is banished. What a banker can express only in technical and culturalist terms needs to be interpreted politically: 'The intermediaries [in the Stock Exchange] who are starting to develop research capabilities hesitate to recommend a sale even when it is a matter of "profit taking", for fear of being criticized for "undercutting" the market. [. . .] We find it difficult to get across the idea that *for there to be a market, there must be some actors who anticipate a rise and others a decline. It is not possible, and not even desirable, that everyone be of the same opinion.* In a word, "sheeplike" behaviour is frequent, as in all markets, but, *as far as we are concerned, the intermediary who leaves the flock first brings down the wrath of all the others on his head, and becomes a "scapegoat"*'.[30]

When reality is hard to control, 'you need make-believe to establish trust, by the virtue of language alone' – only this way can all danger be kept at bay. For, in finance more than elsewhere, 'words are, in this area, surprisingly effective; they are able, in the twinkling of an eye, to pull down buildings that had appeared solid, to undermine the foundations of a community, to ruin the forms that seemed the most stable'.[31] This is why the fiction, too, requires a little constraint.

The social foundations of a debt economy

The profound social embeddedness of the financial system gives us a glimpse of the functions of control or even repression that it can exercise – or, more precisely, it enables us to understand how the financial system is invested by relations of force, how the relations of power that structure the politico-financial system enable a process of mutual control and domination to exist. The repressive dimension is generally underlined by the analyses of classical political economy: the financial system, in this view, is mobilized in order to strengthen political authority, to counter a potential opponent or quite simply to reduce the impact of any potentially dissident scrutiny. The work by Clement Henry Moore that I have frequently quoted analyses this relation within the context of financial liberalization, and attempts to draw a parallel between financial repression and political repression. It is interesting in the way it looks at the political and economic spheres together, and shows a fundamentally political grasp of the financial system. But it reduces the political sphere to the games of politicos and relations of power to an instrumentalization handed down from on high. The political elites in power, starting with the Head of State – whether his name be Bourguiba or Ben Ali – and his accomplices, have certainly used the cogs of the financial machine to establish their domination, eliminate every competitor and prevent any hypothetical opposition from being financed. But these disciplinary or repressive actions, brutal and, it might be said, coarse in nature, are in the final analysis extremely rare and concern only a very limited number of actors, who themselves form part of other segments of this elite.

The symbolic value of political intrusion

Two affairs, and only two, come to the mind of any Tunisian when you mention violent political intrusion to him: the Moalla-BIAT affair, and, more rarely, the Bouden affair. But their intrinsic importance appears marginal. Rather, these affairs comprise fables, and are more part of that '*stratégie du pourtour*' which aims at 'frightening people, making an example, intimidating':[32] the banker who dreams of the political, the wheeler-dealer who discovers that he is virtuous, the financer who wishes to free himself from consensual rules. These symbolic gestures are part of a highly elaborate political discourse and in this sense show how efficient they are: they condition behaviour, and try to model the way people think about relations of power and to impose the model of an omnipresent and enlightened state, which needs to be simultaneously feared and loved.

In the Tunisian *imaginaire*, the affair of the BIAT (*Banque internationale arabe de Tunisie*) illustrates the impossibility of there emerging, within the politico-financial complex, any opposition (even virtual) to the supposedly 'good government' of the central power. The BIAT was created in 1976 by Mansour Moalla, the former Finance Minister of Bourguiba, thanks to his mastery of the administrative world, to his political acquaintances, and to his business links (especially in the circles of Sfax). His success could be gauged by the lightning speed with which, as early as 1982, he was able to become the third bank in the country and the first private bank, thanks to Moalla's connections, both political (Bourguiba's son was a founding member of the BIAT and a member of the board of directors) and technocratic (his links with the public and parapublic world were numerous). However, the BIAT succeeded in being a showcase for the new Tunisian openness and its policies in favour of the private sector, the very example of the emancipation of the economic from the political.

This was the case until, on 11 May 1993, in an interview with *Le Monde*, Mansour Moalla expressed certain reservations about the reform policies being carried out by the government. On 19 May, Tunis Air started to withdraw its assets from the bank. Subsequently, other public businesses followed its lead; as a result, having lost 20 per cent of his deposits within a week, Mansour Moalla was forced to step down from all his official functions so as to save the BIAT. From that point on, thanks to the cooperation of the Central Bank, and thanks to the interbank credit authorized by it and to techniques of rediscounting, the bank, temporarily chastened, was able to continue its ascent.[33] This episode was simultaneously interpreted – and continues to be so – as a desire on the part of power to avoid a business becoming too important and growing too rapidly, an opportunity to undercut a potential competitor on the eve of the 1994 elections, which Ben Ali won with 99.9 per cent of the votes, and a chance, too, to bring into line the Sfaxian networks that were suspected of wanting to free themselves and compete with state power. This urge to control a nationally prestigious bank is periodically reactualized by political interventions of various sorts: the replacing of certain members of the board of directors under pressure from Carthage, or the enforced sale of shares, allowing representatives of the central power to enter the bank's board of directors.

The affair of the *Banque Franco-Tunisienne* (BFT) was of a quite different nature: it illustrates the, so to speak, sacred character of the fictive world mentioned above, and the impossibility, for the politico-financial complex, of allowing any hostile scrutiny to focus on the operation of the black box of the bank system. In 1982, the *Société tunisienne de banques* (STB), owner of the BFT, decided to sell off 50 per cent of the latter's capital to the Arab Business Consortium International Finance and Investment, ABCI – based in the Caiman Islands and representing Arab capital. The Tunisian authorities were keen at that time to foster alliances with Middle Eastern interests. However, when the transfer was signed, the principal shareholder of the ABCI turned out in reality to be Abdelmajid Bouden, a French-Tunisian lawyer, a wheeler-dealer apparently close to the then Prime Minister, M. Mzali. He was intending, furthermore, to participate actively in the management of the bank.

For a while, Bouden accepted the classic practices and arrangements of this milieu; but, for reasons that have remained unclear involving his private life, he refused any compromise after 1989, broke off negotiations with the Tunisian authorities, and henceforth pursued the logic of judicial confrontation alone. From that time on, right up to the present day, a permanent struggle, with resort to the national and international justice system, has set Bouden against the public authorities and the local establishment, in a struggle over the conditions of sale of the BFT, the management of the currency set aside for its purchase, and, in particular, the management of the business, with the protagonists accusing each other mutually of bad governance, or even of plain and simple misappropriation. The affair has still not to this day been settled, even though Bouden has benefited from several judgements in his favour: national judgements that have not been enforced, and international judgements that have not been recognized by the Tunisian authorities. But he left Tunisia in 1992 in rather incredible conditions, and has since been pursuing his fight from Paris, while attempting, recently, to come to a closer understanding with the opposition.[34]

For the business world, this episode has nothing to do with that of the BIAT. In the case of the BFT, the central power did not issue a warning to the whole of the financial establishment. Rather, it catalysed and expressed a general feeling: the plain and simple rejection of an intruder into the closed world of the bank, and the refusal to see its practices questioned. Thereafter, the only solution lay in the exclusion of the troublemaker. Furthermore, the different treatment meted out in these two affairs underlines the nature of their status: the first was largely made public, not officially, of course, but by rumour, over dinners in town, and during discussions in the corridors of power. On the other hand, the second was totally concealed, even by financial circles and among the bourgeoisie of Tunis. The history of the BFT, indeed, cannot be told in the tones of the fable of the 'wicked regime' versus the 'good society', precisely because the obligatory final moral of the tale – people coming to an agreement, the consensus being renewed – could not occur.

We could add many other examples of interference with the Stock Exchange, of bankers resigning, of political interventions in favour of or against eminent personalities. All of this is true, to be sure, even if certain details may be approximate, exaggerated, or even plain false, while others are underestimated or hushed up. This stems from the nature of the information – rumours, information passed on in confidence, in secret, off the record – and even more from the absence of press freedom, the lack of any independent information and of any critical thinking. But that is not the question, insofar as it is collective representations and interpretations more than anything else that count in the fictive world of Tunisian finance. Even if an intervention has real economic foundations, the actors involved 'do not think of it in isolation from the other aspects of social life'.[35] The message then appears in all its sharpness, presenting the clear image of an omnipotent state, a central power – Carthage, the Palace, the President in person – the only master of developments, alone able to enact norms and define the limits that must not be transgressed.

The political reading of these events – or even their political over-interpretation – is directly linked to the context in which they occur. The BCT constitutes the main channel via which the central power exerts its control of the banking sector. In the public banks, the presidents, the directors and the whole decision-making hierarchy are directly appointed on political criteria and on the basis of their direct allegiance to the Head of State, and indirectly to the single party. These banks also participate in partisan clientelism and, here too, any alternative is immediately crushed. The *Banque du Peuple*, set up in 1964 by Habib Achour from subscriptions of the members of the UGTT (*Union générale tunisienne du travail* – the single trade union in Tunisia), was thus absorbed as early as 1968 by the *Banque du Sud*, closely linked to the power of Bourguiba:[36] in no case could the emergence of any alternative source of finance, of any clientelism or any patronage other than those of the single party, be permitted. Likewise, in the 1980s and 1990s, and unlike what was the case in other countries in the region, no Islamic bank has been able to develop its activities within Tunisia.[37] Monopoly and vote-catching are nowadays deeply rooted in banking practices. They go back at least to the Coopérative tunisienne de crédit, set up in 1922 and run by Mohammed Chenik. After experiencing various vicissitudes within the Tunisian elite, the Coopérative became an instrument of the Neo-Destour and financed the national movement and its clientelist policy, mainly in Tunis and the Sahel.[38] Under the Protectorate, all other financial institutions were in the exclusive service of the colonial power, both public and private.[39]

These days, private banks are also affected by this normalizing, disciplinary scrutiny: the director and the manager must themselves be approved by the Head of State – otherwise they have to get involved in fights that they inevitably lose, as the experience of the BIAT showed. This interference also affects banks whose capital is mainly foreign. Thus, in 2000, the BNP, the main shareholder of the UBCI, had decided to appoint a Tunisian president who was unlucky enough not to have met with the approval of the public powers; the pressure was such that the French bank had to give way and appoint someone close to the Presidency.[40]

The Central Bank also constitutes a breeding ground for directors and executives for the commercial banks, especially private banks. These reliable men are important cogs in the spread and, especially, the perpetuation of the politico-financial complex; they contribute to the maintenance of a social order held together by tolerance of bad debts, support for businesses in difficulty, laxity about the criteria for loans, and, more generally, a consensus on this highly specific operating of the debt economy. In short, everyone has to behave in such a way that nobody disturbs the fictive world of finance.

The Central Bank is always run by a man in the President's confidence: Hedi Nouira was its governor under Bourguiba after independence and throughout the socialist period, mainly so that he could watch over the process of 'statisation' and 'Tunisification' – but also to counterbalance the policies of Ben Salah, the principal shaper of the policy of collectivization.[41] From 1999 to 2003, the governor was M. Daouas, the nephew of President Ben Ali. This was also taken to be a signal, with the BCT appearing as an essential cog in the machinery of power.

Less visible, but just as symbolic, the *Association professionnelle des banques de Tunisie* (APBT: the professional association of Tunisian banks), set up and for a long while run by Bourguiba's son, continues to be a significant communication channel for the central power, via the appointments and the transmission of unwritten directives and circulars from the BCT. According to the bankers of Tunis, it does not play any role of intermediation for, or representation of, the profession; it essentially acts as a link between Carthage and the financial world.[42] Likewise, professionals speak of the *Association des intermédiaires en Bourse* (AIB) as if it were 'a cash register'; its only function, apparently, is to ratify decisions that have already been taken by the public powers.[43] In addition, the way the whole society is controlled by the cells of the RCD also affects, and perhaps to an even greater extent, the banks: all of them, even if they are private or controlled mainly by foreign interests, possess a professional cell that exercises a real activity of supervision and normalization over what its employees do. The cells participate actively in the financing of electoral campaigns and symbolic actions, such as the *Fonds de solidarité nationale* or the *Banque tunisienne de solidarité*, whose capital comes largely from the more or less constrained participation of the banks of Tunis.[44]

The regulatory function of political interference

It is thus indisputable that central power uses the financial sector to its own advantage. It instrumentalizes it, invests it, perhaps even more these days than previously, with privatization and liberalization. Spectacular actions, symbolic acts, the spread of rumours and authorized interpretations all converge to transmit the idea of a Promethean state that leaves no room for manoeuvre and suppresses the merest hint of autonomization. This interpretation is shared by financial circles as well as by the population as a whole: everyone agrees that the bank is a state matter and that absolute control renders any alternative and any antagonism impossible. When the BIAT was brought into line, this was understood by everyone as a reaffirmation of the centrality of the state.[45] More diffuse signs and types of behaviour contribute to reinforcing this Promethean impression. In the regions and small towns, political pressure and relations of force, blackmail and various kinds of arrangement often pass through the banking institutions. On instructions from the delegate or the governor, banks can carry out a discriminatory policy when it comes to allocating credit, tolerating delays in payment, or in legal proceedings.[46] The central power and its representatives do not hesitate to use the bank to transmit their messages of disapproval, or their sanctions, on to persons and groups suspected of independence or openly hostile to it. The most recent symbol of this disciplinary function is the 'leaking' of the list of the 107 people most deeply in debt in Tunisia. This mentioned the gross debts of all the big names in the Tunisian business world on the basis of data from the Central Bank; it started to circulate at the end of 2003, and was the object of endless discussion within the Tunis bourgeoisie and in opposition circles. This leak should not, of course, be understood as a desire to 'clean up the sector'. Nor should it be viewed as an error of evaluation, news of which led to the governor's resignation, as the rumour would have it. This list is not trustworthy, as only data about current credit were provided, without any mention of the assets of the debtors named and their solvency. It suggests, rather – over and above the concentration of the supply of credit – the fantasmatic character of bad debts. In particular, it materializes the exercise of a disciplinary power, which aims to show that power knows who is doing what, and could, should the need arise, act.[47]

If we go no further than these explanations, however, we remain trapped in a Manichean conception of political domination, conceiving relations of power as the relations of an owner to his property. The detailed analysis of the Tunisian debt economy aims precisely at entering more deeply into this interplay of relations of force, and of helping people to understand in greater detail what was happening behind these theatrical performances. The abovementioned affairs are perfect indices of the system, with its inextricable interweaving of public and private, the lack of transparency, the fundamentally political dimension of credit, the existence of accredited intermediaries who can be neglected only at the risk of running into problems or facing punishment. These affairs simultaneously bring out the existence of a self-contained world closed in on its fiction, and at the same time of an infinity of social relations structured by financial activities.

The more financers serve central power, the more they need to protect themselves from it. The more the central power needs financers, the more it plays with them, and plays them off against each other. But these relations do not stop with these dualistic confrontations. Financers are not outside the state, but within it. Unlike what might be supposed from the functionalist interpretation, the Tunisian authorities cannot generally go too far in a confrontation with hypothetical badly behaved bankers, or else they risk upsetting the equilibrium of the whole society. Confrontations always happen in a cork-lined room, so to speak, where everyone knows the customs and manners. The central power does not exercise any absolute power of domination over financers, just as the latter cannot impose their conditions in any authoritarian way on the central power. On the other hand, there are 'friendly exchanges of services, which end up establishing relations of friendship when these do not exist at the start'.[48] These exchanges make possible what Jean-François Bayart has called a process of 'reciprocal assimilation of elites'.[49] In the interviews they successively granted me, bankers often repeated as much: 'We need to be "on good terms" with power, since we are in contact with it every day, in order to obtain accreditation or authorization, to open up branches, place new products, or develop our relations with other countries' and, quite simply, to 'develop our activities'. More than relations, they need to 'show a lot of tact' with the power, and this tact 'is a question of culture'. It is necessary to 'weave several alliances, to educate people, to carry out consultations, not to frustrate those in power, to be able to manage difficult files, to choose your staff carefully, to compromise . . .' 'You need to take all this into account in order to guarantee the stability of management.'[50] In this way, the brutal political intrusions mentioned above merely reveal, at a given moment, the state of the relations between society, the economic elite, finance, and the central power. Moreover, it is striking to see that bankers are not overwhelmed by panic when such events occur and that, in the final analysis, arrangements can be made quite easily.

These actions, in the shape of warnings, bans, or acts of repression thus constitute, first and foremost, regulatory moments in the financial world, attempts to keep the financial microcosm together (or put it back together) – in particular, the social order.[51] Such actions admittedly work to the advantage of the central power, since the arrangements transform bankers into scroungers, but the repression is never absolute, if only because the debt economy is a process of mutual dependence: certain individuals can be expelled from the complex and repressed so thoroughly that they vanish from the Tunisian scene (M. Moalla, A. Bouden), but actually, reintegration is the rule. Banking institutions continue to exist. The BIAT has not disappeared; neither has the BFT, and the court cases concerning its future are still ongoing. In particular, these political manipulations of the world of finance take their meaning only from the inscription of the relations between 'politics' and 'finance' in ever-more diffuse configurations of power, which do not merely link bankers to the state, but also link most economic and social actors with one another.

Because he fails to take into account the social foundations of the debt economy, Clement Henry Moore concludes his detailed analysis of the Tunisian scene by asserting that the financial system there has very little power. The 'regime' monopolizes it, he says, and cannot permit any financing from alternative sources of authorities, parties, associations, trade unions – in short, of any entities independent of the state. The analysis of the debt economy has shown quite the opposite, in particular how bank credit constituted the keystone in Tunisian political economy and its social order. So there *is* power – a power that is not monopolized by the Tunisian authorities, or even by the Head of State in person, but a power exercised in an extremely diffuse way, via relations deployed in several different directions and enfolding bankers as well as entrepreneurs, consumers, administrative authorities, partisan entities, and foreign partners. I do not deny, of course, that the central power exercises domination through finance. It seems to me to be difficult, on the other hand, to accept the vision of a power allegedly monopolized by the Head of State, or shared between him and finance, because of the existence of a regulation of the implicit social order that includes the entire, or almost the entire, population.

The modalities of implicit social order

The 'credit bourgeoisie' is indisputably the great beneficiary of this debt economy insofar as social capital is indistinguishable from the ability to borrow, and insofar as personal relations are predominant. 'The more you borrow, the more credit you have'[52] could be its slogan. The transformation of prestige into liquid assets or, conversely, the transformation of assets into prestige creates dependence and sustains a whole network of relations between debtors and creditors.[53] Credit works as a mode of social control since being in debt creates a relation of dependence. Debt, especially unpaid debt, is the foundation of a social order built of redistribution and the construction of accepted fictions. But credit also works as a sign of power: the entry into a political economy of massive debt is made possible only by the previous existence of a certain social capital made up of relations between members of a family, or friends, or inhabitants of the same region, or of administrative and professional relations, acquaintances within the party, and so on.

Jean-Yves Grenier's remark on the subject of the Ancien Régime also fits contemporary Tunisia perfectly: 'These characteristics [. . .] are inseparable from a certain ambiguity residing in the conjunction of a simple economic situation sustained by credit and of a more complex dimension that emerges from a social representation that links together [. . .] wealth, power and prestige'.[54] Only within this context can power insert itself within the skein of acquaintances and relations of force in order to exercise control, discipline or normalization: credit is then transformed into a central institution of individual relations of domination. Prosecutions and sentences for unpaid credit, for embezzlement, for fraud, and for tax evasion all happen in accordance with the personality and above all the status of individuals; the law on bankruptcy is applied in varying ways, depending on the 'quality' of entrepreneurs; the management of arrears is a reserve of local political capital. The cancelling of bad debts or arrears is an obvious favour to the ruling class and the economic and financial elite, but it is a favour that is distributed skilfully, applied variously, and dispensed individually. It authorizes a process of differentiation within the elite, which enables someone to be brought down and dragged through the mud by a treatment which can sometimes be compared to that suffered by the lowest classes or 'enemies'.[55]

Generally speaking, however, this exercise of power is neither blind nor repressive; it is a 'positive' exercise of power, comprised of arrangements and compromises, of negotiations and pressures. Even without having to follow any direct injunction, as often as not the entrepreneur 'knows' that if he maintains a certain degree of sociability, especially with influential party members, he will obtain his credit more easily. He 'knows', too, that he can use these various mechanisms in order to prosper, in particular by creating bad debts or holding up payment. Unlike what is often stated, this social and political dimension of credit is not proper to the 'authoritarian' nature of the 'Ben Ali regime' alone. It has issued directly from the structuring of society, from the relations that have unfolded within it, and thus from its historical trajectory.

The politico-financial complex is also based on more popular practices: consumer credits constitute a real 'democratization' of the financial system and the debt economy. The well-being of the middle classes, the rhetoric preferred by the Tunisian authorities, is not without its concrete realizations – quite the contrary.

BATAM symbolizes the democratization of credit and consumption. The founders of this private business for the sale of domestic electronic appliances are the Ben Ayed brothers, who enjoyed success and prosperity in the 1970s and 1980s. With liberalization and the spread of 'western' lifestyles, the business realized, in the 1990s, that it could create a sales explosion by offering consumer credit to its customers. In a legal vacuum, it offered credit at usurious rates. Within a few years, BATAM became, so to speak, one of the central institutions in the reproduction of the Tunisian political economy, in response to a veritable 'social demand', endlessly reproduced and endlessly growing. The business found itself in difficulties in 2002 and, in 2003, was forced to file for bankruptcy and apply for a legal settlement.[56] Numerous factors can explain this bankruptcy: overhasty expansion, mismanagement, under-capitalization and excessive debt, laxity of the authorities as well as that of the board of directors and the management, and blind trust in the system of personal acquaintance and reputation. For the banks, the debt of BATAM seems to have risen to 185 MDT and for businesses to 115 MDT, that is a total of 300 MDT, a figure far higher than the turnover in the best year (240 MDT in 2001).

In the Manichean interpretations that characterize any closed political system, the fall of BATAM was interpreted as 'punishment' for an opportunistic alliance between those close to the President: indeed, Hedi Jilani, the Tunisian boss of bosses, and other members of the Trabelsi clan had entered the capital of the business. The Ben Ayeds thought that they here had at their disposal instruments that would enable them to develop their businesses, in particular the obtaining of new credit. The bankruptcy was interpreted by some as an abandonment by the banking sector at the behest of the central power, and by others as completely the opposite – as the Central Bank and the Tunisian authorities taking a strategic sector back under their wings.[57]

The reality is not so simple, however. The chain of dysfunctions that accompanied the fall of BATAM gives us a glimpse of the complexity of interdependences that such an activity both makes necessary and enables. Without any attempt at exhaustivity, we can cite the absence of vigilance of the board of directors and its complicity with the exuberant remuneration picked up by the directors and the members of their families, with excessive recruitment drives and investments; the lack of any reliable and continuous IT monitoring of the forty sales points; the indulgence shown by the auditors, especially when faced with such opaque accounts, not to mention tacit agreements, 'affairs' and other kickbacks; the passivity of the bankers, duped by the attractiveness of an expanding turnover and by the profits obtained from the rediscounting of its bills; the strategy of diversification adopted by the group (which in reality included sixteen businesses) aimed at fiscal optimization, of a cavalier financial attitude, of an increase in the capacity for debt and of a response to competition organized with the arrival of Carrefour; the laxity and laissez-faire of the Central Bank and the absence of any supervision on the part of the Committee of the financial market; an absence of control of the level of household debt; a speculative and playful conception of business, based on the lack of transparency of accounts and the circle of debt dependence; the inanity of financial controls and the complacency of stock exchange dealers; and the impossibility for there to be any independence on the part of rating societies paid by the business itself (and thus inevitably complicit with it). The blindness of the financial system as a whole is characteristic of the functioning of the debt economy and the fiction that characterizes it: the banks did not switch on their alarm systems, and this goes for the most 'modern' and dynamic of the banks, whether foreign (Citibank, UBCI) or national (BIAT, Amen Bank); they sounded the alarm only very belatedly, in October 2002.

The systemic interventionism of the public authorities effectively relieved these banks of responsibility; they could always count on being bailed out by the Central Bank. This explains the kind of behaviour they indulged in, as does the system of loan management resting above all on a name and a reputation, and conversely the absence of any risk analysis or management analysis. Likewise, the bodies in charge of financial regulation and supervision (BCT and CMF) allowed themselves to be lulled by the flattering label of new 'national champion' and, once the disaster had occurred, did all they could to keep that fictive world over which they stand guard alive: silence, hedging, and the absence of any sanction all characterize the way the situation was treated, but more generally the way power by credit operates. And this too is not just a Tunisian characteristic. As Jean-Michel Rey notes with regard to credit in the eighteenth century, 'in general, credit is to some extent silent about its overall functioning. Many things that, from its point of view, are essential are never stated; the community is forced to accept them as an inheritance, in accordance with a necessity that is apparently always standing back. So it is, above all, a series of strange silences that are transmitted [. . .]; silences that partly constitute the symbolic basis of a community, and that feed indefinitely into political thinking'.[58]

The salvage plan of BATAM shows that consumer credit is a mechanism, fundamental even though implicit, of Tunisian social reproduction. While the business and its managers should have gone before a court for deliberate non-payment of suppliers (delays extending for between 18 and 36 months) and for abuse of social property, the reflex, on the contrary, was to react by defending the economic and social order. 'National protection' was the line of conduct of the authorities, which, instead of allowing the liquidation of BATAM to proceed, if only to serve as an example to everyone else, appointed as attorney a man from the Central Bank, Ali Debaya, former CEO of two of the biggest banks in the country (STB and BNA), and obtained an amicable judicial settlement. Everything was done in order to avoid collapse, and a crisis cell met for months, twice a week, trying to reschedule the debt, consolidate the accounts, restructure the debt situation and obtain new loans.[59]

So, the popular interpretation has it that the central power intervened because the collapse of BATAM could have destabilized the country and undermined social order and the contract existing between the 'Ben Ali regime' and its middle classes. The idea of an exchange lies behind this interpretation: in the case of a conflict with Power, even if we leave to one side the vacillating wish to reach a rapprochement with a simmering opposition at the end of the 1990s, consumers would all have something to lose in terms of well-being, standard of life, and lifestyle. The crisis of 2002–3 was dangerous, on this reading, precisely because it threatened the social contract based on the exchange between an increase in the standard of living and an absence of liberties.[60] This interpretation rests on the implicit idea that consumers and households in debt have something to defend – their material well-being – and they would never rebel in case they were stripped of it. In other words, a tranquil state of debt, over-consumption and corruption would seem to be the price paid, consciously imposed by the 'regime', to ensure social peace and the absence of any political commitment.

This is the idea of depoliticization as a political strategy. Paul Veyne has provided a very fine critique of this idea in his book *Le Pain et le cirque*, a very subtle historical sociology of the political sphere in Rome. In it, he denounces the idea that depoliticization was a Machiavellian calculation on the part of the Roman authorities, with something being offered in exchange for the granting of satisfactions to the people. For Veyne, people do not conform to the ideal of autonomous and politicized citizens; on the other hand, 'politics, from the point of view of those governing, consists in behaving in such a way that the governed will get involved as little as possible in what concerns them; more exactly (and everything hangs on this nuance), the government manages to be the only body to get involved in it, since the governed are, I do not say conditioned, but rather spontaneously disposed to let it do so; a qualification can be added, of course; there are states that are more repressive and mystificatory than others. But the depoliticization dear to dictatorships is nothing other than the enforced culture of a natural apoliticism'.[61]

If we follow this line of argument, we are not in the presence of a concatenation (consumption, debt and corruption) whose aim is to depoliticize the population and maintain it in a cosy apoliticism. We need to analyse things the other way round: it is not the central power which authorizes the system of debt and fosters credit consumption in order to depoliticize the middle classes; but, accommodating to the whole complex of the debt economy, it tries to avoid this complex from becoming politicized by not refusing it access to a particular lifestyle. 'Depoliticization? At the bottom of this hazy notion we find the vague idea of an exchange of satisfactions; but politics is not an exchange, even an unequal one, of homogenous quantities; it is an accommodation with heterogeneous situations,'[62] as Paul Veyne points out.

If there *is* a social contract, it takes the form of the defence of a social order. Consumer credit and household debt can then be understood in terms of submission and accommodation to an economic system and social relations that lead them to run up debt; in terms, too, of adherence to a lifestyle and a particular mode of liberalization, democratization, and economic modernization. It is especially difficult to change lifestyle when satisfaction levels rise with an increase in access to consumer goods. Household debt is the other facet of the democratization of access to consumer goods. BATAM and its avatars, just like the 'average Tunisian consumer', constitute shared symbols of material comfort, of an improvement in the standard of living, of modernization – in short, of a successful Tunisia. For the 'credit bourgeoisie', subjection is expressed first and foremost in the negotiating of the status of the star entrepreneur. Coercion, control, and discipline constitute only one dimension of the contemporary Tunisian political economy. The elements of adherence and recognition cannot be concealed.

At the end of this chapter, repression by finance appears to be quite marginal; on the other hand, the analysis of the politico-financial complex has shown the extent of mutual interdependences and the influence of different actors on these interpendences. It then becomes easy to understand why the banking system constitute an ideal introduction to the study of how power operates in Tunisia and how the political anatomy of financial details make it possible to grasp the modes of domination and coercion. The analysis of the concrete operation of the debt economy, in fact, has showed that control, framing [*l'encadrement*], discipline, training, the impossibility of antagonism, the construction and the workings of a fictive world are central and effective in the exercise of a power of domination – more than techniques of repression properly speaking. Of course, the latter exist, but they are marginal, and what dominates is indisputably a muted but still permanent negotiation, as well as a central power that seeks to control by investing the relations of force, the inextricable overlaps between public and private, and the full vigour of social relations.

I reckoned that it was more important to show that the interweaving of relations and interests was such that, in the very absence of repression, central power exercised an equally firm and ubiquitous control over society as a whole, precisely because social bonds have more force than do the laws of the market. Credit remains this central institution of individual relations of domination in the configuration of debt and the loan of monetary advances. Consumers and businesses may see their arrears and their bad debts being waived so long as they do not leave that political economy and the relations of power associated with it. As was the case in Rome or in the French Ancien Régime between the property owner and the tenant farmer, an account is perpetually kept open between the debtor and the creditor, between those in debt and their bankers – an account which is never closed so long as these relations of dependence are accepted.

Part II

Constriction and Adhesion

My analysis of the banking sector has shown that there was an indisputable element of support, and that this passed in particular through the acceptance of many relations of dependence and the way different actors played on these relations. I also suggested the weakness of repression properly speaking, whether it is carried out via financial intermediaries or directly by way of police mechanisms on economic actors. All the same, nobody in Tunisia is unaware of the weight of the two institutions, generally considered as *the* repressive institutions par excellence, namely the police and the single party. The object of this part of my book is to explain just this apparent contradiction and to understand the way these two processes go together. The following pages will enable us to go into the functioning of the traditional mechanisms of political domination and control, in an attempt to grasp the ways they fit into this interplay of mutual dependences and, eventually, into the processes of accepted obedience.

In the course of the various interviews that I carried out on the methods of political domination and control, one reply struck me as particularly revealing: the formula *'quadrillage, verrouillage et maquillage'* or 'grid, clampdown, and make-up' suggested by two main players in the opposition and proponents of the independence of the judiciary – the judge Moktar Yahyaoui and the lawyer Raouf Ayadi. The country and its population is kept under surveillance by means of institutions of control and repression, starting with the police, the set of services attached to the Ministry of the Interior, and the single party. There is a clampdown on press activities and any political expression, but also on any potential institutions and places of critical thought and action. The figures are falsified, as are data and situations, so as to construct the image of a docile and well-behaved Tunisia. The policing objectives and disciplinary aims of economic policies are also falsified and disguised, as are social programmes, charities, and public services. If these definitions suggest the diversity of the very modes in which power is exercised, they also have in common a way of presenting a figure of this power as autonomous, external to society, powerful, voluntarist and omnipotent; a unilateral action on the part of the 'Ben Ali regime', a power which dominates and manipulates Society.

What can we learn from this representation, this Manichaean and (all things considered) naive vision, inseparable from the 'myth' of the omnipotent *'zaîm'*[1] and its corollary, an 'undifferentiated and subordinate mass' that is totally passive?[2] Why is this imaginary construction so significant, even among the very small active part of the population that plays on the relations of force with the central power and is thus well acquainted with the subtlety of modes of government? In an attempt to advance our understanding of this over-interpretation of power, the analysis of the traditional mechanisms of political domination and control will focus on better grasping its cogs and wheels, all those techniques which make both constraint and support possible.

3

A Meticulous Grid

As we have seen, repressive techniques, in their extreme and visible forms, touch only a very restricted number of people; on the other hand, daily life in Tunisia is characterized by the conjunction of an apparent normality and a constant and intrusive police presence. Given this, how are we to analyse this mode of government? What roles do these different – and not strictly repressive – techniques play in the exercise of power? What role does the police play, and can we really talk of 'police power'? As Hannah Arendt points out: 'No government exclusively based on the means of violence has ever existed. Even the totalitarian ruler, whose chief instrument of rule is torture, needs a power basis – the secret police and its nest of informers. Only the development of robot soldiers, which, as previously mentioned, would eliminate the human factor completely and, conceivably, permit one man with a push button to destroy whomever he pleased, could change this fundamental ascendancy of power over violence'.[1] The question that rises is ultimately that of knowing whether the – 'softer' – forms of police control, censorship or surveillance by the services of order and the single party can by themselves embrace the relations of power.

The omnipresence of the police, or a net of fear

Police omnipresence is indisputably the first practice denounced by human rights organizations; it is the most visible and best known of the expressions of repression. The number of police hovers, depending on whom you talk to, between 80,000 (as estimated by foreign observers in Tunisia) and 133,000 (probably exaggerated statistics supplied by the Tunisian opposition) for some 10 million inhabitants – which is, however you look at it, a somewhat impressive percentage. The ratio of police to ordinary Tunisians thus varies from 1/67 to 1/112, whereas in France, the most heavily policed country in Europe, it is 1/265 and in the United Kingdom 1/380.[2] If we wish to include the activity of policing as such, we need to include, over and above the agents with the official title of police officers, certain soldiers on police duty, different categories of 'informers', and also members of the single party. To one degree or another, everywhere in the country, in the regions, in administrative offices, public companies and even in the big private enterprises, on the roads and on public transport, at places of work and in bars and places of relaxation and entertainment, all of these agents are keeping people under surveillance and carrying out a continuous check on citizens, travellers, employees, school pupils, students, believers, car drivers, readers, parents, consumers, passers-by, lovers and tax payers.

The police, a moral authority

The ubiquity of the Ministry of the Interior is not merely physical. It is also moral, administrative and political. Moral first and foremost, in the sense that all public policies or economic projects have taken on board the watchwords of stability, security and public order. All the other administrations depend in some way on the Ministry of the Interior: in the civil service, since at least the start of the 1990s, it has been the Ministry which decides on new recruits. It verifies that a job-seeker is affiliated to the RCD. The National Police Force carries out an inquiry to see if the candidate personally – or any friend or family member – is a sympathizer with Islamists or, since around 1998, a sympathizer with the opposition, of whatever tendency. And even once the civil servant has been duly recruited, the state can still put an end to his contract (with no fixed term) merely if the Minister of the Interior – sometimes not even in writing – so instructs. Justice, too, is subject to police domination when it is not purely and simply following police orders. It thus happens relatively frequently that a sacked civil servant will be given a favourable decision when he appeals to the administrative tribunal – but this decision is then never applied.[3]

This omnipresence also finds expression in the diversity of police services that have a political character: state security, the special services, the general intelligence services, the guidance services, the municipal police, the presidential security forces and the services of the National Guard, of course, but also the Customs services, the interior revenue, the health services, the department of foreign trade, and the CNSS, which can all be used in the pursuit of police objectives. This is why the Tunisian authorities were able to deny the attacks on Sihem Bensadrine, a female opponent, and reject her accusations against the government by claiming that 'there is no political police in Tunisia'.[4] To some degree, that is true: all the party's services and administrative services, whether of the police or not, can be mobilized with great effectiveness to meet the objectives of surveillance, control, intimidation, dissuasion, and even punishment; there is no need for a political police. This shows in particular 'the ability of police institutions to mobilize the panoply of institutions in accordance with their own aims and objectives, to "infect" public logic and seep into the way everyone behaves'.[5]

There are countless mechanisms that play a role here. Intelligence dossiers doubtless constitute one of the most effective techniques for surveillance, intimidation and dissuasion. Whether you are seeking a job or developing some activity, requesting help from the administration or registering at university, and so on, the intelligence dossier is an open sesame or, conversely, an insurmountable obstacle. Everything depends on the answers you give to questions about prayer, the veil, the friends and family you regularly see, your way of life, professional career, prior relations with police services – or, more reliably, it depends on the police's own inquiries into these questions. The network of surveillance of districts is another example: police HQs, party cells, *comités de quartier*, municipal services or the *omda* – all of them have to refer back, officially or not, to the Ministry of the Interior. Its services can also have more direct functions of control and training. When opening a café or a hotel, as well as requiring the authorization of the Ministry of the Interior, you have to put up with an employee acting as an informer, and customers (as well as employees and management) are subject to surveillance . . . If you wish to obtain an invitation to tender on farms, privatization of public entreprises or economic projects, the authorization of the Minister of the Interior does not depend on how good the candidate and his project are, but on how his political and social normality are judged.

The case of taxis is a good example. For the population, this corporation is synonymous with 'nosy cops'. 'A taxi means the police' – as one taxi driver himself told me. If they may occasionally lead to shadowing, or even hamper the freedom of movement,[6] they do not generally act directly. Rather, they are there to listen, to demonstrate that people's conversations are being listened to, to spread the idea that everything is being listened to, including the most anodyne discussions, those in taxis when people merely chat about the weather – in other words, they enforce the idea that the police are everywhere. There is another fact, less well-known but just as important: the police, in this broad sense of the term, also perform various tasks of integration: the Ministry of the Interior, as in many other authoritarian countries, is doubtless the branch of the administration that has modernized most rapidly, in particular by recruiting young skilled people, especially jurists and IT experts.[7]

The trivialization of the police

The development of police institutions and mechanisms constitutes the main characteristic of the modes of government since the end of the 1980s. The way the single party spreads into everything, the fact that the state administration is doubled by a party bureaucracy, the surveillance to which the whole country is subject, or even the cult of personality – these have been attributes of the exercise of power ever since independence.[8] And from the end of the 1980s onwards, they have been supplemented by an intrusive, private dimension that could not be better exercised than by the police. Contrary to what is often claimed, 'ever-increasing police penetration' is not actually due to Ben Ali in person. Abdelkader Zghal, for example, noted how the institution of repression increased its power at the end of the 1970s, and Ahmed Tlili, in his open letter to Bourguiba published in 1975, was already denouncing the unshackling and extension of the police institution.[9] Be that as it may, the rising power of the Minister of the Interior and police mechanisms is a concrete expression of this passage from control over society to control over the individual. To be sure, the police is a state apparatus like many others, but it possesses the specific feature of being coextensive with the whole social body, as it can handle the most minute details.[10] Police power is indisputably the best placed to develop this science of the population and the individuals in it, because it intervenes in the most exhaustive way possible, in the interests of the established social order. It thinks of itself as an absolute instrumental force of command over all the domains to be governed, starting with the individual, without any unnecessary compunction about intrusions into private life or any possible excess of government.

The personal repression of individuals and their private affairs is aimed at ensuring public order. For Tunisia, Mohamed Kerrou shows that this configuration is not new. It is written into a historical trajectory, and possesses the particular feature of having always institutionalized the control of morals via the figure of the *mezwâr*.[11] These days, the *omda* and the police officer have to some extent taken over his function, in an admittedly quite different context, notably by being set within modernized institutions that have issued from colonization and independence. Sadri Khiari demonstrates the same thing in other terms when he speaks of a desire for political desocialization aimed at making individuals dependent on central power by isolating them from each other.[12]

In this situation, the police becomes the primary expression of the political realm, and its main function is not to enforce the law. Rather, the police 'are perhaps the place where the proximity and the almost constitutive exchange between violence and right' is found.[13] The police founds the law, as Walter Benjamin put it, and thereby imposes violence as the foundation of power: 'It is law-making, for its characteristic function is not the promulgation of laws but the assertion of legal claims for any decree, and law-preserving, because it is at the disposal of these ends. [. . .] Therefore the police intervene "for security reasons" in countless cases where no clear legal situation exists, when they are not merely, without the slightest relation to legal ends, accompanying the citizen as a brutal encumbrance through a life regulated by ordinances, or simply supervising him'.[14] In the prisons, of course, but also, for example, in working-class districts, or even in the fiscal services of the central administration, the exercise of police power in Tunisia sends out a message that is loud and clear: what must be respected is not the law as such, but the law of the stronger, that is the law of the police, superior to all other powers, there to ensure that the law is respected but especially to impose its own law, taking advantage of its total impunity and able at any time to exercise its power by violence. In other words, 'fearing the police and collaborating with it – that is the law'.[15]

The violence of the relations of power in Tunisia is nothing new. It has characterized the country's political history ever since the end of the nineteenth century at least. The struggle between the Destour and the Neo Destour, the opposition between the supporters of Bourguiba and those of Ben Youssef, the attacks on the Zitounians,[16] the Fellagas who fought for national independence, the Communists, and then on the Arab nationalists, the student left and the Islamists, the assassinations and attempted assassinations, and the brutality of strikes and the brutality with which they were suppressed – the whole contemporary political history of Tunisia shows how recurrent violence has been, and how deeply it has been incorporated into Tunisian modes of government.[17] The colonial experience played a foundational role in this degree of coercion constitutive of the exercise of power.[18] The repression of discontent and uprisings could be brutal. Tunisian historians concur on the absence of overt violence and forced labour, contrary to what happened in sub-Saharan Africa, for example. But they also show that the violence was no less real, and was inflicted by spoliation, recruiting labour from outside on a massive scale, displacing populations, and so on.[19] The expropriation of land, for example, was carried out 'on amicable terms', but, behind the formal consultations of tribespeople, what happened was in reality a form of legalized plunder.

Generally speaking, placing Tunisia in a state of economic dependence was transformed into a vast operation of juridical seizure of the country's resources. Sana ben Achour traces the sources of modern law in Tunisia back to colonial practices which performed 'a codification of Moslem law, a reappropriation of the precolonial reformist past, and a makeover of local law in terms of the categories of French law'. She shows in particular that this process – characterized by a focus on the 'Tunisian question' and the desire to gain acceptance for French sovereignty by drawing support from local sources of law – was inseparable from the exercise of violence by juridical normalization of the colonial order. More precisely, the differential use of juridical systems was the product 'of a settlement that was *forced* and *imposed* by the colonial power'.[20]

The (recent) increase in power of police institutions, procedures and mechanisms is, however, symptomatic of a new situation, 'in which the state, either through its powerlessness, or by virtue of the internal logic of any juridical order, can no longer guarantee by the means of that order the empirical aims which it desires at any price to obtain';[21] in other words, a situation in which 'power is threatened' and 'begins to collapse'.[22] Hence the recourse to what is to some extent institutionalized violence, real, concrete violence, potential and virtual violence, or implicit and latent violence. However, in Tunisia, there is a certain ambivalence in police power: it is at once central (in its practices as well as in its disciplinary and pedagogic functions) and banal (insofar as there are many other mechanisms of surveillance and normalization). I would therefore like to bring out the way these complementary procedures operate, since they suggest the increasing diversity and refinement of the exercise of political domination.

The party, or the snares of social mediation

The minute network of surveillance of the country constitutes one of its central modalities. After the police, the bodies of the RCD are indisputably the most significant and most systematic means of surveillance. This is illustrated by the (physical) omnipresence of the party through the thousands of cells spread across the entire territory (7,500 local cells and 2,200 professional cells) and the construction of its new seat which, symbolically placed at the entrance to the business district, is meant to exhibit its flamboyant modernity.[23] The cells in particular, in residential as well as work districts, fulfil the function of acting as alarm bells should the norms not be respected. In spite of the apparent figures – 2 million RCD members for a total population of some 10 million inhabitants, in other words one in two working people – this permanent control is due more to the personal involvement of its active members. In fact, it is not known what exactly these official figures mean: there are many supporters who are not willing members, and some people are affiliated without even knowing it. Furthermore, the figures are mere conventions, and the systematic quantification of the party is part and parcel of the discursive staging which tries to conceal the absence of any public debate.[24]

On the other hand, if a state of tension or crisis arises, the cell has to report on the situation, and is held responsible for it. This explains the constant vigilance, with a maximum degree of control over the life of the district or the village, over public places (cafes, bars or cybercafés), over economic and social situations (access to jobs, reception of social programmes, activities of associations), and over sensitive categories of the population (young people, the unemployed, former Islamist voters, believers, day labourers, illicit street vendors). The space of Tunisia is entirely coded by the functional siting of these cells. The places chosen for these cells are spread out across the territory, in a response not merely to the necessity of keeping it under surveillance, but also to the necessity of creating a useful space for the deployment of relations of power.

The party cell, intermediary of central power

However, the main function of RCD cells is not security.[25] They are, first and foremost, intermediaries of the central power, its main driving belts. They are the relays of modes of government and political regulation, and deploy their mediating actions in numerous directions. The directing authorities and the cells are the main places of diffusion of official discourse, in every domain, about the terrorist 'evil' and the legitimacy of the 'eradication of Islamism', about the decision to implement economic openness and find a rapprochement with Europe, about the indispensable solidarity and anchoring of social preoccupations, the progressive process of democratization, economic success, and the virtues of the 'Tunisian model'.

The cells do not merely indulge in the art of commentary. They contribute to transforming those discourses into acts by taking it upon themselves to convince Tunisians to make gifts, by setting up and running associations, by providing information, and by contributing to the success of this or that economic or social policy. The RCD cells and the local *comités de quartier* have been transformed into essential cogs in the machinery of the struggle against Islamism – and, to a lesser degree, against the extreme left and the opposition in general – by acting as agents of police administration, and handling with insistence and often without any great subtlety the registers of blackmail, of intimidation, of physical threat and in particular of social, economic and financial warnings.

If we are to believe the number of supporters and the official figures, the cells are, however, popular. Nonetheless, this popularity seems real only for older people, those who were able to participate in the historical trajectory of the Destour, 'one of the few political parties in Third-World countries that can draw on a tradition of political mobilization going back to the 1920s',[26] and who witnessed its ideological hegemony during the period when the national state was being constructed. Today, it would certainly be an exaggeration to speak of popularity: the relative dynamism of the cells is, first and foremost, linked to the role they play in the promotion or active support of economic and social opportunism. The RCD has always sought – successfully – to extend its influence across a great proportion of the population by promising social mobility, professional success and an increase in wealth. In this sense, it is a vector of a process of individualization that is mainly expressed by an exacerbation of individual competitiveness within society and by a widespread sense of mistrust.

Another form assumed by this role of intermediation is illustrated by the very nature of the RCD. This latter operates and behaves much more as a bureaucratic apparatus than as a political party, with, in particular, a very high level of centralization and a parallel hierarchy to that of the administration. Inspired by the Soviet system but immediately reinvented, this doubling up is carried out in Tunisia to the advantage of the state bureaucracy: the equivalent of the *omda* is the president of the cell, that of the delegate the head of the constituency, that of the governor the head of the regional committee of coordination, that of the central administration the ruling apparatus of the RCD. This is, then, an administration rather than a political party, because in the absence of any public debate, and given the relentless censorship, politics has only an evanescent existence in Tunisia. Unlike in the 1960s and 1970s, political debates internal to the single party have vanished, conflicts between barons have been hidden by the need for permanent allegiance to the Head of State, the 'political entrepreneurs' have disappeared.[27] Party cells are understood and conceived as intermediaries for the execution of decisions from Carthage, or even from Ben Ali in person, and they seem to have acquired the means for this even if the reality is indisputably more complex.

The appropriation of state resources, and indeed their real privatization, brings out this change from party into administration.[28] Thus, it is estimated that there are over 10,000 civil servants detached from their posts with the RCD. These members of the civil service work entirely for the party, but are still paid by the state. The public authorities do not merely provide this intellectual qualified personnel, but also offer car parks and public offices. For example, in the council of Jendouba alone, over one hundred administrative offices are occupied by the party for its various activities. The take-over has recently become definitive, thanks to the sale, for one symbolic dinar, of certain of its flats to the single – definitely single – party. Finally, the administrative dimension of the RCD is reinforced by the way it is perceived by enterprises and individuals. The latter behave towards the RCD as they would towards an administration, that is by considering this relation as inevitable but non-voluntary, a cog in the machine of the unavoidable process of negotiation and integration into society.

This role as intermediary is not restricted to the public sector. In the private sector too, cells play on their influence to guide social and professional life. The members of the RCD are simultaneously active in the trade union sections of the great enterprises, in regional and national structures; they contribute to disciplining the *Union générale tunisienne du travail* (UGTT) and to making it more docile to central power. The professional cells of the RCD enforce a real control over the organization, the structure, the internal management, and even the economic direction taken by businesses and companies. They operate simultaneously as a recourse and as a cog in the wheel of the exercise of power within the economic entity, denouncing the 'bad' elements and congratulating the 'good' ones, getting involved in social management, in professional promotion or, on the contrary, in the dismissal, the sidelining or the punishment of each of the employees.

The party cell, apparatus of redistribution

In these conditions, the process of (re)distribution is fundamental. As such, the RCD does not possess any real means of giving and dispensing. In any case, it does not have any official book-keeping at its disposal, which gives it the double advantage of immunizing it against any accusations of misappropriating or embezzling money and of protecting it against any possible seizure and any material consequences of any potential unfavourable judgement.[29] However, as an intermediary, the RCD is extremely wealthy. It has at its disposal financial resources that it can constantly and rapidly appropriate through sums of money regularly gathered from individuals and, in particular, private and public businesses, depending on their degree of prosperity. In particular, it possesses indirect resources, which do not belong to it but which it can manage and which it glories in: social programmes, mobile health services, Eid presents. But its main strength lies in the ability of its members to influence and act with savoir-faire. In close collaboration with the police, the RCD turns out to be a necessary stage in the obtaining of authorizations (taxi permits, building permits, authorization to open a shop, a restaurant, or a bar, and, generally speaking, any economic activity, whether it be legal or illegal), in the acquisition of accreditation, and the facilitating of requests to the administration (obtaining documents to show one's civil status, lodging a complaint with the state prosecutor), in the granting of certain ranks ('families in need', 'the poor', 'zones of shadow'), and in the real benefit of certain forms of aid (such as 26.26).[a] Ramadan meals, sheep for Eid, and, previously, the World Food Programme, are also in the remit of the RCD.[30] During Eid 2003, for example, the ceremony at which aid was handed out to the needy was co-presided over by the Minister of Social Affairs and by the General Secretary of the Party. Generally speaking, being part of the RCD means that you can benefit from its capacity to intercede within society, it means taking advantage of its role as a facilitator and its status as an essential mechanism in the exercise of power, it means being able to solve local problems, pull strings, accelerate procedures, make use of various advantages, and so on.

In contemporary Tunisia, the RCD (like the PSD and the Neo Destour before it) thus appears as an unparalleled mode of social integration. The official statistics aim to suggest that almost all of Tunisian society belongs to the 'party in power'. Beyond this discourse, it is true that it takes in individuals both young and old, rural and urban, illiterate or college-educated, Arab

---

[a] These so-called 'zones of shadow' are geographical zones defined by the government in accordance with criteria of poverty and enclaving, or even – though this is not said – of difficulty in disciplining the population; these zones are beneficiaries of the presidential programme, the *Fonds national de solidarité*, also known as 26.26 after the number of its postal account. (*Translator's note.*)

nationalists or pro-Americans, of a secular or an Islamic cast of mind. The cells, scattered across the whole territory, within businesses and administrative offices, in urban districts and villages, are there to gather and reply to the population's requests. No ideological backdrop distorts this desire to include all segments of society. The RCD is a network of interests and clienteles that provides employment, grants, administrative facilities, aid of every kind, lodging, banking facilities, free cards for medical treatment and transport. Nothing is officially demanded in return, but people are drawn along by example and by a desire for effectiveness, and so the member of the cell will take part in public meetings, will make a point of being present on election days, will support this or that social activity of the party, will not take part in strikes, will come along to applaud the President, a minister or some prominent figure from the Destour, and will not join any independent association. It has to be said that it costs little to join (5 DT per year in the cells of the civil service, for example) for advantages that are often worthwhile, at least for those on lower salaries (aid at the beginning of the school year corresponding to 20 DT per child, envelopes handed out at religious festivals, in particular Eid-el-Kebir).[31]

Nonetheless, the very nature of these mechanisms makes it impossible for the party to be used too much as an instrument by Tunisians. In fact, the RCD is a machine for giving and controlling, keeping under surveillance and distributing, on the individual and not a collective level. The members – and many of them behave in this way – often remain passive, barely motivated by the activities of the cell and its satellite associations, belonging out of necessity rather than conviction. But at one moment or another they are directly and individually controlled on concrete results, for example their participation in an election or their ability to raise gifts on 8 December, the national day of solidarity. They are then obliged to cooperate, on pain of being placed in the party's black books otherwise. For 'belonging to a party doesn't mean anything', whereas if you don't belong, 'you rule yourself out'.[32] In rural milieus and in small towns where the social microcosm is particularly restricted, it is a guarantee that you will be served last, that you will be the target of administrative hassle and delay, and will not be able to benefit from social aid and social programmes. Belonging to the party is a very effective instrument, since it determines citizenship, or at least social and economic citizenship. It is difficult to carry out economic activities and to succeed – obtain grants, add an extra room to your offices, gain access to seeds for sowing, profit from a subsidized credit, benefit from postponed repayment deadlines – without going through the RCD.

The party cell, vector of integration and of restrictive adhesion

But these mechanisms of integration cannot be understood solely in terms of clientelism, or a system of exchange, or the operating of a centralized and autonomous system imposing its modes of action and governance. The mechanisms of surveillance and discipline are made possible only by their high degree of social integration. As we have seen, the RCD is representative of society insofar as it equally integrates all Tunisians who so desire. The party thereby absorbs within itself the conflicts, the struggles, the rivalries, and the relations of force between personalities and segments of society. And even a certain amount of debate. RCD cells constitute, without the least doubt, the only places where it is possible to speak, admittedly in a conventional manner, respecting the limits that have been interiorized by everyone, but – to repeat the expression used by an experienced observer of the Tunisian political scene – they have become 'ghettoes of discursive democracy'.[33]

At the summit of the party, all the regional notables are represented and participate in its ruling organs, in Tunis, relaying local and even particularist requests.[34] At its multiple extremities, the cells register and permit the renewing of oppositions and balances between different groups and traditional structures of negotiation, arrangement and agreement. As long as he gives his allegiance to the central power and manages to find points of understanding with the official position, a notable is all-powerful, almost untouchable, and he can claim and hand out significant advantages to his group; but the centrality of his position can rapidly be damaged if the interests of his own people or his clientele run up against the desires from 'on high', or if he does not manage to find a compromise in the limited space for negotiation left him by the central power. In other configurations, the local representative of the state can, on the contrary, adopt the strategy of 'intervening indirectly in order to maintain the situation of tension and conflict between the representatives of family groups' to 'forestall any attempt at a coalition' between them.[35] The RCD cells thus appear simultaneously to be the sole authorized places for the expression of the grievances and aspirations of the population.[36] This mechanism, particularly strong in rural milieus, is replaced, in urban milieus, by a multiplicity of similar systems inserted into relations of work (professional cells), leisure activities (satellite associations of the party), and the social relations of the local district (*comités de quartier*).

As historians and sociologists have shown, the tensions between big families and tribes, between old lineages and former political tendencies, between regions and districts are made permanent and ceaselessly reactivated within cells, constituencies and committees of coordination in the course of highly concrete struggles over the attribution of resources, the definition of economic and social policies, the outlines of urban renovation, and country planning.[37] Sometimes, the central power is allied with local, regional or tribal notabilities; sometimes, it exploits local tensions and conflicts to ensure that an unpopular policy is put into effect, impose a personality from outside, or override resistance. It is on the basis of these balances, these negotiations, and these arrangements with notabilities that aid and grants are distributed, jobs awarded, access to advantages facilitated and the benefits of impunity permitted – and public policies are also transformed, remodelled, placed in difficulty, or even stymied.

This general context enables us to understand why belonging to the party constitutes a formidable engine for social ascent, and why the party is invested in such an intense way. As we have seen, the active members of the RCD are not members out of either conviction or ideology, but in the hope of advancing their own interests, obtaining something, giving voice to desires, expressing a grievance or an aspiration, resolving internal conflicts or, on the contrary, exacerbating confrontations between groups.[38] The extent of these material demands has been grasped, but the symbolic and social dimension cannot be concealed. In the rural world, local elites focus on the party in order to use the cells as places of 'mediation between local interests and the politico-administrative institutions of the state'.[39] In cities, however, it is neither the traditional businessmen nor the bourgeoisie who constitute the bulk of the party's battalions, precisely because they already benefit from being recognized. The lower middle classes and the poorer classes are in the majority here, not only because they are indisputably the most numerous demographically speaking, but also because they have everything to gain from a reinforcing of their positions in the relations of power. They need the party in order to climb up the social ladder or quite simply, in these times of crisis, to maintain their positions. Thus, in five or six years, the president of a district cell becomes a notable and can, for example, build himself a desirable residence or open up a profitable shop.[40]

Social revenge thus appears as a significant dimension of the functions filled by the RCD and incarnated by the head of the party – the President himself – in person. And even more, his entourage. This is doubtless one of the explanations – but not the only one – for the widespread corruption and predatory behaviour in the presidential circle, also filtering down to the party structure. Or, to be more exact, one of the interpretations of this phenomenon by the national bourgeoisie, the traditional elite and an important fringe of the middle classes:[41] coming from a modest background, Ben Ali and his entourage thus seem to be assuaging a thirst to join the bourgeoisie and a huge need for social recognition. While this conclusion is indisputably a caricature, it nonetheless suggests the existence of a certain form of politicization, or at least the vigour of social relations. It thus shows up the importance of social differentiations, the stakes of power that they cover, the hidden conflicts, and the tensions and modifications in the relations of force between different social segments and between segments of the elite.

Thus, 'a driving belt, a structure of control, a channel for grievances and a space of mediation and upward mobility: the cells of the Destour show many different faces'.[42] The image of the political economy of repression in Tunisia is gradually becoming clearer. More than being mere offices for the registering and spreading of orders from on high, the cells appear as places of power that authorize a process of subjection in the double sense of the term, that is as submission to an exterior rule imposed unilaterally, a technique of domination in its own right, and simultaneously as a form of belonging and active support.[43]

Supervision from below, or grid surveillance by the individualization of control

The RCD cells are not the only ones that keep the country under surveillance. Associations, official and unofficial 'informants', permanent or occasional, the *omdas* and delegates representing the decentralized administration, female social assistants who depend on the central administration, the managing agents and caretakers of apartment blocks . . . whether they are individual actors or representatives of institutions, all of them have as their main mission the ordered scrutiny of society.

Overt supervision: national organizations and local committees

National organizations are big machines that were originally conceived of as relaying the central power; they have since been integrated into the institutions of surveillance and control. The *Union tunisienne de solidarité sociale* (UTSS – Tunisian Union of Social Solidarity) appears as the archetype of this first category of associations, those that were conceived and intended right from the start to supervise the population.[44] By itself it brings together almost all the techniques of control at the disposal of the authorities that depend on the RCD and the central power. The UTSS organizes, guides and manages its interventions in close collaboration with the RCD: the 'solidarity restaurants' and the distribution of financial aid organized during the month of Ramadan are in the remit of the party's local and regional cells; the financing of these operations is divided between the UTSS and the RCD, without it being possible to determine exactly who runs what. In particular, the UTSS has only a marginal voice in the choice of beneficiaries and is in fact obliged to accept the selection carried out by the RCD's local structures on the basis of the local files of the National Programme for Aid to Needy Families (part of the Ministry for Social Affairs) and on the basis of clientelist concerns:[45] thus, 'certain beneficiaries are not really in difficulties',[46] whereas 'people who really are poor [find themselves being] refused occasional aid, either because they are not members of the RCD, or because they are not among the crowds who acclaim the President when he makes his official visits'.[47] Furthermore, this official character of the 'main NGO' deceives hardly anyone. According to one sociological inquiry, the beneficiaries of the actions of the UTSS consider the latter as actions carried out by the state, and not as private actions, and they feel grateful to the state, with the RCD being considered by them merely as a service provider for the latter.[48]

Comités de quartier present a rather more complex image of an increase in the policing of everyday life that does not stop people taking the initiative and attempts to develop a social movement. An analysis of these committees illustrates the capacity for recuperation of the Tunisian authorities. It also reveals the stakes of power within a society that is forever able to find margins for manoeuvre, spaces of liberty and, in particular, to play on the relations of force and the permanent tensions in place in order to try and modify situations, to make other voices heard, to express new expectations simply.[49]

The El Mourouj II committee, constituted by the trade union members of the *Régie des tabacs et des allumettes* [authority responsible for the sale of tobacco and matches] who have recently arrived in this part of town, took as its initial objective the closure of a public rubbish dump near people's dwellings, and the improvement in local conditions.[50] Indeed, the social movement had originally begun with the inhabitants, on the basis of material and civic demands. Created in 1988, the El Mourouj II committee turned itself into an association in 1989 and the administrative and political authorities immediately interpreted this movement as an attack on public order, as a potentially subversive movement that might contest their hegemony – but also as a supplementary opportunity for control and discipline, an instrument of normalization. Thus, as well as attempting to supervise the El Mourej II committee, the party and the police encouraged the creation of other committees throughout the country, with the result that there are now over 5,000, bringing together nearly 35,000 volunteers.[51] These committees are counted as among the 8,000 or so NGOs in which the Tunisian authorities take such pride, but there can no longer be any doubt about their degree of autonomy: all the members of the *comité de quartier* are also members of the RCD and report to the local cell as well as to the Minister of the Interior. Their juridical situation is, however, ambiguous: the committees, considered as NGOs, do not have the status of associations. No juridical text mentions them directly, but they have little by little been regulated *de facto* by means of organizational decrees coming from the Ministry of the Interior.[52] Thus they are now completely brought within the logic of political control thanks to their subordination both centralized (general management of Regional Affairs) and decentralized (division within each governorate). Their daily operation requires some of the normalizing techniques characteristic of the disciplinary exercise of power: emulation and rivalry between committees, personalization of power, working for the glory of the President, creation (by decree) of a presidential prize for the most active *comités de quartier*, with a far from negligible prize of 25,000 DT financed from the budget of the Ministry of the Interior.

Officially, the role of the committees is to ensure the cleanness and 'proper' operation of a district – in terms of morality and delinquency – to meet the elementary needs of its inhabitants and to allow their demands to be expressed. Unofficially, the members of the committee also participate in the police surveillance of the district by drawing up a list of 'good' and 'bad' citizens, keeping the inhabitants under surveillance, keeping the population (especially opponents of the regime) in check. In fact, the *comités de quartier* operate rather like representatives of the authorities in the district. But they can fulfil these functions of discipline and security only because they are active in local life: the members of the committee are familiar with the inhabitants, they resolve – or attempt to resolve – their daily problems, and they deliver welfare provisions. This makes them fully part of the official practice of solidarity and the clientelist system that goes with it. People, especially those from the lost underprivileged social classes, those who need support, have got into the habit of going through them, without this involving them in any particular support of the party. These activities, halfway between providing services to citizens and keeping them under supervision, are recognized and required: in this way the public authorities insist on 'the spirit of solidarity and mutual aid which marked the creation and development of *comités de quartier* from 1991 onwards and brought out the noble values that have become anchored in civil society'.[53] But these *comités de quartier* are themselves controlled by the RCD cells and by the Ministry of the Interior, so as to forestall any attempt at autonomization, any swerving away from or undermining of discipline, indeed even the most anodyne attempt that might set in motion a process inevitably interpreted in terms of independence. Any deviations, even if only alleged, or interpreted as such, are rapidly stigmatized. Thus, it seems that several members of the UTICA, fully paid-up members of the 'establishment', were called in and reprimanded for having participated, at the request of the *comité de quartier*, in the financing of a mosque in their region of origin (the Kairouan and Djerba case) without having referred the matter to the higher authorities of the RCD and the President's Office.[54]

Diffuse supervision: an infinity of associations

On the other hand, matters are more complex when it comes to the very dense network of thousands of small associations of which hardly anything is known and whose creation was suggested or fostered by political circumstances, then by the state – but which have received no official mandate and are thus not officially integrated into the structures of para-state supervision. According to the figures of the Ministry of the Interior, civil society has never been in better health, as is proved by the number of associations which rose to 8,386 in 2003 as opposed to a mere 1,807 in 1987 with, for the year 2003 alone, the creation of another 279.[55] These quantitative data need to be viewed with the greatest caution as it is very difficult to know what they are really measuring – and as this figure is also politically constructed.[56] The RCD has played a fundamental role in their creation or the way they have been subjected to surveillance. Its force resides in its ability to federate the actions of these various organizations and to recuperate them when they are inventive, when they attract individuals, or when they are potentially subversive; it then re-orientates them to its own profit and makes them redound to its glory. The functional character assigned by the authorities to these associations suggests that they are, first and foremost, a branch of the administration and a structure of supervision. In addition, it is estimated that at least 5,000 of these NGOs are linked to the Ministry of the Interior or to the party, and that they are mainly confined to activities that can be considered as inoffensive and festive: over 80 per cent of these associations are cultural, artistic and sporting in character. From 1988, their growth, often spontaneous, was indisputably fostered by the end of the period of Bourguiba's rule, by demands for democratization, and by the climate of openness and the new President's speeches in support of this. Given its inability to stem a potentially autonomous movement, the central power has opted for a soothing discourse on civil society and the benefits of associations, which in reality betrays the same desire to control as with national organizations.

As is suggested by the remarks of an association president, the state party also exerts its power to guide and divide the forces within this same civil society which it is attempting to control down to the finest detail: 'Initially, I belonged to an association which looked after economic matters and then, one day, the governor of the region called me and told me that I should now move into the association which I now preside over. It's less interesting (in my view) than the other association, but never mind . . .'[57] The state party also exerts its power by recuperating activities and structures which are judged to be dynamic or astute and which correspond to the legitimate expectations of the population. The examples of *comités de quartier* and associations for microcredit financially monopolized by the very official *Banque tunisienne de solidarité* demonstrate as much.[58] The organizer of a development association noted this, and said, with some bitterness: 'Every time an operation is set up, our wish is that something be left in place. [. . .] We would like, when we go, to leave behind an informal or formal structure, but each time, that has turned out to be impossible: the local political and administrative structures always contrive together to absorb the project once we've gone'.[59] However, one should not overestimate the dynamism of the associations: they often run into huge difficulties in recruiting volunteers, in getting members to pay their subscriptions, and in broadening the circle of participants. The best symbol of this is certainly provided by the *comités de quartier*, who, if we are to believe the official statistics, comprise merely 35,000 volunteers for 5,000 committees, or an average of 7 militants per committee! This can only relativize the ability of these associations to perform their tasks of surveillance and supervision.

The associations are integrated into relations of power, simultaneously performing at least four functions. As the last example suggests, the first of these is indisputably pedagogic: to create – by a discourse that is repeated over and over again, by the creation of a multitude of entities, by their continuous mobilization, by the organization of initiatives to their glory – an impression of omnipresence, in which power can keep everything within its totalitarian gaze. In Tunisia, nobody is taken in by the nature of these associations, and their proliferation is there precisely in order to reinforce this utopian sense of absolute control. Contributing to surveillance constitutes another role assigned to the associations: not leaving any empty space, structuring it in accordance with its own preoccupations, its own vision of the territory, occupying a place as soon as a new request, a new need, or a new expression makes itself felt. In addition, the submission of the associations makes it possible for various modes of control over the individuals who take part in them to be set up and diversified. This preoccupation took concrete form with the creation, in 1993, of a data base and four institutions whose object it is to supervise their activities. Their very name summarizes the desire to supervise and needs no particular commentary:[60] the Commission for Financing the Activities of Associations, the Commission for Activities of Associations and the Goals of the 'New Era' (another name for the Ben Ali regime), the Commission for the Realities and Perspectives of the Action of Associations in Tunisia, and the Commission on the Role of Associations in the Work of Development. It is, furthermore, clearly stipulated, in the 1992 organic law on associations, that they cannot be political in character. The associations are under permanent surveillance precisely because control cannot be absolute, and emancipation, or indeed opposition and protest, are always possible – we need merely recall the history of the tumultuous relations between the central power and the Tunisian League of Human Rights since the end of the 1980s.

The fourth and final function is certainly the most important and the most complex of them all: to discipline the population. The associations also exist in order to spread the objectives, the ideas, the fears, the preoccupations and the priorities of the moment throughout society. They play a part in the definition of safety nets and the social policies that compensate for liberalization, going along with or taking over from the state, in what is ultimately a classic scenario largely shared by the donors.[61] But their mission is also to lend support to liberalization directly, as well as to the upgrading and the policy of competitiveness of the Tunisian authorities, by attempting to shape behaviour and to condition the economic reflexes of individuals. Abdelbaki Hermassi, former Minister of Culture, expressed this clearly when he wrote: 'By their efficiency and their adaptability, associations are in a position to make upgrading a daily preoccupation of society, in all its component parts, and to avoid the risk of perceiving upgrading as a project imposed from on high and lacking in any social and cultural support. [. . .] Even if the state devotes itself full time to the task, it cannot by itself meet all of these conditions [to succeed in upgrading and liberalization]. Thus the intervention of associations is necessary so that the latter can prove that they are contributing to the accomplishment of these great tasks of civilization'.[62] Thus their mission is also to channel people's personal dynamism, to co-opt and guide individuals' energies, to track down and denounce deviants, to encourage and congratulate the zealous. The illusion of civil society, and the supervision of association, must show that space is controlled, that a 'healthy emulation' exists, that 'good' individuals are supported and favoured, as the National Associations Day, every 23 April, reminds everyone.[63] So associations make it possible to classify individuals, to select them, to keep them under surveillance and, if necessary, to punish them.

The confinement of 'independent civil society'

Thus, associations constitute one of the main means of controlling and subjecting the population to a network of surveillance, now as before.[64] When this form of training runs into resistances, everything is already in place to make life difficult for them. There are now only ten or so of these rebel associations: the *Ligue tunisienne des droits de l'homme* (LTDH – Tunisian Human Rights League), the *Association tunisienne des femmes démocrates* (AFTD – Tunisian Association of Democratic Women), the *Conseil national pour les libertés en Tunisie* (CNLT – National Council for Liberties in Tunisia), the *Association internationale de soutien aux prisonniers politiques* (AISPP – International Association in Support of Political Prisoners), the *Association de lutte contre la torture en Tunisie* (ALTT – Association for the Abolition of Torture in Tunisia), the *Rassemblement pour une alternative internationale de développement* (RAID/Attac Tunisie – Rally for an International Development Alternative).

The 1992 law which established the classification of associations had two complementary objectives:[65] on the one hand, to classify, evaluate, organize, master and define the 'good' and the 'bad' associations; on the other, to tame the LTDH. But the techniques for bringing these associations to heel are much more numerous and diversified than that: they include the instrumentalization of texts and laws, generalized surveillance, intimidation and manipulation of fear, the use of violence, the drying up of funds, cooptation, recuperation by promotion, the granting of favours or, sometimes, 'raising people to the ranks of the notables'. As for Islamists, it is striking to observe that, ever since the years 1999–2000, the forces of order have been using above all juridical and economic procedures rather than police methods, even though the latter exist and can be practised, often brutally. Officially or not, they can prevent or interrupt meetings, follow and harass militants, encircle meeting places, force their way into premises, attack militants physically, call the relevant people in for questioning in police stations or at the Ministry of the Interior, organize tendentious and defamatory campaigns in the press, launch prosecutions and institute proceedings, and organize break-ins into professional and private offices. So police activities are real and pernicious in their effects of intimidation, and the spreading of fear and physical violence, even if they fall behind the years of the great repression

(1991–1998), during which *ad hoc* support committees were not even tolerated and petitioners were immediately suppressed and arrested.[66]

So it is not my purpose to underestimate these police practices but to bring out other apparatuses – those which are much less visible and, as often as not, by their subtlety, all the more powerful. Ever since 1992, the law has stated that if the administration has not expressed any justified objection within four months, the association exists legally. While there has indubitably been a liberalization in the spirit of the legislation, the same cannot be said of the facts. The extremely ambivalent character of the laws and decrees regulating associations, their multiplicity and redundancy, explain the redoubtable efficacy of the juridical mechanisms:[67] this vagueness authorizes all kinds of interpretations, or more exactly enables the essential aspects of the content and the juridical practices to be carried over into decrees of application and interpretations.

As a result, non-recognition is often used. This first technique is not, properly speaking, juridical since the legislation does not require any procedure of recognition; what we have here, rather, is a procedural ruse of repressive character. Theoretically, associations are supposed to deliver the requested documents (status, executive members . . .) to the governorate and pick up a receipt attesting to this delivery. Within four months, if they have not received any motivated letter of refusal from the Minister of the Interior, they write to the *Journal officiel*, the equivalent of The Gazette or the Congressional Record, for publication. Now, the best known of the independent associations, CNLT, RAID/Attac, Centre pour l'indépendance de la justice, or ALTT, have met with various snags: either they have never received a motivated letter explaining the refusal, *and* have never received the receipt attesting to the delivery; or, belatedly, they receive both the receipt and a letter of refusal. The associations are then forced to operate in the margins of legality. So they put themselves into a delicate situation, since they have not been able to publish their association in the *Journal officiel*, which is an obligatory procedure. From then on, they are extremely vulnerable, without any protection when faced with police demands. In addition, the Minister of the Interior can also request the judicial authorities to dissolve any association in the name of an infringement of public order or morality, or by pointing to the political nature of the association.[68] The absence of any judicial independence and the latitude of interpretation allow the central power to do whatever it wishes in this regard.

In the domain of juridical instrumentalization, a second technique consists simply of practising entryism and using, in a haphazard and perverse form, the principles of direct democracy within associations. This strategy, which makes manipulation, recuperation and interference all possible, can be performed thanks to the law of 2 April 1992, which completes the process of political supervision, specifying that associations 'cannot refuse membership to any person who is committed in his principles and his decisions'.[69] The battles within the LTDH can be rapidly summarized:[70] the law of 1992 aimed, as one of its objectives, to allow members of the party to enter the League and to prepare a congress – that of 1994 – to take over control of its managing committee. Since that time, members of the RCD have played a full part in the League. Negotiations or struggles between different tendencies drag on, sometimes opening the way for arrangements, sometimes leading to show-downs and open conflicts. In every section, the composition of the management is the object of wheeling and dealing, and membership cards are generously handed out. This explains the episodes that occurred in 2003–5. Having sealed up the offices of the League and cancelled its 5th Congress, the authorities endeavoured to block the sessions of the regional sections so as to impose a management subject to them, thanks to a manipulated vote made possible by the very presence of members of the RCD who had been brought over to a very 'specifically Tunisian' vision of human rights.

A third juridical procedure of control, doubtless less systematic, consists in drawing on legislation that had been considered obsolete just a short time before. Thus, to supervise all activity on the part of organizations appealing for public subscriptions, the beylical law of 1922 – which had been forgotten for decades and which the law of 1959, revised several times over, was aimed precisely at replacing – was reactivated within the framework of the struggle against the Islamists at the start of the 1990s and against independent associations at the end of the same decade.[71] According to this law, the authorization of the Prime Minister is obligatory whenever public argent is being requested by associations pursuing a goal of welfare and assistance. In practice, however, the rule has been extended to non-public financing from outside and to associations 'of a general character'.

We could also mention the creation of competing bodies, the refusal of jurisdictional control over the constitutionality of the law on associations or the way the latter is brought into line with the repressive laws on the press, meetings and public demonstrations.[72] All these procedures, juridical in order, cannot be simply interpreted in terms of 'falsification'. The persons concerned are obviously not taken in by these techniques, with their repressive, policing aspect – and to some degree the latter are indeed not meant to be credible. They allow a discourse to function, and to convince those who want to be convinced. But, as in many other authoritarian situations, juridical norms and the apparent respect for the forms are part of the democratic fiction, and contribute to the process of international legitimization and the consolidation of internal legitimacy. They also constitute symbolic resources of power as well as a mode of appropriation of the Weberian state, in this case the former colonial state.[73] The element of unrealism and subversion does not hamper the power of state order and discourse. It might even reinforce it.

Over and above the legislation and its often tendentious interpretations, the economic and financial arm is widely used in an attempt to bring into line recognized organizations and associations. The techniques here too are many and varied. They all have the aim of preventing their concrete operation and, in particular, any influence they might have beyond the (very narrow) circle of their organizers.

Administrative or police measures can be used with the sole aim of affecting organizations financially, and thus operationally. The obligation they are under to ensure that all external financing goes through a state structure allows one ministry, that of the Interior, of Foreign Affairs, or of International Cooperation, to deny or suspend funds arbitrarily. In tandem with this, the reactivation of former laws can prevent any system of internal financing from being set up on the basis of individual contributions. Phone lines can be cut or bugged, access to the Internet as well as available content can be controlled, people can be prevented from hiring premises (thanks to pressure being applied to the owners), passports can be confiscated from militants, and they can be forbidden to participate in international networks, which are often the only ones which make financing possible. These are all so many techniques which constitute definitive obstacles to the day-to-day operation of associations.

In the harassing of the LTDH, it is less the trials than the attacks on associations' finances that have severely affected its functioning. Economic agents have, to this end, been transformed into policemen. It was the bank in which the League opened an account that informed it of the arrival of money from Brussels, but also of the necessity, if it was to get its hands on these funds, of presenting the 'authorizations required in conformity with law 154 of 7 November 1959, notably the dispositions of articles 8 and 14', even though the law of 1992 does not demand such documents.[74] In this way, two important sources of finance have been blocked since 2004: the second tranche of European financing and the financing from the World Fund for Human Rights.[75] Finally, the enclosure of so-called civil society is aggravated by the very context of the political and social life in Tunisia. Associations which are not registered simply have no access to the populations they seek to address, as any advertising of their activities is strictly a matter of their degree of allegiance, the publication of their communiqués is controlled by the Minister of the Interior, and public debate is impossible.[76]

The impossible game of foreign partners: the example of European aid

However, the importance and efficacy of these mechanisms cannot be understood without taking into account the significant extent to which Tunisian society is part of the international scene, and is thus not immune to the new rise to power of 'international civil society' and trends in favour of human rights, democratization and the rule of law.[77] So foreign actors go along with this movement in all its dimensions: the economic and integrative dimension, with overt support for development associations; the political and exclusive dimension, with its implicit struggles (together with that of the Tunisian authorities) against the Islamists; the security dimension, with the priority being given to the struggle against 'illegal migrations', 'terrorism' and 'regional instability', without any real consideration of the repressive forms that this struggle takes, especially in the way it stifles all other social expression.[78] The deployment of this movement is indisputably handicapped by the significance of the mechanisms of police crackdowns and other forms of repression. However, it manages to find an intermittent hearing for itself, through actions of cooperation and the international networks of NGOs. The development of these international activities, the rhetoric of 'good governance' and the necessary democratization of southern countries as the well as the increased space devoted by the western media to violations of human rights throughout the world have doubtless made police crackdowns and other forms of repression less 'acceptable'. This global dynamic has become exacerbated at the margins of the western world. Tunisia today is the object of sustained observation by the European media – primarily that of the former colonial power.

It is within this framework, too, that we need to understand the use of these veiled measures, in which physical violence is neither central nor systematized. The Tunisian authorities have gradually embarked on a real apprenticeship of external pressure and how to manage it, and thus a 'refinement' of the modes of repression. As Mohamed Talbi puts it, crudely but clearly, 'the authorities no longer dare torture people systematically and then throw the body of the torture victim out onto the road. As far as I know, there are no longer any people who are tortured to death.'[79] Under international pressure, as well as pressure from within, the regime was obliged to make concessions'.[80] When the repression was too flagrant, countries such as France and the United States or the European Union could only intervene, urged on by associations, concerned politicians, influential individuals, and networks within administrations. This has been seen in connection with certain opponents who were imprisoned or harassed: the intercession of France *vis-à-vis* the central power enabled one person to be freed, and another to leave the country. On the other hand, when repression occurs discreetly, by less visible and direct methods, foreign institutions are largely deprived of any means of action. Since the end of the 1990s, the Tunisian authorities have come to realize this clearly: arrests and tortures, especially of Islamists, still occur but, in order to muzzle the opposition and the associations for the defence of human rights, the authorities now operate less by unlawful arrest, imprisonment, torture and trial than by delays in the legal process, confiscation of passports, telephone tapping, harassment, continual physical and moral pressure, and drying up of sources of income. Faced with these methods, which are just as effective but all the more difficult to describe and above all to prove, the bureaucracies of democratic countries do not know how to bring their influence to bear, especially insofar as they are bogged down in their strategy of support for a reliable ally, one that is fully committed to the anti-Islamist struggle.

So, paradoxically, these new procedures of repression and supervision are accepted, unconsciously (of course), tolerated, or indeed gone along with by the very same people who claim to denounce them and fight against them. The example of European financing enables us to distinguish between five different modes in which repression is adjusted.[81]

Firstly, the majority of donors do not cast any doubt on the principles of cooperation as defined unilaterally by Tunisia. Via the MEDA funds, the European Union thus accepts the conditions fixed by the Tunisian administration.[82] The financing of associations needs to be directly handled by the state or to be officially agreed by it. It can, in addition, concern only organizations recognized by the Tunisian state, which may lead not only to the exclusion of organizations that would be best placed to defend that for which this financing was set up, but in general reinforces organizations which are now fully disciplined.

Secondly, the national and international organizations of cooperation are not by nature ready to engage in a show of strength, even less to risk scandal. Under pressure from the European Parliament and lobbying from numerous European human rights defence associations, the Commission found the ingenious solution of inventing a new procedure, outside the MEDA funds. The 'European initiative for democracy and human rights', indeed, has the aim of getting round the rules controlling finance as imposed by the Tunisian authorities and succeeding in contributing effectively to the budget that keeps the LTDH going. But the Commission's response was quite flabby, and it did not become involved in any proceedings or envisage any sanctions when the offices of the League at Monastir (which were, however, financed by it) were broken into and occupied by the police on 2 June 2002; nor when, in the same town, the lease contract of the League's new office was denounced by the proprietor, who herself was being pressed by the Tunisian authorities at the end of 2002; nor when the police forces prevented the League's Congress in Gabès from voting on 19 October 2002, when other European funds meant for the League and passing through the coffers of the state were suspended and even when the funds of this credit line were blocked by the banks on the instructions of the Minister of the Interior. As a result, the inventiveness of the Commission hung fire and the LTDH finds itself yet again without any European financing other than rather insignificant subsidies for the organization of seminars or internal meetings. The caution, or even the shame-faced support, find negative expression in the lack of significant symbolic gestures: European representatives were not present at the inauguration of new offices that they had partly financed, and their protests are quite inaudible – apart from the fact that they accept incongruous, not to say absurd explanations.[83]

Thirdly, we can observe a sort of 'Tunisification' of local representations of foreign and international organizations. In spite of these and, sometimes, in spite of the injunctions of their headquarters, these latter are caught up by the Tunisian political economy and thus integrated into that mechanism of control, intimidation and persuasion, of supervision and self-censorship. If we exclude the League (financed from funds directly managed by Brussels), the Delegation of the European Union, for example, in the final analysis finances only associations co-opted in accordance with a strategy whereby many small sums of money are handed out to large numbers of associations per governorate – a strategy defined by Carthage. The 'democracy' projects of MEDA are channelled by the recognized intermediaries of the Ministry of Foreign Affairs and International Cooperation and, following the official paths, are transformed into support for the OVG, those *'organisations vraiment gouvernementales* [really governmental organizations]', as the Tunisians call them, which are really not authentic counter-powers.

Fourthly, the procedures set in place by these international organizations are often poorly adapted to local contexts, in particular to the low-key repression of the Tunisian authorities. For instance, in order to reply to a European call for bids, one needs to have an office equipped with computers, continual access to the Internet and national and international telephone lines, adequate and up-to-date information, and so on. So, in fact, the practical preconditions of access to these conditions are constantly being hampered by the favourite activities of the Tunisian forces of law and order.

The absence of autonomy left in the definition of the subsidized programmes suggests a fifth and final form in which external financing is inadequate. The projects are defined by the Commission with priorities (women, young people) which do not necessarily correspond with those which the organizers of the main movements would like to see subsidized, for example the struggle against torture or the denunciation of the situation in prisons. In addition, the finances provided concern only the associations that are implanted on the two shores of the Mediterranean, with the NGOs or associations of the North *de facto* dominating those of the South, for the material reasons mentioned above. This is true both in the case of the management of the project as in the very definition of the subjects, thereby reproducing 'an asymmetric field of power in which the effects of the competition, hierarchy or exclusion are intense, and which in simple terms reflects the global division of wealth and influence'.[84] Likewise, the ways in which aid is provided are not inevitably the best they could be. Hence the Euromed Network for the Defence of Human Rights essentially finances travel and seminars for militants who are already fully convinced and committed, without any effect of proliferation and diffusion amid the Tunisian population since these meetings occur abroad and they are not publicized by the media within Tunisia.[85] In other words, European financing allows the reproduction of an 'independent civil society' without any influence on the Tunisian population as a whole.

So we find ourselves in a situation that is less ambiguous than perverse. Shame-faced support for a very small group of people who are already personally involved enables the European authorities simultaneously to buy themselves a clean conscience, to reply in part to public opinion in the Union, to seem to respect international commitments (article 2 of the Declaration of Barcelona), and so on, without thereby inconveniencing the authorities, or having to manage any delicate situations. This is certainly not deliberate and results from progressive shifts that are the results of tensions, negotiations, concessions and the fundamental decision to remain in Tunisia. But in fact what happens amounts to a return to the status quo: an indisputable but circumscribed support to people who are already fully committed and work together without any impact on society; and thus an absence of any real support for the extension of activities aimed at defending human rights or the struggle for democratization and the rule of law, and also an absence of any questioning of this action and even of any evaluation of this aid. This is a support which never questions 'grand' politics, the politics of commercial agreements, of financial aid and security cooperation. The effect of this situation is to give succour to the Tunisian authorities by calming the most untimely protests without thereby modifying their behaviour, except in the form of the apprenticeship effect analysed above.

From 'informers' to social workers: individual surveillance on a day-to-day basis

Surveillance is also a matter of individuals attached, whether formally or not, to the apparatus of police and party. The 'informers' are without any doubt the best known of them, even if, in the final analysis, thanks to the nature of their work, little is known of their sociology and their daily lives.[86] Some of them are apparently paid by the police (the wages are generally low but sometimes rise to 300 DT per month), which will give them an income if they no longer have a job, or an additional source of income which is often necessary for the improvement of their living standards. Others receive no money for their services, but benefit from material or relational advantages, such as access to patents and licences (for cafes, restaurants, taxis, bars and so on), the obtaining of administrative facilities, the buying of immunity (several 'informers' are, in a configuration that could hardly be more traditional, former common-law criminals), or else the possibility of using the public highways, indulging in illegal street vending activities, or any other informal activity. This is why the proprietors or employees of cafes and hotels or the managing agents and caretakers are supposed to report on the activity and behaviour of people they regularly come into contact with, and why travelling salesmen are allowed to pursue their 'illegal' activities with impunity, in exchange for information. The 'informers' are managed by the Minister of the Interior and financed or otherwise rewarded thanks to the slush funds of the sovereign ministries (the Prime Minister's office, or the offices of the Interior or of Defence) without these remunerations being subject to parliamentary control.

The techniques of surveillance by individuals also assume unexpected and less grossly police-controlled forms. Administration bosses and head teachers in lycées and schools, for instance, can also play the same role of informer and intermediary: they provide information to the police services, to the *omdas*, to the base cells or to *comités de quartier*, but they also transmit information from the latter to the individuals whom, as a secondary task, they are supposed to be keeping under surveillance.

The example of welfare workers is particularly interesting if we are to understand the historical roots and the contemporary meanings of these highly specific forms of supervision, intimately linked to social control.[87] These women, functionaries of the Ministry of Social Affairs, have historically been recruited from a political base: at independence, women who had been militant in the national movement, even if they were illiterate, could obtain a post. This way of rewarding the active members of the struggle against the colonial power has persisted until our own day, in the form of partisan clientelism and co-opting, with no account being taken of the necessities of professionalism and the 'technicization' of practices. Welfare workers are members of the Union nationale des femmes tunisiennes (UNFT – National Union of Tunisian Women) and have their offices in the premises of the municipal authorities. It is not unusual for their education to be inadequate from the point of view of the effective exercise of their profession, without this being any source of guilt for them since their social work is not to be dissociated from their work for the party. They carry out surveys for obtaining social accommodation, getting a job for girls who have not finished school, for an invalid permit, for financial aid amounting to 109 DT per term for those who have no family to help them . . . For all these interventions, the Tunisian authorities require a favourable verdict on the part of the welfare workers. Within the context of surveillance and police control analysed above, it is easy to understand that they are simultaneously performing an activity of supervision for the benefit of the state party. In order to benefit from this aid, it is, for example, essential to be a member of the RCD and, in the case of women, to belong to one of the 800 local sections of the UNFT; in the case of men, it is necessary to have been part of the local cell of the party for at least three years – to avoid (obviously!) any purely egotistic and self-seeking opportunism. During the elections, welfare workers participate actively in party canvassing, going from house to house, threatening the poorest members of the population by blackmailing people with the prospect of aid and subsidies. But, conversely, their work is made possible by the way they are deeply embedded in the local society whose most vulnerable members they help, protect and keep under surveillance. Being sensitive to the difficulties of some people and the problems of others, they assist them individually in their efforts, and in particular in the adoption of 'good' behaviour.

In the administration, too, a central place is given to individuals scattered over the whole territory. The *omda* constitutes the last rung of the central Tunisian administration, behind the delegate and the governor. He is the direct descendant of the sheikh, representing local power, who in the eighteenth and nineteenth centuries was often opposed to the central power. Before colonization, the sheikh's role was to manage the affairs of the locality, defending local positions *vis-à-vis* the central power. Under the Protectorate, he became the representative of central power *vis-à-vis* the localities, and his first fiscal agent, while remaining a notable, and representing the family, the tribe and then the village. At that time, in spite of this process of centralization, he maintained his credibility and legitimacy among local populations. With independence, on the other hand, this dimension disappeared and the sheikh was, rather, chosen from among the dynamic members of the party. Until 1969, sheikhs were recruited from among young men of between 20 and 30, in accordance both with a logic of reward and with an economic and social logic, especially in the idea (already) of fighting unemployment. The sheikh became *omda* by the law of 27 March 1969, and the decree of June that same year sealed his integration into the single party. Henceforth, and up to the present, the *omdas* are chosen by him although they are, once appointed, functionaries of the Ministry of the Interior.[88] Unless they are dismissed, they are appointed for life.

This brief historical overview enables us to gain a better idea of this role and the nature of the supervision that *omdas* provide. Sheikhs were originally bearers of traditional legitimacy, and have become holders of a legitimacy derived from state and party. With independence, the conflicts between them and the authorities of the single party have been exacerbated, but they have been rapidly resolved by the way the sheikhs are kept in check. Many of them were dismissed, or neutralized thanks to the infiltration of members of the single party into the assemblies which elect the sheikhs. They have found themselves confined to a reduced number of administrative functions, whereas their political and police functions increased.[89] Nowadays they exercise essentially a power of information; they transmit administrative and judicial decisions; they deliver identity cards, attestations for the CNSS and social organizations, residence permits, attestations for the granting of bank loans, and so on. The role of the *omda* cannot, however, be understood entirely unless we recall the primacy of the administration, which party structures have never managed to supplant. In each place or district, the *omda* echoes the base committee of the party, called the cell. The president of the cell is best placed, in a rural milieu, to become an *omda*, and in the best position to rise in the party hierarchy, for example by becoming a member of the steering committee, then president of this committee, then RCD delegate in the local village, and finally governor. Between the two hierarchies, each person keeps tabs on the other.

The *omda* is more important in the rural world because he is often the sole representative of central power there, the sole authority in situ, the sole permanent presence of the state. Indeed, the services of security are present, physically and continuously, only at the level of the delegation, in a bigger village or town, and cover the localities of several *omdas*. The same applies to the council services. So in one sense, the *omda* usurps priority from the delegate, or even the governor, insofar as he is, in rural communities, irremovable, and his superiors make only rare appearances. His function is vital. He is the eyes of the administration watching the local commune; he oversees everything; he is asked for everything – to carry out a survey into a project (the establishment of an electric line, the building of a school . . .), to allocate cards for 'those in need' and the 'indigent', to distribute aid and subsidies, to deliver authorizations and attestations. He plays a key role in the electoral system and gives instructions; he is the direct collaborator of the security services. Under the beylical system, the sheiks were already performing more or less the same function. Now, the relations of domination have been reversed, and the party and administration have become auxiliaries of the police service. As for the party cell or the *comité de quartier*, the controlling function of the *omda*, however, is inseparable on the one hand from his role in clientelism and in the granting of economic opportunities and, on the other, from his ability to represent different segments of the local community and express their expectations and interests – or, more exactly, some of them. His effectiveness comes from the concentration of his powers: by himself, he fulfils all the roles of a municipal authority, since the full range of state entities exist though him, and he supervises between tens and hundreds of people. Admittedly, the *omda* is chosen by the administration and the party, but he is chosen on the basis of local balances and relations of power between different groups in the locality.

In a town or city, however, his importance is less, since the security services are based here and are physically present. However, the *omda* owes it to himself to know all the people in his district. Here too he gives them their civil status papers, as well as certificates of poverty or indigence, in particular for the obtaining of free cards (healthcare, transport). He simultaneously fulfils a social task and a policing task, even if the latter proves more important if any tension arises between his roles: he transmits judicial decisions and summons people to the police station, to do military service, to the law courts, etc. He draws up reports on the individuals in his constituency, and this policing task has a direct influence on his administrative work. In association with the welfare worker, he hands out aid on the basis of thoroughly subjective and political criteria.

In the exercise of his power, not everything, however, is negative. Knowing 'his' population better than anyone, he is also, without the least doubt, the best placed person within this system of permanent negotiation to perform a favour, to obtain aid, to facilitate relations with the administration, to act as an intermediary with the police, to pass up requests and wishes . . . By so doing, he does not hesitate to pick up his reward and sometimes to pass off his own interests as directives coming 'from on high'. But this self-interest does not take away from the positive dimension of his influence, in the city and especially in the countryside, and more particularly it in no way diminishes his importance as a tribune. This apparent confusion of genres is not illegal, and even less a deformation or anomaly: all these practices are known, systematic and openly affirmed; they reveal a mode of government founded simultaneously on scrambling the borderlines between public and private, on the absence of specialization and professionalization, and on the primacy of allegiance. Indisputably, the *omda* is considered as a cog in the wheels of the party's surveillance and police control, one who simultaneously does people favours and plays the role of an intermediary. The driving belt he incarnates indisputably functions from top to bottom, but he can also function from bottom to top, bringing the grievances of individuals or groups and other perceptible tensions to the notice of the authorities while evaluating the tolerable limits of an intrusive interventionism.

These varies different modes of surveillance allow us to understand better the way political control and domination work in Tunisia. It is impossible to separate the 'cops' job' (enrolment in the party, surveillance, supervision and the fight against any suspicion of independence) from a whole series of practices of inclusion, which can take many forms, such as the financing of the party's branches and mechanisms, of course, but more especially daily participation in the community's social and economic life via channels of mediation, intercession and social ascent, or the creation of economic opportunities. These practices of inclusion play a central role in modes of government since, in the absence of debate and of any politicized expression of conflicts, they simultaneously foster the arrangement and mechanization of normalization. This centrality can be a synonym of support, notably when participation in these forms of supervision opens the way to obtaining advantages, to economic integration, to the expression of aspirations, and to the desire for recognition. But, more often than not, this centrality is neither total approval, nor blind belief in government rhetoric: far from it. Belonging to, and participating in, these bodies is often partial, intermittent, even passive; the number of active members in associations is considered to be disappointing, by the central power itself; the party cells are understood, first and foremost, as places for creating and obtaining economic and social opportunities. The fact remains that these institutions and these individuals play an exemplary disciplining role, if only by their omnipresence, imaginary and real, and, in particular, by their ability to hamper the emergence of any credible alternative.

4

The Normalizing Activity of the Bureaucratic Apparatus

It is impossible to consider modes of government and techniques of subjection if we leave the state administration out of the picture. In parallel with, and in concert with, the party's organizations, the bureaucratic apparatus is fully part of the systematic network of surveillance of the territory and, even more, of people's behaviour. Apart from the police, the central administration and the judiciary constitute the two main bodies in the service of this exercise of domination. For the state party is, as we have seen, a party that operates like an administration; but it is also a state bureaucracy regulating the whole of daily life and imposing its logic down to the smallest detail.

Bureaucratic centrality

Tunisian bureaucracy is omnipotent, or so it is claimed: even if it needs to be qualified, this commonplace remark is not necessarily false and can be evaluated from two different standpoints. According to the Tunisian authorities and their foreign partners, the administration is 'a high performer' particularly when judged by the standards of the other countries in the region or middle income countries.[1] Donors praise the coherence of Tunisian demands, the efficiency of administrative services that manage international aid and credit, the rate of absorption of external finance, the effective management of foreign currency and debt, and the ability to respond to the expectations of donors in terms of the organization and quality of the partners. Foreign investors established in free zones are happy with the way checks are exercised lightly.[2] However, for the others – local actors, national entrepreneurs, foreign investors working onshore, citizens and tax-payers – the omnipotence of the administration is apparently made manifest through its oppressive weight, its ability to slow down and hamper developments, and its often intrusive character.[3]

Both of these evaluations reinforce the cliché of the omnipotent administration, a cliché that has largely emerged from national history and the legacy of the Ottoman and French empires: the pyramid-shaped organization of the administration and the exercise of a hierarchical gaze seem to have made it possible for police power, both partisan and personal, to spread and become characteristic of Tunisian modes of government. In the framework of this book, my objective is not to carry out a specific analysis of these *a priori* views of the administration, which are inevitably simplistic and one-sided. On the other hand, I *have* attempted, by analysing certain economic policies and certain everyday activities, to try to understand the operation of the administration within the general framework of the practices of supervision, control, and discipline.

Hierarchy and allegiance

The extremely hierarchized character of the administration allows it to share out the roles between different bodies on a strict basis, to politicize the bureaucracy, and to exert a hierarchical gaze. Party allegiance does not, however, constitute merely a constraint and a burden: as has been said for businessmen and wage earners, for citizens or for tax-payers, civil servants also benefit from several advantages. These can be social advantages, given the nature of their positions and their social roles as mediators within the RCD as within their administration; they can be material advantages, since they can benefit from a house and a car, with free petrol (200 litres per month for a section head, 300 litres for an assistant manager, 400 litres for a manager) or a mobile phone; financial advantages in terms of salaries and bonuses, but also in terms of possible perks, for instance with regard to the age of retirement, theoretically fixed at sixty years. Even if they were not set up with this in mind, allegiance and politicization allow all subordinates to be kept under surveillance: thanks to the pyramidal organization of the administration, the 'boss' – head of services, assistant director, director, CEO, general secretary, councillor – controls the behaviour of the employees; so he exerts a real normalizing power that is made possible by this chain of advantages and benefits that simultaneously fulfil roles of attraction, intimidation, or even punishment.

The disciplinary gaze spreads across the whole administrative hierarchy, at every level of the staff. The system of training for supervision – the *École nationale d'administration* (ENA – National School of Administration) – socializes young civil servants by internships in governorates and public companies. Likewise, at the other end of the pyramid, civil servants at the base perform a crucial function by closing off the system of surveillance. This applies to the *chaouch* [approximately, an usher] whose traditional function emerged directly from the Ottoman Empire. These days, he continues to help administrative activities to function properly, by digging out documents filed away, photocopying texts, bringing files for analysis, serving tea, and welcoming visitors. In the Tunisian political situation, as a result not of legislation but of social practices and the nature of power relations, he simultaneously plays a part in the surveillance of civil servants. On a day-by-day basis, this organization, associated with 'the discipline of office'[4] exercises a real power of domination. But this is in no way specific to Tunisia. Max Weber noted that at the beginning of the century, thanks to hierarchical dependency, all central power benefited from a total 'power of disposition' on the part of the administrative apparatus.[5]

This discipline, a set of relations made of protection, perks, persuasion, conditioning, routine functioning and surveillance, is increasingly felt to be a burden for a certain number of civil servants. That is why, especially since the 1990s and the occasions permitted by liberalization, senior civil servants are 'deserting' public administration in increasing numbers, sometimes to take refuge in international administration, sometimes to launch themselves into the private sector, sometimes to seize the opportunity of setting up on their own.[6] The analysis inspired by Hirschmann in terms of *exit* and *voice* (or resistance) is incomplete. These people are, admittedly, no longer cogs in the disciplinary machine comprised by the Tunisian state apparatus, they are no longer subject to the discipline of serving which weighed so heavily on them; but they do remain fully integrated into a system of relations of power that is particularly tightly supervised. Abroad, too, they will be subjected to surveillance, they will experience the close attentions of the party and will be all the less able to escape it if they wish to rise up the social ladder, bolster their economic success, ensure that they have a quiet life and come back home.[7] They will not necessarily be able to break free of mesh of interests and social relations, but they will formulate their discontents, their doubts, their detachment, their lack of zeal, their need for new horizons – and also, quite simply, their desire for change or the longing to grasp an opportunity – by modifying the places of expression and the modes of action available.

This mobility is doubtless evidence of resistance – not so much in the form of opposition to power, rather as an integral part of the political game and the evolution of relations of force, fully integrated with the exercise of power. The functionaries who express real opposition or are the object of personal or family sanctions rarely choose this path, quite simply because their life after leaving the administration would then be rendered impossible for them: how can they start a business, set themselves up on their own account, or invest, unless they are in contact with the administration? How to prosper without maintaining economic and social relations that are necessarily part of the space of negotiation with the many representations of the Tunisian authority? So, as often as not, they are simply put 'on the shelf' or 'into cold storage', keeping their salary and title but barred from promotion, bonuses, professional and even social life. The hierarchical gaze and the discipline of the service explain that most civil servants are simply 'adhesives', to use Bismarck's ironic term:[8] they acquiesce and are satisfied with strict subordination to their hierarchical superior.

Centrality and the waiting-game: the paradoxes of Tunisian administration

The myth of an omnipotent and efficient administration is thus sustained by the force of official rhetoric, by its pyramidal organization, by its centralism and its capacity for control and discipline. In the facts, however, this force and this effectiveness are largely overestimated, or even imaginary. Certain techniques conceal the failings of the system by their force of persuasion and their power to guide the real. The Plan, for example, lays down everything in advance but, in fact, it particularly structures administrative action in its tiniest details and determines, almost in advance, the results to be obtained.[9] The discourse emphasizes action. This dimension even comprises the essence of the 'reformist' government, – one, in other words, that is sensitive to reforms, to openness, and to moderation – which constitutes the pride of Tunisians. Nonetheless, the reality is often much less glorious, underlining yet again the limits of voluntarism. François Siino, for instance, has shown how the politics of scientific research, which had been the object of highly structured discourses right from the earliest days of independence, was realized in concrete form only over twenty years later . . . on the basis of actions taken by teachers and researchers, and not by the administration on the basis of its own projects.[10] In the same way, Mustapha Ben Letaïef and Sana Ben Achour have brought out the size of the population living on land acquired informally:[11] only 50 per cent of the title deeds are registered in urban milieus, which suggests that, among the 80 per cent of families which the Tunisian authorities pride themselves on having turned into property owners, a great number have become so independently of any state action.

The management of the floods in May 2000 illustrates the negative performances which Tunisians can experience in their daily lives.[12] From 27 May onwards, the rural zones of the delegation of Jendouba, the Ettatwer district ('development' district, the shantytown of Jendouba) and the town of Bousalem were affected by severe flooding. With neither electricity nor drinking water, the town was left without assistance for three days, and the Tunisian authorities intervened only at the end of the fifth day for electoral reasons: the municipal elections were to be held on 28 May, and the ballot could not, of course, be held up! So these delays can be explained politically: the region of Jendouba was always been 'badly treated' by the central administration and, yet again, this has found concrete expression both in their relative casualness but also by the discriminatory treatment of the material consequences of the bad weather, as the authorities refused to consider these zones as having suffered damage, so as to avoid having to provide extra financing.

But the absence of interventions also has purely bureaucratic causes: once the municipal elections were over, it took until the restricted Ministerial Council (2 June) for the media to be permitted to mention the floods, and the different organizations allowed to begin to supply help; the Red Cross, for instance, intervened only three days after the bad weather. These failings stem from a form of behaviour in which fear is interiorized, in which the hierarchical gaze paralyses, in which disinterest and the fear of being contradicted by one's superior inhibit all action. Local administrations did not warn the population about the (inevitable) floods because they work in a routine manner and cannot make decisions. Subsequently, symbolic aid was distributed in a clientelist fashion by the RCD and the regional administration, often after being diverted; this aid was devoted to the infrastructure and to farmers even though the people most badly affected were town dwellers in poor districts. This example might be described as a caricature, but it underscores the Tunisian style of government (obsessed with the political and security dimensions) and, in negative, the emptiness of its supposed administrative omnipotence: the municipal elections of Bousalem were postponed 'because of the rain, which was good for agriculture'; the forces of order suppressed any young people who expressed their anger, and did not provide any aid; in the final analysis, the situation was sorted out 'politically', by manipulating the results of the national competitive exams and granting the high-school pupils in the town results that were far higher than the average.

Behind the effects of media announcements and harassment, the administration mainly appears to be demobilized. The organization and nature of relations incite civil servants, in the positions they find themselves in, to profit from the advantages of that position, and they are more concerned to preserve or indeed to broaden their networks of relations than to work hard. They even carry out, in full view of everyone, a second profession, with this practice being officially encouraged for obvious budgetary reasons. The bureaucratic apparatus then appears in another light, with only partial control of human beings, without any real capacity for development. All of these interferences together explain the policy of wait-and-see and the sense of immobility that characterize the Tunisian administration: decisions are taken slowly and applied even more slowly, precisely because the necessary sanction of the restricted Ministerial Council, or even of the President in person, fosters spinelessness in a bureaucracy that is already used to self-censorship.

However, the logic of inaction needs to be understood. In this system, it is more important to survive than to act, especially because employment is not guaranteed and because the politico-administrative situation is not always easy to decipher. The civil servant knows that, in the absence of a perfect acquaintance with the networks (which are by nature extremely fluid), he always runs the risk of colliding, in spite of himself, with particular interests or with some individual connected to the Head of the State and his entourage by a chain of relations (of family, region, friendship, or clientelism). It is within this framework that we need to understand the implementation of state actions and the (often huge) gaps between discourse and concrete reality.

This does not mean, however, that the oppressive character of the administration is politically orchestrated. The causal link rather goes the other way: because the administration is largely ineffective and suffers from slow and cumbersome operation, political interference can be deployed easily, and the relations of power can flourish in the cogs of the administration.

Apart from the total absence of autonomy on the part of the personnel, demobilization results partly from the pre-empting of bureaucratic action by the party, to its sole glory and profit. The RCD passes off as its own the initiatives of the public authorities and recuperates the expertise of the state apparatus. This strategy is made possible by its institutional and (especially) its personal presence at every level of the administration, as well as by the absence of critical thinking and of any audible expression of disagreement. This is the case of the mobile health forces or the programmes of aid for the least well off.[13] These actions are conceived, programmed and managed by the administration, but they are presented to the population as coming from party cells and organized by them. This recuperation generally affects the conception and implementation of public policy, but also its beneficiaries, who are, first and foremost, eminent party members, those close to the *omda* and the local delegate and their clients. The interpenetration of the state apparatus and the party apparatus is organized around an unequal sharing out of work. The conceptualization, implementation and management belong to the administration; the publicizing, the choice of beneficiaries, the financial and social advantages and, above all, the legitimacy all belong to the RCD.

This inveiglement is possible only by means of the extremely hierarchized and disciplined organization of an administration closed in on itself. But it is not exercised only for the party's benefit. Inveiglement is also a personal activity, carried out by the President, who then exercises an almost privatized power by appropriating the public policy implemented by the administration. As Hannah Arendt showed, the notions of public, private and social are extremely relative. Today, in Tunisia, this overlap is clearly part of the modes of government.[14] It is sometimes analysed in terms of a loss of sense of the state or of its collapse:[15] translating a normative vision of state operations, this interpretation is unable to grasp new or incompletely conceptualized modes of government. However, these inveiglements and these rampant privatizations can be interpreted as 'positive' techniques of the government, modes of intervention like the others, but also as less easy to interpret because of their apparent novelty.[16] State power can also be exercised through intermittent and delegated modes of action, passing via sometimes distant intermediaries of power and often autonomous, but linked to the central power by relations, affinities, alignments, and complex networks of dependence. The situation in Tunisia is in this respect ambiguous. In spite of delegation, the role of the administration remains paradoxically irreplaceable: the pre-eminent form of public action is bureaucratic action, direct and regulatory. The administration remains the inspiring and inventive power behind these measures, and makes them effective (or not). Conversely, the process of delegation, whether voluntary or involuntary, contributes to removing responsibility from the administrative apparatus by ensuring that the interventions are carried out in a discretionary way. It aggravates the demobilization of civil servants by leaving other actors to monopolize the legitimacy of public policies.

In spite of a relatively well-organized structure, cadres who are often competent, and a state tradition that is profoundly interventionist, the inertia and immobility of the administration can be explained by the undermining effect of the critical and populist discourse of systematic denigration of the bureaucracy – a denigration that is all the more powerful in that it is relayed by the President in person. Austerity measures also mean a ceaseless reduction in the operational budget of an administration which thus has fewer and fewer means at its disposal. The repressive and cumbersome procedures of the hierarchized and politicized organization deprive civil servants of any motivation and any capacity for innovation, and this even applies to the most dynamic of them. Untimely but sovereign interventions on the part of the most fully qualified intermediaries are always to be feared, as is the inveiglement of the administration not by general interest but by private interests close to the Palace. This does not mean that the administration has lost any of its centrality. Nor that it does not have intense effects of power on those it administers.[17] More than ever, it operates as a 'house of servitude', to use Weber's term. For, when it comes to deciding the way in which affairs are to be carried out, 'bureaucracy does it incomparably better than any other structure of domination'.[18]

'Society must be defended': justice in the service of normalization

Justice is in particular demand in Tunisia. Currently, over 1.5 million cases are being considered by the courts, for a population of 9 million inhabitants, which means, in a rough and ready way, that one person in every three goes to law.[19] Different and even contradictory interpretations can coexist to explain this situation: the legitimacy and credibility of the judicial system, as is confirmed by the way the wage-earners and trade union workers who resort to it perceive it;[20] the way conflict is built into social relations and the ultimate absence of consensus; the importance of illegality; the resort to justice as the central modality of mediation in Tunisian society; the existence of new spaces of expression that leave a place not for democracy and pluralism, but for the exercise of certain rights by the populace.[21]

It is hard for me to go into details in an analysis that would need in-depth research all by itself. However, in the course of my work, certain data have struck me as interesting, and worth integrating into an initial overview of the disciplinary function of Tunisian justice. Even if the figure is exaggerated, the information which states that some 50 per cent of economic cases before the courts concern spoliation contradicts the image of consensus and moderation which the authorities seek to give of their country; it suggests the significance of economic cogs in the managing of relations of power. In fact, it is easy to create economic difficulties for an individual via the courts. These receive the complaints of people who are trying to get their goods back – but such people may be the 'despoilers' as well as the 'despoiled'. This information helps us to refine our analysis of economic arrangements as cogs in the machinery of discipline – in two different ways. On the one hand, it shows that the practices of inveiglement of wealth cannot – contrary to what the opposition often claims – belong exclusively to circles near the Head of State, but that they are spread diffusely throughout society as a whole. On the other hand, it suggests that justice constitutes another mode of these techniques of control and that it is intensively drawn on in the managing of social relations.

In fact, judges, public prosecutors, and magistrates as a whole have acted as driving belts of the central power, notably in cases of crisis, to fight successively against student movements, leftist movements, the Baathist movement, popular revolts, trade union movements, the Islamist tendency (of course), and democratic demands.[22] Interventions aimed at influencing counsel's speeches and verdicts are commonplace and reinforce the power of normalization, especially since common-law courts are competent to judge certain political misdemeanours.[23] When the economic stakes of a judicial decision are significant, intervention is systematic, or almost. Sentences passed on people for non-payment of credit, for embezzlement, for fraud or tax evasion depend to a large extent on the personality of the persons judged. So, in concrete terms, and contrary to the Constitution, the judicial apparatus is in the hands of the executive power.

A functional justice system

This increase in the power of the executive is realized through the way verdicts and sentences are influenced; it takes concrete form in particular in the way the latter are carried out, or rather not carried out. We need to linger for a moment on this last point. An official statistic, issued by the Institut supérieur de la magistrature and published in the daily newspaper *Ach-Chaab*, is striking: 85 per cent of verdicts in civil courts are not actually carried out.[24] At least three factors can explain this situation. First and foremost, the authorities can block the execution of these verdicts by abstaining from helping the bailiff-notaries in their work, which after all requires the intervention of the police and sometimes other state actors. The insolvency of those found guilty, in addition, can be easily and rapidly organized by the simple act of signing over their wealth to their wives, children, parents, brothers or cousins; this means that the guilty are no longer in possession of the goods to be seized or the fines to be paid, and the sentence cannot be carried out. Finally, there is no means of constraining the state.

Generally speaking, however, it is difficult to interpret these dysfunctions in terms of political will and repressive instrumentalization, in the first place because it is mainly anonymous persons who resort to the law and are forced to discover how ineffectual it can be. The great majority of cases concern the 'average Tunisian', who comes up against more powerful economic or partisan interests. Sometimes, he comes close to those in the elite who are near the Head of State, as we find in the cases of illegal appropriation of land and houses in the smart suburbs of Tunis. More often than not, however, he merely annoys networks of relations and imperatives of a social kind: the defence of squatting on private land in the desire to avoid social disquiet and movements on the part of the least well-off populations; the defence of reluctant creditors in the context of rising unemployment and the necessity of keeping up the appearances of the banks; and tolerance of the organization of insolvency in the hope of calming the discontent of the middle classes. The 'average Tunisian' can, in addition, use justice in an attempt to protect himself from the illegality of other Tunisians, who are just as 'average' as he is. In these (very numerous) cases, illegalities are more akin to ruses for survival than to spoliation or embezzlement. We need for example to remember that, in the last few years, the judicial system has been so overwhelmed by the number of bouncing cheques that a draft law of 1999 set out to depenalize this infraction.[25]

Of course, such practices can be knowingly used for repressive ends against political opponents, as is proved by the case of Judge Yahyaoui who never managed to recover his piece of land, the businessman Majid Bouden who never managed to recover the sums of money owed by his bank, the various Islamist candidates, real or supposed, who never managed to return to work as civil servants . . . However, this permanent and unwarrantable interference needs to be seen as what it is: not, usually, as an explicit desire to exclude, to punish, to intimidate or convict, even if this dimension does exist for avowed 'enemies' and greedy 'friends'; but rather as the expression of a totalitarian conception of social relations and relations of power, of a mode of government which must leave no place for any distinction and for any alternative.

This is the case of the bankers analysed above, who never manage to recover bad debts by legal means, or private entrepreneurs, who refuse to take any part in the national political economy. A flourishing industrialist, for example, had refused to give a favourable response to the government's request that he manufacture locally an imported product needed by farmers, in spite of assurances of a state guarantee and a public bank. Feeling protected by the law, the industrialist cited technical and financial reasons for his refusal. But he was punished for precisely this: whereas the auditors designated by the judicial system drew up a report establishing that the enterprise was in good shape and its books balanced, the business was still put into judicial settlement.[26] There was nothing political in this affair, as in that of the bankers and many others; rather, what we have here is a totalitarian view of social life. In order to face an economic and social demand, and to avoid any aggravation in the deficit of the trade balance, all means are permitted, including abuses of power and the flagrant violation of the law by the executive. And this conception does not concern merely major economic activities and social elites. The little greengrocer, the craftsman or shopkeeper can be the victims of injustice in the same way, quite simply because it is not the law which is imposed, but the law of whoever is the strongest in society.

The judicial system contributes, by intimidation, fear and social control, to stigmatizing and punishing whoever wishes to set himself apart; it thus appears as a central mechanism of the power of normalization. This control is not exercised on a group of people, a social or professional category or a class, but affects everyone, individually. It operates less as a system of justice and more as a system of individual control; it operates less as a judicial mode and more as a mode of social protection. As is suggested by the systematic way in which, in cases of litigation, judicial decisions favour enterprises,[27] Tunisian justice is a functional justice, and its function is essentially to 'protect society' – or rather to protect a certain order of society – and to ensure the proper functioning of measures of security and the realization of the pact of security.

A justice system under pressure

The independence of justice is a pure illusion in this totalitarian conception of power. This also explains the importance of the struggles and conflicts in the profession. Everywhere else, disapproval, discontent and even resistance are expressed in muted terms, drawing on relations of force and a respect for social order. In the sector of the judiciary, on the other hand, an open opposition can be expressed and its members – not just a few individuals but a significant number of them – try to break away publicly from the logic of politicized clientelism, from discipline and training. The emancipation of the profession happened gradually. In June 2001, a huge majority of lawyers elected Béchir Essid to the post of president of the barristers, beating the official candidate. The Tunis bar, the *Conseil de l'ordre* and the sector-based associations, such as the Arab Organization for Young Lawyers, play a role in denouncing violations in public liberties, as do lawyers in independent organizations (LTDH, for example, or CNLT). The open letter from Judge Yahyaoui, published on 6 July 2001, which denounced the absence of separation of powers and the systematic political intrusions in the operation of justice, had an enormous impact, not only abroad.

Judges can exercise their powers by producing verdicts that are in conformity with the law, but not with 'normal' modes of government.

Administrative justice is thus much braver than common-law justice and, in cases brought against the state, it has preserved a certain credibility. Even if it knows that its verdict will not be carried out, it does not hesitate to condemn the administration for its failure to allow a former opponent to register as a student or get his old job back. On other occasions, the lawyer will be led, for the good of his client and the effectiveness of his action, to behave in ways which he in other respects disapproves of and openly criticizes:[28] he will ask him who are his socially useful relations and acquaintances, how much money he has to call on informal intermediaries or mediators and to use procedures that are neither codified nor regulated. This naturally produces advantages in terms of efficiency and application in conformity with the law, but at the same times fosters a social order and modes of government in which the predominant features are negotiation and persuasion, with the prince's arbitrary will as the ultimate factor.

Lawyers constitute the profession that is the most exposed and the most sensitive to the vicissitudes of Tunisian modes of government, by virtue of the very nature of their activities: managing conflicts between individuals. Because they daily have to face, via their clients, police practices but also the arbitrary nature of administrative decisions, techniques of control and surveillance, acts of predation and intimidation, they constitute the socio-professional class that is most politically committed. A significant number of them suffer from and resent these practices; they denounce them and try to oppose them. The foreign (and especially French) media reported at length on the hunger strike undertaken by Radhia Nasraoui, who was attempting to alert foreign opinion to police violence and intrusions into her private life. Over and above this personal case, which met with considerable media interest, the high number of complaints made by lawyers for harassment or brutality – according to organizations for the defence of human rights, over seventy of them in the two years 2001 and 2002 alone were never investigated by the police – confirms the recurrence of this technique.[29] It is interesting to dwell on certain of these practices because they suggest the importance of economic and social measures in attempts to normalize a 'dangerous population'.[30]

The first strategy used to control this rebellious profession is a tried and trusted measure. Ever since the end of the 1980s, the surveillance of lawyers by police and party has been carried out by professional RCD cells.[31] Inside all the organisms of the profession, representatives from the cells relate the words and deeds of their colleagues. These reports are presented to the RCD and the police, they list what is happening in these gatherings, who are the subversive elements present, who are the reluctant figures and the dissidents or, conversely, the most zealous. When the barristers' president asks a member to represent the bar at a foreign conference, a lawyer affiliated to the RCD is sent in tandem by the party to monitor his colleague's words and take note of them.[32] If any lawyer expresses a reserve or a doubt, not on the politics of the Tunisian government but on the way justice works there, he is immediately classified as an 'opponent'. This fact is transmitted to the party, to the ministry and the police and, as a result, the undisciplined lawyer is excluded from the lucrative markets involving the defence of public administrations and enterprises. Furthermore, the police can intervene directly *vis-à-vis* his clients, or those who had been planning on becoming his clients, by turning them away from certain law firms and guiding them towards others; offices can be encircled by policemen in civilian clothes who prevent clients or colleagues from going in, or keep their comings and goings under scrutiny. The offices and homes of these lawyers are under constant surveillance; they are the object of acts of vandalism and aggressions; their post is seized and their telephones tapped.

Everything possible is done to weaken the power of the barristers and to undermine lawyers' morale: economic temptations should be able to discipline them, normalize them, or exclude them. Ever since the start of the 1990s, in parallel with the merciless struggle against the Islamists, the central power has been ceaselessly working to reduce the lawyers' field of intervention. A series of measures of a legislative order have been enacted, with a common underlying logic: to reduce the lawyer's juridical usefulness – for instance in the case of justice in individual cantons or in fiscal affairs.[33] Likewise, qualified intermediaries – unregulated juridical counsels or civil servants from the legal department – can act as lawyers in an increasing number of situations. Such is the case in the conciliation boards, when the state's responsibility is in question, or in administrative disputes, as with attacks of the administration in responsibility, indemnification by the administration or problems of expropriation. All in all, between the years 2000 and 2001, eighteen juridical texts were enacted, reducing the role of lawyers, especially in economic affairs, without thereby clearly establishing the function of different groups. This is a well-known procedure: advantage is taken of a juridical void and of incompatibilities between different bodies, as well as juridical disorder and, in short, a sort of state of exception.

The attempt to train lawyers also finds expression by measures that are quite simply meant to stop them working and make their conditions of social and professional life precarious. Pressures on public or private clients can be brought to bear just by advice from friends, directives from the party, a visit from an acquaintance well placed in the police or in some economic administrative body, or by more overt means such as blackmail based on one's tax record or, even more severely, on one's social security cover. This, for example, is the case with the lawyer Abderrazak Kilani, who seems to have gradually lost all his public clients and his main private client, the Bank of Tunisia, for political reasons linked to his standing in the elections for the presidency of the lawyers' section in Tunis, his defence of the judge Moktar Yahyaoui, and the creation of the Tunisian Centre for the Independence of Justice.[34] In order to reinforce these pressures and dissuade him from instituting proceedings, the Finance Ministry asked to see his tax returns. A second method consists in harassing the lawyer in his daily tasks, for example, when he needs to pay subscriptions or rent or buy an apartment in order to set up a practice. For the Council of the Order of Lawyers, it is even difficult to find, temporarily, any premises for purely cultural activities; under pressure from the authorities, hotels can cancel reservations that had only recently been accepted. The development of conciliation in matters where blows have been exchanged and wounds inflicted, and in everything concerning material damage, constitutes a third technique which directly impacts on the lawyer via his clients. By avoiding the legal department, there is admittedly a speeding-up of justice and sometimes a resolution of the litigation that is as fair as possible. But this measure does not merely cause severe harm to a suspect intermediary; it also contributes to making the clients' social and, above all, private life increasingly fragile.

Of course, the profession is not a unified and indivisible whole, and there are lawyers who are more or less cooperative, more or less reluctant, more or less committed, more or less indifferent to the smooth operation of justice, more or less sensitive to pressures and in particular to attacks on their standard of life. The material arm is definitely the most effective. The mere fact of having assigned the legal department of state affairs to lawyers who are members of, or close to, the RCD, starting from a list given to administrations, to public enterprises and public banks, has had a major impact on the modification of relations of force within the profession: this list has gradually grown longer since 'people need to live'. In these conditions, the central power can easily attain its goals and get round the established rules. Like those entrepreneurs who relay the practices of control and discipline, certain lawyers act like driving belts of the central power: they address enterprises and tell them to take care, their lawyer isn't necessarily the man for the job, or say that this colleague is more efficient than that one. But insofar as they are influential intermediaries in society, certain lawyers also transmit other kinds of advice in the area of tax, social security, and relations with this or that administration. Ever since the middle of the 1990s, the distinction between 'good' and 'bad' lawyers (but also between 'good' and 'bad' doctors, or chartered accounts, etc.) has existed in a very concrete form. This distinction was initially based on a blacklist of lawyers nobody should work with, and was then transformed, after intense and widespread protests, into a 'whitelist' of lawyers everybody could work with. This list is handed out to general secretaries of administrations, to CEOs of enterprises and state companies, to the headquarters of governorates, and to local councils: it is thus known to everybody.

These few fragmentary and certainly incomplete elements still enable us to understand that it is impossible to distinguish between individual strategies and conceptions on the one hand and, on the other, the overall workings of the judicial apparatus. This latter is not subjected in any uniform and general way by decisions from on high, in other words from the regime, just as it does not face any autonomous and sporadic acts of resistance. It is through individuals that the strategies of normalization pass, as well as the protection and defence of the social order that are important aims. All of this is integrated into a general political economy which turns justice into a technique permitting the exercise of certain rights by the population and, simultaneously, a disciplinary whose major function is an essential cog in the wheels of the police state: just like the administration, the judicial apparatus participates in the objectives of the growth of the forces of state and society, but a growth that respects the established social order.

Bureaucratization and disciplinarization of intermediary economic organizations

On the margins of the bureaucratic apparatus, organizations of an economic nature, notably trade unions, have been more or less systematically and more or less intensely integrated into the mechanisms of discipline. They play a particularly central role in these techniques of domination insofar as they constitute unavoidable intermediaries in everyday economic relations.

The UGTT, 'broken in' by economic means

The history of the UGTT and its evolving and ambiguous relations with the central power – the state bureaucracy, the party and the seat of power in Carthage – has frequently been analysed.[35] I am not going to offer any additional interpretation but, on the basis of this literature and my personal interviews, I shall be trying to understand the nature of the involvement of the trade union organization in the set of practices of surveillance, political domination and discipline in the contemporary period. The following pages will bring out the techniques by which the trade union is 'held in check' and the power plays which occur within it.

The recent centralization of the modes of organization and operation of the UGTT, which goes together with the way it is rather forced to toe the line, reflects an objective economic and social situation characterized by structural economic changes, a demobilization of the world of work, the ambiguous effects of liberalization and globalization, and the obsolescence of the former structures of the struggle to realize social demands. It also results from a disaffection vis-à-vis the confederation, fuelled by its lack of firm direction and its conformity. This – new – situation is symptomatic of a process in which the only institution that for a long time was a competitor of the single party was blocked, and symptomatic, too, of the transformation of its function and its position in the system of power. Unlike what happened in the 1960s and 1970s, and even at the start of the 1980s, the trade union is no longer a vital force these days. Now, the confederation is an essential driving belt for the political authorities, even if this function is not always carried out with the docility and efficiency that these authorities might wish for. It is now simply one component of the central power among others, a fundamental one, admittedly, and one which sometimes betray a hankering for autonomy, but constrained by the limits imposed on it, limits with which it is more or less precisely acquainted. The permanent conflicts and de facto competition between the trade union and the single party have disappeared.[36] This leaves only the functions of an intermediary and, often, a pure and simple appendage to power. 'The function that the UGTT is now expected to fill is that of relaying the wishes of the Palace of Carthage: first and foremost, it must guarantee social peace, contribute to the circulation of the official discourse, place its own legitimacy at the service of the legitimacy of power, involve workers and trade union members in the clientelist networks around Ben Ali and his supporters, join in the general policy of depoliticization and denunciation of the opposition, repress dissident trade union workers and even help out the police activity in enterprises (by informing on Islamists, for example).'[37]

This process of training the UGTT was not obtained by the use of force in its most brutal form or of any institutional legerdemain. As opposed to what had happened at the start of independence, especially in 1956, and during the three following decades, there was no creation of any parallel trade union organizations, nor any massive waves of arrests after the 'Change'. Since the 1990s, there have indeed been several imprisonments, but this 'cleaning up' process was mainly carried out by the confederation itself. Now, discipline is maintained first and foremost by an attempt to reach a compromise and by persuasion on the part of the leaders. It is in this way that the 'voluntary gift' to the *Fonds de solidarité nationale* (or 26.26 mentioned above) was set up with the explicit authorization and active collaboration of the trade union confederation. The latter reached an agreement with the public authorities that the sum representing one day's work would be officially taken out of the annual base salary of employees.[38]

The material dimension of supervision takes several configurations. UGTT contributions are retained at source and transferred by the administration to the confederation, so this procedure can be used to prevent an undesirable candidate from standing, to diminish the weight, within the confederation, of this or that trade union deemed to be rebellious, ideologically unsound or refractory, or indeed to modify the weight of the UGTT within the apparatus of power.[39] In order to do this, it is enough merely to say that a particular candidate has not paid his dues or to increase the number of contributors of a particular trade union deemed politically loyal. Another – very classical – configuration resides in the handing out of various advantages. It is difficult to know whether, as critical trade unionists think, the UGTT apparatus is indeed 'corrupted by money', but what is certain is that corruption, which cannot be understood independently of these relations of power, exists and is spreading. The bureaucratic hierarchy of the state and the party gives instructions for different administrative services to hand out advantages to trade unions, and, above all, to their leading members. Trade union secondments (during which the salary remains paid by the state) are the object of frantic competition, in particular because this situation enables the trade union member to be freed from his work while benefiting from substantial advantages. The practice of a second job is general, and it is quite common also to see the leader of a sector-based trade unionist seconded to the UGTT working in a complementary or competitive activity.[40] It then becomes easy to 'keep hold of' those trade unionists who are rendered vulnerable by dishonest compromises and advantages. If they become too critical, if their positions are considered to be inadequately adapted or unsuitable, if a need for renewal, punishment or a change of direction starts to make its presence felt, these files are opportunely made public, which, generally speaking, quickly encourages the persons concerned to toe the line again. The same is true for senior trade union figures who are given positions in the administration. These appointments are transformed into a means of control at the level of the promotion thus obtained, which in certain cases may be extremely rapid, not to say unhoped-for: sometimes a secondary school teacher or a barman has become a director in an office or agency.[41]

The handing out of material advantages is also quite effective in calming the trade unionists' demands for better pay or conditions. So the President of Tunisia recently decided to extend the customs exemption of vehicles in the administrative area to members of the executive bureau of the UGTT. As a result, the latter now ride around in grey-metalled Peugeot 406s – a material symbol of their submission to the administration. Only two members, it appears, have rejected this advantage, arousing a general outcry.[42] As an institution, the UGTT is, furthermore, relatively rich, benefiting from a twice-annual payment of PAYE from civil servants who are members of unions, of occasional financing from the Palace, meant in particular to influence negotiations in progress and, in addition, one-off payments, for instance provided to the CNSS to organize seminars or colloquia. This clientelism does not belong to one management organization rather than another; it already existed in the years preceding the placing under supervision of the UGTT, but it has developed much more widely since then and has been perpetuated since the replacement of its general secretary in 2001.

Some authors thus talk in terms of a '*syndicat managérial*'[43] or a '*syndicat gestionnaire*',[44] that is a managerial trade union, in acknowledgement of this new position, in which the UGTT is no longer seen as in opposition to the other organizations of the state party, if only in terms of workers and salaried employers, but instead shares, just as the other institutions do, in the developing of economic policies, contributes to the regulation of the labour crisis and ultimately to the maintenance of 'public order' and 'social peace'. This dimension makes it possible to understand the place of the trade union confederation in relations of power: it is a cog in the machinery, one that is not necessarily controlled, nor entirely submissive, but a fundamental factor in the quest for order, stability and tranquillity. In fact, the slowness in privatization, the maintenance of protection, the attempts at a social handling of unemployment, and the often illusory nature of liberalization, are all explained by the way demands are relayed, and sometimes called into being, by the trade union.

In fact, clientelism and the relay function of power are themselves made possible only by the role of intermediation and redistribution which the trade union plays for its members. We again find the same configuration as analysed above for the RCD, the *comités de quartier* or the *omda*, at a perhaps more intense degree thanks to its deep integration into working relations, but also, more broadly speaking, in the mechanisms of redistribution and in the practice of permanent negotiation. The UGTT's power is bolstered by the distribution of goods, influence (career opportunities), symbolic gestures (notability, upward mobility, and even moral promotion), aid, travel, holiday camps for children . . . At the time of the elections, this means so many votes that have been rustled up. And, conversely, again following the set-up in place within the single party, the UGTT is also the place in which the expectations of the world of work can be realized – a world whose fears, doubts and above all demands it relays.

This mediation does not reach concrete form only in an open discourse that criticizes and proposes new economic and social guidelines for the government. But the mobilizations organized or controlled by the UGTT act as a safety valve and an early warning system for the central power. In 2003, for example, the trade union confederation found itself mainly focused on the struggle against low-security jobs, informal commerce and fraudulent bankruptcies. It thus alerted the central power to the extent and the consequences of a phenomenon that affects an increasing number of salaried employees, while attempting to circumscribe the discontent that it arouses and preventing accusations from being directly addressed to the main actors in this development, often close to the President's circle.

While the confederation needs to steer a careful course to maintain a status that is forever crumbling before the attacks of an increasingly dominant central power, it must also take into account an increasingly reluctant base when faced with changes in the role and inner operations of the UGTT. The divergences and indeed conflicts between the 'summit' and the 'base' are increasing, and the confederation recurrently collides with the demands of its supporters. As a result of this very anchorage in social and economic relations, the confederation cannot be perfectly disciplined. As a result, too, of its history, the conflicts are still more significant than elsewhere, even if the bureaucratic apparatus of the confederation always – or almost always

– emerges victorious from the battles or masked conflicts with individuals, trade unions that belong to it, or the 'base'. The defeat and silencing of the oppositions within the UGTT, however, constitute more a strategy of waiting for better days than an alignment or an alliance. The multiplicity of networks, of clienteles, of friendships and alliances enables a subterranean competition to arise, and, in certain circumstances, allows oppositions to express themselves. It is not unusual for the council of executives of a sector-based trade union to be disowned by the ruling apparatus of the UGTT, which imposes its solution.[45] This also explains the ambiguous support for workers when the bases decide, in spite of the injunctions of the confederation, to embark on action.

Dissent and division within the UGTT are also revealed by the tumultuous relations between the latter and independent associations. In various very specific conflicts that have been developing since the start of the 2000s – those of Moknine and, more generally speaking, textile companies that used to be public and have been 'badly' privatized, in offshore enterprises that close down from one day to the next, in certain hotels in Hammamet – the discussions about walk-outs, occupations, and hunger strikes are as often as not carried out by very particular trade unionists:[46] they oppose the current line of the UGTT but do not wish to abandon trade union action, and so they act individually, leaning on other organizations, notably the LTDH and RAID/Attac-Tunisie. The defence of workers is now the object of open conflict between these institutions.

The UGTT is a central, albeit declining institution due to economic transformations and political pressure: but this does not mean that it is either totally 'submissive' or totally 'aligned'. Beyond the myth of consensus, its analysis brings out the extent of the tensions, latent conflicts and negotiations in Tunisian society as well as in the exercise of power, and undermines the image of an entirely repressive action on the part of the central power. It also brings out the absence of homogeneity in an institution whose leadership is indisputably integrated into the process of disciplinary normalization, but whose base does not seem so docile and easy to control. We should certainly talk in terms of an unstable cohabitation between a neutralized leadership and an uncontrolled base, rather than of any alignment. The UGTT is aware of its declining powers and is also trying to risk its survival by trying not to lose what is left to it.

The historical retreat of the UGTT and its increasing dependency are both the result of the way the social structure has changed, and of transformations in the world of work. In the private sector, the number of people in trade unions has been very low ever since 1987. Many trade unions are merely idling and in certain enterprises, such as textiles, the right to join a union does not, in actual fact, exist. In addition, the RCD is a particularly efficient competitor in its strategy of redistribution and upward mobility. Finally, the UGTT has been made vulnerable by the relative rise of the UTICA (*Union tunisienne de l'industrie, du commerce et de l'artisanat* – Tunisian Union of Industry, Commerce and Craft). As an entrepreneur in textiles told me, during a conversation in 1997, 'the UGTT is very strong in the sector, but the bosses are too, thanks to the policies of Ben Ali.' The need to control and discipline the world of work has indeed passed, ever since the current President came to power (and this also corresponds to the implementation of structural adjustments), by a new balance of power between the working-class trade union and the bosses. This new balance of power did not come about entirely smoothly since, at the moment, three out of every four conflicts at work seem to concern the failure to respect the executive salary agreement signed, every three years, between the UGTT and the UTICA, under the aegis of the government.[47]

The UTICA, official appendix and intermediary of the partisan power apparatus

Historically, the UTICA, which has no historical legitimacy since it was created by the state party after independence, has never set itself in opposition to the central power, or even acted a critical adviser. On the contrary, it has always constituted an appendage of the apparatus of party power, without any initiative of its own. The great majority of leaders of the UTICA are active members of the RCD, and even, as often as not, form part of its elite. As contributions from members are relatively low, the bosses' organization is largely financed by the state, either via a percentage of the tax on turnover, or via direct aid, or indeed through the inveiglement, with the explicit authorization of the government, of foreign funds, for example financing from the Konrad Adenauer Foundation.[48] This submission has increased since the 1990s thanks to the activation of strategies of alliance and networks of power that straddle the business world and the politico-administrative world. The UTICA is one of the privileged bodies for the exercise of this strategy of training, which passes largely through practices of intimidation, sanctions and perks. It is an important element in the policy of order, peace and social stability with clear and overriding objectives. In fact, it fulfils, as often as not, the role of a pure and simple driving belt for the central power.

Two almost too perfect illustrations of this are provided by the *Fonds de solidarité nationale* and by the policy of 'upgrading' of enterprises. In the first case, the UTICA has signed an agreement of, so to speak, subcontracting with the power of the President and so it is the UTICA which, in the name of the President and in cooperation with the CNSS, sends the forms and money orders for payment to the employers, so that they can pay the sums due on the 26.26.[49] In the second case, the UTICA has played the role of faithful disciple in spreading information about the benefits of the 'upgrading', contributed to the choice of those selected in the experimental phase of the programme and, later on, rallied the troops when it turned out that the entrepreneurs doubted the bureaucratic process set up by the administration.[50] The bosses sometimes makes suggestions about modifying a policy or an arrangement in operation, but it cannot, at best, do any more than propose corrections and nuances. These authorized criticisms can be articulated only by certain bosses, those whom Jean-Pierre Cassarino calls the 'official opponents' who belong to the UTICA and often to the RCD, who also benefit from a very good knowledge of the mechanisms at work in the apparatuses of power and thus know with great precision the limits that must not be crossed. Warnings and even motivated reactions to public policies (for instance in opening up the economy, liberalizing services or restructuring of banks) are rare and, when they do exist, they are expressed belatedly, in tones that are softened down and often timid, and are always accompanied by repeated reminders about the 'benefits of the Change'. The UTICA participates fully in this political economy of the unsaid, of the impossibility of criticism, and of the myth of mere statistics and perpetual progress that contribute to shaping the fiction of the economic miracle.

In these conditions, the majority of entrepreneurs, including those who belong to the bosses' union, deplore its inconsistency when it comes to relations of force. The UTICA is rarely considered to be a bosses' organization playing its role as a defender of entrepreneurs, and even less as a lobby facilitating collective action so as to promote innovative and productive strategies, contribute to the spread of information, participate in training and research programmes, foster the development of relations between entrepreneurs, organize debates and critical discussions, and create industrial districts or 'clusters'.[51] It is perceived, rather, as an intermediary in the service of the central power, a politicized body without political power, as the institutional representation par excellence of the interpenetration of the economic and the political. In Tunisia, studies have shown that entrepreneurs made an effort to appear pleased with themselves and with government action; that following the programmes of the bosses' organizations was a measure of timidity; that professionals were unable to unite in order to promote their activities collectively; that economic and social dialogue was not much encouraged . . .[52]

The submission of the UTICA is particularly easy to obtain as there is within it no consensus on what economic policies to follow, on the instruments to be set in place, on the level and especially the modes of state intervention, on the managing of integration into the international scene. As opposed to what has been observed in Morocco, the Tunisian 'bosses' have not become an instrument of influence in the hands of entrepreneurs, or a place in which alternative policies can be developed.[53] It is still destined to spread the official discourse, largely supported by the party and by those segments of the elite that are most linked to the central power. It is a space for the one-dimensional spread of information and the economic opportunities of the moment, on the express condition that those involved behave in accordance with the rules of consensus.[54] In the universe of a discourse closed in on itself, the absence of consensus, and even of convergence, can find expression only in silence and the consummate art of commentary. Support for these norms from entrepreneurs is to a very large extent faked, and real behaviour is a stubborn silence rather than any acquiescence. There are no public debates or any contradictory development of a consensual position, since the joint definition of economic policies is really more of a myth. The business community has few means at its disposal for influencing the administration, for getting coherent demands across, or for articulating support or opposition to any reforms.[55]

This situation is explained first and foremost by the significance of interventionism, of a statist concept of the economy and a Third-World view of international relations.[56] These 'traditions' are deeply rooted in people's behaviour and modes of thought, including among self-declared liberals who are often the same individuals as the convinced statists of previous years – and this in spite of the overt liberalism of the years since the 1970s and even more since the 'Change'.[57] This situation is aggravated, furthermore, by the heterogeneity of the enterprises and the sector-based and entrepreneurial interests represented within the UTICA. It also includes bosses of the conglomerate as well as individual entrepreneurs, modernized enterprises, working in export and associated with foreign interests, family enterprises resistant to any transformation in their mode of management, enterprises in the electronic sector and textile and plastics enterprises . . . One example will summarize these insoluble contradictions better than any other. Illegal activities are indulged in by powerful actors of the economico-political elite that is also represented within it. The latter come up against the interests of the vast majority of small and medium entrepreneurs and even major enterprises operating with a certain legality, notably in textiles, garments, leather, and small consumer goods.[58]

However, the bosses' trade union is not totally subject to the disciplinary demands of the central power. Like the different trade unions within the UGTT, the different federations sometimes have more nuanced positions than what the UTICA allows to be seen on the public stage. Off stage, tensions are expressed, always more filtered and coded than in the world 'of work', never made public, but no less real for all that. As a consequence, the bosses' organization fulfils an (admittedly limited) function of intermediation: it relays 'moods', in particular those of the mass of small manufacturers and small professions who constitute the vast majority of the industrial fabric of Tunisia.

As a result of this almost total submission, the UTICA appears emptied of its meaning. The fact of belonging to the bosses' organization – as well as to other professional organizations – represents nothing concrete. It acts essentially as a 'symbolic value',[59] signifying consensus: you are not against, you are not opposed, and yet you are not inside. Supporters do not consider the UTICA as a representative organization and participate, so to speak, by default, since there is nothing else, since, above all, not to participate would constitute a dangerous act of suspicious singularity. Behind this alignment and the deafening silences that go along with it, we can perceive the doubts, the reluctance, the tensions and latent conflicts that, at the individual level, pervade the relations between entrepreneurs, and between entrepreneurs and public and party organizations too. Opposition is rare, but if support exists, it is powerfully constrained and always supervised.

Between supervised support and bureaucratic normalization, Tunisians seem to be definitely kept 'in the status of "political minors" '.[60] The previous developments have suggested the extent of demobilization, lifelessness, and at all events their enforced withdrawal from the public scene thanks to censorship, the increased level of the 'policing' of everyday life, the destructive effects of the *stratégie du pourtour*, manipulations of every kind, surveillance and supervision by the party, the process of perpetual allegiance, the shutting down of debate and the straitjacketing of thought . . . As a result, Tunisians usually consider themselves to be subjects and not citizens.[61]

The analysis proposed hitherto does, however, enable us to understand another dimension of the mechanisms of discipline and political control: the latter are not necessarily envisaged, conceived and implemented on the basis of a voluntarist and disciplinary conception, they do not emerge from some all-knowing state, from a brutal cynicism that attempts to force people to believe in a false openness so as to increase their direct grip on society. Rather, the intrinsically indeterminate character of juridical, political, economic and social instruments makes them suitable, in specific circumstances, for fulfilling such a function. These different modes of surveillance also suggest the significance of economic and social mechanisms, the depth of their integration into relations at the heart of society and the impossibility of understanding 'repression' – or rather, control and domination – by sticking to a strictly political analysis. If we look more closely, we will thus find tensions, negotiations, arrangements, in short a whole series of non-repressive modes of operation, also made up of partial support and sometimes shared understandings. We realize, above all, that domination is not a uniform machine regulated in advance, but that when it is put into action, this is a process with its full share of imprecision, clumsiness, uncertainty and arbitrariness. Discipline, but indiscipline too, occur in the interstices of the relations of power. The following pages will focus on just this theme, within the framework of Tunisian capitalism.

Part III

Negotiations and Consensus: The Force of 'Insidious Leniencies'

My ambition in this part of the book is to go a little further in understanding the various forms of domination, this time concentrating my analysis on more local configurations rather than those associated with policing – those which are less juridical, and less institutional, attempting rather to grasp power in its economic and social extremities. There is nothing new about taking this dimension into account: this becomes clear if we read the founders of the historical sociology of the state, starting with Marx and Weber. In their day, they devoted a great deal of their activity to demonstrating that the economic dimension had something to do with coercion: 'to "appropriate" something is to acquire rights. [. . .] More precisely, these are powers whereby one has something at one's disposal (*Verfügungsgewalten*)'.[1] The political or sociological analysis of 'authoritarian regimes', however, often neglects the economic dimension, which is not to say that the latter is purely and simply forgotten. Those who, like Juan Linz and Alfred Stepan, do take it into account, for instance in terms of 'economic society', do not go into its mechanisms, or into the 'anatomy of the detail' that alone enables us to understand its political meaning.[2] As for liberal political economy, it tends to analyse authoritarianism as a mere 'exchange' between, on the one hand, economic and social well-being, guaranteed employment and a certain degree of social protection and, on the other, the violation of public liberties on the basis of a macroeconomic and economicist conception of the political dimension.[3]

Given all this, it seemed to me more innovative to dwell on the more concealed procedures of domination, on the little, day-to-day, anodyne interventions, on the various arrangements that link people together by considering economic reality as inseparable from relations of power. This intellectual method is not simply the fruit of various theoretical influences. It is also a response to what I have learnt from 'fieldwork', which brought out a continuum between daily life and the exercise of power – a continuum which threw up hints such as 'the system which controls is also the system which provides' or – what comes down to the same thing – 'what weighs down on us is at the same time what protects us'. So I would now like to take a closer look at these ambivalences, these reciprocal relations and these permanent comings-and-goings which also enable power to be exercised in a disciplinary and coercive way, but which simultaneously result in people not only accepting that power, but to a degree – indeed, a significant degree – supporting it.

The expressions quoted above reveal a voluntarist conception of the 'Ben Ali regime' and the image of a demiurgic and omnipotent President. An entrepreneur indisputably senses the constraints of the political system and, at least at certain moments, does indeed perceive the latter as a system of observation and control. Nevertheless, this same entrepreneur will be the first to assert, and not only by interiorizing constraints and the norms of political correctness, that he 'owes it to the "regime"' that there is social peace and geopolitical stability, that the constraints are, so to speak, 'rewarded' by a series of highly concrete benefits, such as the protection of the markets or the obtaining of tax exemptions. Likewise, an individual may consider that 'the regime may drive me to starvation', thereby suggesting the interference – broadly considered to be hostile – of the political in his everyday life, but he will at the same time acknowledge that the government and even the 'regime' has a certain legitimacy, thanks to its ability to 'offer a way of life', a sense of well-being relatively higher than elsewhere, a rising level of consumption, and a definite social stability.[4]

If we were to accept this interpretation in terms of compensation, inevitable punishments or rewards, and consciously planned government machinations, we would be reducing the political dimension to the 'regime', considering the exercise of power as an exchange of satisfactions, just like some commodity. However, if we criticize this position, we should not thereby be led to ignore what the actors themselves say. All of them – entrepreneurs, civil servants, consumers, craftsmen, shopkeepers – are actually stating something fundamental: administrative, economic and social mechanisms are by nature ambiguous and equivocal, simultaneously making it possible for opposites to coexist: control and a margin of manoeuvre, domination and resistance, economic constraints and economic opportunities, financial costs and financial advantages . . . In other words, economic actors as well as individuals are subject to disciplinary power, but they also relay it, feeding into this logic of negotiation, arrangements and accommodations.

This is what I shall be trying to analyse in the following pages, starting with an analysis of the relations of power in the field of economic activities. With this aim in mind, I shall be setting out from the dominant interpretations of the relation between capitalism and political domination in order to integrate fully the ways in which actors understand their integration into society. These interpretations have two aspects, partly contradictory, even though they are sometimes found uttered by the same actors or written by the same analysts. In simple terms, the first reading might be called 'interpretation by constraint' and summarized as follows: enterprises and, more generally, the business world are subjected to the constraints of authoritarianism and more specifically the particular forms of the 'regime', combining corruption, nepotism and the blocking of any attempts to set up a strong economic pole; as it is omnipotent, the central power can ceaselessly intervene, creating an unpropitious climate for the flourishing of economic forces. The second reading might be baptized 'interpretation by collaboration' and summarized by the following argument: on the national level, the objective alliance of a parasitic bourgeoisie and the state enables a *rentier* economy to survive; since the 'regime' needs resources, it responds all the more favourably to the demands of international capital in that the latter are first and foremost centred on a strict and hierarchical control of the world of work. My critique of these two interpretations is an attempt on the one hand to show that it is impossible to distinguish between capitalist logic and political logic and, on the other, to suggest the existence, over and above the permanent negotiations and the strategies of accommodation, of a security pact that reveals relations between the state and its population that are much more complex than an objective of absolute control and repression.

5

Between Hidden Conflictuality and the Permanent Search for Compromise

The interpretation by constraint is particularly widespread in the business world, in the Tunisian and especially the Tunis bourgeoisie, in the world of the opposition and among critical intellectuals, and also (albeit in a slightly different form) in the international community. It consists in emphasizing first and foremost the interferences of Power in the economic world and pointing out the drawbacks, inefficiencies and perversions it causes. On the basis of concrete examples drawn from the tax relations and the strategies of deployment of Tunisian entrepreneurs, I aim to conduct a critical analysis of this interpretation by underlining the complexity of the bonds that are thereby woven between those who govern and those who are governed – in other words, the complexity of relations of power, notably the fact that a business is the locus of relations of force and that it plays an active part in shaping the outlines of political 'constraint'. The most political of public actions is, in every case, taxation. If we analyse this, we will be in a better position to grasp the political meaning of a historically situated economy, in this case that of contemporary Tunisia, and in particular to gain a better understanding of the inseparable character of economic practices and the relations of power.

The twists and turns of tax relations

In Tunisia, the tax system is rarely viewed as an economic instrument. Tunisian jurists have demonstrated the overall lack of coherence of the reforms which have succeeded one another ever since independence, and have pointed to the recurrence of fiscal modifications that have emerged from the accumulation of contradictory measures and the interweaving of economic logics that are not always mutually compatible.[1] The succession of measures and counter-measures, amendments and administrative interpretations, has tended to cast a veil over the outlines of the economic rationality of taxation. On the other hand, it seems clear that the tax system is first and foremost conceived as a financial instrument which varies widely with the state's budgetary demands, national and international circumstances, and international agreements.

The state's current revenues rest totally, or almost totally, on money from taxation – indirect taxation in particular, as VAT is forever increasing, but also direct tax thanks to the tax levied on the income of wage-earners. We will fail to have a complete overview of the fiscal situation if we do not take into account the social security of the private sector, which in Tunisia plays a role quite close to that of the tax system:[2] the *Caisse nationale de sécurité sociale* (CNSS – National Social Security Office) is in surplus, and at present constitutes a veritable financial power. It grants loans (car loans within the framework of the programme of 'popular cars' and, for the most part, property loans), realizes capital gains on the management of its portfolio (as was the case with accidents at work in the mid-1990s), builds up capital thanks to the profits it makes from its operations (advantageous returns on government bonds and accessories bonds), invests in the capital of profitable businesses (the CNSS is a shareholder in the biggest private clinic) and can thus afford the luxury of being able to help close the budget gap (financing the deficit), being the main contributor to the financing of social solidarity (by participating in the 'needy families' programme, the *Fonds de solidarité nationale*, help for students without grants, divorced women and the unemployed) or indeed financing the resolution of social conflicts.[3] So these contributions are broadly considered as taxes by economic actors, following the idea – it hardly matters for our purposes whether it is right or wrong – that in Tunisia the contributions paid to the CNSS are relatively high and the benefits obtained very low or even nonexistent.[4]

Given this, how are we (in spite of this crucial financial function) to interpret the vision, widely shared by the business community, of a tax service in the service of political repression? When you ask an entrepreneur about the Tunisian tax system, you almost automatically get the reply: 'it's an intrusion of Power or the Administration' and 'the inspectors are incompetent'. And if you venture to ask whether there are economic instruments of political control in Tunisia, the reply is unanimous: the tax system. It strikes me that this idea needs to be taken even more seriously in that, financially, the Tunisian authorities have decided, ever since independence at least, to impose a low rate of taxation: it represented only 20.5 per cent of GDP in 2003 (as opposed to 21.5 per cent in 2002 – a level which has been more or less stable since the end of the 1980s, a slight rise on the 1960s and 1970s), a very low figure, whereas the budgetary resources taken from borrowing have continued to increase. This intuitive evaluation of the tax system has, so to speak, been corroborated and theorized by certain studies.[5] The characteristics of the tax system, it is claimed, reveal the significance of a repressive regime and of the constraint weighing down on the economic world, notably with 'punishments' in the form of tax inspections; taxation is illegitimate as a result of the state practices of intrusion and the non-democratic nature of the 'regime'; tax evasion is an act of dissidence or, at least, of opposition.

These analyses implicitly take up the classic political theory on the relation between taxation and political representation – the traditional 'no taxation without representation', inverted for *rentier* states into 'no representation without taxation'.[6] They underline the difficulties there are in reforming the tax system, the stagnation of tax revenues (or even their diminution), as well as a tendency to replace taxation by external debt. Resorting to borrowing, it appears, means 'also and above all the inability of a state of non-law to set in place any real fiscal reform accepted by the taxpayers [. . .] the absence of the rule of law [cannot] but encourage the actors to adopt *rentier* behaviour, accustomed as they are to expressing political allegiance in exchange for economic privileges'.[7]

The legitimacy of control as evasion

Be this as it may, there is in fact a certain legitimacy in the state's intervening and establishing powerful checks, quite simply because people do actually evade paying taxes. If we are better to understand the role played by the tax system in the exercise of power, a more detailed analysis is required – one which examines the cogs in the microeconomic and macroeconomic mechanisms of the tax system.

At the end of the 1990s, the new managing director of the tax inspection service made it publicly known that he estimated that the shortfall in tax due to fraud and evasion represented 50 per cent of the revenue drawn from different taxes.[8] Already in the middle of the 1980s, the IMF had estimated tax fraud to be more than 50 per cent of the expected revenue.[9] As in Morocco, in Greece or Portugal, other countries which I have studied, two characteristics are mentioned which might give some legitimacy to tax inspections.[10] On the one hand, fraud is significant and widespread: the absence or underreporting of declarations and the low rate of recovery actually combine to diminish tax revenue significantly. However, we need to treat the figure of 50 per cent with considerable caution: concretely speaking, this figure allows inspections and tax levies of every kind to be justified; it also authorizes the discredit of the economic and financial world, and thereby the process of surveillance and negotiation with businessmen. On the other hand, the state apparatus is presented as having the technical capacity to discover the main areas of fraud and to target taxpayers from whom money needs to be recovered: while the competences of the tax administration are often subject to doubt and caution, the administration of the CNSS has a very good reputation in this domain.[11] Precisely because it is considered as the most efficient, it is the most feared and, depending on the entrepreneurs interviewed, it constitutes the apparatus most likely to be used for political ends.[12]

Tax inspections have increased since the years 1997–8, to make up for the shortfall resulting from the drop in revenue from oil and the free exchange

Agreement with Europe, evaluated by the Tunisian authorities at approximately 70 per cent of customs revenue, i.e. 18 per cent of tax revenue.[13] Thanks to the significance of tax evasion, the administration has transformed adjustment into a tax instrument like any other, following a financial logic rather than a logic of justice or law. In addition, the drop in customs duties has led to an increase in VAT rates and the broadening of its base. A freeze on VAT credit on 31 December was imposed in 1998, in draconian conditions, without businesses reacting any more than usual. Entrepreneurs were warned that tax credits had been abandoned and that they would eventually be repaid later. Most businesses decided that it would be more sensible to give up their VAT credits, including foreign investors.[14] Those who, out of principle, and feeling sure of their rights, decided to follow the arduous paths of legality were subjected to an in-depth tax inspection as soon as the procedure for recovering their TVA credit had been launched, the sums being finally repaid incorrectly and in piecemeal fashion, in ever smaller tranches.[15] It is within this context that entrepreneurs complain that the inspections are arbitrary, and the adjustments slow. It has to be said that, during three decades, the under-taxation of economic actors was the rule – and it still is for agriculture, which is still tax exempt. In particular, tax evasion has been tolerated so as to foster the development and constitution of a national bourgeoisie,[16] which the current context (one in which revenues from oil, gas and phosphate are declining or even disappearing, as are liberal norms) no longer makes possible – at least not as well as before.

These new conditions do not, however, deprive taxation of its political role or its role as mediation. Although it is, of course, never said, tax fraud, a current practice among the vast majority of entrepreneurs, continues to be tolerated and even fostered. Sometimes, this tolerance is involuntary, explained by the very way the chain of decisions operates. There is often a big gap, in time and in content, between the President's speech, the passing of the law, the decrees of application, and the reality. The documents are often inaccessible and very sparingly distributed, and it is not unusual for one to search in vain for the wording of laws enacting certain decisions, even though they are being fully applied.[17] This situation is aggravated by practical difficulties: the inadequacy of printed matter, the impossibility of declaring deficits on certain of them, the absence of standardization of annual accounts, and the omission of a site for the exempted revenues. It is also fuelled by the 'increasing weight of formalism in the administration', as well as by the 'real limits of judicial censorship and the limits in the channel of diffusion of the administrative doctrine both within the administration itself and between the latter and the taxpayers'. As a result, there is a risk that 'personalized applications will be perpetuated, from one centre to another, from one taxpayer to another'.[18] The rise to power of the executive in legislative domains and the development of improper interpretations of the legislation also explain how it is easy to evade tax, consciously or not. Tax specialists cite the case of the extension of the amnesties on direct taxes to indirect taxes or that of the setting of the conditions of non-imposition of indemnities and advantages on salaries by the administration.

In particular, the wording of tax regulations can sometimes be so vague that 'it sometimes happens that answers given to similar questions at close dates contradict one another',[19] *de facto* creating real encouragement for fraud. This is, for instance, the case for VAT, with its many various special dispensations, the complexity of the rules of retrieval for tax credits, the difficulties introduced into the texts for groups composed of subsidiaries, or its problematic coexistence with consumer rights.[20] This is also the case with the system of fixed taxation, for which there was, on the part of the legislator, an evident desire to leave small entrepreneurs and the huge breeding ground of SMEs – 90 per cent of physical persons subject to task on industrial and commercial profits – in a lax system which favours them: the average taxation of the 260,000 taxpayers at the fixed tariff – which means the same number of families, which thus represent a significant proportion of taxpayers, 70 per cent of them in 1997 – is of the order of 50 DT per year whereas a primary school teacher, for instance, pays 500 DT per year.[21] 'In Tunisia, the fixed rate has, over the years, turned itself into a veritable refuge for numerous taxpayers whose main objective is to escape paying tax, either totally or partially,' writes S. Zakraoui.[22] This state of affairs has been interpreted as a desire to create a certain tranquillity in the area of tax, and to calm the relations between the administration and the taxpayers.[23]

This tolerance of evasion is also illustrated by the very low number of tax-payers subject to the system of fixed taxation who actually do pay their taxes. Thus the same sources mention that in 1997 the rate at which these declarations were submitted was only 57.9 per cent.[24] The reform of the fixed rate in 2000 does not seem to have changed the situation; it may even have aggravated it, since in 2006, 65 per cent of taxpayers had opted for the fixed rate, paying an average of 73 DT tax per year, whereas at the same date wage-earners were paying 72 DT . . . per month.[25] Likewise, the technique which consists in reinvesting all the profit in the creation of a new company, instead of consolidating and recapitalizing the existing company, is not opposed by the fiscal authorities, even though it constitutes a clear strategy of tax evasion.[26] On the contrary, it is favoured by the legislation, which was definitely conceived with quite a different end in view, but which in concrete terms encourages the creation of new entities by tax advantages.

Another mechanism favourable to the development of fraud is linked to budgetary techniques. Each new finance law modifies the investments code, as well as various fiscal regulations.[27] Furthermore, these laws are often backdated, with the result that businesses – or their accounts, jurists or certified accountants – can spend an entire year working without knowing with any precision how much tax they will actually have to pay.[28] Also, entrepreneurs constantly use an argument to which the Tunisian authorities are particularly sensitive: the risk of undermining the 'Tunisian miracle' as a result of the financial strangulation of entrepreneurs by the Inland Revenue. Since September 2001, the tax administration and the CNSS have thus demonstrated a benevolent indulgence towards the tourist sector, and units that are struggling are temporarily left alone by the inspectors.[29]

What we have here is a vicious circle, or a virtuous circle, depending on the point of view adopted: on the one hand, entrepreneurs practice tax evasion, sometimes in spite of themselves, both as the unexpected effect of a poor understanding of the rules in force, as a way of lightening their tax burden, as a survival strategy when faced with competition, as a relation of force with the Inland Revenue, as a preventative tactic when faced with future tax levies, and as a 'counter-conduct' in relation to the behaviour of an administration that is *a priori* considered to be intrusive and arbitrary; on the other, the existence of tax evasion gives the authorities a legitimate excuse to interfere in economic affairs. These adjustments can sometimes be so significant that they imply a negotiation between the hierarchy of the tax administration and the taxpayers. For the biggest of them, this negotiation is carried out directly between the manager of a business and the President's personal councillor.[30] One of the biggest groups in the country, which was to be subjected to an adjustment of the order of three or four times its annual profit, is said to have managed to reduce this adjustment by half, after paying into the 26.26 and putting one of its companies onto the Stock Exchange. A certain implicit haggling does indeed lie at the heart of current tax practices, as is suggested, *e contrario*, by the case of perfectly legal businesses which allow themselves . . . not to contribute to the 26.26! Contrary to what it claims, the business community probably does not lose out – at least financially – in this game. It is not certain that it is such a powerless victim when faced with an omnipotent central power and a pitiless administration.

The political importance of tax relations

So tax avoidance cannot be interpreted as an absence of control on the part of the Tunisian authorities, as a resistance on the part of 'civil society', as a safety valve generously provided by an omnipotent central power or as a counterpart to the absence of any political representation and the lack of democracy. Negotiations, arrangements and uncontrolled concatenations can, for example, explain how a vast majority of entrepreneurs live perfectly tranquilly while evading tax. Everything works perfectly well until the day when a more powerful competitor activates his acquaintances, when one activity causes offence, when it is necessary to make an example, or when financial needs necessitate a tightening of fiscal discipline . . . These practices also help us understand why the authorities accept behaviour that is on the margins of legality when the latter, contraband, informal activities, racketeering or levies, penalize them. Whereas fiscal fraud procures significant financial advantages and sometimes the sense of being cunning, it offers the Tunisian authorities points of anchorage for its desires to control and intimidate.

Conversely, and in a complementary way, the ability to control and levy can be used to arouse fear, to exert one's authority, or to punish. This, for example, is the case with one measure in the tax laws which can ultimately lead to a business going bankrupt thanks to the automatic tax procedure. The latter may be the culmination of a tax inspection and may give concrete shape to the failure of the process of reconciliation set up for this purpose; it then corresponds to a recovery measure and the desire to increase budgetary revenue.[31] But it can also be the object of a political, or quite simply disciplinary instrumentalization, thanks to countless legislative procedures which can always justify an intervention. The taxation is then arbitrary or out of all proportion with the sums really due and, in the framework of revision of the books, the tax administration will order an exorbitant sum to be paid.[32] The entrepreneur may, of course, attack this decision, refuse the review and ask for help from lawyers to embark on judicial proceedings. But if he does this, he will have to pay the administration 30 per cent of the arbitrary sum demanded as automatic taxation. In addition, the chances of winning the trial are extremely reduced.[33] It is easy to understand the function which this procedure can then play: it may at any moment trigger a mechanism of intimidation, negotiation and punishment. In actual fact, this measure is reserved for the most important businessmen, who, within the framework of the *stratégie du pourtour*, are now considered as dangerous or quite simply annoying, especially as far as 'friends' at court are concerned. In this way, a well-targeted tax adjustment apparently made it possible to consolidate the private monopoly of trips to Mecca, and the main shareholder in a big commercial group was subjected to an automatic taxation aimed at forcing him to accept the sale of his shares to people close to the President.[34] As we can see, the tax system enables this or that entrepreneur to be made more vulnerable or stronger, members of the economic elite and other notabilities to be differentiated from one another, their positions to be bolstered or, conversely, the vulnerability of individuals to be insinuated.

These developments suggest that while the tax system is not important from the macroeconomic point of view, thanks to the low level of the rates of taxation, it can be so in terms of political economy. This interpretation of the tax relation, comprising simultaneously constraint and laxity, control and tolerance, undermines the idea that it is impossible to tax the population – businesses in particular – in the absence of a certain democracy. I will not go over the criticisms of this thesis, which have been made for a long time, and which the examples analysed here corroborate.[35] I would prefer to emphasize two complementary and yet convergent criticisms. Firstly, the quantitative dimension is not significant in political terms: the low level of the sums collected can, on the contrary, reflect the intensity of the tax relation.

Secondly, fraud and tax evasion, the extent of exemptions, advantages and negotiations on the amount of tax to be paid – all these practices tell us nothing about the political conditions of a society: they may be compatible with a process of democratization, as is suggested by the examples of Greece and Portugal.[36]

The emphasis on negotiations and arrangements helps to understand how the tax arm can also be transformed into pure repression, particularly as, after all, it is considered by everyone as one of the main places in which struggles, relations or force, and accommodations can find expression. This conclusion stems in part from a romantic and certainly biased interpretation of Tunisian history. It is striking, in this respect, to hear Tunisian entrepreneurs these days referring indirectly to the fiscal *mehalla*[37] and the symbolic dimension of their exercise of power, envisaging the tax system as a system of rewards and punishments, considering taxation only in terms of negotiation and the absence of submission, drawing a direct link between closeness to the centre of power and minimal or even non-existent taxation – all themes which historians have brought out since independence, often in a much more subtle fashion.[38] The simplifications are obvious and historical analogies are dangerous. But the Tunisian imaginary draws nourishment from the myth of resistance to taxation as a mode of expression of support for the national struggle or of opposition to power 'from outside'.[39] It is fostered by the *stratégie du pourtour,* which can be materialized by sanctions as well as by laxity or tax amnesties. The object of these latter is to calm relations, remove anxieties and enable rapprochements to take place.[40] Taxation is indisputably perceived as a major locus of power. When a 'friend' is, or senses that he is about to be, disgraced, his first reflex is to try and shield his wealth from any fiscal punishment, by the use of front-men, by practices of transferral, by investments abroad, by the use of certain laws, especially that on bankruptcies passed in 1995.

It hardly matters whether this strategy works or not: what counts is, in this case, the perception of the tax system as an instrument of punishment *par excellence.* This perception is particularly significant insofar as events interpreted this way and presented as 'real illustrations' of this repressive function of the tax system ceaselessly reactivate this imaginary. When there is a tussle between the authorities in place and recognized political opponents, taxation is indubitably one of the first repressive measures to be mobilized. For example, the property of an entrepreneur who is also a member of the LTDH has been sequestrated . . . on the excuse that his brother had arrears with the CNSS after one of his businesses had gone bankrupt.[41] In this case, as in many others, Social Security uses its juridical specificity to sequestrate property. It is, in fact, the only body able legally to define its own jurisprudence, deciding itself on the sentence and its execution, without passing via justice. We can clearly see how this exorbitant right, linked to the role of 'state piggybank' and to its independent function as tax system, can open the door to excesses. Another example is provided by Judge Yahyaoui, now a symbol of the struggle of justice for its independence in Tunisia. It is particularly revealing that this judge embarked on his fierce struggle with the Tunisian authorities and President Ben Ali on the basis of his personal tax history.[42] We again find one of the fundamental ingredients of the Tunisian repressive system, which affects private life, one's intimate details, and the overlap between private and public.

At the end of this fiscal detour, two conclusions can be drawn. In the first place, external constraints appear extremely small in this domain. In spite of the pressure from foreign donors, the tax system is rooted too deeply in relations of power to tolerate modifications, even if they are not central, in its structures and above all in its mode of operation. It constitutes a fundamental political capital which props up the position of the elites, the notables, the well-connected and the leaders. It makes it possible to exploit tax evasion as a relation of force between these elites and the central power. It makes both strictness and laxness possible, but in particular makes a considerable number of accommodations possible for the vast majority of the population. In the second place, the repressive function does not appear to be fundamental. The tax arm, when it wants to be exercised, is undeniably the most effective and most systematically used instrument. But previous developments mean that we can add two corollaries to this statement: firstly, the motor of the tax dynamic is not essentially, or even mainly, this disciplinary function: constraints of revenue, bureaucratic logics, adaptations to the constraints of the international environment, clientelist tactics and economic and social activities broadly define the outlines of taxation. They then underline the fact that 'fiscal punishment' rarely falls 'from on high'. In the – ultimately rare – cases where the fiscal arm intends clearly to assert its control and domination, its use is rendered possible only by the existence of a whole series of behaviours and mechanisms which offer anchorage points for the tax administration and for political power.

The national and international deployment of Tunisian enterprises

Over the last few years, the analysis of the relations between 'Power' and 'entrepreneurs' in terms of hostile political interference has tended to be generalized to economic activities as a whole. The authoritarian dimension of the 'Ben Ali regime', it is claimed, leads to two types of behaviour that are problematic in terms of rationalization and competitiveness:[43] one the one hand there is caution, or even a strike, when it comes to national investments and, on the other, a strategy of dispersion in an attempt to protect oneself from an avid central power. For the more solid and structured of economic groups, it appears, there is also a more or less constrained internationalization.

Staying small to stay free?

On this view, entrepreneurs are hampered by their fear of direct interference on the part of 'family', 'clans' and 'friends', by the generally predatory and corrupt atmosphere, by anxiety over arbitrary and unforeseeable tax levies, by the absence of the rule of law and by juridical insecurity, by the business climate and the degradation of the environment, by the worry that they might appear too powerful and thus arouse the possessive desire of power, becoming caught up in the *stratégie du pourtour*. As a result, it is claimed that they prefer to remain 'small' and minimize their potential power by increasing the number of small companies that are all independent from one another. They also adopt a low profile, reducing their investments and associating themselves with foreign companies so as to protect themselves from predators and ensure that their activities can increase to a significant extent without drawing the wrath of power down on their heads.

The facts are there to give support to this interpretation: there is a propensity to diversify businesses rather than to consolidate them; family structures are maintained and outside capital is authorized only to a limited extent; and the number of big and even medium-sized businesses is extremely limited.[44] The biggest of the Tunisian groups, Poulina, for instance, is a conglomerate of 71 subsidiaries for just 6,000 salaried workers.[45] Likewise, when it comes to investment, the performances are not really good: representing 30 per cent of GDP in the years 1983–6, investments represented only 25 per cent of them in the years 1996–2003. While they are not embarrassingly bad in terms of regional comparisons, they are disappointing in view of the encouragements and programmes of support for investment.[46] In particular, they to a great extent fall within the public sector and foreign donors esteem that the missing private investments represent at least 3.5 per cent of GDP in spite of the upgrading programme.[47] Finally, for some years we have been witnessing rapprochements with foreign businesses: the biggest groups, for instance, have allied themselves – either by association or capital sharing – with multinationals or foreign groups, especially in agribusiness, wholesale distribution, and chemistry; in the area of tourism, the alliance has assumed concrete form in exclusive representations or management contracts and long-term or rental agreements;[48] and one of the most solid companies – the Chekira group, specialized in ceramics – would prefer to invest abroad (in this case in Portugal) rather than continue to invest in Tunisia.[49]

However, this strategy of dispersion is far from being explicable solely by the fear of political interference. As its presence in the productive public sector and among the foreign enterprises of the offshore sector suggests,[50] many other variables are needed to explain it – first and foremost, the narrowness of the Tunisian market. In a market of just nine million inhabitants, the level of saturation of a sector is rapidly reached, especially when the country's entrepreneurial structure is dual and the exporting businesses function almost exclusively offshore, without any link to the fabric of businesses that are turned toward the national market. A dynamic business leader has every interest in diversifying his production into other industrial sectors, into building or, if he has the means, by exporting his capital.[51]

This kind of behaviour is all the more rational in that there are other purely administrative, economic or fiscal factors that might well support such a choice.[52] Up until 2001, the absence of any juridical framework for holdings prevented regroupings and consolidations. The fiscal advantages for certain sectors and for the creation of new structures constitute other incitements to diversify. The proliferation of units in the same group makes it possible to lighten the constraints of the labour laws; the personnel 'turnover' from one company to another every four years, the maximum length of fixed-limit contracts, or else one of these entities manages the entire workforce by subcontracting. The absence of consolidated accounts and of a data bank on businesses favours strategies of transferral between companies, since deficits can be dumped on one of them or, conversely, be spread out among several companies. The fierce competition between entrepreneurs does not encourage consolidation and, from a strictly management point of view, the dispersion of activities also enables risks to be shared out.

Social constraints may also circumscribe activities and favour choices that, in other circumstances, would be considered as non-rational: the strategy of diversification can also result from the sharing of capital and profits between different members of the family, or else from the lack of confidence in potential sub-contractors and the choice of vertical integration (the yoghourt, the yoghourt pot, and the packaging, for instance). Dispersion – what Moncef Bouchrara calls 'rampancy' and Pierre-Noël Denieul 'the proliferation of the units of production' – also stems from the decision not to change modes of operation, not to break the logic of 'subterranean' or informal resources, not to undermine the way of doing things. The wish of entrepreneurs to remain within family structures and not to open either their capital or their accounts is to be explained less by political constraints than by human factors, such as the desire to keep control over a business created from scratch, the fear of transparency and any gaze from outside, the preference for DIY jobs, ad hoc arrangements, and playing fast and loose with the tax authorities or any other administrative authority. It is easier to 'cheat' with and between little structures than within a big group under surveillance and subject to much more rigorous techniques of management.

One of the dominant myths of the politico-economic history of Tunisia is that of the vulnerability of the 'powerful', including the economically powerful: central power, it is claimed, has never liked rich businessmen, perceived as potential competitors who are all the more dangerous in that Power is presented as external to society; they became too 'big' and were all disgraced.[53] Moreover, it is in these terms that we need to understand the current reactivation of the fear of political interference, subsequent to attempts on the part of the Tunisian authorities to foster economic concentrations within the context of the privatization of public enterprises and 'upgrading', both of them being perceived as instruments of control.[54] This preference for discretion and dispersion may be perpetuated by predatory practices, and even more by rumours about these practices and the fear that that might occur.[55] But dispersion is in no case the direct result of these. In any case, there are significant counter-examples. The Aziz Miled group is entirely focused in tourism.[56] Poulina illustrates the theory of integration as much as that of dispersion. Admittedly, the group Abdelwahab Ben Ayed, started out in poultry, invested in chemistry, mechanical engineering, reconstituted wood, ceramics and tourism; but it has also penetrated into the fields of agro-industry, materials for aviculture, animal foodstuffs and freezers. The weight of repression needs to be minimized – or rather, we need to understand that the latter can operate only as the result of a multiplicity of factors, rationalities and behaviours which lead the actors to adopt such a strategy.

Internationalization and investment strikes, a political overinterpretation

Certain cases, for instance that of Poulina, rumoured to have forged an alliance with Danone for political reasons, corroborate the way that internationalization can stem from fear of predatory acts on the part of the central power. Nonetheless, this interpretation can also be questioned, if only by reason of the fact that those close to the President's office may themselves also choose this strategy in order to prosper. This is the case of Hédi Jilani, the 'boss of bosses', who has links – both family and financial – with the President, the Mabrouk group or entrepreneurs such as Aziz Miled or Chekib Nouira. In these cases, the alliances are even encouraged, *inter alia* because they promote a vision of modernity and openness in the Tunisian economy.[57] The example of the BIAT suggests the coexistence of multiple and potentially contradictory logics: the alliance with Natexis may be considered at one and the same time to be a way of protecting historic shareholders against the central power and as an alliance of prosperity on the part of shareholders close to it. Associations with foreign actors stem, indeed, from several different rationalities: the search for normalization, for know-how, for external markets and new products; the desire to prepare a succession within a context of liberalization; an apprenticeship in expertise from the international players and a modernization of the process of production; the need to overcome the constraints of a narrow market economy and a non-existent regional market; the strategic decision to find a way round foreign competition . . . It is, moreover, the most dynamic of businesses – and this is why we also come across groups close to the 'family' – which forge alliances in this way with foreign enterprises, by total buyout, selling off parts of the capital, or joint venture.

The idea that internationalization is a reaction to interference from the central power also rests on the hypothesis that foreign partners are in a position to protect Tunisian business and to resist the desires for political control, clientelism and predation. This is far from being the case, as is proved by the processes of 'Tunisification' of foreign enterprises, in which the foreigners adopt the apparently most efficient practices in the Tunisian political economy. Foreign enterprises may even be more vulnerable than Tunisian enterprises, if they do not comprise part of the big international groups with significant powers of negotiation. They are not really integrated into the social fabric of Tunisia and their know-how is less able to protect itself from the growing appetite of certain wheeler-dealers. They may be led to make up for this deficit by the use of intermediaries who are not always reliable.

The last strategy mentioned is the investment strike. I will be even more brief here, since this thesis is the result more of self-fulfilling prophecy than of reality. It may be true that the proportion of public investments is particularly significant in the whole set of investments, representing about half of these, that the investments realized in the framework of upgrading are less than predicted, that the objectives of the IXth plan have not been achieved and that the biggest investments are those made by offshore enterprises: nevertheless, the level of Tunisian private investments has not slackened due to an environment that is, or is no longer, business friendly.[58] The rate of private investment in Tunisia has been at around 13 per cent for two decades, whereas in emerging countries it reaches 25 per cent. In reality, statistics suggest less an investment strike than a very slight slowing down, with the rate of private investment having passed from 13.5 per cent of GNP between 1970 and 2000 to 13 per cent between 1990 and 2000. They show, above all, that investments are rare in industry and in sectors that are open to competition. As a result of fiscal encouragements and the low level of international competitiveness in Tunisian onshore businesses, entrepreneurs are investing, against all economic and financial logic, in protected sectors (food processing, service industries) or tax-free (agriculture), or in assembly industries and industries of tradable goods (building materials, ceramics, glass) and rents (construction, property).[59] As for the slowdown in investments, it can easily be explained by the economic context of Tunisia: there are numerous uncertainties, born of liberalization, the prospect of free exchange with Europe, and the slowdown in growth, itself linked to the national and international conditions. The banking situation, especially the extent of unpaid bills, weighs heavily on the profitability of investments while the technological backwardness and unattractiveness of the entire region do not favour the conditions sought for investment.

Imaginary submission, real submission

However, these interpretations cannot be read simply in terms of fantasies or of political over-interpretation. Economic practices, after all, are inseparable from social representations, in particular from the link between wealth, power and prestige. The business world is invested by the field of relations of force, and the power relations that are deployed within it may allow an effective process of control and domination. Sometimes, the action is spectacular, and political instrumentalization operates via the implementation of disciplinary or even repressive measures. The ruling political elites then use the economic machinery to bolster their domination, eliminate competitors, increase their material base, and to prevent the economic and social consolidation of a potential competitor. The mechanisms, in this case, are tried and trusted: private preserves and the creation of a de facto monopoly;[60] advantages and nepotism, of course, but also appointments within businesses; rapid modifications of the law or the regulations suddenly authorizing a certain activity hitherto forbidden or strictly controlled, or modifying the rules of the game across a particular market segment;[61] capital inflow with or without the entrepreneur's consent; reserved privatizations; falsified calls for bids . . .

In this area, the instrumentalization of 'corruption' constitutes one of the most powerful arrangements for arbitrary decision-making. Favouritism and agreements, embezzlement and abuses of power keep personalities imprisoned in particular power relations, and the public nature of these acts makes it possible for them to be punished and expelled from the political field, on the occasion of individual transgressions, political events, delicate social situations, conflicts between segments of the politic-economic elite or quite simply depending on the mood of the prince. This does not, however, mean that 'corruption' is a diabolical creation of the Tunisian authorities. These quite simply profit from its inevitable presence in society and in those very political business circles in order to exercise their power of inclusion or exclusion. For a long term, know-how dominates and nothing is done to check transgressions. The threat of incrimination hangs like a veritable sword of Damocles over the head of the corrupt, those who commit a breach of trust, and the dishonest, and it can fall at any moment to punish this or that person 'in the circle' who is sufficiently powerful to be considered as potentially dangerous, or quite simply to make an example of him, to arouse fear, to remind everyone that wealth, like the other attributes of power, is subject to the principle of allegiance, to chance and discriminatory factors. The fact that the punishment is without any common measure with the acts denounced means that we can call this 'repression'. The *stratégie du pourtour* is clearly visible: a person can serve as an example, demonstrate the limits of the norm, show, above all, the controlled exercise of power.

This political interference needs to be interpreted in terms of normalizing chastisement and training. Punishment appears as an element in a dual system of gratification and sanction (in Michel Foucault's terminology) or of glorification and intimidation (in Roland Barthes's). 'To punish is to exert discipline':[62] the art of punishment is aimed neither at expiation, nor at the pure and simple disappearance of the behaviours denounced, but rather discipline. The interweaving of public policies, aids, living standards, and social recognition explains how the worst of punishments is bankruptcy.[63] When the entrepreneur is constrained to sell his goods or go into exile, or when the wheeler-dealer is imprisoned, what we have is primarily a differentiation between 'good' and 'bad' actors, a definition of 'honoured' acts and 'reprehensible' acts and the imposition of norms. But we could also add that to humiliate is to exert discipline. When a businessman is dethroned, or a wheeler-dealer beaten up, this is meant to remind us that perpetual allegiance is indissociable from the mechanisms of power, that social ascent, success, or economic failure are inscribed within relations of force, that autonomization is illusory, that humiliation – like chastisement – is a power of normalization, with simultaneous effects of homogenization and individuation.

However, these intrusions are made possible only by virtue of the oppositions and conflicts that crisscross the 'business world'. Far from being unified, the latter is – like everywhere else – the scene of rivalries, jealousies and mean tricks. When I was carrying out my interviews, rivalries between different groups or interviews of a single sector were rarely hidden. Sometimes the weight of political connections, one's role in the financing of the RCD or the archaic nature of the practices involved were simply taken as read. Other interviewees, conversely, loudly and clearly denounced the 'corruption' of this person or the 'stupidity' of that one. While talking about one of his colleagues, one of my interviewees even told me, in a fit of boasting, that he had gained the agreement of the party and the President in person 'to kill him', and pretended to be naively astonished: 'I don't know why they still haven't given me the go-ahead'.[64] This is a very clear example of how control is exercised, too, by intrusion into ongoing conflicts between persons or between visions, by the instrumentalization of these rivalries to decide between different businessmen, to maintain uncertainty, or to discipline the milieu. But nor does this prevent these same businessmen from themselves instrumentalizing these political relations for their own ends.

Which interventionism?

These cases are limited to the big entrepreneurs, of whom, in the finally analysis, there are not many. For the vast majority of businesses and independents – 97 per cent of businesses, if any reminder is needed, employ fewer than six salaried employees – interference is much more insidious, passing as it does via the most commonplace mechanisms of everyday life.

Incessant and routine interventions

The first of these, and probably the most obvious, is the way one can play with laws and regulations. Jurists and political analysts have brought out a certain number of legislative characteristics which facilitate these interferences: the instability of the laws; the very short duration of the legal rules in force; the dispersion of legal texts across different codes, laws, regulations; the sheer number of points of intervention of the administration by the proliferation of organs of regulation and administrative bodies; the rising power of the executive; the increasing number of texts with different statuses; contradictions between texts; the proliferation of derogatory regimes that are forever being revised.[65] The cyclical character of legislation, the centralization, the compartmentalization of bureaucracy, its increasing lack of responsibility, the slow pace and inertia due to massive overmanning and an excess of reforms – all this renders administrative functioning very arbitrary and susceptible to political instrumentalization.[66] Nobody can be completely within the rules, due to uncertainties, inevitable flaws, gaps and vagueness in the legislation supervising private economic activity, in particular fiscal law and labour rights.[67] This is especially true in that 'no legal text can oblige the administration to communicate the data and documents that it keeps stored.'[68] It is easy to see how the relations of power can then play within these interstices: favouring this or that entrepreneur, leading one of them to lose markets while the other wins them, putting some at fault and privileging others because of easier access to information. Without being the Machiavellian creation of an all-powerful government, instability and uncertainty can however make it possible for the administration and the local authorities to interfere in economic activities and thereby in the conditions of economic success – or failure.

It might have been thought that the passage from administrative authorization to liberalization would modify the situation by reducing the number of state interventions, and especially their discretionary character. But, as all the economic actors interviewed have pointed out, what has happened is rather a growth in the number of possibilities of interference on the part of the mechanisms of power,[69] confirming, on an initial impression, that in Tunisia, whether we mention socialism or liberalism, 'these labels do not have much significance [. . .] when we realize that in every case they permit the establishment of an identical system for controlling individuals'.[70] As for authorization, the administration held at any precise moment the absolute power of granting it or withholding it. But in the liberal political economy, the definition of the requirements contained in the contract and their control, for example, produce a great number of different places in which arbitrary decisions, favouritism or even corruption can be applied. In many cases, furthermore, guarantees and rules of operation are non-existent, difficult to find out or, quite simply, not respected.[71] Sometimes the terms of reference of the contract are so vague that they can permit both an interpretation and its opposite. In particular, the administration may or may not follow the requirement laid down in the terms of reference, it may or may not implement checks, it may or may not respect the rules that it had itself fixed, it may be lax or severe . . . All of these are points at which power can be exercised; it can favour, praise, reward or, conversely, put someone back in his place, supervise, control, punish, correct. This makes it easier to understand how the policies of 'state disengagement' have increased the importance of the networks within the administration and the world of the party, the sole means of access to financial and economic resources, and especially to information.[72]

What we have just mentioned with regard to juridical texts is also encountered in the way institutions work when they come into contact with economic actors. The way overdue payments are dealt with by the tax authorities or the CNSS, or delays in repaying banks, vagueness in work regulations, the effective application of norms, rules or standards defined with greater or less precision opens several opportunities for clientelism and interventionism. At the local level, the administration of public health and municipal administration fulfil the same role. Insofar as the RCD is more an institution of mediation and clientelism than a political institution, it also intervenes in this set-up. Just like those great businessmen who enter the Central Committee or ally themselves with the presidential family in order to succeed, the 'small businessmen', depending on their degree of social integration, their place of residence, their initial wealth and their ambition will enter the party's cells or federations, establishing links with local notabilities, with the well-known Destourian families in the region, attending meetings called by the governor, and ostentatiously giving to the 26.26 or to the activities of the party.[73]

Within the context of the control of economic success, the extremely frequent practice of non-respect and non-application of sentences needs to be remembered. Social ascensions may happen on the back of unpaid rents, taxes, or contributions, or of bad debts; conversely, failures may ensue from irregular distraints, unrealized retrocessions, or unapplied acknowledgements. A judicial decision is or is not implemented, depending on political decisions and often on anticipations of what the authorities would like. The systematic character of these arbitrary arrangements is itself comprised of coercive practices in the administration: if a conscientious intermediary, a policeman or a civil servant, tries to apply an undesired judicial decision, he is quite simply transferred.[74] This clearly brings out all the ingredients that make the procedure so efficient: coercion, intimidation, a specific use of authority and in particular of arbitrary measures, but also an integration of the different actors in the interplay of economic relations and the interiorization of a certain social order.

As a result, we can no longer limit ourselves to talking of economic repression. A whole system of more or less anodyne constraints and little favours keeps society as a whole going and enables the relations of power to be deployed in the interstices of these social practices. In local town districts, any little shop, any stall or commercial outlet, any practice (a lawyer's, a certified accountant's, a doctor's) is subjected to the incessant round of party members of *comités de quartier*, representatives of the police or other disciplinary administrations, 'informers' of every kind, asking for money or a commitment to their cause, sometimes for the 26.26, sometimes for an association, sometimes for a club. These intermediaries, whether authorized or not, openly proclaim, 'We can do everything to make life easier for you'. Concretely, a photo of President Ben Ali stuck up in a man's shop, his lodge, his office or his residence, a nicely framed certificate attesting to the financing or provision of work for the well-being of the district or the payment of gifts to the 26.26, the party or the organization for the 7 November celebrations all constitute forms of laissez-passer. On one level or another, these lubricate the wheels of control. They make it possible for certificates to be obtained authorizing the free parking of one's professional car or banking credit facilities, they smooth over relations with this or that economic administration, they sort out problems with the tax authorities, customs department or social security, they open up the network of relations able to favour economic activity, to mollify health services or get the *omda* on your side.

Widely solicited interventionism

My argument might meet with the objection that these economic or financial choices, or even the dysfunctions in justice, have been caused deliberately by the public authorities so as to instrumentalize these now unavoidable interventions.[75] This interpretation seems to me to pander to the voluntarist illusion which grants the state a coherent vision of its role and of the guiding lines of its economy, and even more than that: a quasi-absolute capacity for action.[76] It underestimates the degree of its impotence and the entrepreneurs' ability to 'make do', to use the *arts de faire* described by Michel de Certeau; it smoothes out the life of the world of business and does not explain the tensions, the conflicts, the opposed interests, and the great variety of activities carried out within it. Police power is incapable of imposing any organization meant to discipline the economy so as to supervise the toiling masses and rally national and foreign capitalists. And that is, generally speaking, not its aim. So we need to seek elsewhere for the function and, above all, the reason behind these daily interventions. My hypothesis is that these 'incessant interventions' are less imposed and suffered than they are accepted, used, and even actively sought by the economic actors themselves. They are accepted because they are painless, because they are commonplace and because, above all, they can be reversed. An extract from one interview enables us immediately to seize the logic of reciprocity and mutual advantages that stem from 'insidious leniencies', to use Foucault's terms.[77] 'It's not painful, and you can cope with it even if, in the long term, it's exhausting', but it's also 'very beneficial, since nothing is impossible in Tunisia!'

These interventions are simultaneously requests and intercessions. In offshore enterprises, for instance, it is not unusual for the services of the governor or the delegate, or even those of Health and Safety, to provide one or two employees. This practice is very widely accepted: 'Since we need protection, we cope with it; we accept one or two people provided by the authorities, they don't cost us anything'. When there is a showdown between the entrepreneur and the authorities, the RCD or associations linked to it inevitably come after a gift for it: the reaction, 'it's a nuisance, but all's fair in love and war' is quite normal. For such interventions are often desired. These days, for example, it is quite usual to hear the actors of Tunisian tourism stating that the problem of ghettoization and the low level of diversification of supply 'is a problem of encouragement; today, there's no encouragement to open bars, restaurants . . .'.[78] Interventions are expected in the domain of the financial restructuring of hotels, in the protection of the textile sector or in the processes of privatization. Perhaps what we have here is a systematic 'demand for the state' on the part of a 'parasitic bourgeoisie' used to aid, to grants, to exemptions and *ad hoc* agreements.[79] 'This system of relations, of systematic interventionism, is also a favour to the enterprise: thanks to it, there are no lost causes,' we hear. It is possible to use these relations to allow the enterprise's demands to be met and its vision of things 'set up', but also, more prosaically, to bring a conflict to an end, to 'get a message to the trade union', to 'overlook a stupid mistake' or 'sort out a misunderstanding'.

This explanation, however, is incomplete. It neglects demands that are just as urgent on the part of employees and salary-earners, demands for job protection, the obtaining of positions, and administrative facilitations. It also forgets the urgings of the state itself for this objective to be met, for this programme of solidarity to be made visible, for this international financing to be obtained. It also ignores the coercive nature of certain of its actions. Rather than 'parasitic bourgeoisie' or '*rentier* bourgeoisie', we ought rather to talk in terms of mutual dependencies.[80] To take up the expression of an entrepreneur I interviewed, those who hold power should not so much 'create dependencies [. . .] as play with them'.[81] The RCD can approach entrepreneurs to get advertising across or to call in sums of money since it is one of the main transmission cogs of their demands. Conversely, it is quite usual for entrepreneurs to be taken to one side by these intermediaries who then remind them that 'they haven't given for nothing' and that 'we can offer you certain favours'. Central power can control only because such intermediaries exist in society, and also because its 'incessant interventions' encounter permanent demands and echo various preoccupations on the part of economic actors. So the latter cannot be considered as being merely dependent on omnipotent political and administrative actors; entrepreneurial strategies also shape politics and its modes of intervention. This is how we should understand the remark of one entrepreneur who was interviewed: 'In Tunisia, the interventions are never-ending but you have to admit that they are very well "driven" [. . .] Even in the offshore domain, "they" control things very well, even though they are aware that offshore activities are vital for the economy'.[82] Nothing can prevent the 'regime' from intervening, but the shape this interference takes is limited by economic constraints that cannot be eliminated or even neutralized.

The example of entrepreneurs invested with a national role speaks volumes. Via the rhetoric of 'participative citizenship' and the celebration of 'National Enterprise Day', the implementation of these new national heroes is an attempt to symbolize the integration of the objectives of growth, development and accumulation in the national project. In any case, this practice is not new and goes back to the beginnings of the construction of the independent state even if it was then less theatrical than today.[83] The central power shows that the political realm can have an impact on the behaviour of individuals and that it alone can reward the devotion of businessmen. However, the example of Poulina suggests that this scenario demonstrates relations that are more complex than a mere act of allegiance. 'Poulina's personnel is proud of belonging to our institution and Poulina can exist and develop thanks to this personnel. Every honourable person becomes, at the end of his tenth year of work, a Companion of Poulina, renamed Companion of the Change in honour of the Change (7 November 1987)', as the group's presentation document puts it.[84] Honouring certain individuals appears above all as a social practice that simultaneously stems from nationalism and paternalism. It obviously suggests the opportunism of a cunning businessman, but it is an opportunism that cannot be analysed solely in terms of submission, but much rather in terms of a certain play in relations of force with a central power that also attempts to instrumentalize it.

This emphasis on negotiations, agreements and canvassings 'from below' qualifies one of the major interpretations of politics in Tunisia, namely the pairing submission/sedition and the strategies of 'exit option' and 'hidden disaffection'.[85] It also casts doubt on the thesis (mainly mythical) of the independence of entrepreneurs.[86] All the previous examples underline, rather, the centrality of a state of conflict that dare not speak its name, hidden as it is by transactions that are as incessant as interventions, by temporary conciliation, and also by a consensus partly constructed by contained violence and partly by enforced support. In the Tunisian political economy, submission, sedition and the exit option are in the final analysis exceptional because opposition is never frontal and the modes of disciplinary domination also create spaces of liberty and systematically leave room for accommodation.

Political ambiguities of consensus in the economic sphere

Certain observers bring out just this dimension to underline the original nature of the modes of government in Tunisia, especially in economic matters. Sensitive to the theme of reform, the public authorities – these observers claim – 'tune in' particularly to the economic world, being aware as they are of its difficulties and its demands, often deemed to be legitimate. This 'tuning in', they say, is expressed by means of a discourse on the necessary integration of entrepreneurs into the life of the city and their economic and social responsibility, as well as by means of the rhetoric on 'participative citizenship' symbolized by the handing out of decorations. It assumes concrete form in the proliferation of programmes defined in agreement with professional organizations and by the participation of these in the implementation of economic policies and reforms. Among donors, this characteristic is sometimes interpreted in political terms; the consensus methodically constructed by discussions between economic partners indicates the path towards an authentic democratization. It also, in this view, explains the current tensions that have arisen from the absurd gap between a relative freedom of expression in the business worlds and a total political clamp-down. For others, the economic crisis and liberal reforms have fostered an increased autonomy in the private sector; the importance of the industrial bourgeoisie in negotiations, it is said, is increased, and this triggers a process of democratization.[87]

In fact, many if not all of the economic actors interviewed emphasized a certain 'tuning in' and a real desire on the part of administrations to go along with businesses. If we also remember the significance assumed by commissions, meetings and restricted ministerial councils dedicated to economic questions, there is no doubt that the rhythm of growth, the conditions in which economic activities can flourish, and the improvement in the job situation constitute authentic preoccupations for the state.[88] These same actors, nonetheless, quickly add that government discourse is largely 'ill-adapted' to the real problems experienced by businesses, and that the problematics developed within administrations are 'artificial' when faced with the preoccupations of the PME. The actions centred on 'participatory development', they also claim, do not really work, and 'public/private cooperation is still difficult', with the authorities being unable to understand the 'real preoccupations' of the private sector.[89] Research has shown in very concrete form how the consensus was obtained: first and foremost by subjection to administrative and political logic, the rule being 'the appearance of "concerted" decisions with, in fact, the government as principal shaper'.[90] As a result, 'business ultimately appears to be an extension of the administration, thereby placing the economic domain under the tutelage of the political'.[91] So the consensus is constructed administratively, but also by fear and the effectiveness of the *stratégie du pourtour*, by silence and enforced acquiescence and by strategies of accommodation on the part of entrepreneurs, who are mainly worried about not sticking their necks out in a confined environment, being ready for compromises and half satisfactions rather than uncertain relations of force.

Finally and above all, the interpretation of consensus in terms of democratization betrays a narrowly economicist and mechanistic vision of this political process and suggests the ambiguities contained within this portmanteau word. Most foreign investors and most donors, those 'naive apostles of "liberal democracy"' do indeed share the belief that 'democracy and the generalization of liberal values and institutions necessarily accompanies the expansion of capitalism'.[92] Donors are led to legitimize their interventions in favour of capitalism – a 'real' capitalism, of course – by basing their arguments on the positive relation between political liberalization and the spread of liberal capitalism.[93] And yet, over a century ago, Max Weber already magisterially criticized 'economic monism': he showed that the historical sequence that had come into being in Europe was unique, and definitively disproved the existence of any automatic link between capitalism and democracy; he emphasized the plasticity of social forms that make it impossible to prejudge the necessary connections between variables, for example between economic liberalization and political liberalization, or between capitalism and democracy.[94]

Although the inanity of this thesis has long since been demonstrated, it is amazing to see it being restated so categorically, just as the opposite thesis is restated, this time by the Tunisian authorities – the thesis that a certain interventionism (not to say authoritarianism) is the most highly performing system for an economically underdeveloped country.[95] Highly detailed fieldwork suggests, however, that the ways of development, like those of democracy, are more than disconcerting. For Taiwan, Françoise Mengin has brought out a much more tortuous relation, passing via foreign actors, contrary alliances, blocked initiatives and misunderstandings. She shows, above all, how the developmentalist model of the state is not inevitably mediated by an authoritarian interventionism as efficient as it would wish to appear and that democratization does not result from an explicit demand on the part of industrialists.[96] There is no point, now, in going over the inconsistency of such theses that sin by excess of functionalism and, in the apt words of Amartya Sen, by 'sporadic empiricism'.[97] It is striking to note than consensus and unanimity are interpreted as vectors of democratization, indisputably expressing a particularly impoverished definition of democracy insofar as the latter is not the negation of the conflict, but its institutionalization.

Economic actors, then, are largely apolitical. In the name of their particular interests, and sometimes in the name of a certain general interest, they ask for more freedom of enterprise, more transparency and predictability, more debate, fewer arbitrary decisions and more 'rule of law' – which does not mean that they are asking for more democracy.[98] They regret the existence of blockages that stem in fact from modes of government, but they do not express this in the political terms of a democratic deficit. They demand the juridical and regulatory conditions that should enable them to maintain their dominant position, not a 'change of regime'. They deplore 'pernickety interventionism', 'bureaucracy', 'administrative hassle', the 'incompetence of local civil servants', 'unfair competition', 'corruption', 'intercessions', and, for foreigners, 'exacerbated economic nationalism'.[99] During the interviews I conducted with entrepreneurs, many of them – despite their implicit criticism of political constraints – told me, often in similar terms, that 'if Ben Ali has done at least one good thing, it's breaking the power of the trade union', that it was 'a good thing that the UGTT should be a driving belt', or else that 'it's really good that that there is only one trade union that negotiates a protocol once every three years'.[100] The absence of any explicit demand for democratization cannot, in my view, be explained by the *rentier* nature of Tunisian capitalism.[101] The apoliticism of entrepreneurs is partly constrained: preference for silence and aversion towards frontal confrontation also result from the political conditions and the latent violence of a closed world in which criticism is forbidden. This does not have a great deal to do with the '*rentier*' or parasitic nature of the bourgeoisie – but it does explain how 'the capitalists will never take to the bush';[102] between their prosperity and political change, the entrepreneurs have clearly made their choice.[103]

The thesis of 'political constraint' weighing down on the business world thus appears, to say the least, to be unilateral and in part a fantasy. In particular it sins by political overinterpretation. In the context of Tunisia, the central power shows itself to be less powerful and omnipotent than preoccupied by incessant negotiations and the search for compromises that are continually being refashioned and presented as a natural consensus.

6

Negotiated Accommodation

We thus have one thesis on constraint and the (hostile) interference of the political into the business world: but there is another thesis widespread in Tunisia, of Marxist or dependentist inspiration, which on the contrary insists on the elective affinities that supposedly exist between economic liberalism and authoritarianism. Although marginal in its explicit and sophisticated form, this interpretation, or rather certain elements of it, is shared by important segments of trade unionism and the civil service and by several critical intellectuals. The submission of individuals to Power, it is claimed, passes through an alliance between the regime, on the one hand, with the 'parasitical bourgeoisie' thanks to the constitution of rents and the submission of labour by the 'marginalization of the social' and, on the other hand, with 'international capitalism'.[1] This interpretation stresses the fact that the profusion of local processes – not directly involved with security – contributes to shaping domination and discipline by 'putting the population to work'. On the basis of their Marxist backgrounds, these authors show that political power is no stranger to economic relations: rationalization of the techniques of power and economic rationalization are concomitant phenomena.

So they partly share the analysis proposed in this work on the basis of a Weberian and Foucauldian tradition.[2] By looking at tourism and the textile industry, however, I would like to highlight the multiplicity of relations between technologies of power, development of the productive forces and modes of economic and political regulation. I would also like to suggest, on the one hand, that 'material conditions' and 'constellations of interests' are far from being the inevitable determinants of political development and that, on the other hand, it is impossible to separate out spheres – capital, the regime; capitalism, political domination – that are fixed and precisely demarcated.[3] I will be showing that capitalism and discipline are indissociable, without however being reducible to one another.

Offshore zones and just-in-time methods

The Tunisian economy remains organized on a dual model of production, with a dynamic but unstable offshore sector, and an onshore sector largely dominated by agriculture and unsophisticated services. Foreign investments represent only 10 per cent of productive investments, but they represent over 34 per cent of the total number of exports and about 65 per cent of manufacturing exports, create 17 per cent of jobs and cover 80 per cent of the current deficit.[4] Their crucial character can thus be understood.

The advantages of dualism

For the authorities, the advantages of this model are obvious in terms of foreign currency and jobs, but also in political terms: this dual organization is no threat to Tunisian producers, it exerts no pressure for an acceleration in structural reforms, it does not exacerbate the protectionist demands of entrepreneurs, it allows the central power to keep hold of the levers of action on the national level.[5] Confinement can thus be understood as a fully fledged technique of power. Subsidies, interest rebates, a lax attitude towards bad debts, successive aid programmes for investment can all be interpreted as instruments which enable uncompetitive Tunisian enterprises to survive and dualism to be preserved.[6] These practices have survived into the present, in fact, in spite of the free exchange agreement and the international pressures in favour of liberalization. The advantages granted to investors, created in the 1970s, are renewed quasi-automatically and the Tunisian authorities strenuously negotiate the maintenance of a system that should have been suppressed in 2002. Those in charge, indeed, openly affirm that 'Tunisia seeks foreign direct investments for export, not for the national market'. Unofficially, they add strength to their words by emphasizing the significance of *rentier* situations, the need to protect non-competitive national productions, and the positions gained.[7]

In fact, everything has been done to attract offshore investments: real salaries are subject to a downwards pressure even if they remain comparatively high; the single trade union has largely been brought under the public powers; the waiting period for businesses to be set up is relatively short; official organizations, in particular the *Agence de promotion des investissements* (API – Agency for Promoting Investments) and the Foreign Investment Promotion Agency (FIPA) offer benefits – provision of documents, procedures to be followed, legislation enacted – that are appreciated by investors.[8] The effects of this policy are undeniable: apart from privatizations, all IDE have been carried out offshore.[9] Surveys show that, for the latter, the choice of Tunisia results from a whole series of factors: order, political stability, and individual security always appear as major advantages.[10] While the foreign investors of offshore zones escape the essence of administrative relations in Tunisia, and many of the social relations too, they share with the majority of their Tunisian counterparts an ethos which sees stability, security, order and discipline as the most certain values, and consensus as the social quality par excellence. To judge from critics denouncing the absence of any effect whereby offshore investments are driven into the national industrial fabric, dualism (and thus the strategy of confinement of foreign investments) seems to be effective:[11] exports are practically produced in a self-sufficient manner, without this being considered as problematic by the Tunisian authorities.

Jean-Pierre Cassarino has shown how this dualism was organized:[12] applying the 20 per cent rule – according to which offshore enterprises can, with official permission, sell up to 20 per cent of their production on national territory – would have been made difficult by the administrative, customs and regulatory procedures defined by the law of 1993, but also by the decree of 1997 that was supposed to improve the situation. The authorities adopted this strategy quite knowingly. Confinement is, in any case, taken quite far in Tunisia: as opposed to what happens in other countries, customs control is carried out at home. This method betrays a security-minded conception of offshore, and a rather basic vision of control, which must be direct and administrative. This vision is corroborated by the existence of other extremely strict rules that regulate offshore enterprises: access is denied to persons not belonging to the enterprise, the name of the latter is not written on the buildings, the walls have been built so high that nobody can see the factory from outside, people are forced to work behind locked doors and with barred windows ... which itself raises certain security problems.[13] Even though certain companies apply these rules with considerable zeal, the rules themselves are drawn up by the legislators and implemented by a bureaucracy that conceives surveillance and watertight compartmentalization as absolutes.

However amazing it may appear, this confinement is also found in tourism. The ghettoization of this activity is partly the fruit of a state strategy, for reasons similar to those of offshore.[14] At a period when internal tourism was not envisaged, the geographical concentration on the coast, in well-defined areas, generally far from urban conglomerations, resulted from strict planning and the rational vision of an engineering state. Tourist zones were defined and the areas laid out and made viable by the administration following plans that it had drawn up itself; in order to benefit from the several advantages granted to the sector, it was essential to invest in one of these zones.[15] These days, confinement also takes the form of a preference for clubs and package deals – medical tourism, tourism for pensioners. This tendency was initiated by the big tour operators, but it suits the Tunisian public powers perfectly well: in hotel complexes, they discourage contact between foreign tourists and Tunisians, who are, for example, forbidden entry to hotel enclosures and the night clubs and bars that belong to them. Whereas in the 1960s and 1970s the young people who frequented night clubs often had their heads shaved by the police during morality campaigns, there is now a law targeting Tunisians who annoy tourists.[16] All these measures, some of them stemming from professionals and others from the authorities betray the same vision.

The image of a Tunisia that is safe, smooth, without theft, rip-offs or flirtation is simultaneously a guarantee of the success of family and popular tourism, an assurance that foreign currency can be obtained and international recognition won. In spite of the intrinsically globalized nature of the sector, Tunisian tourism mainly remains in the hands of national actors:[17] foreign operators intervene directly only very rarely and, as with the textile and garments industry, exert their influence (one which is very significant) as principals.

This dualism reinforces and legitimates disciplinary measures by putting to work, in a capitalism mode, workers and employees, by strictly localizing activities and rigorously controlling the movements of goods and especially of people. Offshore is fully part of the national economy and, in spite of successive adjustments and programmes of liberalization, it is fully protectionist – and thereby easier to keep under surveillance and to normalize. To paraphrase Janet Roitman and Gérard Roso, we might say that the country favours the offshore domain so as to remain national.[18]

Just-in-time methods and disciplinary government

The disciplinary dimension of international capitalism goes further than that. The 'just-in-time' mentality, and the flexibility of the workforce that are characteristic of current globalized capital, particularly concern a country like Tunisia, which attracts relocalized enterprises whose production is situated at the end of a globalized chain and depends on foreign principals. This also applies to tour operators, who consider tourism as a mass industrial product, standardized and subject to the same demands for price cuts (chartered flights, low cost and last minute deals, and so on). Enterprises demand above all an extreme flexibility in the workforce and adaptability in organization of labour. Concretely, in industry as well as in services, Tunisia offers them these conditions. The perpetually renewed use of fixed-term contracts by rotating the staff and appealing to structures of sub-contracting, transforming a group into various companies on the basis of which it is possible to get round the rules for employment and dismissal, the prolonged employment of trainees, flexibility of very cheap youth jobs, tolerance on the part of the authorities of a partly informal work, including in foreign enterprises, arrangements of every kind – all of this ultimately makes it possible for the right to work to be extremely adaptable in spite of the regulations protecting salary earners.[19] Even if discussions drag on forever, in the case of a strike, sequestration of bosses or occupation of the factory, flexibility is not undermined.

All this is recognized by the very same people who uphold these principles: the World Bank underlines the fact that Tunisian regulations are well adapted to the needs of enterprises, that the regulatory and administrative conditions of working are rather good, and that labour flexibility has now been achieved;[20]

European candidates for relocation agree on wage-cutting and the importance of incentives for offshore investments.[21] Labour flexibility is nothing new in Tunisia and dates from the liberalization of the 1970s. At that time, it was obtained by the intensive use of apprentices, part-time and overtime work, etc. These days, the modes of flexibilization have become more varied, with systematic resort to sub-contracting and workforce companies, and also a certain reorganization of labour, a more frequent use of piece work in factories and multi-skilling in service jobs.[22]

Flexibility is an aspect of the more general "just-in-time" organization that symbolizes the new disciplinary formula of capitalism.[23] The just-in-time system does not concern merely the delivery of goods; it is first and foremost a reorganization of work and an individualization of the relationship with salaried employees. So Jean-Pierre Durand explains that 'in accepting the principle of just-in-time system, there is no need for a boss to impose discipline: discipline is in the just-in-time system [. . .]. Accepting the just-in-time system means accepting the discipline that it imposes; so there is no longer any need for a disciplinary middle management. This is the deep meaning of the paradoxical concept of *constrained involvement*: the salaried work implicated in "just-in-time" becomes active and involved because he has no choice, as the flow requires all his faculties to be maintained in a state of last-minute preparedness. To some degree, we could say – with the slogans of 1968 in mind – that 'the flic is in the flow'. In other words, the social control of previous times carried out by a boss or middle management is no longer required, since the employee conforms to the demands of the just-in-time system as he has accepted its principle of operation.'[24]

Social control and putting Tunisians to work

Getting the Tunisians to work in this way is obviously not confined to organization in the just-in-time system; it also concerns the more Taylorian organization of work, in small and medium enterprises and on the shop floor.

Putting Tunisians to work – capitalist style

In the case of Tunisia, the disciplinary function of work is all the more effective in that businesses are organized on the Fordist model.[25] This model applies even more for the small enterprises of a few employees and for those enterprises which work wholly or partly in the informal sector. The foreign offshore domain is concerned as well, perhaps even more so, since the Tunisian entity is ultimately concerned only with paying its workers and performing a materials accounting (i.e. an accounting of the goods that enter and leave the business) without concerning itself with its own management, or even its accounting.[26]

'Putting to work capitalist style' is done through several commonplace techniques:[27] the continual surveillance of work stations, which is intensified in big businesses by Internet usage; a relatively long working schedule – 8 to 9 hours a day, 6 days out of 7 in the textile industry; the enforcement of procedures and norms; the hierarchized and centralized organization of work, which leaves little place for delegating work or taking personal initiative; cross-checked controls and external audits for the biggest businesses. Furthermore, there is a practice proper to Tunisia, which reveals, perhaps, more than any others the disciplinary nature of Tunisian capitalism. The questionnaire, which is a legal obligation, forces employers to ask their workers in writing for details of absences, illnesses, accidents, or professional mistakes.[28] Even though employers had not asked for it, it came into common use thanks to the fundamental place which Health and Safety ascribes to it; when a conflict arises between the entrepreneur and one of his employees, the Health and Safety inspector asks to consult the questionnaire, which decides the matter. If an absence or a mistake is not mentioned, the inspector will, for instance, give the employee the benefit of the doubt rather than the employer. The role of the questionnaire is easy to understand: it constitutes for the employer an internal control imposed from outside, and a technique for disciplining the labour force, while at the same time it is, for the administration, a means of playing its role as intercessor, while keeping an eye on the business and its actors.

It is within this context that we need to understand the recurrent complaints of business bosses about the lack of punctuality shown by Tunisian employees, on their absenteeism and irregularity at work, on the lack of discipline shown by employees and their 'cultural' need for a boss – and finally on their irrationality, which apparently explains their inopportune resignations or their 'excessive' holidays during Ramadan and the summer months.[29] The managers of foreign businesses have often told me, in interviews, that 'discipline on the political level is not found on the level of work'. Tunisian employees, they claim, are not 'completely available mentally, affectively and physically' for the business, they do not express any 'support for the culture or the objectives of the enterprise'. In other words, they are not 'mobilized'.[30]

These comments can be interpreted in terms derived from E. P. Thompson: such behaviour is not the result of any indolence, laziness, childishness or lack of discipline proper to the Tunisians, but should be interpreted as an act of rebellion, resistance, and refusal of a discipline imposed, and as a partial rejection of constraint. They could be understood as the expression of 'a labour force which is only partially and temporarily "committed" to the industrial way-of-life'.[31] We should not see in these 'defects' either a criticism of capitalism, or a protest against the loss of autonomy and humanity in work, but rather as a quest for the resolution of conflict between the world at work and the world outside work.[32]

But these comments can also be read as a construction produced by a mythical representation – that of an undisciplined people who need a leader in politics as they do at work – which justifies domination and entrepreneurial paternalism in a similar way.[33] This perception is largely relayed by the Tunisian authorities through moralizing language. 'It is high time that easy-going practices give way to discipline and that every Tunisian man and woman gets back to work,' Ben Ali was already saying in 1988. The interiorization of discipline is also given concrete expression in discourses centred on work as the fundamental value as well as on the immorality of leisure and unruliness: 'Work is not just a livelihood, but also an attribute of citizenship as well as a reason for attachment to the earth'; 'We are imperiously summoned to rehabilitate work as a value of civilization, society and the economy. We need to give back to work its value and its sacred character as a better means of fulfilling oneself and contributing to the glory of the homeland. There is no progress without serious and unstinting hard work.'[34] These ringing quotations sound like pale copies of other authoritarian situations, Mussolini's Italy, Salazar's Portugal or present-day Malaysia.[35] The organization of work and the surveillance of the population are thus all the more inseparable since the interiorization of discipline does not follow just from an economic process but stems from an ethos transmitted by institutions, by a discourse, by a mode of government.[36]

An open and diffuse paternalism

The social control of the workforce operates via a diffuse paternalism, sometimes openly assumed, sometimes denied – but no less real. The first case is illustrated by that boss whom I interviewed and who quite simply declared to me: 'We are in a paternalist society and I have to confess that I benefit from it'; while the second is illustrated by those managers of modern enterprises who reject the charge: 'There is no paternalism, it's a permanent dialogue'.[37] We may doubt this, however, when we take into account the daily discourse within the business: 'So Poulina is the fertile hen, she has laid her eggs and each time an egg is transformed into a chick, she gives it something to do that will help the family. And then time goes by and the family never ceases to develop. Then Poulina becomes a grandmother; she has contented herself with looking after, advising and maintaining contact with her chicks by developing the strategies and the general policies of the Group', as the presentation of the conglomerate states on its Internet site.[38] 'Poulina is our mother,' says one worker, while the manager of one branch agrees that 'Poulina is an organic group akin to a big family with written rules', and an executive notes, 'The fact that it is the only guarantor, i.e. that it alone can grant special dispensations, is important [...]. As for the way the system works, there are some very formalized aspects with procedures, and an adaptability that is guaranteed by M. Ben Ayed'.[39] The system of aid is largely propped up by social surveillance:[40] paternalist bosses sign their employees' bank credit, act as their guarantors or themselves give them consumer credits; they agree to pay advances on their wages; they contribute to financing medical treatment; they use their networks of acquaintances to obtain an appointment with a doctor or a civil servant . . .

But first and foremost, paternalism has a function of discipline at work: business managers choose certain employees to sub-contract production in total dependency; they use and abuse the metaphor of the family within the business; they 'control in order to help' and behave like fathers bringing up their children; they keep their employees' lifestyles under surveillance, for instance forbidding them to smoke 'for their own good'. The boss is the only person who can infringe the rule and allow his employees to do the same.[41] In these conditions, entrepreneurs say that they prefer to recruit in the neighbourhood or through female workers already in the factory, precisely because they know and control their milieu.[42] This, indeed, is one of the reasons that explains why the fathers of young girls accept this kind of work: the girls are still controlled by the local society and there is no significant disruption of the sexual segregation that structures spaces and traditional activities. In addition, the sexual division of the tasks and fields of intervention is transformed only moderately. On the basis of surveys on the way decision-making is shared out in a family, one anthropologist has thus shown that women have so far kept their traditional prerogatives and that, in spite of all the actions taken in their favour since independence, they did not seem to have acquired any ability to take strategic decisions, or have any major say in family life and the public space.[43]

This paternalism is shared by foreign entrepreneurs. It is doubtless in this way that we need to interpret their remarks, with their averred culturalism: 'They are children'; 'they like to be ordered about'; 'the man who orders other people needs to do so strictly, he must be authoritarian'; 'they like to have a father with a big stick'; 'the company [i.e. the business] is seen as something external to them; they seek to draw an immediate profit from it, that's all; and if they do have any sense of belonging, it doesn't go as far as giving them any sense of responsibility'.[44] All groups agree about the role of the ideal boss in the business: paternalism contributes to legitimating a disciplinary organizing of the workforce and a security-conscious vision of work in the factory. It is especially significant insofar as it is based on the one hand on a shared imaginary of the strong man and the 'need for a boss' and, on the other hand, on the myth of the state that is outside society and its corollary, the 'culture of rioting and sedition'.[45] Capitalism and disciplinary power form a whole, in particular because individuals share an ethos which sees in discipline a guarantee of the stability and security necessary to prevent a disorder that is always a possibility.[46]

Overt social control

One other element needs to be mentioned in this analysis of the disciplinary character of capitalism: the bureaucratization and the subordination of the Tunisian trade union movement. 'Before, there were two powers to be managed, the trade unionist and the politician; today there is only one. When you have a problem with the UGTT, you call the governor and everything's sorted', one entrepreneur explained to me. Another went further: 'The UGTT exists for the symbol but it isn't dangerous, either for power, or for the business'. 'If there's one good thing that Ben Ali's done, it's to have brought the trade union to heel', said another, even more clearly.[47] These remarks are unambiguous, as is the view of strikes expressed by President Ben Ali himself: 'Resorting to strike action, even if it is guaranteed by the law, indicates a lack of efficiency and dialogue, and a deficiency on that level, because, in a democratic society, *social peace is a capital imperative towards which all social partners should tend, and the realization of which depends on the degree of efficiency of the dialogue and the mastery of its channels*'.[48] Paternalism goes hand in hand with neutralizing the trade union.

However, social control is not expressed by the submission of the UGTT and by paternalism within enterprise alone. Other practices simultaneously make it possible to integrate the discipline of work and to keep the wheels of political domination turning. For instance, the young girls who work in the textile industry are recruited from the neighbourhood of the factory by already employed female workers: 'That way, we can go and see the family, the neighbourhood and keep them more under control'. Control works both ways: for businesses, it is apparently more effective to benefit from direct contact with the family and the neighbourhood and thus know why there has been an absence or a delay; it is also more convenient to be able to bring in the female workers on a Sunday or in the evenings if there is an emergency.[49] For families, it makes it easier to keep an eye on their girls, via the neighbourhood, the relatives who are already there, and qualified intermediaries – or directly, when the business happens to be in the locality of the relatives.[50]

The same analysis could be made of the over-valorization of the weight of the family and, more generally, of the fact that one's position in the social hierarchy is of much greater significance than personal aptitudes. Surveillance also operates via the apprenticeship or practices of spin-offs, in other words via controlled sub-contracting.[51] It is quite simply the result of the codes of life in society, as one boss in the PME reminded me when he told me in no uncertain terms, 'In your questions, you insist too much on relations with the administration; that's not the only thing that's problematic and even, for an offshore enterprise, the administration isn't a big deal. For me, it's even more problematic in relations with all my private business contacts, the suppliers, the customers, the craftsmen who come round to do repairs, the drivers'.[52]

There is nothing political about any of these practices. Recruitment is primarily a question of relationships, resting as it does on networks of family, region, friendship, or neighbourhood. When it does play a role, the clientelism of labour offices seems less a matter of party than of regional affiliation. The choice of markets, the obtaining of contracts and the selection of the sub-contractor operate through these same relations. In Tunisia, the business is not a place of political control. In certain cases, 'there are loads of informers', as a certain number of entrepreneurs repeatedly told me. All the same, there was no desire, on the part of the state party, to recruit them. They are not 'set there by the powers that be' in order to control, but once they are in the business, employees may be approached by the police, or by other authorities, to provide information against the cancelling of a POS, administrative facilities, or financial advantages. In other cases, 'you don't feel like you're in a police state at all'.[53] In fact, the UGTT cells are not very common in private enterprises and RCD cells are even less common. As for the customs official, the sole representative of the administration who is constantly present in the business, he does not play this role and when he oversteps his professional duties, it is for strictly personal – and lucrative – reasons.[54]

It is easy to understand how businesses, unlike associations for instance, do not need to be observed. There reasons for this 'neglect' of the obsession with security are at least twofold. On the one hand, the surveillance of society is such that it is not necessary to invest a place that does not harbour a category of the population not already under surveillance: workers male and female are known by the members of the *comités de quartier*; company directors are known by the bosses' federations, by agents of the tax authorities or social security. Furthermore, all groups fully master the disciplinary rules that they have long since interiorized: people know what they can and cannot say, and they rarely venture to discuss things at their work places. On the other hand, businesses are not subversive places, they are not considered as dangerous places because they are controlled and 'made safe' in other ways, by the discipline of a certain capitalism.

Relations of force and hidden conflict

The occasional but recurrent exercise of repressive actions or openly security-based pressures vis-à-vis 'capitalists' suggests, however, that capitalism cannot be identified solely with its disciplinary nature and that other dynamic forces are at work. When the administration imposes rules that handicap the tourist sector – for example by forbidding Tunisians to frequent certain public places or by taxing drinks at exorbitant rates – a trial of strength between professions and ministry is inevitable, even if it remains hidden. The same applies when a boss is summoned to see the governor, who demands that he forces one or other of his female employees to remove her veil, intimating to him, thanks to a list opportunely left on the table, that he knows exactly the number of veiled women in every business in his governorate. This is the case, finally, when a governor calls in the manager of a factory and orders him to dock the pay of each of his employees by a few dinars or when a foreign company leader, on the first day he takes up his job in Tunisia, receives a visit from people who claim they have links with associations or entities close to the central power.[55] Indubitably, these activities clash with other of capitalism's mechanisms (autonomy of decision-making, economic, sector-based or financial logics, respect for a certain hierarchy within the business) and, aware of these interferences – considered as negative – foreign investments, in any case, are not established in Tunisia in any great numbers.[56] Those who decide to do so are rarely branches of big international groups. They are, rather, European SMEs or the executives of big groups setting up their own businesses and looking for reconversions after experiencing difficulties in their home countries.[57]

The historical sociology of the economy reminds us that capitalism is conflict, less as a result of the resistance of certain actors than because of the multiplicity of logics at work within it and the plasticity of relations that it entails.[58] Jean-Louis Rocca's research into Chinese capitalism and the use he makes of the concept of 'getting people to work' found in Henri Lefebvre have the interest of reminding us in very concrete form of the way in which, these days, capitalist logic by its very nature entails conflicts, contradictions, violence, inequality, injustice and crises. In Tunisia, where the watchwords are 'security', 'stability' and 'social peace', the conflicts inherent in capitalist logic are not, however, absent. They are simply masked by the several various techniques of disciplinary normalization, in particular by the construction of a largely fictive consensus. I would like to show here that these conflicts are more numerous than the monotony of Tunisian political and social life would like it to appear, and thereby suggest that the disciplinary nature of capitalism does not comprise capitalism's whole nature and above all its logics of action.

Tensions and the stifling of conflicts in the workplace

The intensive resorting to justice is a first symptom of these tensions. There are, as far as I know, no figures, but during my interviews, the representatives of the UGTT 'on the ground' insisted on this practice, and not a single entrepreneur interviewed told me he had been able to avoid justice, especially in the framework of managing labour relations. Employees appreciate a justice that decides most often in their favour and, for the same reasons, employers systematically denigrate it. But this system is not synonymous with the application of the decision – quite the contrary, in fact: the economic administration and in particular the police – in the broad sense of the term – are sensitive to the strictly financial and economic logic of capitalism.

The foreign manager of an offshore enterprise summed the situation up in these words: 'These days, the authorities act with greater subtlety, they are more realistic and less nationalistic, as *they have a good sense of the relations of force*'.[59] It is indeed, first and foremost, a question of relations of force, as is also suggested by the difficulties encountered by the entrepreneurs who wish to lay off workers. The observation that, ultimately, these entrepreneurs have indeed obtained satisfaction and that the 'regime' really has favoured 'capitalist interests' does not mean that agreements and negotiations, but also opposition and tensions, do not exist between the different groups. The flexibility of labour, for instance, has required long struggles, it has involved justice, and various administrative mechanisms have tried to stem the scourge of unemployment in a logic of the need to 'defend society' that goes against the logic of liberalism. This is how we should understand the attempts to limit the number of layoffs, especially in the case of foreign businesses, the obstacles set up by the administration to stop bosses taking their employees to court, the pressures brought to bear by the police or the governorate to stop an employee being punished and encourage his reintegration into the factory, the multiplicity of financial and regulatory agreements to foster employment.[60] All these dealings show that social stability is largely merely a superficial harmony and that the number of latent conflicts should not be underestimated.

The public powers intervene directly only if discontent starts to intensify and they need to avoid social unrest. It is not illogical for this lack of involvement on the part of the authorities in conflicts to be interpreted as a disguised form of support for employers. However, it is difficult for the Administration and Politics to be so clearly distinguished from one another, even if there is a tendency towards administrative autonomization. Tensions arise, rather, from a complex interplay between divergent interests, for instance – in greatly simplified terms – between on the one hand the defence of the middle classes, a central pillar of the 'disciplinary regime', and on the other the defence of capitalists, who comprise a central pillar of the 'developmentalist regime', that is that facet of the Tunisian state which aims at fostering, through its choice of economic policies and direct interventions, the development of the productive sector. Tensions have also arisen from different logics of action, for example – and again simplifying dramatically – between the protection and maintenance of a standard of living, on the one hand, and competitiveness on the other – or between jobs and the quest for currency, between security and attractiveness. The government is affected by all of these crisscrossing logics at the same time: everything can be done to favour the demands of businesses and at the same time everything can be attempted to avoid layoffs. The public powers, after all, are aware of tensions on the labour market and the fears which unemployment arouses within the population.

Recently, its increasing interventions have been linked to the ever more numerous hunger strikes, occupations and illegal strikes.[61] For the authorities, these conflicts must be kept invisible since they meet with a favourable response among the entire population. However, they are managed in a very real way: everything is done to solve the problem at its source and as quickly as possible, via the interventions of the UGTT, delegates and provincial governors, RCD networks, labour inspectors and general secretaries of town councils, as well as with the financial support of the CNSS. Disciplinary normalization is carried out on a softly softly approach, often in an insidious way. Protests appear on the public scene only if the way the employers behave is clumsy or fraudulent, if the authorities misjudge the situation or if the local social context allows political protest movements to slip into these interstices.[62] Nevertheless, discontent is neither political, nor organized, nor oppositional. People fight to keep on to their jobs and preserve a certain social guarantee. Even when this conflict is politicized by the intervention of organizations such as the CNLT and, above all, the LTDH or RAID/Attac Tunisie, the strategy of negotiation is more important: repression affects only the members of these organizations and it operates essentially on the basis of intimidation. Negotiation and containment are the keywords here.

Logics and objectives that do not necessarily converge

The fact that economic or security policies attempt to reinforce the disciplinary nature of capitalism in no way prejudices the efficiency of the 'regime' in guiding the behaviour of 'its' entrepreneurs. The unfinished nature and plurality of logics at work explain it, but so does the plasticity of social forms and relations between variables. The contingency of situations arises precisely from the multiplicity of objectives, representations and ways of understanding the notion of security.[63]

For entrepreneurs, for example, tactics for reducing trade union constraints are numerous and not always deliberately implemented: the development of the fixed-term contracts, temping, piece rate and so on mean that only 'people with a head for work' are given permanent posts; it is also possible to buy employees with money, or the hope of promotion, so that they will not set up a trade union cell; a more or less regular contact with the delegate or the governor makes it possible 'to get the message across'. More generally, the decrease in trade union influence in Tunisia can be explained as a result of an increase in working conditions, by the pursuit of ostentatiously paternalist anti-union policies, by the development of sub-contracting and outsourcing thanks to the proliferation of small non-unionized units and, in the more modern businesses, especially foreign ones, by a modification of modes of supervision that softens the forms of command.[64] Within this context, external employers and observers may consider that the subjection of the union by the central power is a significant contribution to the entrepreneurs' strategy.

The historical analysis of the union movement has, however, shown us that the UGTT was indeed something different, mainly a political actor. It is precisely for these political reasons, and not for economic reasons, that it was subjected: it represented a potentially competitive force and so needed to be disciplined and controlled. An institution like the UGTT has a memory and this is translated by microdecisions and modes of thought that perpetuate behaviour and, in particular, kinds of understanding that no longer essentially correspond to relations of force and present concrete situations.[65] This memory thus leaves less room for class struggle than national unity, the building of the nation-state, and contribution to social peace.[66] The misunderstanding is, right now, a working misunderstanding, and the political bringing into line of the trade union confederation serves the current capitalist dynamic, but dissensions within the UGTT and the growing gap between a summit co-opted by the central power and a base that is increasingly mobilized in favour of employees might undermine this convergence.

The same applies to the dualism described above. The voluntarist policy of the Tunisian state is not the only one that explains the 'success' of this strategy of confinement of offshore enterprises. The latter results from numerous factors. An industrialist established offshore will have no interest in entering an unattractive internal market that is segmented and unintegrated, and he will try to minimize his relations with an administration that is judged too pernickety, to get round the elements 'out of the market' that it is difficult for a foreigner to master, to beware of bad debts and 'the culture of unpaid bills'. Likewise, in the domain of tourism, the nature of the clientele, the strategy of tour operators and the development of 'Club' or 'all inclusive' formulas, the relative lack of supply outside hotel complexes, the administrative burdens, the Tunisian ways of life . . . all of these contribute to the ghettoization of tourism mentioned above.[67] The thesis of a dualism consciously conceived and voluntarily constructed thus appears too simple. It does not take into account the many reasons, sometimes proper to Tunisian society, sometimes dependent on globalized economic and financial strategies, sometimes more on grossly simplistic representations or highly individual interests.

In short, the disciplinary nature of capitalism cannot be read as the expression of any particularly attentive 'listening' on the part of the 'regime' to the expectations of Tunisian entrepreneurs. The relations of power undeniably serve capitalism; however, they serve it not in the sense of 'doing it a service', but in the sense that they can be used in various strategies.[68]

The multiple paths of negotiated accommodation

In the domain of employment, as in that of economic success, repression as such is thus the exception rather than the rule. What works are very fine mechanisms of control and normalization that may, at very precise moments (of their nature rare) be transformed into harassment, chastisement and exclusion pure and simple – but which are most often expressed by pressure and sometimes victimization, by the use of arbitrary measures and favouritism, by the mobilization of individual interests, by petty obstacles and day-to-day administrative hassles, and even more by a strict delimitation of economic and social possibilities. In these conditions, the question that is posed with the greatest urgency is that of 'voluntary servitude': what 'keeps' people and the system in thrall? If the principles of absolute obedience and pure and simple constraint are not central, what exactly has this effect? Is it support? Negotiation and accommodation? Probably a mixture of all of the above, made materially possible by a multitude of imperceptible and insidious mechanisms, which ultimately form an environment that simultaneously produces constraints and advantages, economic opportunities and opportunities for training, conditions of domination and emancipation.

We can now return to the remarks made by entrepreneurs as mentioned in the introduction to this part: 'what weighs down on us is at the same time what protects us'. The mechanisms that are sensed as constraining are deliberately sought out, since they are simultaneously protective, enriching and reassuring; what can be represented as listening to people can also turn out to be an instrument of control; conversely, what may be perceived as submission may just as well result from a convergence of different logics and interests. If we take this detour through labour relations and the working of businesses, we will better be able to advance in the understanding of 'what keeps Tunisians in thrall' by suggesting the ambivalences of domination, the many different modes through which the political is inserted into existing relations of power and the concrete modes of this accommodation with constraint and surveillance.

Assent and habit

A first mode of accommodation resides in pure and simple assent. What external observers may present as constraint, or even a form of coercion, a power of normalization and discipline, is as often as not experienced as a mode of normality, in other words as a set of interiorized rules.[69] Only the systematic nature of incidents, the ban on unavoidable debates or the appearance of contradictions between principles of action make these practices unpleasant or even intolerable. In Tunisia as elsewhere, this explicit assent can be explained, first and foremost, by an absence of any questions being asked about the environment in which individuals live and work. Neither consent, nor rejection: most of the time, they are absolutely not bothered by constraints on their work, by accommodations forged on the basis of politicking and wheeling and dealing, by the disciplinary workings of the business, the administration or any economic organization, or by the exercise of certain police control. Then, when intermittently or temporarily such constraints do exist, assent operates thanks to the generalized apoliticism of the actors and their relative lack of awareness of the mechanisms of training.[70] These mechanisms, inseparable from the concrete nature of economic policies, social programmes, aid and subsidies, are not necessarily perceived for what they are. So long as they do not suffer from any massive rejection or confrontation, so long as individuals accept them because to some extent they derive an advantage or a sense of satisfaction from them, there is no critical distance here. Most Tunisian entrepreneurs do not reason in political terms when they criticize the administration's incessant interference, the requests for money from the party and its multiple satellite associations, or when they deplore the absenteeism of the workers. Most employees do not reason in political terms when they regret the increasingly precarious nature of work and the spread of liberal norms. For all these groups, it needs some traumatic event, or at least something exasperating – often of a personal order – for these petty regrets and disaffections to be transformed into resistance, and thus into a political act. Finally and above all, assent is explained by the participation, including involuntary and unconscious participation, of economic actors in disciplinary power. As the above examples have shown, it is much less a matter of 'creating dependencies' than playing with and on them.

A second mode of accommodation resides in the painless and, so to speak, invisible character of constraint and even coercion, made possible by the way interventions and the exercise of power become ever more routine. Or, in the terms of Max Weber, by the way they have 'become a day-to-day phenomenon' (*Veralltäglichung*) and in the words of Étienne de La Boétie, by 'habit'.[71] 'They drive the nail in gradually'; 'it's a gentle, non-violent interventionism, which we don't even feel'; 'it's natural, it's always been like that': all these remarks suggest the invisibility of training and normalization.[72] In the world of work as in social relations as a whole, the tactics of power are not necessarily visible because they are mediatized by beliefs and representations. The internalization of constraint is so strong that it is blurred by the deployment of a certain ethic – or moral rhetoric – around the values of work and the nation, or else the good of the country, well-being and growth, and the citizen's moral duty:[73] 'in Tunisia, we have a feeling for family and community', 'it's for the good of the nation', 'we do it for the country', 'it's the Islamic sense of solidarity' . . . The exercise of power, too, is understood in the terms of religious belief, of national unity, or Tunisian-ness, all of which bring all individuals together, in the fabric of social relations, in the chain of microscopic dependencies. The campaigns of moralization, the Islamization of social life, or the discourse on the tradition of moderation of Tunisians are all part of these mechanisms of the mediation of discipline.[74] In this context, the process of normalization is imperceptible; once transformed, it becomes acceptable.

Between adhesion and distancing

The dynamic of the relations of force and the play of relations of power constitute a third mode of accommodation. The absence of 'rebellion' felt towards a relation of domination or systematic surveillance is in no way a synonym with acquiescence. Forms of resistance may exist that shape relations within business, within society, between business and central power, without thereby undermining the general economy of control and domination. These resistance or 'counter-conducts' define, at a given moment and on a given subject, activities that do not necessarily tend towards normalization. They express the state of relations of force at a specific moment but they are neither sufficiently powerful, nor fixed and definitive enough, to be able to describe an activity. In the business world, as in society, there is rarely opposition, dissidence or revolt. As one of my Tunisian interviewees summed it up, 'capitalists don't like vagueness and risk, they won't get involved in dissidence'.[75] Employees who are recurrently absent during festivities and family events, wage-earners who 'don't support' the business and don't make it 'their own', are not thereby opponents.[76] There may be a strike and even a hunger strike, sector-based and one-off resistances, and social conflicts without this having entailed the development of any critique of economic and social practices, even less of mechanisms of discipline and surveillance.

As the adage has it, 'you obey but you don't enforce'. The way individuals behave is forever swinging between support and distance, between the attempt to exercise a certain power and subordination, between 'the loan of self' and 'the withholding of self'. Identity at work or within society is most often experienced in the mode of doubling, a controlled doubling of the relation with one's self and others, in other words a 'constant effort of reappropriation of one's being', at work as in society.[77] These activities cannot be transformed into rejection unless the deterioration in living standards, services offered, and working conditions becomes too significant and if, in other spaces, one's fears encounter more political demands. So as not to feel torn apart and to come to some accommodation with these situations, every individual perpetually negotiates, with himself but also with others, the acceptance of his involvement, with the result that what is objectively a constraint is transformed into a voluntary commitment.

What Jean-Pierre Durand calls a 'paradoxical contentment' can be extended to every relationship within the society: since 'involvement is constraint, escaping from the paradox resides in the voluntary construction of the acceptability'[78] of work as of life in society. In other words, surveillance and domination do not stop individuals from at the same time managing to invent for themselves margins of manoeuvre, and their own spaces for action. The relations that are deployed in these worlds allow both discipline and a softening of discipline to exist, as well as spaces of freedom: 'To work is constantly to labour, in the tension between instituted norms and personal autonomy, to perfect the conditions that will make it possible to tolerate the constraints of work'.[79] On the side of 'capitalism' as on that of the 'regime', there is no brutal domination, unless we consider those limit cases constituted by 'examples', the occasional theatricalization of force and the *stratégie du pourtour*. Relations of power are greeted with support but also resistance; the latter leads the central power to develop a strategy to maintain itself, one that is deployed with all the more cunning in that resistance is powerful and persistent. So there is a continual movement, without any stability in spite of the emphasis always laid by the Tunisian authorities on this intrinsic quality of the 'regime'. Accommodation does not express 'the glum and stable domination of a uniformizing apparatus' but quite simply the simultaneous nature of support and resistance in a 'perpetual and multiform struggle'.[80]

Nonetheless, this negotiated accommodation may also result from a much simpler situation, namely a partial but still real support for discipline. Acceptance may stem from the expectation of concrete and material advantages. Certain segments of the elite thus support a logic of cooptation and differentiation, with the secret hope of becoming one of the 'elect', of being 'chosen', even if the corollary of this is possible disgrace. This active support is thus inseparable from the desire to always serve better, which conceals the constraints, and highlights only improvements and progress. The same is true of entrepreneurs who aspire to stability and security and would like to benefit from an even more disciplined and normalized labour force; of the middle classes who are anxious about delinquency and the 'dangerous classes'; of workers in the tourist sector or offshore enterprises who share a certain access to modernity and 'western life'; and of citizens who accept discipline because it brings them a certain standard of living, basic infrastructures, and social peace, even if all of these are obtained at the cost of practices that have more to do with coercion than with persuasion. As La Boétie put it: 'In sum, we get to a point, through the favours and sub-favours, profits and paybacks that one has with tyrants, that we find in the end almost as many people to whom tyranny seems to be profitable as of those to whom liberty would be pleasant'.[81]

However, the advantages of discipline and domination can be the fruit of more subtle games with styles of life and constitution as subjects. Female Tunisian workers in offshore factories are admittedly subjected to strong discipline, to constraints of time and organization, but they simultaneously find in their work an indisputable source of revenue and complementary resources, of emancipation and transformation of their life styles. The social status linked to work also brings satisfactions, pleasures and considerations, which also goes to explaining why 'work, even in its negative repercussions, is acceptable and accepted'.[82] Contrary to what has been advanced by authors such as E. P. Thompson or, more recently, A. Ong, the discipline of capitalism and urban modernity does not merely introduce new social relations and new relations of power that favour domination, control and surveillance.[83] The prospects of autonomy, of freedom and the obtaining of material or immaterial advantages appear clearly.[84] The female offshore workers can thus prepare their dowries and play a part in financing the household, either their own or their parents'. The social relations of these young women have indubitably become modernized, even if paternalist behaviour remains massively present and social (in particular family) control just as oppressive.[85]

The multiplicity of the meanings of work and the plurality of ways of experiencing it come from the profound heterogeneity of perceptions of reality: simultaneously discipline and emancipation, submission and access to a certain freedom, rigidity and new latitude of action . . . The same might be said of life in society, of the role of the party, of administrative or political interventions. This proliferation still makes it possible – or almost possible – to find points of acceptance, use and convergence that render disciplinary power tolerable, acceptable or even desirable. Freedom and obedience appear indissociable: both are anchored in relations of power and take form only in the detail of concrete situations. This makes it easier to understand what this voluntary servitude means, one which cannot be reduced to the love of domination.[86] 'Servitude is not the blind and frank acceptance of the established order; the opposite of servitude is not simply the rebellion that regularly shakes the established order', but rather the link and the permanent tension between the desire to rebel and the desire to serve.[87] It means submission and the fear of power, but also an appropriation and a bending of power to one's own ends, a using and benefiting from power. 'The intervention of a limitless political power in everyday relations thus became not only acceptable and familiar but deeply condoned – not without becoming, from that very fact, the theme of a generalized fear [. . .] it became both an object of covetousness and an object of seduction; it was desirable, then, precisely insofar as it was dreadful'.[88]

7

The Outline of the Tunisian Security Pact

The exercise of power does not involve merely obedience and prohibition, fear and violence. It also claims to foster growth and bring in foreign investments, to create jobs and a business-friendly environment, to protect activities and guarantee social stability, to favour well-being and consumption, to reduce inequality and encourage solidarity. The many different paths of negotiated compromise suggest that power is not imposed from on high, but that it plays, too, on people's desires, on the positive elements that lead individuals to act. So desire is 'accessible to governmental technique'[1] precisely because it is also a 'desire for the state'.[2]

This demand for the state, which has been nursed ever since independence (and was there, to some extent, also under the Protectorate), is a powerful force in Tunisia, as the political economy of 'incessant intervention' shows. The example of the banking system and the chain of debt suggest, as we have seen, that an implicit social contract lies at the heart of modes of government. In the following pages, I would like to show that it really is there. It is a diffuse presence, and might be described as a 'security pact', a phrase that echoes the government rhetoric of the National Pact of 1988, signed by the entire Tunisian political class straight after the assumption of power by Ben Ali, and (even more) the celebrated Fundamental Pact of 1857, the first expression of a certain number of fundamental political principles whose literal translation is, fittingly, the 'Security Pact' (*Ahd al-aman*).[3] And the phrase also echoes the Foucauldian analysis of the mechanisms of security.

The security pact, or how to ensure peace and order

We need to make one thing clear first. A pact is completely different from an exchange. It does not aim to give something in return for something else, for instance to procure growth, guarantee jobs, ensure a standard of living, or make security prevail even in exchange for police brutality and the reduction of public liberties. A pact is a much more complex relation between the state and its population; it expresses the permanent and ubiquitous solicitude of the state, the way it claims to present itself and legitimatize itself in the eyes of its population. A security pact is a relation within which the state attempts to forestall all uncertainty, risk and danger.

Economic and social security as a defence against the greatest dangers

In Tunisia, danger is the keyword that guides the different modes of government: there is the Islamist danger, of course; but also the danger of poverty and inequality, those vectors of Islamism; the danger of an over-pronounced westernization that fuels Islamism; the danger of an economic crisis that fosters unemployment and desocialization, those factors of Islamization; the danger of globalization, opening the country up to foreign influences and foreign competition . . . So what we have here is a veritable political culture of danger, ceaselessly reactivated. As the reader will already have realized, the ultimate danger is Islamism. The role of the political and the state is to ensure security and order in the face of Islamism, by repression and the *stratégie du pourtour*, but also and above all by positive measures, social programmes, public policies, economic guidelines, and international alliances. The Tunisian president justifies his actions in these terms: 'I can only repeat to you my conviction that the deep root of fundamentalism is extreme poverty. Hence the importance of fighting it by ambitious economic and social reforms'.[4] In the same way, the RCD has, on the margins of its purely police techniques, developed an overall approach aimed at guaranteeing against these dangers: ever since 1987 and in particular since 1989, the pursuit of the policy of educating and promoting women more widely, the de-ghettoizing of the country's underprivileged provinces, and the importance of social transfers (estimated at 20 per cent GNP) have been presented as techniques directly aimed at maintaining security, seen as a sacrosanct task.

What is sought is principally a security that might be described as 'societal', so as to differentiate it from the 'social security' that in western countries is guaranteed by real institutions. In Tunisia, security is less the result of institutional mechanisms than of social relations and a system of interdependences in which the central power deploys its action, drawing on these entanglements.[5] The state dispenses goods, and modes of life and social being and, via these mechanisms, guarantees society against the dangers that threaten it. The state draws on solidarity, the fight against poverty, police surveillance of potential destroyers of social order . . . If there really is any legitimacy of power, this is where it resides – and, more specifically, in this ability to offer ever more economic and social security, ever more prosperity. This situation is not found in Tunisia alone, of course, but extends to all those cases in which the disciplinary exercise of power is associated with a sort of economic and social productivism.[6] The positive evaluation stems from the fact that the authorities thereby appear 'responsible', the government 'attentive' to material demands, the state 'anxious' to ensure the country's prosperity.[7] Security mechanisms are indisputably arrangements that foster protection – or 'systems of protection' to use a different terminology, that of Polanyi.[8] This too explains why these interventions happen on a daily basis: they are better adapted than is the law to protect the population against the dangers that threaten it, and they represent the 'ubiquitous solicitude'[9] of the state.

What, in concrete terms, is the security pact in Tunisia these days? It is clearly the assurance of order and tranquillity. From a material point of view, it is the good functioning of a certain society of consumption and well-being. The Tunisian authorities thus make it a point of honour to enumerate the benefits that they are bestowing on their middle classes, and it is no coincidence that speeches focus on precisely this dimension: growth annually rises to around five per cent, fostering a real development in the country; nearly 80 per cent of families own their own accommodation; cars are made more popular both by programmes that provide purchasing aid and, in periods when petrol prices go up, by oil subsidies; electrification and water conveyance affect over 90 per cent of the population; telephones are increasingly accessible, as is the Internet; birth rates have fallen and demographic growth has been limited thanks to an active family planning policy; etc. The Plan is the main indicator of the pact's effectiveness: as a technique of assessment, it attempts to order everything so that the objective of security can be attained.

Debt is the central mechanism in this process: power by credit, life on credit, credit as the mainspring of the security pact. This makes it easier to understand the centrality of the political economy of credit and debt which I described in detail at the start of this book. The bank is simultaneously an institution of protection and security and an institution that creates dependency, control and surveillance. Credit is particularly central in that, in a period of liberalization, the classic modes of support and intervention are partly under fire. Nowadays, in Tunisia, the financial burden of subsidies and compensations is continually decreasing. Some people have even concluded that the decrease in transfers leads to a deconstruction of social relations, the dismantling of the state as protector and dispenser of goods, the downfall of the 'corporatist' state or even the waning of the Tunisian 'extensive and redistributive' model.[10] It cannot be denied that liberalization has entailed a significant drop in subsidies and in state contribution to the operation of the most central security mechanisms.[11] Behind the deconstruction of an apparent order, an outside observer is struck, however, by the persistence of interventions. These are certainly quite different in nature, but they are no less effective:[12] credit, of course, but also the modes (not only statistical) of the social handling of unemployment; a targeting of subsidies to certain categories of the population or to certain products such as oil; the control of a sustained growth in spite of international ups and downs; the construction and preservation of a good image that will guarantee the obtaining of external low-cost credit; and the pursuit of a social policy via largely symbolic but nonetheless functional programmes within the framework of the security pact.

What we have here is a hybrid system in which the state is simultaneously ubiquitous and absent, by the norms of past interventions.[13] The public apparatuses that emerged from the ideas current in the 1930s, originally aimed at taking over the task of proper social protection and ensuring full employment, have actually been damaged by budgetary rigour. However, new mechanisms are being set in place; they are particularly characterized by a certain blurring of the distinction between public and private and a redefinition of the boundaries of interventionism. New modes of exercising protection, redistribution and security are gradually being invented. 'Priority to the social sphere' is not just a rhetorical slogan – it constitutes a fundamental element in the legitimacy of Tunisian power at the same time as it reflects a real fear of the dangers of poverty and its political consequences. The norms of protection and the social conditions of workers are among the highest in the region and, in this respect, Tunisia need not be ashamed by any international comparisons.[14] Unlike other countries which have massively chosen offshore activities, these zones are not 'zones of oppression'.[15]

The security pact conveys the idea that the state is indisputably the only authority able to respond to these demands for justice and attention to the poor, for the satisfaction of basic needs, and for social integration and ascent. Solidarity is established in the name of 'cultural', that is religious, values, but only the state and the direct representatives of central power can concretely bring these policies to a successful conclusion.

Dependence and security: the outline of the pact

This security pact is not, however, limited to the order of material existence. The other facet of consumption, the rise in income and living standards, growth at all costs, is a particular lifestyle. The pact also aims to guarantee a certain ethos, a certain way of being and acting in society. The security and the solicitude bestowed by the state also mean dependence and modes of surveillance. The lifestyle guaranteed by the state subjects individuals: those who cannot or will not gain access to these consumer credits, this banking fiction, these social programmes or these modes of sociability find themselves marginalized by the close intermeshing of institutions. Programmes aimed at redistribution are also mechanisms whereby the 'outcasts'[16] are forced into dependency and controlled.

The use of social programmes is one of the great classic tactics of authoritarian clientelism, as research on Mexico, Angola, Singapore or Salazar's Portugal has shown.[17] They express a desire to pacify social relations, to pursue the objectives of justice and charity, to obtain security in the societal order too and, at the same time, to exercise control and surveillance. Tunisia is no exception to this picture. The political and security guidelines (in every sense) of social programmes are indeed recognized here: the solicitude of the state is inseparable from the dependency that it creates. The more security is offered to individuals, the more their dependence is increased.

In the Tunisian context, in which there is a ban on thinking and a strict supervision of society, solicitude subjects people for the particular reason that it is indissociable from stability, interpreted as the management of crisis by caution, by consensus and by the support of all. This solicitude is rarely brutal, is painless and invisible, and has become natural by force of habit. 'Never take drastic action': power in Tunisia is not exerted by radical measures, by shocks, by assumed antagonisms, but via these many different paths of compromise, these small-scale interventions and halftone measures that ultimately enable everyone, or at least the majority, to come to a compromise, to find out where their advantage lies, to discover a *modus vivendi* in a way that is perfectly smooth but also leads to complete dependence.

This solicitude is indissociable from dependence and the desire for harmony with the state which so benefits the nation: the question of economic and social security is, first and foremost, a national question based on the desire for national unity.[18] Protection from external forces, from the Other, is a mainspring of the activities of the Tunisian state. In this sense, it is indisputably a 'social-national state',[19] in the sense Etienne Balibar applies to western welfare states, in spite of its differences: the intervention of the state in the reproduction of the economy and the education of individuals is systematic here, and the lives of individuals are always subordinated to their status as 'national'.

In Tunisia, the national movement and the struggle for independence were indeed structured around the question of economic and social security.[20] The establishment of the Neo Destour and the radicalization of the national movement were crystallized around questions of development, and also around uncertainties as to the consequences of the economic crisis of the 1930s. The pact was defined against the discriminatory policy of the Protectorate and antagonisms between populations that were created by the colonial authorities; one corollary of this was the need for the economic and social integration of the natives. The colonial state, however, had also sought a kind of societal security, in accordance with the health-conscious state and the positive development of the territory and its population; from the 1930s, it tried to integrate the population by subjecting the territory to surveillance and ensuring a certain amount of redistribution. This heritage comprised the shape of the social policy that was followed throughout the first three decades of independence.[21]

For the equation between citizenship and nationality to come into being, and for it then to hold good, 'citizenship needed to become increasingly, in deed and in principle, a social citizenship'.[22] The discourse of the primacy of social rights over public liberties is, in Tunisia, first and foremost a rhetoric and the product of an authoritarian instrumentalization. But this positive dimension (i.e. the desire for national integration) must not be neglected. The security pact is inseparable from nationalism and the unity of the social body. It makes it possible for the exercise of power to be legitimated and the strategies of control of the populations to be justified. It also makes it possible to exclude, for instance, Islamists 'supported from outside' and influenced by an 'imported ideology'.[23]

Security and laissez-faire: *two complementary facets of the pact*

If they are to be taken into consideration as credible and politically viable, the measures aimed at ensuring security need to be accompanied by spectacular gestures. This explains the public morality campaigns or the successive decisions in favour of Arabization. But these symbolic acts are, in the final analysis, rather few in number. The common lot is, first and foremost, the interventionism and day-by-day solicitude of the state. It is also, paradoxically, *laissez-faire*.

If we look at the economic and social life of Tunisia, we are struck by the way well-defined principles of action coexist with the non-respect of the latter. The case of health insurance is a good illustration of this situation. While the authorities have set up a social security system that is one of the best in the region, and periodically attempt to reform it, it appears that on the everyday level access to healthcare is made possible by networks of family, friendship, profession or neighbourhood, as is access to jobs.[24] Sociological studies suggest that power does not have the influence that it claims to have over social life, for example in the outer suburbs of towns where spontaneous modes of dwelling, anarchic building activities, and informal activities assume mind-boggling proportions – or indeed in emergency situations.[25] In particular, what we find is that extremely strict bans coexist with a systematic by-passing of these bans – a by-passing that is tolerated to an even more significant and frequent degree. This tolerance has sometimes been interpreted as a safety valve in the face of systematic constraints, the strictness of the bans, or the sense of exasperation aroused by the absence of freedom. The tolerance extended is illegal, illicit, and systematically transgresses the law: it has been viewed as paradoxical with regard to the systematic surveillance of society, and to the daily surveillance of economic activities.[26]

An analysis in terms of the security pact makes another interpretation possible: *laissez-faire* is a complementary mode of security mechanisms. In reality, as in discourse, the security pact cannot encompass everything. Control cannot be as absolute as the central power would have us believe, and the imposing of discipline is not complete. If tight surveillance can, in certain circumstances, constitute the most adequate technique for ensuring a certain social stability, to preserve jobs or to even out inequalities, *laissez-faire* can, in other circumstances, and when applied to other objects, appear as a much more effective technique when it is limited. So zones of *laissez-faire* are among the security techniques of power, provided – of course – that not everything is permitted and that the level below which interventionism is not necessary is known. This configuration is illustrated by the examples of the informal economy, of contraband and counterfeits. But before we proceed to these case studies, we need to point out that this *laissez-faire* itself is not entirely under control. The blurred lines between surveillance and tolerance are something which those who govern cannot entirely control: the exercise of the power of domination is also realized by trial and error. Nonetheless, these uncertainties, and the incompleteness of the practices of discipline and *laissez-faire*, do not, in the final analysis, stand in the way of surveillance and domination.

Illicit or even criminal activities are indeed more than tolerated, as is indicated by the extent of the phenomenon and the degree to which is known.[27] So it is difficult to share Michel Péraldi's view that these activities, initially tolerated because they were marginal and considered as inoffensive, have gradually started to represent a danger for the established order: 'So transnational informal commerce is so threatening for the established order only because it assumes the singular appearance of a resistance associated with the economic pragmatism of a political economy, the economy of the personal bond and of the primacy of relationships, which invalidates and renders obsolete the principle of bureaucratic organization as the basis of the ethics by which states attempt to "embed" the economic realm into the social order'.[28]

To speak of resistance in this context would doubtless be an exaggeration. Thus small or medium shopkeepers are mainly after income, profit, monetary resources. They do not think of their activity as a politicized or even politicizable. It is just an activity like others, tolerated all the more insofar as it can be largely managed and ipso facto controlled. The fact that these activities are allowed shows that the political authorities are aware of an effective reality, difficult if not impossible to modify, and that – on the basis of this reality imposed on them – they make it work for them, they try to get inside it so as to derive some benefit from it. Since these activities cannot be banned, a flexible and astute understanding of the security mechanisms makes it possible, rather, to limit the boundaries of the acceptable. On the one hand, the government turns a blind eye to the continual flows of goods – or even persons – who violate the geographic, normative and legal frontiers with the precise aim of fighting poverty, unemployment, underemployment, and destitution: in other words, they act in accordance with the very logic of the security pact. Considered as a survival tactic – which is not necessarily the case, even it remains within acceptable limits – the informal sphere is thus considered as something which this *laissez-faire* can keep under control.[29] But, on the other hand, these activities are largely managed by different networks of power, directly by people at court or indirectly via the many different forms of political supervision, RCD cells, activities organized by the Tunisian embassies or consulates abroad, associations linked to the party, or celebrations sponsored by it.[30]

Finally, the thesis of a possible undermining of the established order rests on the idea that personal bonds and the primacy of personal relations act against state regulation. All the examples mentioned so far suggest, on the contrary, that the exercise of power passes precisely via these social relations and personal bonds.[31] These remarks, furthermore, converge with other aspects of the research carried out by Michel Péraldi and his colleagues. The restrictive measures set up by the European states, notably by France, but also certain Tunisian measures, have transformed the circuits and the nature of informal commerce, bringing new actors onto the stage.[32] So, ever since the end of the 1980s, we have witnessed a decline in the traffic of 'shopping bags' and an increase in the number of 'containers' – in other words, a decline in the small-scale and more or less individual craftsman's traffic and a growth in much more highly structured channels that require much more powerful financial and political support. In particular, all these activities, like theft, and trafficking of every kind, including drug trafficking, are known to the police services. Yet the defrauders, thieves, criminals, and delinquents are not arrested. Detailed records are forever being updated and files completed and, when the right time comes, they make it possible for punishment to be meted out. *Laissez-faire* needs to be understood in this sense, too: liberty is caught within the meshes of fear, of the potential threat of legitimate punishment. For 'we all have something to reproach ourselves with'.[33]

For those who govern, it is thus less a matter of controlling economic activity than contributing to the definition of its image and shape.[34] *Laissez-faire* also makes it possible to encompass things which the central power cannot control. It encompasses them all the better because there are representations, and even myths, which give an added consistency to the view of *laissez-faire* as liberty. In Tunisia, these myths are mainly comprised of the beylical *imaginaire* of a state that is foreign to society and of the autonomy of entrepreneurs.[35] *Laissez-faire* is a mechanism which thus reveals itself as a technique of discipline too, since it permits an increase in the number of opportunities for punishing and designating the 'enemies', whether they be Islamists, delinquents, defrauders, traffickers or crooks. *Laissez-faire* is a technique of control because, as opposed to what the common liberal view claims, there is 'nothing natural about it'.[36]

Economic integration by any means

The major preoccupation is employment. At present, the official unemployment rate is hovering at around 15 per cent, but specialists estimate that it is actually somewhere around 20 per cent or even higher. The fall in figures that has been registered over the last few years seems essentially due to the social handling of unemployment.[37] Recent developments in the labour market can only go to increasing this preoccupation: the employment content of growth is forever decreasing, the reconversion of the textile industry seems difficult, the – relatively new – phenomenon of young graduates is merely getting worse, and job creation takes place in sectors where activity is cyclical and unqualified.[38]

The Banque tunisienne de solidarité; *guaranteed credit*

The *Banque tunisienne de solidarité* (BTS) is one of the fetish instruments of the public powers. It is a security mechanism conceived in order to foster access to jobs and to develop small jobs that just guarantee survival. The BTS reveals the place occupied by credit in the security pact.

Its origins lie back in the middle of the 1990s, when the restructuring of the banks definitively excluded the smallest farmers from access to the *Banque nationale agricole* (BNA). Within the framework of economic liberalization, the idea of establishing funds for the latter, on the model – by now known throughout the world – of the Grameen Bank, started to sprout. By lending money to members who coopt themselves, this organization makes it possible to exploit social pressures to ensure excellent rates of repayment. However, on the pretext of possible Islamist infiltration, the initiatives made up to the mid-1990s were all turned down, and it was President Ben Ali in person, who, on 7 November 1997, announced the creation of the *Banque tunisienne de solidarité*.[39] The language used on this occasion took up the idea that 'small jobs', 'local work' and 'craft trades' should fill the deficit in employment created by liberalization. The role of the BTS would be to help those excluded from upgrading to find financing. Gradually, however, the bank's field of intervention has grown, notably after the establishment of the *Fonds national pour l'emploi* (FNE – National Employment Fund or 21.21, from its post-code) and the realization of the high rate of unemployment among graduates.[40] It now finances more consequential plans, such as opening surgeries or IT services.

Before the activities of this bank could get started, donors (the World Bank and the *Agence française de développement*, for instance) had planned to take part in financing it. But an examination of the modes of action of the BTS eventually dissuaded aid agencies from getting involved in capital: the project turned out to be unsustainable and totally dependent on annual refinancing.[41] The banks in Tunisia then capitalized the BTS, fully aware that they would not receive the necessary return on their investment and that they would never be repaid. They did this, either out of conviction (since this was a request made by the Head of State), or out of self-interest (tax exemptions were offered, to overcome the reluctance of some of them). Tunisian officials have always denied that repayments were low and that there were unpaid bills. However, they were unable to convince foreign financiers. It is impossible for an outside observer to verify the accuracy of either of these analyses, but one question can hardly be overlooked, a question that Tunisian bankers generally ask in concert: how can the BTS achieve positive results, when the rate of bad debts is crushing in the banking sector, and the environment in Tunisia fosters non-repayment? The absence or low level of repayments needs to be analysed in the same terms as bad debts – as mechanisms of protection at the heart of the security pact.

Be this as it may, the capital of the BTS was 'swallowed up' in the very first year and the state, since then, has had to bail it out. But this should not be interpreted as a slide or a failure. This result was unavoidable – this was the very reason for donors not to participate – and, in fact, the BTS had been instructed to operate as a hole in the wall rather than as a bank. The specific organization of the institution confirms this decision: the BTS is a 'bank without bailiffs or secretaries, or drivers, *or files, or reference numbers*' to symbolize precisely its closeness to the beneficiaries of loans and to avoid bureaucratization.[42] It might rather be said, with one Tunisian banker, that it is 'a credit line with a social purpose'. Actually, the bank lends without guarantee and on the basis of a mere interview with the potential beneficiary of credit. It is difficult to know how the money is distributed, but it goes without saying that while the number of beneficiaries has stayed high,[43] access to BTS microcredit is made all the easier if the candidate for a loan is a member of one of the various associations linked to the party; the bank's services also make their decisions on the basis of files provided by these associations, the RCD cells, the *omda* or the police. The desire to control microfinance politically, when it was at that time developing on the margins of legality, was real enough. Thus, Ali Narâghi has shown how the independent associations involved in this activity have interpreted the creation of the BTS as a form of administrative supervision.[44] Microcredit thus became the object of an extremely strict juridical supervision.[45] As for all other kinds of interference, it would, however, be reductive and even wrong to interpret the creation of the BTS solely as an instrument of control, of discipline and clientelism. As a mode of the security pact, the function of the bank of the poor is to foster integration into the professional world. The disciplinary dimension is merely one of the indirect consequences of this desire to guarantee stability and security.

Young people, between control and laissez-faire

According to the latest report of the World Bank, the level of expenditure dedicated to the active handling of unemployment in Tunisia is high, representing as it does 1.5 per cent of the GNP, which corresponds to the upper tranche of what is spent by countries in the OECD. However, this expenditure affects a much smaller number of people – five per cent of the active population in Tunisia, as opposed to ten per cent in the OECD – essentially because it is young people who arouse the greatest anxiety among the Tunisian authorities. In one sense, they are right: youth unemployment is an objectively explosive fact, given the fact that the latter apparently represent over three-quarters of all unemployed.[46] According to 2004 figures, the rate of unemployment was 37 per cent for ages 15–17, 32 per cent for 17–19, 29 per cent for 20–24 and still 22 per cent for 20–29. This is an all the more explosive fact as young graduates are most severely affected: unemployment afflicts up to 40 per cent of young people aged 20–24 who have graduated or have studied at university for at least one year. Furthermore, those aged less than 25 years often find work in agriculture, a particularly unstable activity, and in the textile industry, a sector in a state of severe crisis. This preoccupation is recognized by the highest authorities of the state. In 2004, the first core cabinet meeting, a proper decision-making authority devoted to youth leisure activities was commented on by the official agency TAP in these terms: 'These measures show that the supervision of young people, the need for power to be permanently prepared to listen to their worries, and the desire to associate them with the exercise of responsibility, figure among the constants of the avant-gardist social policy of President Ben Ali, who is untiringly targeting both national and regional development plans, particularly in the area of employment, on young people'.[47] The setting up of various measures, the establishment of a national consultation of young people every five years, and the creation, in 2002, of an *Observatoire national de la jeunesse* (National Youth Observatory) give this preoccupation concrete form.

The difficulty experienced by young people when it comes to integrating into economic life suggests another potential criticism of the thesis of the repression of the 'economically powerful'. It is not just the 'great' and the 'rich' who need to be controlled and, should the case arise, repressed; the whole population needs to be susceptible to security mechanisms. This explains the extent of the efforts set in motion to extend the pact to this sector of the population. Once they have finished their studies, and given the high level of unemployment, they are just as much encouraged to find a job as to go to a job centre. These centres, recently set up as a one-stop agency, provide them with help and advice.[48] They thus have access to vocational training, and to financing, from the BTS, for projects – thanks to cheap credit over a period of 10 or 15 years, to help with setting up small companies, and thanks also to programmes of professional integration. In 2000, the *Fonds national pour l'emploi* (National Employment Fund) was created to help young people to get an education, reintegrate themselves and gain new qualifications. Vocational training under the title of 'Initiation to professional life' was developed for those holding a Master's (SVP1) or the baccalaureate (SVP2), so that they could be temporarily recruited at very low wages (less than the minimum wage) by public or private enterprises, with public financing. We could also cite the establishment of employment-education contracts or funds for professional integration and adaptation. Work sites (*'chantiers de l'emploi'*) are offering young people a job in exchange for financial benefits, some 60 DT per day for a fortnight on-site, or 4 DT per day. They are being used more and more, and in rural milieus they provide a complement to the family income and represent an attempt to limit the exodus from the countryside.[49]

All these measures are mainly aimed at bringing down unemployment and guaranteeing a vital minimum for young people. At the same time, they provide new modes of control. It has to be admitted that young people are reluctant to join the party. There are no figures for the RCD, but it is officially accepted that the proportion of young people who join associations is no more than two per cent, which suggests a disaffection, a veritable rejection of a supervision that they deem to be burdensome, out-of-date and, in addition, relatively ineffective when it comes to obtaining a job.[50] So, given that it is difficult to get them to affiliate to the party or its youth organizations (*Chabiba al Madrassia*), they are introduced into a system of professional observation. Employment measures then function as a form of disciplining, in which unemployment is seen as being 'abnormal', employment or a surrogate for employment as the norm. The preoccupation with security is also expressed by the way aid is targeted: those who have not graduated are barely if at all affected by the active programmes of employment aid, which are targeted essentially to 'dangerous populations', young graduates and men.[51] In order to take up the few available jobs, you have to be ever more loyal, and in particular more zealous than your competitor.

In spite of the voluntarist discourse, the continuing level of unemployment among the young suggests that the measures and help available are barely effective. The informal sector remains an obligatory passage if they are to enter active life,[52] while going abroad is ever more attractive. According to official figures, two thirds of young Tunisians would like to leave and, unlike the previous tendencies, this phenomenon apparently extends to young women – over 50 per cent of them are candidates for emigration.[53] This choice of the exit option is an unprecedented situation, one that is far from desirable as far as Tunisia's image goes, but it is a tolerable situation in the view of the country's authorities. The strategy of the 'centrifuge' does, after all, make it possible for people who cannot be integrated to be expelled from society. This strategy is all the more accepted in that it is applied in a discreet and disguised way. So, officially, there are no (or very few) young Tunisians who head off abroad illicitly – those who do take the leap into the dark are mainly Africans, Libyans, or indeed Algerians or Moroccans. Still officially, Tunisia is not a point of departure, but sometimes merely an intermediary passage for ships setting off from Libya. The facts, though difficult to establish, are nonetheless more ambiguous, and the real number of departures continues to increase. This tolerance reveals another side of the security measures: it is less a matter of really finding a solution to a problem – a job for these young people – than of circumscribing dangerous populations so as to ensure that order and tranquillity ultimately reign.

The *Fonds de solidarité nationale*, or the intolerable shadow

The security mechanism *par excellence*, that which has been made most visible and has become the symbol of the Tunisian mode of government, is the *Fonds de solidarité nationale* (FSN – Fund of National Solidarity). Better known by the name 26.26, from the number of its post code, it was – in the official prose description – a fund aimed at 'eradicating the zones of shadow', eliminating poverty and providing 'basic needs' to populations which had hitherto been excluded from them. Since 2000, while the Fund has continued to operate despite having overrun the limit date, it has not been deemed necessary to develop another argument. But the facts are there: the Tunisian government's social policy now also passes via a solidarity that is imposed on and extended to all citizens. Unlike the other instruments of redistribution, which to a large extent are still in place, the 26.26 has some rather unusual modes of financing and functioning.[54] So at least three elements characterize this new technique: the story of the 'shadow' and the spotlighting of individuals and their activities; the theme of consensus and the participation of all in the elimination of poverty; and the rhetoric of solidarity as a pendant to capitalist and political discipline. Taken together, they bring out one of the fundamental aspects of the pact: the war on poverty is a question of security, because everyone has to play a part in the existing social order. The Fund is thus a fully fledged control mechanism: it controls zones and individuals merely by localizing them and describing them as 'poor'; but it also controls the non-poor, thanks to their 'consensual' participation in solidarity.

The mechanism of compulsory donations

These days it is a well-known fact that voluntary gifts to the 26.26 are largely obligatory: all enterprises and companies have to pay it 2 DT per employee per month; likewise, entrepreneurs are deemed to pay in significant sums at one period or another of the year, often on 7 November, 8 December (Solidarity Day), during an electoral period, or else to attract the benevolence of the authorities, to be seen in the local paper, and to 'ensure or buy a future for themselves'. This obligation is doubtless implicit, but no less real. An entrepreneur who ostentatiously withheld from this duty of solidarity would risk having a hard time of it, encountering tax inspections, blocked access to public markets, and administrative hassles. Bar managers, for instance, are obliged to pay a sum of between 5,000 DT and 10,000 DT per year, on pain of having their licences revoked – these licences being an arbitrary and revocable permit on the part of the governor. The Governor of Jendouba openly warned in public that there was no alternative: either individuals participated in the 26.26 and kept their permits, or they would be replaced by the various people who were waiting in the wings . . .[55] Sometimes the gift requested is one in kind. Instead of levying the entrepreneur in cash, the latter is encouraged to build, at his own expense, a section of road or a canal in the name of the 26.26. In return for future markets with the state, the carrot dangled before his nose is an absence of any problems with the administration or, even more cynically, the maintenance of his accreditation. As for civil servants, they have to pay one day's salary per year, and farmers one per cent of their sales. In the law courts, the Attorney General sends round a circular ordering magistrates and clerks to give up part of their salaries, and even children, from kindergarten to high school, have to participate in this enforced solidarity. Tunisian subjects, whether they reside in Tunisia or abroad, are in addition constantly subjected to this pressure when they have to renew their papers, and in any administrative business. Finally, the state itself makes a substantial contribution to the Fund. It is very difficult to know with any precision how much is brought in by gifts: officially, from 1994 to 2000, an average of 15 MDT came into the 26.26, apart from budgetary endowments. But many observers were quick to shed doubt on these figure: the economist Mahmoud Ben Romdhane estimated the amount to be 24 MDT per year in 1999 for enterprises alone, in other words, twice as much, for example, as the official figure of 11.7 MDT recorded in 1997.[56] Economic circles estimated the figures for this period to be 40 MDT, of which 38 MDT were provided solely by big businessmen.[57]

It is all but impossible to have detailed data about the effective actions of the Fund other than those provided by the official accounts. Even donors have not managed to get hold of adequate information that would enable them to draw up an exhaustive inventory of social aid.[58] There is, so to speak, no real budget, no list of recipients, no flow charts of the management system, no distributional framework for the resources, and no evaluation of the actions undertaken. The analysis of one research centre, the CERES, led to a split between researchers faced with political interference, and finally entailed the non-publication of the complete report. This does not mean that the sums are not distributed: they are, even if in a discretionary and clientelist way, even if the effectiveness of the actions is not always certain, and even if not everything inevitably reaches its destination, as is claimed by the rumours about the 26.27 (an expression that ironically alludes to the 26.26; the '26.27' would be funded by money taken from the 26.26 by the associates of Ben Ali) or about the villas financed by the Fund.[59]

The operational rule is that everyone gives in the name of national solidarity. In the context described above, the means of pressurizing people and collecting their gifts vary from one head teacher to the next, from one director of the administration to the next, from one entrepreneur to the next, or from one representative of the party cell or *comité de quartier* to the next. On the local level, rivalry between cells or administrations sustains pressures, an atmosphere of intimidation, or even repressive practices. Nobody, in the hierarchy of junior or high schools, hospitals, law courts, administrations, public enterprises, or cells, wishes to come last in terms of the sums collected, and the race to reach high figures also operates as an effective mainspring for levying. That being said, there are resistances, and, over time, they increase. What is new is that they are attested by complaints received by the LTDH and the CNLT from parents whose children have been sent home from school, prevented from taking tests, or hit by the head teacher because they had not paid into the 26.26; or the increasing number of entrepreneurs who, in interviews, openly criticize the way the FSN operates and claim that they never give.[60] In spite of all this, the hostility can generally be expressed only in tenuous and nuanced forms. To express his disapproval, an entrepreneur contacted by the delegate from the business's head office and told to make a gift may initially decide not to give anything. But if the pressures become too urgent and if the derisory sums he has finally paid are not deemed to be sufficient, he will find it difficult not to give the sums requested if he does not want his business to be jeopardized.

In the same way, civil servants opposed to the payment of this tribute are, as often as not, forced to accept the deduction of one day's salary from their pay cheques, since the steps they have to take to refuse this practice are tedious and politically dangerous. They will express their disapproval by refusing to participate in the Solidarity Days or other exceptional celebrations that are all opportunities for giving. In the interviews I did, a significant number of entrepreneurs told me that, depending on the period, they had given to associations (for the police, for various party organizations and authorities), to the RCD, or . . . to the CNSS investigation – which clearly expresses the lack of distinction between taxation and non-state levies for most Tunisian citizens; ever since the end of the 1990s, priority had been given to the 26.26, and they gave only to this Fund. Another consideration, more down-to-earth but just as effective, explains the spread and acceptance of these obligatory gifts: to improve the financial viability of the FSN, the sums paid into it are deductible from the tax base.

It is particularly difficult to synthesize the different perceptions citizens and tax payers have of this specific technique of redistribution. Some claim that it is neither more nor less than a racket, others say that it is legitimate to finance a social policy by solidarity. Some see this payment as a form of tax, others as a gift, yet others as extortion. Two evaluations, contradictory but often found simultaneously within each individual, appear clearly: on the one hand, the exercise of a pressure is identical to the act of 'paying', since the latter requires recourse to the administrative or moral authority – the head teacher, the junior school teacher, the director of the administration, the boss; on the other hand, the 'payment' is indisputably considered as part of the security pact. However, perceptions change over time and the 26.26 has now been tamed. These days, some people are tired of giving, while others play the role of intermediaries for the Fund; some can be more openly daring than before in opposing the measure or pleading economic constraints so as not to pay, while others have quite simply integrated it into their system of constraints and their book-keeping. The publicizing of gifts, which for several years constituted one of the procedures of disciplinary pressure, has disappeared, which betrays an ambiguous development; on the one side, the FSN is definitively 'part of the Tunisian landscape' and of its mechanisms of control and supervision; on the other, the revenue from these Solidarity Days seems to be far from high and could indicate doubt, reluctance, and indeed resistance to payment. The administration too has tamed the 26.26. Whereas in the first years it felt itself to be partly dispossessed of a policy and in particular of its legitimating effects, these days it has found its true path and partly recovered its prerogatives.

The 26.26, a technique of subjection

Even if they can act as a burden on the balance sheets of enterprises, or rather some of them, the sums paid to the 26.26 are quantitatively not very significant. The arsenal of state interventions in social affairs has continually risen and the traditional instruments have maintained their importance.[61] But its visibility does suggest the motivations that underlie its implementation. It is a political discourse aimed at the middle classes, with the ambition of eliminating the main 'scourge' threatening order and security.[62] It is a desire for political control over the poor and for the elimination of the Islamists by using methods that the latter had themselves borrowed from the single party;[63] it is also an attempt to get round the pressures of the IMF and the World Bank on the basis of aid and budgetary expenditure. It is a supplementary instrument for arrangements between the business community and Carthage, resulting from the strong relation between, on the one hand, tolerance for the non-respect of certain rules or conflict resolution and, on the other, payment to the 26.26.[64] It is a means of recuperating, controlling and appropriating welfare and practices of charitable giving. It reveals the 'privatization of the state' insofar as the obligatory character of payment and the absence of all control by the public authorities mean that the 26.26 can be interpreted as a private tax system.[65] Finally, it is a symbol of the personalization of the power of Ben Ali, since the FSN was created on his initiative, he is its sole master – in the absence of any control by Parliament or the National Audit Office – and the measures implemented are carried out in his name and not in that of the state or an administration that is, moreover, often criticized.[66]

The 26.26 appears mainly as a security mechanism aimed to eliminate the 'shadow' and thereby forestall the dangers that poverty inevitably provokes. The demand for transparency is a discourse, but transparency is also a form of power. It is a process of subjection because it highlights the localization, the good will, and the activities of certain categories of the population, and makes it possible for procedures of evaluation and classification to operate. The 'deserving' poor person can benefit from bonuses by taking advantage of gifts from the 26.26; the 'undeserving' person is punished by being deprived of access to them. The central power's claim that it will eliminate the 'zones of shadow' makes it possible to create a space of legibility whose criteria are quite obviously defined by the state and by it alone. Aid to the poor has become a crucial component in the representation of the Tunisian central power, which makes the poor more visible but also, ipso facto, more controllable.

As a result, the 26.26 appears as one of the most significant techniques of control of the art of governing in Tunisia. Like the 'examination', in the analysis of discipline by Michel Foucault,[67] the FSN exerts a normalizing gaze and keeps everyone under surveillance; it demonstrates the subjection of those who are perceived as objects and the objectification of those who are subjected; in its exercise of power, it makes visible those subjects who need to be seen; it turns every individual into a case, an individual to be gauged, classified, trained, congratulated, held up as an example, corrected, excluded, normalized . . . Contrary to what is often affirmed, for example by opponents who make of it the symbol of a despotic and corrupt regime, this technique is not new – it has been used in Tunisia before, for instance during colonization: to finance the Universal Exhibition, a collection was organized from the tribes through the intermediary of the sheiks and local notables.[68] What *is* new, perhaps, is the mode assumed by this procedure of levying and control, with a certain rationalization of techniques, a rationalization that has actually been requested: 'Relying on solid experience acquired on the ground level in direct contact with the realities on which it is always acting, the National Solidarity Fund has reached its cruising speed, *having provided itself with a specific methodology*. Its interventions are now characterized by *the rationality imposed at every level by an acute sense of efficiency*'.[69]

In itself, this technique is frankly commonplace. We find it in Africa, now as before; it is used in Mexico as well as Iran.[70] The historians of Antiquity mention its use in Greece and Rome, and those of the French Ancien Régime also refer to it.[71] However, the comparisons concern merely the technique, not its meaning and its socio-political scope. In contemporary China, for example, decentralization makes it possible, on the pretext of a struggle against inequalities, to carry out an informal over-taxation and the enriching of notables and party cadres;[72] but the similarity ends there, since the levies are so high that they have led to a decline in rural revenue, which is not the case in Tunisia.

In addition, this disciplinary technique can work only because it is integrated into the networks of power in which individuals circulate. Entrepreneurs (though the same goes for individuals or families) are admittedly in a position to have to contribute to the 26.26, but they simultaneously act as its relays, since they are the intermediaries of the central power when it comes to levying employees; they benefit from other relations of force (salary discussions, working conditions, and so on) to exert pressure on them; they negotiate this payment in exchange for lower taxes, even for pure and simple tax exemption; they obtain a market, a contract, an administrative facility. The 26.26 can operate only because it finds an echo in the constant demands for security, protection, and facilitation on the part of economic actors. The intermediary elites and the notables, the social and professional hierarchy constitute indispensable links in the chain when it comes to collecting sums meant for the Fund: the entrepreneur with his employees, the head teacher with his staff, pupils and teachers, the director of administration with the civil servants he directs, the *omda* with the cell leaders, the cell leader with craftsmen and independent workers. This role can easily be transformed into a source of local power. Here too, current practices are somewhat reminiscent of past practices, under the beylicate as well as during the Protectorate. At the time, this collection was a source of profit for its intermediaries.

Be this as it may, the population pays too since the demand goes through the notables, the partisan elites and the qualified intermediaries of the central power. 'Thus the tyrant enslaves his subjects by means of one another',[73] as Étienne de la Boétie emphasized. In a similar way, the very acceptance of the principle of the Fund is rooted in popular attachment to the practices of solidarity that were reactivated in the 1980s. The Islamist movement, indeed, had envisaged as much in its programmes, but the very legitimacy of solidarity is anchored in a conception of Islam which has nothing political about it. The principles of redistribution and social development are, indeed, part of the history of the construction of the Tunisian national state and the funds, whether private or public, were part of this logic. In the case of 26.26 as in the others, 'power passes through individuals. It is not applied to them'.[74]

A non-liberal vision of the security pact

Be that as it may, paying attention to desires, needs and demands is not the same as democratization. The very conception of social action is strictly circumscribed. Reading the official texts and written proof, analysing the speeches or interviews of political and administrative leaders, helps us to understand that the latter mainly have a security-, economy- and state-based approach to the social realm. It is a matter, first and foremost, of 'defending society' against the chaos that would ensue from an uncontrolled social situation, against a hypothetical rebellion stirred by the dissatisfaction of the most underprivileged strata, against resistance and even opposition sustained by a low level of integration into society, and against a wave of Islamism fuelled by poverty and unemployment. This conception betrays the omnipresence of the 'Islamist danger' in official rhetoric, but also in the way it analyses political competition. It also reveals the significance of the 'danger of desocialization' linked to international economic vicissitudes, in particular liberal openness. Finally, it suggests an economicist reading of Islam, which it views as the fruit of poverty and low levels of economic and social integration, even though several pieces of research have long since undermined this interpretation. This conception is all the more significant in Tunisia, as it is still very widespread in diplomatic circles and the milieus of international cooperation.

The historical trajectory of Tunisia also circumscribes social action, not so much as a continuity of practices, but as an *imaginaire*. This latter is largely built around the idea that the control exerted by central power is direct and absolute. The beylical administration, at the end of the nineteenth century in particular, took poverty into consideration, viewing it thereafter as a state responsibility. As the historian Abdelhamid Larguèche suggests in his work on the poor and marginal in Tunis, although activities of charity and benevolence continued to be practised completely autonomously, power under Hussein politicized a certain proportion of social action from this point on. In this statist conception, the fight against poverty had clearly ideological aims: 'Civil society in action, although broader (albeit structural) was henceforth perceived in the sources as a poor relation or a complement of true charity: that of the prince, and that of power. The loyal attitude of the traditional elites [. . .] is part of a form of ideological mystification which, by glorifying the prince and, behind the prince, the state, blots out and crushes society. The political dimension ends up overturning the image of the real, transforming the charity of princes into the model of virtue and the major example proposed to the social body as a whole'.[75] The desire for social control and supervision was obvious, as was the determination to preserve the monopoly of the interpretation of social practices.

Drawing on the same motivations, the colonial administration instrumentalized this myth, presented as a tradition, in order to impose its control over the Regency. Since at least the 1930s, the Destour and its successors played a fundamental role in defining and implementing social policies, with the constant aim of ensuring the hegemony of the central power. The desire to construct the nation as a unique representative of society then led the majority trend within the national movement to resort to domination.[76] After independence, in the framework of national construction and the struggle against the presumed partisans of Ben Youssef, against communism and parochialism, the party bodies monopolized access to social services in the rural world, the gift of the sheep for Eid, the organization and financing of Ramadan meals, aid for the beginning of the school year, the distribution of scholarships for students, and the selection of destitute families granted free health care or benefits offered by various of the government's social programmes. Although autonomous charity and voluntary work did exist, these were often instrumentalized. On the other hand, the desire for absolute control is a recent characteristic that dates from the police-oriented evolution of modes of government from the mid-1980s onwards. It hardly matters whether this evolution is to be explained by the weight of logics and reflexes dominated by security considerations, or by the routine operation and even increasing intensity of policing practices and apparatuses. The fact remains that social policy is now indissociable from the disciplinary dimension of the Tunisian government.

In these conditions, the response to the demand for security and prosperity has taken particular forms. In the logic of the single party, the population can benefit from these different forms of welfare only on condition that they participate concretely in the party's political economy: they must attend cell meetings, come and applaud when a minister or the President in person passes through, help gather information and take part in surveillance, contribute to gathering funds . . . And if a certain destitute family does not come to meeting, even if there are practical or health reasons for this, aid can be challenged.[77] This hegemony is illustrated by the impossibility for another mechanism to work, namely charity, which has the specific feature of being an individual practice and, being a good action, is circumscribed to the private sphere.[78] It is all the more marked in that there used to exist in Tunisia, as throughout Muslim world, an active practice of charity. It has gradually been brought into line, precisely because the central power found it hard to tolerate any form of competition. Like other security measures, social policies are a prerogative of the state, which poses as the best protector: 'The state knows best who needs aid [. . .]. The FSN has, in addition, permitted the channelling of gifts and small private donations',[79] as the official press put it, echoing Bourguiba's statement that 'only the force of the state can guarantee the security and well-being of individuals'.[80]

There is no evergetism in Tunisia, and this is doubtless one of the most explicit symptoms of the totalitarian character of the exercise of power in Tunisia. Paul Veyne has shown the implications of evergetism:[81] the spontaneous character of generosity; a personal relation between the evergete and the common people; a contribution to public expenses that was not seen as a form of tax, thanks to its non-obligatory nature; and, above all, political pluralism. On the contrary, ever since independence, the central power has constantly monopolized social action; Nahda's planned solidarity fund was never really implemented. In any case, the FSN is directly inspired by the

Islamists, and the plan formed by the most ardent opponents of the 'Ben Ali regime' is known down to the smallest details thanks to the exploiting of the Nahda archives that were confiscated when the movement was eradicated. Contrary to a widespread idea, the impossibility of any competition was not linked to the religious character of the movement, which had vowed to challenge the state monopoly. Any form of charity, however depoliticized and secular, is banned: witness the recent case of a section of the Lion's Club that had decided to help the poorest in a certain district to pay for the Eid sheep and, with this in mind, had on its own initiative undertaken an investigation to select three or four families from among the most deprived. On the day of the hand-out, the delegate and the president of the local RCD cell intervened to give their own list and to stop anything being given to the families selected by the Club members. The latter refused, and no gifts were distributed.[82] Even a microsocial activity is viewed as potentially subversive, not as such, but in its hypothetical capacity to appear critical, in its possible aptitude for acting as an example, and in its symbolic dimension. As for the members of the Rotary Club, they soon realized this: in 1996 they started to pay money and give computers directly to the Fund; a short time later, they decided to merge their charitable activities with those of the 26.26.[83]

'It's the price to be paid': negotiation and the creation of a 'consensus'

A certain amount of research focused on the practices of resistance to authoritarian regimes now emphasizes the coexistence of very powerful restrictions and of the systematic and tolerated bypassing of these same restrictions.[84] As we have seen, this paradox is sometimes analysed as the effect of a system of power that works with control and tolerance so long as the regime is not threatened. However, this effect can be understood as a mechanism of 'resistance' built into relations of power and, simultaneously, as a practice of compromise, arrangement and negotiation, of a security mechanism that integrates intervention and *laissez-faire*.[85]

Permanent negotiation, the cement of the social order

I would like to turn to this dimension, starting with a rather strange but frequently heard expression in Tunisia: 'It's the price to be paid.' Rapacity, embezzlement and the corruption of the presidential entourage, the systematic draining of the economy or of certain places, the political use of taxation or of social programmes, the tight control of employment and economic opportunities, or the absence of free speech and critical thought constitute the repetitive themes of the debates within the Tunisian bourgeoisie and middle class. But these criticisms are usually accompanied by an 'it's the price to be paid' – the price to be paid for security and the absence of violence ('Islamist', it is often implied), for stability and prosperity in business, for the maintaining of notability and the hope of social climbing . . .

What is the meaning of this constant theme? Is it a simple exchange in which everyone benefits? What role is played by repression and fear? What is the influence of official rhetoric on the economic miracle? What is the element of rumour and fantasy? Whatever the answers given to these questions, it is undeniable that the formula expresses a certain compromise with disciplinary practices, even if the latter are partly experienced as such. Discipline functions much less by repression than by the central power's regulatory capacity as ensured by social and economic mechanisms, as well as by its ability to provide a standard of living, continued growth and stability. It is for this reason that the recent economic crisis (particularly severe in 2002 and 2003) did not, perhaps, represent any real danger for the central power, but did suggest the fault lines and weaknesses in such regulation: the pursuit of a drop in growth, a rise in unemployment, international uncertainties weighing on the national economy, relative restrictions on credit and certain forms of welfare – all could undermine the implicit security pact. With the crisis and the shrinking of advantages to be shared out, the politicization of the economic and social realms appears more clearly. The taxes hitherto tolerated start to appear burdensome, politicized clientelism starts to benefit fewer people, and the absence of critical speech becomes irritating and even oppressive. The concealed political dimension reappears. Of course, the policing and repressive nature of this is never completely absent and growing dissatisfaction is also explained by the increased zest of the disciplinary machine and the difficulty, for the different police authorities, of not using the effective instruments in their possession. However, this dimension does not appear to be the main one, and for the vast majority of individuals, it is eclipsed by the force of security mechanisms; the inconvenience of a seizing up of the economic and social cogs is tolerable so long as the bases of the pact are not affected. Another way of expressing this tacit acceptance is precisely the way it brings out the couple 'security-dependence'.[86] 'The price to be paid' is just this dependence; the more power bestows security, the more it makes people dependent, and the more able it is to subject them.

What holds society together is thus permanent negotiation. Not negotiation in the political domain, since subjection there is total, but the many and permanent possibilities of social and economic negotiations. In a country where growth stems mainly from the multitude of small entrepreneurs and craftsmen, the police cannot govern alone, neither can corruption. There is neither absolute power, nor averred opposition, nor any clear taking of sides. Tunisia floats in a 'mainly minor-key haze':[87] everything is generally negotiated smoothly, with a light touch, on the margins. Wages are officially negotiated every three years, the violations of rules and the tolerance of informality are negotiated too, as are the implementations of legal decisions, listing on the

Stock Exchange, or entering the upgrading programme . . . One's way of life is negotiated too: it is made up of dangerous alliances, of disapproving silences, of being made financially dependent, of redistribution, of the sharing out of advantages. Political control is partly made possible by the significance of social control that facilitates the integration of the single party and the national organisms, which oils the wheels of disciplinary practices and excludes blockages and absences in negotiation. To break this subjection would require above all that the outlines of possible compromises be indicated so that a degree of political autonomy may appear. In the Tunisian case, the latter seems extremely limited as a result of the generalized confusion – maintained by daily discursive practices – between compromise and consensus.[88]

The voluntarist construction of consensus

The myth of consensus appears as a central technology of power. The consensus contributes to persuading citizens that the measures adopted have been adopted by them, or at least with their consent. Ipso facto, it weakens the perception (recent but now significant) of the constraints of the political and the frustrations born from the absence of public debates. This consensus is a construction. It is a fiction which the central power attempts to naturalize, in particular through repetitive speeches and by the rhetoric of *the* middle class and of Tunisian-ness.[89]

The reign of consensus does not, however, belong alone to relations between 'state' and 'society': it impregnates all social relations. Thus, no board of directors can be conceived without unanimity; if the consensus is broken, people are shocked, and the person who questions the consensus is looked at askance.[90] To highlight these consensuses does, of course, show that the different economic and social actors take part in drawing up policies, that they accept choices which thereby become unquestionable; it also shows the unity of a social body whose members, in spite of divergences in their positions, cannot oppose each other.[91] This appears a subtly disciplinary interpretation of a tangible and objective reality: the 'consensus' in fact results from relations of force, from permanent negotiations, and sometimes from coercion, all of which are covered up; if you refuse it, you are opposing the natural social order. When donors and liberal entrepreneurs suggest that there is a contradiction between consensus about the operation of the economic world (and even about public policy), and, on the other hand, the archaic nature of a sometimes burdensome disciplinary control, they take at face value the existence of a consensus, and identify it with democracy.[92] The analysis of economic and social mechanisms that I have been carrying out throughout the present work suggests, rather, that consensus is definitely one of the most powerful cogs in the machinery of voluntary servitude, in particular because it is constructed on a violence that is silent and painless, but no less real.

This situation is not found in Tunisia alone. Research into Italy between the wars has shown the significance of the process of unification and the construction of a consensus in the exercise of Fascist power. It was realized at the very heart of the state, whose main function it was to unify and integrate complexity and social pluralism, to guarantee harmony (thanks in particular to the single party), and to promote moral, political, and economic unity.[93] In Singapore, the construction of the consensus was based on the ideology of communitarianism and pragmatism, the construction of a 'national interest', that of survival in a hostile environment.[94] In Tunisia, consensus is presented as an art of governing harmoniously and as a characteristic ethos of the 'people' or of the 'national identity'. It is a 'fine dust'[95] which conceals the vulgarity of relations of force, of struggles, and of negotiations. Nonetheless, the gap between the complex reality and the language of consensus is not complete; current social relations are interpreted in the light of a history that is forever instrumentalizing the ideal of singleness and of an *imaginaire* comprised of a centralized power and of the negation of alterity.[96]

The motto 'May God give the victory to the man who takes power' expresses this mode of government in which the legitimacy of power resides in its very exercise, in which consensus and unity take precedence over conflicts, opposition and diversity.[97] This myth is forever being reactivated and updated. First, by the struggle for national liberation and by the dominant interpretation – rarely questioned up until now – of the creation of national unity by the voluntarist action of the *Zaîm*. The Tunisian nation, 'which I have created with my own hands during a struggle of almost a quarter of a century, which I have created in its entirety out of a dust of individuals',[98] as Bourguiba put it, is presented as a creation, a break with a past made of chaos and meaninglessness and in particular of divisions and intestine struggles between tribes, between villages, between town and countryside, of dissensions and rivalries within the elite,[99] and thus by denying the 'other Tunisia', that of the South, or archaic lifestyles, of shadow, of poverty, of insecurity, but also that of conflicts, of divisions, of tribalisms and egoisms.[100] Then, by the identification of this nation with Bourguiba and 'the "natural" choice of the single party, the incarnation of the supposed desire for unity felt by the entire people'.[101] Finally, by the fuelling of a nationalism that is still powerful in the terms of 'Tunisian-ness', both as 'civic patriotism' and as 'communitarian nationalism'.[102]

The violence of consensus and the ideology of silence

Now as before, the 'Change' appears as a choice of consensus, born from a pact that embraced all the forces of the country and expressing a total acquiescence in the modes of government, in the silence imposed, in the ways one understands the 'extremists' and in one's attitude towards them . . . The National Pact of 1988, 'the basis of an unshakeable consensus'[103] was based on a 'devastating demand for unanimity [. . .] lying at the foundations of the present regime'.[104] Everyone refers to these catch-all words – such as Islam, nationalism, and reformism – which blot out any dissent.[105] The illusion of the unity and harmony of all in the One – whether this be state, nation, party or Head of State – is still current: it is a matter of 'confronting together our difficulties as if we were a single man', of uniting citizens 'around their patriotism and their spirit of sacrifice'.[106]

Walter Benjamin showed how compromise, 'whatever contempt it may display for all overt violence, remains a product belonging to the spirit of violence, for the effort that leads to compromise does not bear its reasons within itself, but receives them from outside, precisely from the adverse effort, since no compromise, even one freely accepted, can avoid the character of a constraint'.[107] Following him, Étienne Balibar reminds us that consensus, 'far from constituting a condition of democracy, constitutes a redoubtable form of political violence' and 'bears on opinions, customs and manners, and cultural values'. He quotes an expression of Albert Hirschmann, going on to explain that 'what democracy needs [. . .] is a "regular regime of conflict". On condition, of course, that this state of conflict be itself collectively controlled'.[108] *Pace* the upholders of 'consensual democracy', whether sycophants of the regime or 'democratic' opponents, consensus is 'imbued with implicit violence';[109] consensus presents itself as a fundamental ideal of pacification, and at the same time its function is to conceal the violence of a certain exercise of power. It disguises the government's strategies and interferes in relations of force, exercising a repressive if not disciplinary power – for example bringing down an entrepreneur, limiting the activities of a trade unionist, putting the wind up a civil servant, marginalizing an opponent, or imposing 'social death' on an Islamist. Consensus is developed in the fault lines of the disciplinary and security-based relations of power, proceeding simultaneously from violence and its attenuation, as well as the covering up of inequalities and favouritisms. So it is a set of words, but also of perceptions, of ways of thinking and acting in the political space where the 'minor key' rules.

Consensus in Tunisia results from an antiliberal criticism of pluralism, in a reading of state and relations of force derived from the work of Schmitt:[110] the multiplicity, pluralism, and conflicting nature of social forces harbour chaos; the reduction of these can be achieved only on the basis of the unity of a state form and the naturalization of the consensus. The distinction friend/enemy is thus fundamental in the dominant Tunisian discourse: the homogeneity of the Tunisian people comes from its unified action against the external enemy – colonial power, external forces that support internal dissensions, imported ideologies, the Islamist *internationale* . . . Patriotism and nationalism constitute indissociable correlates of consensus, and force everyone to forge a single identification with the nation: exploiting the registers of duality – with/against the nation, inside/outside, for/against the national interest – all opposition is a betrayal, a complicity with an external enemy. One of the organic intellectuals of the 'Ben Ali regime' summarizes the President's project in the following words: his aim is 'to ensure the invulnerability of Tunisia, within the context of a society which is justly balanced and within which difference becomes concordance, and dialogue consensus. This will forever banish the spectres of fanaticism and extremism, and all imported ideologies. There will henceforth be but one single way, that of pluralism [*sic* – B.H.]. There will henceforth be but one ideology, that of patriotism attached to Tunisia, and to Tunisia alone.'[111]

In fact, citizenship is understood in Tunisia only as a relation with nationalism and patriotism. Bourguiba said as much: 'I want you to be convinced that this state is your tribe – the entire nation.'[112] The negation of pluralism and alterity prevents any deeper reflection on access to citizenship and its exercise, confining Tunisians to the status of 'subjects' or 'individuals', not 'citizens', in the formula that is generally used in the Tunisian opposition.[113] Whatever we may think of these substantives, citizenship can be understood only in a scheme in which the individual can, alternately, envisage support and opposition for the state and the central power, in which he can, alternately, pass from obedience to refusal, from command to resistance.[114] In Tunisia, oppositions, criticisms, dissensions, frustrations and disagreements do of course exist; but they are excluded from the public domain, pushed, so to speak, into an enforced privatization.[115]

Consensus, that powerful technology of power, is thus also indissociable from silence. The consent of individuals passes through support and silence, through personal interest and latent violence imposed. 'The capitalists will never take to the bush,' as we have seen: consensus allows the aforesaid capitalists to convince themselves that they will be 'only slightly affected by the negative effects of the regime'; that this imposed consensus 'isn't so serious', that it does not endanger them 'whereas frontal opposition is fatal'.[116] But, by staying silent, they accept positions that go against their interests, and even against their activities and their very way of seeing the world. Because they gradually find themselves being fettered by their own silence, these contradictions are inevitably silenced and even covered up. This fettering has been described as an 'ideology of silence':[117] this ethos constitutes a protection for individuals who do not wish to oppose a dominant order without thereby renouncing what they think. The ideology of silence consolidates a whole order, by masking over the disquieting complexity of reality. But, in spite of Carl Schmitt's statements, this silence is by no means an expression of freedom:[118] it is, rather, a tactic and a compromise, neither complete acquiescence nor complete political rejection. Consensus, and the ideology of silence, are more akin to those 'insidious leniencies, unavowable petty cruelties, small acts of cunning, calculated methods',[119] as Michel Foucault described them in his criticism of the disciplinary exercise of power.

Consensus is an essential element of discourse: it produces knowledge and a normalization of thought and understanding; it creates significant effects of power, starting with the amnesia and silence that spread throughout society, in everyone's activities and everyday behaviour. Among themselves, in board meetings and at dinner parties, in universities and cafes, in the National Assembly and on television, people never diverge from the consensus. The following pages are dedicated to one of the most significant utterances of the consensus, namely the 'reformist tradition' of Tunisia.

Part IV

Discipline and Reform

In Tunisia as elsewhere, an analysis of the 'authoritarian regime' that rested content with explanations in terms of violence and coercion, of populist demagogy and manipulation, of bad faith, ignorance and illusion, of corruption and opportunism, of delusory discourse and over-simplistic pragmatism, or even of discipline and normalization, would be insufficient to grasp the dynamics of the exercise of power. Our preceding discussions of the integration of mechanisms of authority in the Tunisian economy and the increasing number of procedures of negotiated compromise with political domination have shown that such an analysis would evade the question of the full and often active participation of internal actors and the massive support of foreign and international actors who express, in financial and diplomatic terms, their satisfaction with the receptivity of the Tunisian authorities to the 'necessary reforms'. After detailing the material procedures of this involvement, I would now like to turn more specifically to the attraction of political movements, that is to the myths, beliefs, passions, ideals and forms of behaviour, the aspirations and projects that form an integral and significant part of the exercise of power.[1]

This perspective allows us, I believe, to advance in the understanding of the Tunisian paradox that could be formulated in these terms: the practices and modes of government that are most often akin to training and control are largely accepted. Indeed, they are generally appreciated as a 'success' by donors, by foreign partners, and by Tunisian leaders, of course, but also to a great extent by the opposition and by the vast majority of the population. The economic model is a success, political voluntarism is a success, social policies are a success, the fight against extremism is a success . . . My hypothesis is that this positive vision has largely emerged from the problematization of the exercise of power in the terms of reformism.[2] In this last part, I would like to grasp, in all its complexity, what has gradually appeared to me as one of the most clearly structuring factors of 'voluntary servitude' and the 'good' Tunisian government.

Reformism must here be considered in the meaning specific to the Muslim world, and not the way it is generally interpreted as a political form opposed to revolution. This intellectual and political movement, born in the nineteenth century in the Ottoman Empire, was an attempt to respond to the challenges laid down by the European powers by adopting a whole series of reforms: political, juridical, military, educational and administrative. Throughout the twentieth century, this theme of reformism was reformulated, notably in Tunisia, where it became the expression of 'good' government: to be a reformist meant governing with moderation, being sensitive to openness to the international world while preserving national achievements and specific characteristics; it meant to enhance reform as a way of being and behaving.

Far be it from me to venture yet again into the abstract debate over the relation between economic reforms and the nature of the political regime – a debate whose inanity Max Weber had already brilliantly demonstrated, in particular in his writings on Russia[3] – nor, as far its application to Tunisia is concerned, over the relation between liberal reforms and authoritarianism.[4] My analysis tackles the exercise of power in Tunisia on the basis of a historical understanding of the idea of reform, taking the latter very widely, that is less in technical terms than in terms of people's thoughts and way of life, in other words, their ethos. With this in mind, I will set out from what is currently accepted by all specialists on Tunisia and the Ottoman Empire: the authoritarian character of the reforms, in the nineteenth century as well as today; what (following or in parallel with the theoretical work of Barrington Moore on authoritarianism as a conservative modernization) Aziz Krichen and Michel Camau have called 'authoritarian reformism', Clifford Geertz and Abdelbaki Hermassi 'authoritarian liberalism', and Clement Henry Moore a 'modern administrative dictatorship'.[5] My aim is to grasp reformism in all its historical depth, in other words to grasp it in its system of belief, so as to understand the proportion of support and positive values that it transmits, even when the practices related to it are restrictive and sometimes violent. I would therefore like to question the idea that 'reformism is a good thing, that goes without saying',[6] submitting to critical investigation not the idea that reformism is a good (or bad) thing, but the idea that 'it goes without saying', by trying to show how it has been constructed, from what it emerges, and how it perpetuates itself. As Jean Leca reminds us: 'Unfortunately, when a word is used to convey the ideas of self-evidence, self-explanation, historical or natural (or supernatural) necessity and universal goodness, reason (and in particular social-scientific reason) is in trouble.'[7]

8

Reformism: The 'Correct Training'

Reformism immediately appears as the backbone of current official discourse.[1] There is not a speech, not a press article or a lecture in which the attachment of 'Ben Ali's Tunisia' to reforms is not mentioned.[2] But reformism is not merely a discourse. More profoundly, it needs to be understood as a mode of the exercise of power insofar as, beyond the rhetoric, the government of Tunisia insists on showing itself, on being, and on being thought of, as reformist. The economic or social actors are for or against the reforms depending on whether they are more or less 'enlightened'; politicians always pose as reformists, criticizing the 'fake' reformism of the others; exterior constraints are measured by the reforms, whether they hamper them, as often happens, or whether they speed them up, as sometimes happens. The reforms are sometimes difficult and painful, but they are always 'beneficial'. It is easy to see that integration into the public sphere necessarily passes through the reformist prism. If you ask Tunisians what is specific about Tunisia, the reply is unanimous: the 'reformist tradition'. During my nine years of research, I have never heard a single actor, a single intellectual, a single observer, or a single opponent who failed to cite this Tunisian 'virtue' to me; not a single person has ever questioned reformism, criticized it or even subjected it to a detached investigation. This unanimity, this all-too-obvious consensus raised in me first the shadow of a doubt, then a working hypothesis, and finally a thesis: reformism is a myth, a central myth of Tunisian governmentality, its principal *imaginaire*. This does not mean – on the contrary – that it does not constitute an oppressive reality. This latter is admittedly expressed in repeated discourses, but above all in an ethos, in particular ways of thinking and grasping the social and political realms.

Elements of construction of the reformist myth

If we are to believe the official phraseology, reformism is an openness to the West which does not deny Muslim religion and culture; it is the primacy of judicial texts, laws, the Constitution; it is the priority given to order and stability, moderation and the golden mean; it is the expression of a rational exercise of power; it is modernism and integrity.

The current outlines of official reformism

The ruling elites share an essentialist and normative vision of reform and reformism. The latter, moderate by nature, is a process of controlled modernization, careful to preserve the achievements of the past. It is the assimilation of the contributions of the West, combined with respect for Islam and national sovereignty. It is progress, economic and political advance, social advantages; it represents the sensible path of adaptation to globalization; it is an attempt to restore the prestige of the state and respect for the rule of law. It fights against dishonourable behaviour, corruption and laxity.[3] Discourse on reform is a closed discourse, in which nothing is discussed and which no external gaze disturbs, in which everyone finds his or her place around God the Father Khayr ed-Din.[4] The myth of reformism, after all, is indissociable from the myth of the strong man:[5] reformism is elitist, and explicitly presents a dualist vision of society, an uneducated, easily swayed people living in obscurantism and easily overcome by passion, but enlightened by a rational, cultivated, open and structured elite; and saved by the man of providence. So reformism transmits the myth of the state as in advance of society, the only body that is in a position to give concrete form to the implementation of modern, rational ideas thanks to the impetus given by the strong man.[6]

On all these points, state reformism cannot be separated from Islamic reformism, in its demand for the belief in a golden age and the quest for the purity of lost origins, in its support for the reform of institutions, in an effort at rationalization that rejects blind fidelity to the elders and the scriptures and, on the other hand, also rejects the servile imitation of the West. Or rather, it cannot be separated from a *certain* Islamic reformism since it is well known how rich the debates are, and how diverse the positions that could be adopted in this regard.[7] Historians have brought out the consubstantial character of Islamic reformism and state reformism. They have shown how the two reformisms, often presented as opposite, in reality constituted the two faces of one and the same movement. They both issued from the same Islamic culture; Muslim reformism did not hesitate to borrow from the West and was also influenced by its relation with the latter. In particular, the return to the supposedly original ideas of Islam is concomitant with a dogmatic and elitist conception of the exercise of power, which El Ayadi summed up very expressively in the following formula: reformism is 'the ascendancy of dogma over reality'.[8]

In parallel with the attempts at modernization of the bureaucratic apparatus and modes of government, the foundational reformism of the nineteenth century was forever rethinking its relation with the religious realm and seeking a path for modern Islam. In particular, the ulemas actively contributed to the transformation of the state, at its very heart and not outside it, and participated in the debates on the political and social reconfigurations underway, even if fallback strategies could sometimes exist.[9] The discourse of the 'Change' falls explicitly within this 'tradition' and mentions these religious reference points that were constitutive of Tunisian historical reformism.[10] On this point, it also demands a break with Bourguiba, renewing the dialogue, between 1987 and 1989, with the Islamists and, over and above mere words, adopting ostentatiously favourable measures to a certain expression of religiosity.[11] However, current reformism is first and foremost linked to one tradition – among others – of reformism, that of Khayr ed-Din and the Sadiki college that he created to educate the bureaucratic elite, to the detriment of that of Thâalbi and the teachings promoted by the Zitouna, the great mosque in Tunis.[12]

A reading of the official texts and government propaganda suggests that it is less reforms that are glorified than reformism, the definition of which – restrictive and normative – is provided by the Tunisian authorities. Reforms are understood in relation to their contents; reformism is a way of seeing and understanding. Thus the myth of reformism must not be simply understood as a 'Tunisified' version of the general movement of valorization of reform understood as a progressive improvement in the social order, opposed to the revolution as well as to the status quo. In Tunisia, reformism is a posture that takes into account the, as it were, identity-based dimension of a recurrent implementation of reforms; it comprises the main form of historical persistence in social relations.[13]

Techniques of the mythification of reformism

This reformism of the Tunisian authorities is a construction. The central power has at one and the same time pre-empted the contents, the conception, and the very idea of reform, as well as its positive dimension in the social *imaginaire*. Reformism is a discourse of power on itself. It aims to show that the central power – the beylicate, then the protectorate, and finally the independent national state – is the active producer of reforming modernity. In order to achieve this end, the 'Tunisia of the Change' reconstructs the history of the reformism of Khayr ed-Din in function of its own preoccupations and the vision it aims to defend. Even if, in its rhetoric, its themes and its argumentative ploys, continuity with Bourguiba and the Destour wins hands down, the 'Change' was immediately presented as a new version of Tunisian reformism, of a certain reformism that neglects a more intellectual slant and emphasizes action.[14] In order to help people forget their continuity with the Father of the nation, his charisma and his historical legitimacy (but also out of genuine conviction), the 7 November inaugurated a return to long-term history. The references to Hannibal, to Ibn Khaldun, and above all to nineteenth-century reformers, albeit only some of them, are immediate and have remained a permanent feature.[15]

The National Pact of 1988, which expressed the consensus between different Tunisian political forces, draws inspiration explicitly from the foundational event of Tunisian reformism, namely the Fundamental Pact of 1857. It mentions Khayr ed-Din as the inspirer of reforms which Ben Ali and his supporters intended to implement. Here there appears a first element of the construction of reformism as an ethos: the elaboration of a consensus. Reformism is presented as the unifying value, the way of being, thinking and behaving which makes it possible for Tunisian society to be a unity; it provides a sense of national cohesion; it is the bearer of positive values that can be shared by all, whatever their social positions, their interests defended, their visions of life in society. The construction of a sense of unanimity is based around the proper value ascribed to the reforms. Several policies share this objective: reinforcing national integration, promoting the unity of society, and homogenizing the Tunisian population and territory. Press articles to the glory of the 26.26 point to this desire to build unity and above all to maintain unanimity and consensus: the 26.26 acts to 'reintegrate entire swathes of the national territory' and to strive for 'the homogeneity of the nation';[16] the FSN constitutes 'the ever-stronger expression of this desire for unity and, through it [the FSN] for political regeneration'[17]; 'the aim is not so much to attenuate social inequalities as to lay down the bases of a society that is jealous of its indivisibility and whose primary strength lies in the way it is flawlessly bound together'.[18]

Official discourse is a discursive practice like any other. Reformism is a myth: it is the expression 'of the being and the appearance of power, what it is and what it would like people to believe that it is'.[19] This is proved by the plurality and diversity of historical knowledge about the reforms and reformism which are today emerging in every scholarly milieu, but which are however neither recognized nor integrated into Tunisian reformist ideology and official historiography. The diversity of reformist thinking right from the start can be explained by the desire to promote a common future through a change in continuity, in other words by the double attachment to the modern, thanks to the desire for renewal and adaptation, in particular to western modernity, but also to tradition, thanks to the necessity, felt by all, of respecting the laws and values of Islam. It also results from the multiplicity of its objectives and preoccupations, which are often contradictory: to build the state and contribute to the centralization of power, and simultaneously to limit state power; to base activity on elitism while promoting egalitarianism; to rationalize the state and discipline society while striving towards the horizon of freedom; to be pro-European and simultaneously anti-imperialist; to envisage the strategic use of traditional teaching but to reject it as the sole basis for education; to envisage a return to the Islam of the golden age but to seek novelties and historic changes.[20] These original ambivalences explain how very important the debates between reformist trends were,[21] and why, until the present day, the reformist movement has been characterized by its ambiguities, its paradoxes, its plurality and its misunderstandings.[22]

I do not wish to go here into too much detail about the way knowledge becomes de-subjectified, but I do wish to mention briefly the current techniques of mythification of Tunisian reformism.[23] Diversity is left in the shade; the official discourse on reformism shows a negation of differences, a refusal of pluralism, an impossibility of divisions and oppositions. On the other hand, historians have shown that reformist thought always unfolded in accordance with very different modes, traditions, and trajectories; that the reformers had fought each other, even resorting to violence; that their visions of religion, openness to the West, economic policies, the place of the Sultan and the Porte, and later, their position vis-à-vis the colonial authorities were often opposed; that the positions of the different groups were extremely fluid; that behind archaic attitudes a great deal of modernity was often concealed – and vice versa.[24] These cover-ups smooth out the relations of force and meld into a universal consensus. This neglect of differences makes it possible *de facto* to erase the ambiguities of reforming actions. Official historiography sets up as exemplary the 'good reformers' who wish to apply 'good reforms' and have to confront the oppressive slowness of 'archaic and corrupt' leaders and an 'uneducated' population.

Certain techniques have thus made the transformation possible, in particular the simplification of reformism. In the first instance, it is a matter of selecting the right reference points and symbols. The Ben-alist discourse has chosen Khayr ed-Din rather than Tahar Haddad, Mohamed Ali, Qabadu or Bin Dhiaf:[25] it thus lays the emphasis on the statist and technocratic dimension of reformism, since reform has to limit the Sultan's absolute power, with the aim of rationalization and government efficiency. It is this tradition which is currently being highlighted, rather than the purely political – and democratic – dimension. Then, some serious confusions have been perpetrated: so the 1861 Constitution is identified with the establishment of a liberal and participatory democracy; reformism is identified with the ability to reform. In addition, certain realities are underestimated, such as the importance of the Ottoman Empire or the influence of foreign thinkers in Tunisian reformism. Finally, the reformist myth is constructed through the simplification of reformism itself. The use of binary oppositions – traditionalists versus modernists, Zaytounians versus Sadikians, conservators versus reformists – is in fact particularly unpropitious for any real representation of the complexity of social phenomena.

Reformism, an imaginary *polis*

This mythification in no way abates the power or effectiveness of reformism; nor does it lessen the veracity of its historical foundations.

Nineteenth-century reformism is, like the 1789 Revolution for France, simultaneously a founding event and a real myth which is forever being appropriated in contradictory ways.[26] The problem is not the reality of nineteenth-century reformism, the reality of the Fundamental Pact of 1857 and the Constitution of 1861; it is the statement, affirmed by all, that 'reformism has been the specific feature of Tunisia since the nineteenth century', the statement – taken as a principle of truth – of a seamless historical continuity without any break or change in meaning, a smoothing-out which defines a fixed and definite cultural identity.

Masking differences and discontinuities

The construction of current Tunisian reformism, indeed, also proceeds from a specific perception of history, created first and foremost from continuities and parallels.[27] The idea of a continuum in the perception of power and of modes of government – an idea which the confusion between constructed tradition and historical past makes possible – eliminates any breaks and erases social transformations. It seems that, as far as this historicist reading is concerned, it is of little account that the relations between actors, the influence of the latter in society as in political activity, the national and international context, and the demographic, economic, social and political situation are just not comparable.[28] However, the 'reformists' do not come from the same social strata, they do not share the same ideals, the society they wish to reform is not the same ... Certain factors nullify this, in particular demography, education and literacy, urbanization, women's emancipation, economic development, and the complexification of the operation of the country's political economy. And so, objectively speaking, everything has changed in Tunisian society, and it is impossible to apply the analysis and interpretation of nineteenth-century reformism in a rough-and-ready way to the current situation. However, not only does official discourse reify reformism, it also insists on these continuities and direct inheritances. This posture, which 'consists in believing that the generations which succeed one another over centuries on a reasonably stable territory, under a reasonably univocal designation, have handed down to each other an invariant substance' thus appears as 'an effective ideological form, in which the imaginary singularity of national formations is constructed daily, by moving back from the present into the past'.[29] This illusion is also part of the myth, of a myth shared by the political actors and the elites of Tunisia, but also by several recognized observers and analysts of the country. 'Might not the Tunisian "exception"' – as Michel Camau and Vincent Geisser wonder – 'reside precisely in this permanent ambiguity, this political *Tunisian-ness* largely cultivated by the governing as well as the governed, by the dominating as well as by the dominated? The latter must indeed be treated not as a waste product of history in the sense of the culturalists, but first and foremost as a political project, inaugurated by the nineteenth-century reformers, taken up by the national liberation movement, and confirmed by Bourguiba's regime in the days following independence and today pursued by its successor.'[30]

This constitution of the myth did not happen all at once. It was made possible by the recurrence of a common term that nonetheless signified different things. These correspondences and this common language, full of misunderstandings, made it possible to invent a direct relation between nineteenth-century reformism and that of the new independent state to form what was henceforth considered as the 'reformist tradition'. The current myth thus proceeded from a whole series of simplifications, of abbreviated quotations, of historical short-cuts, of confusions between written texts and real actualizations (or between representations and facts), of the neglect of contingencies and conflicts between social groups, of instrumentalizations and procedures of legitimization that were set in motion right from the establishment of the Protectorate. In short, the myth of reformism proceeds from a cover-up of the historicities proper to the various reformist movements.[31]

The first stage of this mythification is concomitant with the establishment of the Protectorate. Whether it emerges from the associationists, the pan-Islamists, the religious reformists or the nationalists, hostility to French colonization is expressed by a systematic reference to the Fundamental Pact and the Constitution of 1861. These texts are seen as the first expression of a certain number of fundamental principles – the equality of citizens before the law, respect for human rights, the primacy of the law against arbitrariness, and parliamentary representation. In spite of the suspension of the new institutions in 1864, and the consequent absence of any real experience of the benefits of the Constitution, the latter represented, for the Tunisian elite under the Protectorate, the political panacea, the ultimate guarantee against the ills of colonization. It was in the mid-1920s that this myth of the 'first liberal Constitution in the Arab world' started to emerge.

The second stage of the construction of the reformist myth came with the country's independence. One the one hand, the religious dimension of reformism is covered up. On the other, the strategy of the monopolization and construction of the reformist stereotype is reinforced by the eradication of the paradoxes and nuances in reformist thought and action. This tendency to a rigid dualism is also expressed in the writing of history: individual trajectories are outrageously simplified (the 'good' Khayr ed-Din against the 'bad' Khaznadar[32] as well as intellectual ones (the 'good' Sadikians against the 'bad' Zaytounians), and the trajectory of men and their ideas becomes linear and unambiguous.

The third and final stage occurred at the end of the 1970s and in the 1980s. The construction of the reformist myth may be correlated with the erosion of nationalism and the loss of the national ideology. This evolution is concomitant with another: the disappearance of the revolutionary thematics. Its corollary is thus the at least partial transformation of the meaning of reformism with the massive reappearance of the Muslim dimension in the political lexicon and its metamorphosis into a real myth. Even if it did not emerge from a complete void, it was from Ben Ali that reformism became reified, endlessly evoked and invoked. Bourguiba was at the centre of everything and he to some extent 'exceeded' the very tradition that he instrumentalized. Ben Ali could not call on the same historical legitimacy, nor on the aura of the 'Supreme Fighter'; he sets himself explicitly in the line of a long history, and draws his legitimacy from his ostentatious reference to reformism. Resorting to this golden age thus appears as a powerful element of legitimatization, and the reformist episode of the nineteenth century is part of a shared historical memory, an *imaginaire* that is common to the whole population.

This view of reformism, including its historical dimension, is familiar to Tunisians. That is precisely why this rhetoric is not merely instrumental, functioning as a myth. 'By constituting the people as a fictively ethnic unity [. . .], national ideology does much more than justify the strategies employed by the state to control populations,' as Étienne Balibar points out, 'it inscribes their demands in advance in a sense of belonging in the double sense of the term – both what it is that makes one belong to oneself and also what makes one belong to other fellow human beings.'[33] This also explains that, in the continued dialogue between heritage and political innovation, reformism can be viewed as an *imaginaire*. Insofar as it sets out to sum up the being of the entire nation and reveal the permanent interactions between past, present, and the projection of the future, it may even be considered as an 'imaginary *polis*'. It is not merely a political unconscious since it indisputably occupies 'the *front* of the stage, and is part of the actors' consciousness'.[34]

Reformism, the obligatory problematic of the political

Reformism is also an element of language, an imposed reading of the political – in other words, a 'legitimate problematic'.[35] These days, those who govern and those who would like to govern can problematize themselves and can problematize their actions only in terms of reformism. When I tested this hypothesis of reformism as a myth on various Tunisian interviewees, I came up against failure to understand, a scepticism, and even a sense of dismay. 'Does that mean that, in its application, every reformism is doomed?' 'I don't see what you're getting at – so is all reformism hopeless?' 'So what's the answer?' In Tunisia, reformism really is the absolute horizon of the political. It structures consensus.

However doubtful, this myth needs to be taken seriously: it does more than inform us about the intentions of the central power and lay bare its ruses.

Social actors refer to it more than one might believe: reformism is not merely a discourse with significant effects of power, but also a vital means of action, a fully fledged mode of government, a process of subjection in the Foucauldian sense of the term, that is a process whereby individuals emerge as moral subjects, 'not in the mode of submission to an external rule imposed by a direct relation of domination, but in that of belonging'.[36] The Tunisian political *imaginaire* is structured around reformism, the myth of which, these days, is shared by all the protagonists of political life: the government, the RCD and the legal opposition, of course, but also – and this may appear at first sight more surprising – the unrecognized opposition, including the Islamists, who had all, directly or by interposed 'independents', signed the national Pact of 1988, which made explicit reference to it.[37]

Islamists emphasize their attachment to the 'movement of Renaissance and Reform', the *Ijtihad* and *Islah*. They point to the desire for modernization recurrent in the history of Islam.[38] Admittedly, they tend to refer to Thâalbi rather than to Khayr ed-Din or Haddad, but they vaunt the same merits of modernization out of respect for a certain original integrity and Arab-Muslim identity.[39] The unrecognized secular opposition, which emerged from the same school of Bourguiba, shares the obsession for moderation and the golden mean, the faith in the providential man – who is very often the one who is speaking – the belief that the reformist tradition constitutes a definite asset and a basis for democratization, or indeed similar definitions of 'good government' and thus of reformism.[40] For example, one of the leaders of the opposition, Mohamed Charfi, defines reformism as a modernizing theory, but a theory that finds effective concrete shape in the sphere of action[41] – a definition that is precisely the same as that given in 1993 by President Ben Ali when he described the RCD as a 'reforming party'.[42] It is even more revealing that one of the few texts ever to have tried to lay the basis for an alliance between the different opposition movements, both secular and Islamist, should have turned reformism into one of the cornerstones of their common work base. In this way, the signatories declare that they are reaffirming 'their faith in the Tunisian people, which very early on in its modern history experienced *a reforming movement*, a people which was *one of the first Arab peoples to endow itself with a Constitution* limiting absolutism by law, a people which has contributed so many martyrs, a people which struggled for decades *for real political reforms* and social development, and *whose elites have always demonstrated great dynamism*, a people which produced *reformers in every field*, including Kheireddine, Mohamed Ali Hammi, Tahar Haddad, and Farhat Hached'.[43]

Political elites, whichever side they come from, have all emerged from the same mould, the same schools, the same universities, the same political experiences: Islamism was born from the nationalist movement and built itself up as an opposition, in the universities, in contact with extreme leftwing movements; the secular opposition was for long associated with the exercise of the central power, during Bourguiba's period, or during the first years of the presidency of Ben Ali; the Destour and Neo Destour were already aligning themselves with reformism – as, indeed, was colonialism.[44] So we might talk of the significance of a kind of non-institutionalized *paideia* which provides the whole Tunisian elite with a 'common imaginary landscape'[45] by giving it the same political culture. Or, as Pierre Bourdieu put it, we may conceive of reformism as a 'field of the politically thinkable' which finds expression by hijacking meanings but also by reinforcing schemas of thought and action implicit in the habitus of the elite.[46] Opponents, defectors and dissidents involuntarily reinforce the discourse of the 'regime', even if not all of them paint the 'common imaginary landscape' in the same colours.

Foreign actors also praise the all-pervasive reformism, without always being aware of its mythical nature. They are often naive about the assertions of official discourse, remembering the simplicity of the expressions rather than the ambiguity of practices and meanings.[47] Donors involuntarily participate in the construction of the reformist myth in at least two ways: on the one hand, they understand the rhetoric of the central power in the western intellectual tradition which sees reform as the opposite of revolution; on the other hand, they participate in various misappropriations which transform practices in the name of reformism in a sense contrary to the essential and ideal definition of the latter. However, all of them – external partners, international donors, and foreign analysts – emphasize the moderate, open aspect of the reforms in Tunisia, which makes them so propitious to democratization. They also emphasize the modernity and westernization of a government considered as favourable to secularism, and the desire to construct a modern, liberal state; in short, the pedagogic dimension of reform and its civilizing mission.[48] Thanks to its polysemia, reformism manages to talk to everyone, and everyone uses it as a point of reference. In a recognized language, which everyone deems to be transparent, it makes it possible to articulate the concepts, ideas and beliefs inherent in Tunisian political practices. This idiom allows people to confront the globalized version of modernity, as it had already done in the recent past with nationalism or, in the nineteenth century, with liberalism.[49] So myth is simultaneously language and metaphor of the political which enables all groups to express different things.

A similar unanimity does not prevent criticisms of the modes of reformism (for example, of the perversion of reformism by the 'regime') from being voiced. This criticism targets in turn the instrumentalization of reform, the neglect of certain of its fundamental elements, the corruption of the term and the degradation of its basic principles; but it never targets the use of reformism as a basic point of reference; it is always made in the name of reformism itself, in the name of 'true' reformism. The debate on its nature – 'good' or 'bad' – actually has no significance here. On the other hand, the dynamics of this evaluation shows that reformism is first and foremost a discourse of truth and that it produces knowledge: a particular actor is disqualified because he is not a reformer, or because he has usurped this noble designation. These days, for example, those in government and secular opponents deny Islamists the label 'reformist' because of their intrinsically archaic nature, their 'anti-modern' behaviour, their 'irrational' political thinking, and their opposition to 'women's emancipation'. The interest of these judgements resides elsewhere, in the mechanism that transforms reformism into an instrument of inclusion and exclusion, a means of classification, and a way of defining good and evil. For reformism is a moral way of thinking, which defines the true and the false, the just and the unjust. Even if, in concrete terms, individuals do not define these terms in the same way, they all aim to incarnate the 'true' reformism and with this aim in mind describe the reformism of everyone else as 'false'. This situation is made possible by the very mythical nature of reformism, an abstract idea and irenic vision of social being, available for appropriation by all.

The social foundations of reformism

National elites and foreign actors are, however, not alone in granting a central position to reforms in their interpretation of the political. The positive values of reformism are widely shared by the Tunisian population. The reformist project is intimately linked with national construction and the formation of Tunisian identity, and so imbues society through and through. But, at the same time, the widespread idea (even found among the shrewdest analysts of Tunisia), that there is a gap between the elites and the popular masses that has caused the reforms to fail, issued directly from the reformist ideology.[50] This apparent paradox evaporates if we stick to a broad conception of the political, which includes the participation of all, through often anonymous actions, in the exercise of power.

Reformism as a process of subjection

The processes whereby the demands of the population are justified can be expressed only in the common language of the governing class, since any other words are inaudible and even unutterable. So these demands are without any doubt shaped by the all-pervasive official discourse. Indeed, this suggests one of the strengths of reformism: by never mentioning the content of the transformations, any break, any continuity, any policy can be included, precisely because it is characterized first and foremost as a step to be taken, a way of thinking, a belief. But the implicit reference to reformism is not a mere evanescent discourse stuck onto an official discourse. It rests on the population's own demands. These are sometimes expressed in terms of 'reform'; often, they are not; but they are definitely never expressed in terms of 'reformism'. However, they imperceptibly contribute to the reformist ethos by means of many wild uncharted tracks: the systematic appeal to the state as clear-sighted and 'in advance' of society, alone able to 'get things moving'; participation in the 'incessant interventions' of the administration and thus legitimization of bureaucracy as principal vector of the reforms; belief in rational progress and material modernization; a shared developmentalist ideology;[51] the expectation that sources of accumulation imperilled by globalization will be protected and preserved; a keen awareness of the loss of national sovereignty and the attacks on the Arabo-Muslim identity of Tunisians; the wish, too, to see rules and regulations respected, nepotism and corruption criticized; and the demand for the rule of law.

So reformism is not simply a state project, nor even a way of conceptualizing the power specific to elites. It is a shared myth and a complex process, bringing into play every individual and the entire fabric of social relations. In other words, reformism is not merely instrumentalized by central power and the elites, but the element of support plays a vital role in its emergence as a legitimate problematic and as an *imaginaire*; reformism can be interpreted as the vulgarization of power *par excellence*, the principal form of historical persistence in Tunisia; the reforms constitute more than an elitist idea and project, but they also benefit from undeniable social foundations; this *imaginaire* is in the final analysis common to all, as is revealed by certain widely read novels and, more generally, by artistic production as a whole.[52]

Over and above perfectly real demands, Tunisians recognize themselves in reformism: its problematic contributes to shaping them as subjects, both in the mode of voluntary servitude (as subjected beings), and in the mode of the support they show (as active subjects).[53] This *imaginaire*, in fact, is indissociable from the 'theology of servitude';[54] reformism appears as an element of integration of political servility and hence its modernization through the administration, that 'house of servitude' as Max Weber called it,[55] by means of the political shaping of Tunisian-ness. Beneath the surface attractions of modernism and adaptation to external constraint, it makes it possible for practices of domination to be perpetuated by being transformed. Starting with socially accepted norms, it puts in place new mechanisms and principles of action. In the nineteenth century, this was one of the functions of the administrative and educational systems, notably the famous Sadiki college. These days, economic mechanisms play this role, for example, enterprises, those zones of modernity constituted by offshore zones, industrial zones and tourist zones, and social mechanisms, such as subsidies and programmes of support and solidarity.

Be that as it may, Tunisians are also constituted as subjects in the mode of active support, 'recognition' and acceptance of themselves.[56] Reform takes on another meaning for the multitude of these individuals on the edge of official reformist knowledge. It none the less constitutes a frame of reference in the behaviour and lifestyle of the entrepreneur adapting to openness and free trade with Europe – whether he does this willingly or under duress, optimistically or pessimistically, by allying himself with foreigners or by exploiting political or administrative relations. It is crucial for the employee confronting liberalization and privatization – he may take part in illegal strikes, increase his productivity, accept a drop in his purchasing power, move house, or organize a hunger strike. It affects the migrant faced with the closing of frontiers – he may abandon the idea of migrating, go illegal, change his destination, decide not to come back, or to wait. It is central to the hotel proprietor who needs to be ready to meet tourists' needs, the smuggler seeking to adapt to new conditions of trade, the trade unionist facing up to transformations in welfare and working conditions, the farmer suffering from a drying-up of financing, the banker seeking to restructure debt, the intermediary needing to accommodate the partial privatization of the state, and the civil servant getting used to the modifications of interventionism . . . Reform produces particular modes of existence, including for the individuals who are deemed to be 'subjected' to reforms conceived at the summit of the state – reforms whose shape, and sometimes even whose very existence, they criticize.

Reformism: a common imaginaire

Reformism, in its effective and mythical aspects alike, is an *imaginaire* to which individuals in Tunisia find themselves linked in one way or another; it is one of the norms they must in their own interests take into account, whether with approval or indifference, constraint or criticism, detachment or misappropriation, avoidance, transformation or conversion.

Such, for instance, is the case with the *Rassemblement pour une alternative internationale de développement* (RAID/Attac Tunisie – Rally for an International Development Alternative), an anti-globalization association linked to the international Attac network. Its criticism of liberal globalization makes it possible to legitimatize the problematic of reform and put it at the heart of public debate. Anti-globalizing rhetoric, a recent development in Tunisia as in the Mahgreb as a whole, does seem to have largely developed as an attempt to tap into the symbolic resources of a recognized world movement. This phenomenon is a new illustration of the importance of the vocabularies imposed and the inevitable instrumentalization of significant reference points: the demands of the RAID are certainly closer to certain elements of the reformist ethos than to anti-globalization properly speaking.[57] In relation to its European counterparts, the Tunisian movement exaggerates the importance of national questions, expressed in terms of sovereignty and independence of development. It fuels reformist rhetoric by over-interpreting the role of liberalism in Tunisia, stimulating ideas about the necessary economic transformations, arousing expectations about state interventions, putting forward and hoping for other types of reform, and highlighting the link between authoritarianism and liberalism.[58]

The strength of the UGTT comes not merely from its active participation in the national struggle, but also from its 'reformism, which confirms on it a certain flexibility and a remarkable capacity to adapt to variations in historical circumstances'.[59] The trade union explicitly stands by its reformism even though it simultaneously attempts to diminish the impact of the reforms set in place by the government. Until the mid-1980s at least, wage-earners, workers, employees and civil servants recognized themselves in this problematization and in this representation of power and the relations of force. These days, the low level of support for the trade union in the world of work needs to be interpreted less in terms of the rejection of reformism and more in terms of a rejection of any total alignment with the reforms put forward and implemented by successive governments.[60] Wildcat strikes and hunger strikes, for example, represent mainly a demand for human dignity and an insistence on access to the material conditions of modernity, not a rejection of modernity itself. During the strikes at the ICAB factory in Moknine, the workers (especially the women) who had been laid off had only one demand: they wanted to find another job, and to be treated properly; the discourses denouncing the predatory and corrupt character of the central power, or the damaging effects of liberal globalization, were entirely constructed by the organizations – RAID, LTDH, CNLT, certain trade unionists – who supported the strikers so as to make their demands more audible on the international level.[61] The various criticisms aimed at the liberalism of the Tunisian authorities express another demand, which the reformist register can include perfectly well within itself: a demand for rules of law defined in advance (i.e. the maintaining of employment promised within the framework of privatizations) to be respected, an insistence on citizenship, and another type of relation to the Other, the state and the administration; and *not* a demand for withdrawal or self-sufficiency, even if the nationalist underpinnings of such an expectation are very strong, notably in terms of sovereignty, national independence and economic development.[62]

The spread of this ethos is thus also found in the business world. Thus, those businesses that present themselves as the most dynamic emphasize the rationality of their approach, the modernization of management procedures, and the questioning of arbitrary and vague rules – all of them themes which echo the reformist rhetoric. Sometimes the vocabulary used makes explicit reference to it. This is true, for instance, of executives trying to stimulate the employees they supervise. The latter, indeed, understand them in these terms, as is revealed by a Poulina worker who states: 'The "setting at a thousand" [a system of evaluation] started with X, I had a fixed wage and now he's told me: "if you want a bonus, you need the *Ijtihad* if you're going to get a result"'.[63]

Reformism: plurality of meanings

This makes it easier to see that, far from the unitary and consensual myth of reformism, the conception of reforms diverges from one individual to another, one social category to another, one interest to another. The worlds of production and the social universes are different, and people's behaviour ambiguous, but reform is common to all. That is why analyses in terms of binary confrontations (for or against the reforms), of opposition or resistance to reforms, turn out to be partial and, in a word, incorrect: individuals certainly do have different positions vis-à-vis the reforms, and to the (themselves very diverse) practical problems which they have to resolve or to which they need to adapt – privatization, liberalization, the opening of borders, public health or social measures, competition, the weight of bureaucracy, and the absence of rules. They express complex and subtle opinions, but they all express them in terms circumscribed by the reformist myth. So the problematizing in terms of reform and reformism does not come merely from 'on high'; it is not merely the instrumental expression of a political will to domination, a technique of control, a mode of the exercise of the centralized and authoritarian power; it is just as much fuelled by aspirations 'from below', by positive demands for transformations and by existential preoccupations.

If we follow the reasoning proposed by Étienne Balibar in his analysis of nationalism and citizenship, we can say that at the heart of the reformism of the 'dominant' dwell the representations of the 'dominated'.[64] The secret power of reformist domination resides in the *imaginaire*, the awareness of identity and the reformist demands of the Tunisians themselves. They all recognize themselves in these precisely because the meaning of reform is plural, not to say 'empty'.[65] Reform is endorsed by the vast majority of individuals, even if this endorsement challenges the reformist logic of the central power and its technique of domination in an attempt to highlight, every individual in his own manner, his own vision, his own strategy, his own logic of action, or quite simply his own desire for survival. That is also why support is partial and partly deployed in the field of representations and in the *imaginaire*.[66] For all these groups, it is not a question of adopting a reformist package, but rather of choosing elements from it, borrowing certain forms of behaviour and rejecting others, of taking certain of its meanings and even of its shapes in order to reject its philosophy or modes of existence. This is the case with middle-class consumerism, which is not merely outrageous consumption, westernization and modernity, or the mechanism of domination by debt, but can be an instrument of social integration and recognition, an effect of distinction, a symbol of protest . . . This eclecticism is all the more significant in that Tunisian reform is disparate, including Arab nationalist thought as much as the Islamization of society, the westernizing as much as the orientalizing of social practices, and a return to origins as much as an openness to the future.

Reformism and 'Tunisian-ness': a diffuse *ethos*

Ever since the nineteenth century, reformism has also constituted the historically constituted mode of extraversion, to use the expression coined in the African context by Jean-François Bayart.[67] Even though she does not use the term, Magaly Morsy offers us a rich re-interpretation of the work of Khayr ed-Din, seen through the prism of a process of westernization that 'cannot be equated with an imitation since it must, on the contrary, impugn passivity in the face of European penetration'; this process carries out 'a necessary return to religious roots' insofar as 'only a reform that is deliberately accepted and integrated into the inner movement of Muslim societies has any meaning'.[68]

The myth of a Tunisia 'at the crossroads of East and West' rests on facts whose importance is doubtless exaggerated but no less real. Historians have shown that incomings, economic resources, political resources, men, and legitimacy all stemmed largely from relations with foreigners and that the confused interplay of foreign powers with the internal quarrels of Tunisia made possible both a certain dependency and, at the same time, a certain autonomy.[69] Likewise, it now seems that the thesis of reformism as a response to decline, internationalization, and the crisis of the nation-state in the Muslim world is a gross simplification:[70] internationalization significantly predates the nineteenth century and has always contributed to the formation of the nation-state; reformism, furthermore, was a response to internal dynamics proper to Tunisian society.[71]

The novelty, in the nineteenth century, came from the simultaneous pursuit of a long movement of emancipation from the Sublime Porte, from growing (and suddenly aggressive and pressing) competition from western empires, from the economically dependent position in which Tunisia was placed by those same European powers, from the emergence of nationalism across the world (more particularly in Europe, but in Tunisia, too), from the reinforcement and centralization of nation-states, and from technological developments. The novelty also provoked this new problematization in terms of reformism as a system of thought that indissociably bound together the process of national construction and openness to (or at least awareness of) the Other. From this moment on, therefore, the project of reform was an essential part of the recurrent operation of the nation-state.

A Tunisian way of being in the world

The reforms of the nineteenth century gave birth to, and fed into, a powerful nationalism by introducing the notions of belonging and citizenship, and by placing its relations with Europe and the rest of the world at the heart of its interventions. But this modern nationalism is not a mere relation with the

Other. It is a relation mediatized by the state, by state interventions.[72] Because state bureaucracy has become rooted and has spread throughout society as a whole, and because reformist ideas have constituted themselves as the structuring ideas of Tunisia, 'Tunisian-ness' is expressed now even more than before by that permanent ambivalence between understanding the other and withdrawal into self, between the demand for a precocious and exceptional openness and a haughty sovereignty.[73]

In official rhetoric, as in its mythical construction, 'Tunisian-ness' is a way of managing global modernity and, simultaneously, the conviction that Tunisia is by nature an exception. This exception, it seems, resides in the perfect synthesis between western modernity, nationalism and a sense of belonging to the Arab and Muslim community – which reformism itself encapsulates. Reformism and Tunisian-ness are thus inseparable, and both of them symbolize the 'specific nature of being Tunisian', as the authorized vocabulary puts it, and marking – right from the start – the profound ambiguity of these mythical narratives. For Bourguiba, 'Tunisian-ness, at the same time as expressing a *project of civic patriotism*, was based on a *communitarian nationalism*. It was demanded and justified in the name of membership of the Arab and Muslim communities. It was doubtless associated with bilingualism as a means of openness to the modern world, in the course of a history whose beginnings apparently go back to Jugurtha. But Tunisian identity in its conquest of historicity was inseparable from the Arabic language, the national language (and language of authority) and to Arabness'.[74] In practice, however, national ideology and rhetoric on cultural identity have also been tools of political domination, transforming the offensive and dynamic project of constructing the national state into defensive and instrumentalist strategies.[75] These days, Tunisian-ness is primarily mentioned as a way of 'remaining oneself' amid globalization or 'trying to find an identity for oneself'.[76] In this sense, Tunisian-ness is indisputably an instrumentalization with populist aims, a skilful but facile arrangement in the subtle interplay between maintaining control over society and remaining open to the international dimension.

But Tunisian-ness is much more than that. It strives to be a value, a Tunisian way of being in the world, one that is deeply anchored in society. All the opposition's texts mention respect for national sovereignty, the Arab and Muslim nature of the community, and the specific nature of Tunisian identity as part and parcel of the reformism demanded.[77] The Tunis Declaration of 17 June 2003, for instance, was a compromise text, aimed simultaneously at reassuring secular opponents and getting the Islamists to sign it. General terms such as 'specific nature of Tunisian identity' are precisely chosen so that everyone can read into them the meaning that best suits them: some will hear it as a synonym of 'Islam-ness', others as 'Arab-ness', and yet others as a reference to the 'western' meaning of reformism, that is a reformism resolutely turned towards Europe. Those who hold power interpret such expressions as the affirmation of their historical legitimacy drawn from the direct heritage of the struggle for national independence, stigmatizing opponents who represent foreign interests.[78] Opponents read them as the pursuit of the struggle for an independence that has not yet been achieved, whether the current dependence be exclusively economic (secular opponents), or cultural (Islamist opponents) or even linked to the absence of a united Arab nation (Arab nationalists).[79]

The ambiguity of 'Tunisian-ness'

In spite of disillusions and 'disenchantment', national feeling remains strong in the population. The national idea is even more than ever integrated into people's self-awareness.[80] These contradictory appropriations are indeed part of the virtues of 'Tunisian-ness' as pedagogy,[81] or of its vices as 'cowardice', as Sadri Khiari calls it.[82] Cowardice in the sense that Tunisian-ness is defined 'negatively', in opposition to Ottomanism, Arabism, or the *umma*, while still being unable to deny those elements that simultaneously constitute it. Or, to be less normative, it is less cowardice than an illusion: the misunderstandings at work here act as the negotiated version of reality, and the national Pact as the tacit celebration of the compromise whereby everyone realizes his own *imaginaire*.[83] In parallel with the discourse on the economic miracle, Tunisia is thus presented as another model, that of national construction and the management of extraversion, notably for the Arabic and African world. Just as reformism is fundamentally a myth, Tunisian-ness appears first and foremost as a 'fictive ethnicity'.[84]

The weight of colonization is evident in this oppositional vision of identity and nationalism. The very concept of 'Tunisian-ness' was, after all, invented by colonizers to prop up their power, by differentiating between the local juridical system and the French system and taking the 'Tunisian issue' into account.[85] As a piece of rhetoric, but also as a feeling, 'Tunisian-ness' has become more precise and stronger with the struggle for independence. It was subsequently renewed in view of new circumstances and new international and national relations of force; defeat in the Six Days' War of 1967 and, more generally speaking, the failure of the Arabic nationalist project, provoked a first shift in the way it was conceived. The idea of 'Tunisian-ness' was again brought to the forefront by the confused situation that emerged from the war in Kuwait (1990–91) and the expansion of the Arab media – and this movement became indisputably more important after the 11 September attacks and the Iraq War. It was also little by little transformed by the exercise of power and by the integration of the rhetoric of cultural identity into the mechanisms of domination.[86] This development suggests the significance of the ambiguities at the heart of Tunisian-ness, which simultaneously contrasts and corresponds with Arab nationalism and Islamism, identifying itself with the Arab and

Muslim world as a whole, while at the same time seeing itself as different. But in the contemporary context where the state is central through its interventions, and even more through the way it structures thought, Tunisian-ness is simultaneously an objective institution of discipline and domination, and a fantasy through which all national individuals tend to perceive the singular character of their own relation of dependence on, and demands made on, the state.[87]

In parallel with the benevolent discourse of President Ben Ali with regard to the West and to the *'primisme'*[88] of the authorities, other discourses aim at underlining the defence – without concession – of national interests.[89] Just as certain editorials exalt the openness of the country in the purest of pro-western reformist traditions, whether they highlight the importance of links with Europe or the boldness of a tentative dialogue with Israel, other articles feed into a virulent anti-westernism, expressing xenophobic, anti-Zionist, or even anti-Semitic sentiments. The difference between the French-speaking and Arab-speaking press is clear, but it concerns less the contents than the form. In any case, it is interesting to note that 'the most western of countries in the Maghreb' is also the one in which the population looks most at Middle-Eastern media – comparatively speaking, much more than at the European media.[90]

In the shadow of reformism, we can observe activities, attitudes and frames of mind that are much more complex, and even frankly nationalistic and hostile to any form of openness to 'the West'. There are many expressions of this, and I shall now attempt to illustrate this ambiguity, starting with the various 'distortions' of the reforms of liberalization that are currently taking place in Tunisia. To gain a better understanding of the extreme complexity and plurality of logics at work behind these consensual myths, the following pages will go into the detail of economic practices and daily administrative procedures.

National preference and limited openness: economic 'nationalitarianism' in practice

Ever since the start of the 1990s, the external observer cannot fail to be struck by the increasing importance of questions of sovereignty. Discussions with foreign partners are held under the sign of respect for sovereignty. Liberalization, privatizations, direct foreign investments and, more generally, liberal economic reforms are read through the interpretative grid of sovereignty. This problematization is demanded in the name of reformism, which, as people point out in Tunis, has been structured around the question of debt and the placing of the heavily indebted country under financial supervision, which led to the French Protectorate and the end of national sovereignty for more than 60 years. The opening of the Tunisian economy to Europe and more generally the world paradoxically thus finds expression by a degree of closing down, and by the establishment of often implicit national preferences – in short, 'economic patriotism'.

An explicit economic nationalism

Defensive nationalism and a keen awareness of the need for sovereignty to be respected explain, first and foremost, how a certain number of national laws are in complete contradiction with international commitments signed by the Tunisian authorities. Whether it is a matter of reciprocal protection for investments or of fiscal conventions, national laws and internal norms take precedence over the international treaties that have been ratified, which creates continual tensions. In spite of the free trade agreements between Tunisia and the European Union, juridical and legal decisions express an open reticence towards foreigners, including Europeans. For example, foreign investors cannot become landowners without the prior authorization of the governor, who controls these permits strictly. Resident foreign companies cannot recruit more than four expatriates without a special exemption from the Commission supérieure des investissements (Superior Commission of Investments), to which it needs to be proved, for each job, that a candidate with the required qualifications cannot be found in Tunisia itself. To recover foreign holdings in Tunisia, prior permission is required, and obtaining this can turn out to be extremely difficult, and in any case a laborious bureaucratic process. In addition, by law, one needs to have resided for at least two years in the country before one can become the managing director of a company; and, in practice, nothing is done to make it any easier to obtain permission to stay, or the annual renewal of residence permits.[91]

A foreign shareholder of resident service companies that are not totally devoted to export cannot hold a majority interest, which frequently hampers the strategy of large international groups. This is the case with the insurance group Allianz (ex-AGF), which owns 36 per cent of the shares of the local company Astrée, which managed to increase to 42 per cent but proved unable to benefit from the departure of Axa in 2002, or that of Generali in 2003, to become a majority holder. So, in 2004, it decided to leave Tunisia and sell off its shares to nationals as well as foreigners – in this case, the Crédit mutuel-CIC – which had had the good taste to opt for the Tunisians' favourite strategy, namely that of sleeping partners.[92] Generally speaking, a system of prior authorization is always a live option for a certain number of activities, in particular when foreign holdings are higher than 50 per cent of the capital. The Commission supérieure des investissements is strictly obliged to give its prior agreement to potential foreign investors.[93] This rule concerns strategic sectors such as transport, communications, and caretaking and education services, which all affect national sovereignty – sectors which, in every country, are relatively well protected, such as public works and finance, but also areas that appear much more innocuous such as tourism, supplying buildings with electricity, laying tiles, mosaics and false ceilings, shaping plaster, or checking roofs for leaks . . . sectors which are certainly not strategic in terms of national sovereignty but which can turn out to be extremely sensitive in terms of employment and accumulation of wealth for the ruling elite.

It is also becoming easier to understand what nationalism means: not just an ideology, but the central power's fear of losing its control over the economy and having to manage an unstable situation. Thus, the disciplinary instrumentalization of nationalism, what Hélé Béji felicitously calls 'nationalitarianism', is not confined to the sphere of ideas. It can be, as Max Weber would have put it, 'economically oriented', allowing domination to operate through the control of economic activities and behaviour.

The example of the liberalization of international trade

This is the case with international trade. The liberalization of international trade is mainly negotiated not merely with international donors and organizations, but also with the different Tunisian economic actors. The decision to appear as the 'good pupil' of the WTO and, above all, of the Euro-Mediterranean partnership cannot happen against the interests of entrepreneurs or, to be more exact, cannot come about in a way too opposed to their interests. But these can very easily be taken into account thanks to the decree of 29 August 1994, which authorizes all sorts of restrictions, and thanks also to the temporary safeguarding measures included in the agreement on association and article 28 of the latter which authorizes prohibitions and restrictions for 'reasons of public morality, public order, public security, protection of the health and life of people and animals'.[94] These juridical arrangements make it possible for 'distortions' in openness to be legalized – distortions which thus do not seem to be a violation of the free trade agreements.

Systematic technical controls have been used, for instance on tyres, to limit their import: when there are no Tunisian norms, European norms are applied, but their verification is still implemented by the INNORPI, the Tunisian organization which administratively controls all imports and can, very opportunely, deem them unsuitable for home consumption.[95] Respect for the terms and conditions, including the extremely numerous conditions that need to be respected for the imported product, is scrupulously controlled, and when a competitor has already implemented all the administrative and technical procedures required, the new importer is obliged to repeat every step, even though the product imported is exactly the same.[96]

In addition, the lowering or indeed suppression of customs duties is often purely cosmetic, with the suppressed tax being surreptitiously transferred to other levies. This is the case with cars: while customs duties for a 4 hp car were 27 per cent in 1995, and consumption duty 30 per cent, the former actually disappeared in 1998 after application of the free trade agreement with the European Union, but the latter had been raised almost as much, reaching 55 per cent.[97] If there are any uncontrolled developments in the balance of current transactions, or a lack of currency, the Central Bank gives oral instructions to the banks and public organizations to limit imports. The modes of intervention are varied: customs formalities may be multiplied, there may be restrictions on the provision of currency to importers and obstacles to obtaining documentary credit, delays in the arrival of products with the harbour authorities being urged to slow down customs clearance procedures and access to the necessary documents, occasional and unofficial increases in customs duties, unfavourable judgements on the import of the product due to production defects, and absence of adequate information or, quite simply, substandard quality . . . Admittedly, all exports are in principle free, but, for this to be valid, one must have an accommodation address with a qualified intermediary. In addition, there is an unofficial list of products that are excluded from this liberty, a list containing (in particular) the most lucrative products, especially the export of olive oil.[98]

It is clear that protectionism and nationalitarianism are both vectors of favouritism and socio-economic inequality. When import depends on subjective judgements, more or less unofficial administrative procedures or the quality of personal relations, protection becomes an obvious instrument in the service of the central power and its objects of control.

The many instrumentalizations of 'nationalitarianism'

However, these protectionist practices do not result merely from administrative decisions, but more from their convergence with economic strategies (both public and private) as well as from a heightened sense of national awareness. The colonial episode founded the defensive character of Tunisian nationalism and the preoccupation with what might be called a 'national preference', expressing the desire to build up a nation-state that was also economically independent and to draw up a security pact.[99] That is why this economic nationalism, too, appears in a particularly obvious guise: under a fully liberal ideology, it expresses and cements a general resistance on the part of the Tunisians, not to openness, liberalism or globalization in general, but to a real or supposed dissolution of national independence.[100] National-liberalism, a strange alliance of liberalism and economic nationalism, is thus not created by a voluntarist project of the state; it expresses the ambiguity of an entanglement of different ways of being, more or less well-thought-out strategies, tactics of power, and economic and political activities.

The example of the obstacles placed in the way of foreigners entering helps to understand the complexity of processes at work.[101] In the sensitive sectors – banking, insurance and telecommunications – we observe the convergence of different interests ensuring that a highly technical sector of activity, which might have been able to benefit from expertise and a specialized, internationally recognized know-how, remains in the hands of national actors (the case of insurance and consumer credit) or in the hands of foreign actors chosen for their docility and their grasp of national interests (the case of the mobile phone industry), even if it means going astray down dead-ends and incurring grave crises (the BATAM affair and spiralling household debt) or not benefiting from the best technology and logistics offered on the market (the case of the second GSM licence, for which Telefonica was ousted in favour of ORASCOM, an Egyptian-Emirates operator). Or we could point to the ill-will of the Tunisian authorities in the negotiations on the readmission agreement with France or Italy, in particular the financial demands linked to that demand; the fixing at unrealistic levels of the minimal sums demanded by the Tunisian authorities when privatizations are carried out or concessions granted, leading to the failure of several operations; the refusal to grant more flexibility for ad hoc recruitments, as with the Alcatel group in the framework of the creation of the platform of qualifications in the area of technologies and information, or with the BNP (*Banque nationale de Paris*) in the framework of its majority holding in the UBCI (*Union bancaire pour le commerce et l'industrie*), or for the resolution of conflicts, as with the dispute over property with France; or indeed the national preference granted de facto in the case of privatizations.[102]

Over and above all these facts, one must point out, too, that these decisions and attitudes did not in the main emerge from bureaucratic and political apparatuses. In the insurance case mentioned above, the refusal to see Allianz rise in the capital of the national company is in reality the result of a profound agreement between the ministries concerned, the *Banque centrale de Tunisie* and the economic and financial establishment. This agreement bore on the simultaneous maintenance of secure incomes, opportunities for interventions, possibilities of control and perpetuation of the system of mutual dependence making accumulation and disciplinary normalization possible.[103] In the case of the UIB (*Union internationale de banque*), the *Société Générale* found it difficult to reach a clear and complete vision of the real situation of the company as a result – of course – of the hostility of the management and the departing team (implicitly supported by the public powers), but also because of the absence of transmission of strategic information on the part of the firms' executives. These 'nationalist' reflexes of closure and distrust in particular can be explained by the fear of being called a 'collaborator', an 'informer' and a 'traitor',[104] a fear exacerbated by the nationality of the buyer, by institutional reflexes akin to private protectionism, and by the hegemonic positioning of certain actors in the different niches of activity. Generally speaking, these activities make themselves known under the benevolent gaze of the authorities (as with the importing of certain makes of car) or with their support (as with the production of certain products with the setting up of normative or health-related checks which prevent or de facto put a brake on competitors' imports).

If we adopt a technical, normative and liberal vision of these and similar nationalist practices, there is no doubt at all that they need to be analysed as contradicting the openness espoused by reformism, representing economic 'distortions', 'bad habits', and 'irrationalities', '*rentier* behaviour' and 'unhealthy protectionism', or even 'irrational moves guided by an old-fashioned blanket support for the Third World'.[105] On the other hand, an awareness of political, social and symbolic dynamisms obliges us to abandon any normative evaluation: nationalism is neither good nor bad, 'it is a historic form for interests and opposed struggles'.[106] In spite of its emotional character, which as often as not drags the analysis into the perilous paths of denunciation or justification, it needs to be taken as a total social given. These practices need, then, to be understood as the expression of a complex appropriation of openness and a now inevitable international integration.

The previous examples have shown that a practice described as 'nationalist' can at one and the same time be the result of an explicit nationalist demand in the name of national sovereignty; of a political, populist or opportunist instrumentalization aimed at legitimatization; of a public and state interventionism; of strictly bureaucratic logics; of a classical protectionist policy operating in the name of employment, upgrading, apprenticeship, or adaptation to competition; of an inability to find an adequate mode of action; of the sense of a dead end and a desire to conceal problems, hassles and difficulties; of an anti-westernism and a reasoned struggle against neo-colonialism; of a diffuse nationalist awareness; of a reminiscence of colonial domination and the economic discrimination that accompanied it; of a desire for political control; of a policy of integration and implementation of measures of economic and social security; of a clientelist strategy or of corruption; of a determination to keep control over the levers of action on the national economy; and so on.

Those who (like Arab nationalists, groups on the extreme left, or indeed many individuals without any political affiliation) criticize the authorities' lack of nationalism underline in their turn this plurality of meanings and this instrumentalization. Their criticisms bear first and foremost on the behaviour of elites in pursuit of their own material interests (and not the pursuit of the service of the ideal of the country's general interest), on the instrumentalization of the nationalist ideology for clientelist and nepotistic purposes, and on the failure of economic policies to meet the objectives of full employment, growth or industrialization. For – *pace* those who believe in consensus – Tunisians do not defend identical positions in this regard, since some of them defend a clear economic nationalism (middle classes, employees, civil servants, trade unionists), while others play the card of a systematic alliance with foreigners (certain big entrepreneurs, certain segments of the state), while yet others do not have any cut-and-dried position, being principally preoccupied by their own economic situation (small entrepreneurs, migrants, tradesmen, workers in the informal sector), while others, finally, wish to preserve their powers of negotiation (senior civil servants, the ruling elite, certain major entrepreneurs, party members) or are moved by demagogy (the popular press, certain segments of the central power and the RCD).

In the abovementioned examples, the different logics have converged to create the image of a defensive and timid nationalism, or even an 'exacerbated nationalism'. But these cases mainly display a quite individual configuration which brings in actors seeking to protect their rents and their positions within society, defending a social reproduction in which they benefit from a privileged position and instrumentalizing nationalism for power. These are all perfect illustrations of economic 'nationalitarianism'. Nonetheless, this is not always the case: more often than not, the ambiguity and incompleteness of different and indeed contrasting logics proves decisive.

National-liberalism, a complex management of international integration

The practices characteristic of national-liberalism are indeed often less unambiguous than the previous examples suggested. In reality, there are many who, while having internationalized their activities and their behaviours, are just as much preoccupied by their national integration and yet, while continuing to claim that they are nationalist actors, are no less 'globalized'.

Multiple logics of action

In fact, the figures of national-liberalism, a contemporary economic version of reformism, are diverse and ambiguous. There is, of course, the out-and-out nationalist reformer, like Khayr ed-Din and today the higher civil servants who simultaneously conceive the great reformist projects and nationalist and protectionist strategies on a day-by-day basis. We also find the technocrats of diverse administrations who implement the reforms of liberalization and at the same time the various ways of side-stepping these; the members of agencies who promote bureaucratic modernity while at the same time piling on the paperwork and fuelling an administrative hierarchy that deprives anyone of real responsibility; elites trained abroad who have passed through international institutions and hamper the internationalization of Tunisian capitalism; the big bankers and businessmen who steer a course between Paris, London or New York and Tunis, but who are the first to demand that the CEOs of banks or enterprises should be nationals.[107]

But we also need to be aware of the whole mass of anonymous individuals who hope to become an integral part of international modernity while at the same time behaving like easily offended nationalists. There are entrepreneurs who support 'upgrading' and free trade and form alliances with foreigners, while requesting subsidies and defending a preference for national interests. There are industrialists who accept foreign acquisitions of holdings, sometimes with a majority stake, and at the same time never stop demanding the application of discriminatory measures against foreigners. There are members of associations that share the ideology of modernity, democratization, and an international lifestyle, while denouncing European neocolonialization. There are individuals who consume Coca-Cola, dream of MacDonald's and Pizza Hut, equip themselves with the most up-to-date household appliances, and simultaneously demonstrate against American imperialism in the region, criticize western materialism and listen to *Al Jazira* or *Al Manar*. Bankers and tradesmen contribute to the spread of consumption and modern lifestyles, but also to a political economy comprised of clientelist interventionism, and of networking on the regional, family or friendship level. Workers in free zones, and employees in tourist complexes are, by day, the best allies of international capitalism and of foreign consumers and, by night, the faithful representatives of a traditional Islamism (reformist or not), of a vengeful 'Arabo-Muslim' set of ideas, of family and kinship values.

When set out like this under an external gaze, these types of behaviour may appear contradictory and reveal more or less naive illusions. In reality, they merely reflect the plurality of logics of action, and the diversity, too, of the interpretations of national-liberalism by one and the same individual, and the complexity and ambiguity of any social practice. In this case, any appropriation of globalization is equally complex – and the individuals concerned do not register, as such, what is commonly called 'hybridity' or *métissage*.[108]

The example of the informal economy

A separate place needs to be reserved for those who apparently seem to undermine the reforming projects of the central power but who, in reality, participate in this reformist and nationalist political economy. The many different actors in contraband are the archetype of this, as historians have shown for the eighteenth and, especially, the nineteenth centuries.[109] A rapid survey of economic activities and the organization of markets will allow us to convince ourselves of the permanence and the current dynamisms of such practices.

In Tunis, 'Moncef Bey' and, everywhere in the country, the 'Libyan souks'[110] materialize the centrality of informal activities. Towns such as El Jem or Ben Gardane make of these a speciality, while, in all municipalities, fairs are organized each year on the eve of Eid or New Year's Day, or the days preceding the beginning of the school year.[111] These permanent or occasional markets sell off products that entered the country illegally, or at least via networks of commercialization operating on the margins of legality; they also offer second-choice products, such as the products from bankrupt factories or factories from which certain batches of products have been rejected by the principal.[112] Contraband occupies a great many actors: inhabitants living on the borders, in the case of Algeria and, especially, Libya; émigrés on holiday, false émigrés who take advantage of national dispositions to go in for street peddling, housewives, students, the unemployed, young people who specialize in business trips to Paris, Marseilles, Naples or Istanbul, recognized local tradesmen who commit customs and harbour fraud, protected wheeler-dealers who develop these activities on a large scale.[113] Contraband concerns every type of product destined for the Tunisian market, exploiting price differentials, policies of subsidy and taxation, and practices of tax evasion.

Second-hand clothes provide an opportunity for a subtler mode of contraband based on the activities of sorting, recycling and re-exporting material from the United States and Germany destined for the poorest countries.[114] These activities are official and even encouraged by the authorities because of their contribution to the inflow of currency and the statistical swelling of exports. But they also permit an illegal spread of second-hand clothes across the Tunisian market and the appearance, at extremely competitive prices, of clothes and fabrics that barely resemble second-hand clothes at all.[115] The informal sector is consubstantial with production. It is not necessary here to go over a point well-known in Tunisian studies:[116] how to enter into the accounts the activity of these thousands of independents and this mass of enterprises that have fewer than six employees, and which represent 85 per cent of the total of Tunisian enterprises – the activity, too, of middle-sized and large enterprises which underestimate their production and do not declare the total number of their employees or hours worked. Fakes are numerous, too, rising sharply since 1995, with Tunisia now constituting 'one of the traditional zones'.[117] Although a law of April 2001 penalizes this activity, fake products remain extremely common, destined for export, in the luxury sector (Vuitton bags, Lacoste clothes, brands of perfume), in objects of everyday use (lighters, biros, razors), in electronic equipment (Schneider circuit breakers, Moulinex products), in the agribusiness (cheese), and even in the best-known logos, with GrandOptical in Tunis, for instance, operating without an official brand name.

In the first analysis, informal activities weaken the strategy of modernization of the national economy by diminishing the tax base and promoting imports rather than local productions. They undermine the rule of law by acting illegally. They sap the Tunisian authorities' desire for control of commercial balance and of currency by basing their activities on foreign goods ... But, at the same time, these practices are indissociable from openness, and comprise another of its modes. They play against certain techniques of market regulation, while constituting the supreme form of that same regulation: as a result, they promote liberal reform in configurations that are different from, but probably more powerful than, those of formal commerce. Thus, they sustain the reformist dynamic, outside the rules of law and bureaucratic normalization – but, indisputably, in accordance with the logic of the policing state and the mechanisms that underlie the security pact. Thus they play a part in the spread of capitalism and its reproduction, even though national-liberalism aims to look after the domestic actors of international competition and reduce the impact of the latter. They contribute to liberalization, investment,[118] the modernization of mass consumption and the cultural unification of society, growth and employment, apprenticeship too, and a certain degree of professional training, town and country planning and the integration of deprived populations (the South and South-East zones in particular).[119]

Informal activities play a part in the process of economic centralization: they constitute a practice of inclusion for the multitude of individuals caught up in these networks;[120] they play a part in the mechanisms of social reproduction;[121] they contribute to the desire for national unification precisely insofar as the smugglers' markets bring together local logics, activities and networks (regionalist, tribal, family) with, on the other hand, state activities, networks and preoccupations.[122] These practices play a part in the increasing degree to which Tunisia is integrated into the international scene, and sometimes in a certain modernization of its productive economy, by the development of fake goods and increasingly specialized imitations and by an increase in the productivity of certain Tunisian infrastructures designed for international trade.[123]

Above all, informal activities involve the full set of Tunisian actors: consumers and investors, marginal players and wealthy wheeler-dealers, entrepreneurs operating partly or totally on the edge of legality, émigrés, people of dual nationality and Tunisians from Tunisia, police and customs officers, those close to the central power and actors who are members of 'the resistance' . . . We could almost repeat word for word what Dalenda Larguèche describes with regard to the nineteenth century: 'A marginal activity, a parallel and illicit economy, a disguised social resistance, a strategy of survival for disadvantaged social groups or illegal but lucrative activities with dynamic and rising elements – the contraband sector [and that of all illegality] is a space in which is expressed a whole series of contradictions, precisely because it simultaneously includes actors with different and even contradictory interests'.[124] Like other economic sites, contraband, the informal sector, fake goods and all other forms of traffic constitute spaces of negotiation, association, and mediation, which make it possible for the social domain to be articulated in different ways. They enable poor and marginal groups to live but also enrich notables and businessmen; they express a tactic of resistance or avoidance but also a strategy of influence and diversification; and they structure both the state and the groups that gravitate around it. In other words, the reformist dynamic can act outside the rules of the bureaucratized space of the national economy and the rule of law.

What do these examples tell us? Quite simply that, beyond myth and fiction, reformism and the economic form it takes, and national-liberalism as a mode of management of extraversion, appear more as heterogeneous practices, and uncertain and unstable makeshifts. They show individuals and groups that are certainly not passive even if they are far from dominating the space of their field of action. I have tried to show that Tunisians are fully part of globalization, in its various facets, starting with the effects of domination that it transmits and produces: to be in globalization and to take part in it does not mean that inequality and domination are avoided – quite the contrary. In a country like Tunisia, domination appears self-evident, as the main fact of globalization, and it even entails a neglect or a euphemising of previous and inner effects of domination.

'Reformism' and 'Tunisian-ness' appear as deceptive words which make it possible for tensions to be defused, problems to be concealed, and strategies to be legitimatized, but also for heterogeneous practices to be fostered, as well as divergent interests, varied visions of the world and Tunisia's place in it. The sacralizing of these terms is an effect of power: it opens the way to consensus and unanimity, the main vectors of discipline; to respect for authority; and to the indisputable character of the government's political guidelines, plans, programmes, and economic strategies. This is also why these portmanteau words, which need to be understood in their historicity, need also to be demythified. Such a task brings out the processes of exclusion that have always been present alongside the processes of integration that alone have been highlighted in discourses and myths. We need to understand that the nationalist practices and rhetorics of withdrawal are neither good nor bad. Our previous analysis, after all, has shown that actions performed in the name of nationalism often concealed political logics of quite a different nature, in particular effects of power, relations of force, and a certain free play in internal social relations. This, too, is reformism.

9

Reforms in Perpetuity: The Success of Reformism

Support for Tunisian modes of government, therefore, cannot allow us to neglect the effects of internal domination, nor the element of coercion. If we interpret these reforms, from a technical point of view, as a transformation of public policies and modes of government aimed at abolishing precisely identified failings, we can only acknowledge the failure of such reforms, which remain perpetually on the agenda. Have not people been talking about the reform of the tax system Tunisia ever since the middle of the nineteenth century and right up to the present day? Or about the burden of debt and the restructuring of the financial system? About the dependency of the productive system and its need to adapt and catch up? About the need for modernization? About reform as a response to crisis and decline? And about the inability of reforms to face up to these challenges, in particular those that come from outside? Are these failures not repeatedly analysed in terms of external constraint, of resistance on the part of the people and the archaism of the elites – yesterday the ulemas, today the economic and political bourgeoisies?

On the other hand, if we view reformism as a mode of government and a process of subjection, then the recurrent nature of the reforms – which Mohamed Tozy has described as 'reforms without change' in connection with Morocco, and which might be paraphrased in connection with the 'Tunisia of Ben Ali' as a 'change without reforms'[1] – cannot be seen merely as a 'failure'. Or, to be more precise, the 'failure' of reforms can be understood as an effect of power, with the succession of cycles made up of reforms, the realization that they have failed, the persistence of the problems and new reforms needing to be analysed as a whole.[2]

Reforms are not solely synonyms for the project of modernization; they are not simply a form of social behaviour determined by a certain ethic, for example solidarity or modern Islam; their main object is not to acquire increased respect for the rule of law, the improvement of market mechanisms, an increase in the competitiveness of the economy, or the guarantee of a securer income for the state. Perpetual reform makes the exercise of power possible. Reformism is thus a mode of control that 'implies an uninterrupted and constant coercion, which watches over the process of the activity rather than its result'.[3] It is for this precise reason that perpetual reforms can be considered as a success. Reformism is simultaneously a space of encounter and a vector of discipline, of social control, of the normalization of individuals. This is what I would now like to show concretely, starting with two examples: privatization and the upgrading of enterprises.

Privatization softly softly, or how to defend 'Tunisian-ness'

The development and conditions of privatization constitute, without the slightest doubt, one of the activities for which it is the most difficult to obtain information and to discover with any minimum of precision how far the process has actually advanced. In Tunisia, there is no detailed evaluation of the public sector. Of course, decrees and laws define public enterprises but, on the one hand, the definitions of what is considered as public vary over time and, on the other, no exhaustive and definitive list of enterprises that are totally or partly public has ever been published.[4] As it has been presented officially, for example on the government's website, the portfolio of the state does not correspond to the information provided by the laws that regulate the supervision of semipublic entities. From one year to the next there circulate lists (always different) of enterprises to privatize, but they are always partial and restricted.

According to the IMF, in 2001 there were still at least 120 public enterprises in all sectors of the economy, representing a fifth of the total added value of the country. Even the Bretton Woods institution emphasizes mainly the lack of information given by the authorities and their inadequacy when it comes to reaching any precise evaluation of the public sector: it is still extremely difficult to gain any accurate idea of all the enterprises subjected to the state's direct control or to non-commercial considerations, with several of them being classified in the private sector.[5] According to European experts, the number of enterprises to be privatized is even higher, mainly due to the complexity of cross-over shares and the financial arrangements of the periods of socialism (1960–9) and even more of the period of interventionist liberalism (1969–87),[6] but also of current liberalization: takeovers and mergers, restructurings and the presence of supplementary functions, stock transfer in joint ventures and the failure of privatizations in the Stock Exchange do not enable us to identify with any certainty these holdings, especially in the financial and tourist sectors.[7]

An attempt at evaluation: the weakness of foreign investors

Some information is provided by the Tunisian authorities but these data, highly sensitive politically, should be used with extreme caution. I will not go over in detail the various techniques of opacity that I have analysed elsewhere:[8] modification of the base of the calculation, systematic neglect, over-general and truncated information, confusion between forecasts and eventual figures, and the lack of systematic information, with some of it being published in percentages, others in absolute values, etc. The only thing certain here is that this opacity concerns the process of privatization as much as the result and the monitoring of the privatized enterprises. In this latter case, for example, from one year to the next, the sample of enterprises investigated is not the same, and so it is difficult to draw up a balance sheet for a given period.[9] As far as the holdings of foreigners are concerned, information is presented in the form most favourable to the donors who urge the public powers to deepen the process, mentioning the sums brought in and not the number of operations. This presentation conceals the marginal nature of direct foreign investments, contrary to the discourse on the openness and attractiveness of Tunisia. As for the names of buyers and the exact amount of each operation, they were inaccessible until 1998. Since that date, certain information has been published. If the sums collected by the state are now systematically provided, the same does not go for the quality of the buyers: in the list made public by the Tunisian authorities, the buyer is often indicated in terms of proprietor... 'various Tunisian buyers', 'several individual Tunisian entities' or 'various purchasers'![10] These difficulties in gaining access to detailed and coherent information are not the monopoly of independent university researchers alone, but concern donors just as much.[11]

Between 1987 and 30 April 2004, 176 enterprises, it appears, were privatized and restructured for a total sum of 2,359 MDT. These operations were mainly privatizations, either total (53 per cent) or partial (18 per cent), and liquidations (22 per cent), with the opening of capital by public share offer concerning only 6 per cent of operations and the concessions just 1 per cent.[12] Until 1997, 79 enterprises were privatized with no public information being given, for a value of 455 MDT, i.e. 5.76 MDT per enterprise. These figures are not published and I have calculated them by subtraction:[13] by showing the very low value of the sale of the first privatizations, they are, indeed, in a position to open up a forbidden debate. The official explanation, which can be found on the government's website, is that until 1994 the privatizations mainly concerned enterprises that were showing a loss. But one can justifiably doubt this. How can one explain the low level, too, of the income drawn from the privatization of surplus enterprises between 1994 and 1998? How, in particular, can one explain the adoption of this strange strategy that consists in starting with the least attractive?

With more certainty, this low level may be explained first of all by privatizations that might be described as 'cosmetic', since they have mainly given rise to re-namings or re-descriptions.[14] The desire to privilege national actors, and more precisely certain of them, then becomes evident: the official site provides more accurate data only after 1998, the year which corresponds to a certain openness to foreigners – and even here we need to note that certain operations do not mention the name of the privatized business. Quite unlike current practices in developing countries, in particular in the Maghreb,[15] until 1998 practically no public enterprise was sold off to non-Tunisian private groups. The latter were not, of course, formally excluded from the competition, but they were rapidly discouraged by administrative blockages that they encountered, or by the inadequacy of guarantees and information necessary for them to become properly involved.[16]

However, after that date, the cement industry and then other sectors opened up to foreign interests, mainly as an effect of financial constraint and the state's need for currency. As a result, foreign investment seems to represent, for the period as a whole, nearly 82 per cent of the income from privatization in industry and 74 per cent in services. These data justify the satisfaction of the Tunisian authorities and the donors in terms of openness. A comparison of these overall figures with the detail of operations, however, gives us a much more ambiguous picture of the situation: the 82 per cent figure for the industry is obtained almost exclusively from the privatization of four cement factories[17] – which brought in 771 of the 782 MDT in the industrial sector – and the 74 per cent figure in the services come essentially from two operations that provided 788 MDT out of the 973 MDT of the sector – the transfer of the second GSM licence and the 52 per cent privatization of the UIB. So, in reality – contrary to appearances – the foreign beneficiaries of Tunisian privatizations are still very few in number: out of 176 privatizations, 4 have benefited foreigners associated with nationals, and 15 have benefited foreigners alone – not to mention the fact that these operations sometimes concerned only partial sell-offs. In other words, hardly 10 per cent of operations benefited foreigners, even if the later brought in over three-quarters of the total income from privatization.[18]

The many different forms of state and bureaucratic redeployment

The state remains central because privatization is an extremely complicated process. Procedures of liquidation, restructuring and privatization are slow to achieve concrete shape, due to the many different institutions and state actors concerned and the historically contingent character of the holdings.[19] The laws passed in domains as diverse as taxation, personnel management and land questions are sometimes contradictory. The number of operations necessary for a privatization is also to be explained by social reasons (the need to maintain conditions of employment) and by political reasons (the need to control capital).[20]

The very conception of the process of privatization illustrates the extent to which Tunisian state control is deeply rooted: the carrying out of the transfer is realized by specialized public organizations – the *Comité d'assainissement et de restructuration des enterprises à participation publique* (the CAREPP – Committee for Improving and Restructuring Enterprises with Public Holdings) or the *Comité technique de privatisation* (CTP – Technical Committee for Privatization), depending on the extent of privatization and its degree of sensitivity. In particular, the terms of restructuring are broadly defined by the public enterprise undergoing privatization. In a situation of flagrant conflict of interests (i.e. in a completely subjective situation), and sometimes in a state of total juridical and technical incompetence, the latter itself defines the strategy of privatization of which it is to be the object and the obligations imposed on the buyer. According to the follow-up inquiries on privatization, almost half the privatized enterprises have run into difficulties in following the terms and conditions, in particular due to land problems, or fiscal and social problems that were not resolved before privatization, and as a result, too, of the imprecision of information provided by the public enterprise before the sell-off, for example on the equipment – often non-standard, or even old-fashioned and obsolete – and even the status of the workforce.[21]

The impossibility of seeing the state withdraw from the economy is also demonstrated by all those 'false' or very partial privatizations:[22] the operation sometimes leads to better management, sometimes to budgetary income, or even to improvements in the statistics, but always to the maintenance of a control of these enterprises by public bodies. This was the case with the *Compagnie de phosphate de Gafsa*, the *Groupe chimique*, or the *Banque du Sud*, up until 2005. This was the case, also, with those companies of whose capital just 20 per cent, 5 per cent and even 2.3 per cent is transferred, in particular in tourism but also in the electronics, machine and chemical industries. State control is still exercised even after privatization, via administrative interventions, in particular by the head office for fiscal controls and the CNSS. According to rumour, but also according to the same follow-up reports on privatized enterprises, many of these recently privatized enterprises have been subjected to fiscal or social control, over a period prior to privatization.[23]

In the rare cases where the buyer is a foreigner, state intervention is perpetuated by at least four procedures: the presence of a Tunisian partner for the foreign buyer, who is usually linked to the state bureaucracy or the central power; the somewhat restrictive terms and conditions in the social domain; regulating of the national market (price, regulations, norms, and import conditions); the presence, especially, of at least one enterprise in the sector which remains within the state fold and to some extent acts as a Trojan horse for the government. The Gabès cemetery, situated in the south of the country, a region deemed to be a political as well as a social 'hotspot', is one example. But a systematic analysis of Tunisian state control cannot fail to reveal the permanence of the interventions requested by the buyers (legal entities or natural persons) from the state, in terms of banking facilities, tax exemptions, or other advantages or privileges that enable there to be a monopoly, a lesser degree of competition, or protection from foreigners: the formula 'let us get on with it, but give us plenty of protection' of French manufacturers of the eighteenth century, addressed to the administrative authorities of the day, can be applied with magnificent relevance to Tunisian entrepreneurs.[24] All these tendencies are accentuated by the new bureaucratic independence of the administrative bodies placed in charge of privatization – an independence frequently encouraged by donors. As a result, it would probably be correct to describe the process as a bureaucratization of privatization.

The objective of job protection is shared by the administration and by the formal or informal structures linked to the central power. Unemployment is analysed as the principal vector of instability, disorder and protest. It matters little whether the desire to limit unemployment be motivated by social, economic, political, security, or even party-political reasons. The main thing is that this preoccupation chimes in with the worries of Tunisians, and echoes the demands of the trade union world and the employees, of course – but also echoes the expectations of certain segments of the business world, the bankers' prudence, and sometimes even the opportunism of the buyers who, though unmoved by altruistic considerations, aim to put themselves into the good books of the authorities while still being able to justify any potential by-passing of market rules or the demands laid down in the terms and conditions, for example in terms of conditions of investment, modernization, the suppression of protectionist barriers, or the lowering of prices.

These occasional convergences do not eliminate the tensions between the different groups. In spite of the muzzling of the world of trade unions and associations, the UGTT does not hesitate to use its weight to sound the alarm about delicate situations,[25] notably ever since it has faced competition in this area by more independent actors who support strikers and circulate petitions. The government's discourse asserting that the privatizations have had a positive impact on employment needs to be understood within this context: it tries to act as a counterweight – apparently without much success – to developments that affect people much more intensely, in particular to irregular layoffs (in Moknine and Ben Arous, for example) and the hunger strikes that followed them, or to the rise of jobs that are insecure, casual, and temporary.[26] The attention paid to the social realm explains the slowness and timidity of the traditional forms of sales of assets. On the other hand, creeping privatization, on the margins of public policies and thus of official rhetoric, is now occurring in several sectors.[27] The simultaneous nature of these processes demonstrates the complexity of the role of the state, which must both respond to the expectations of the UGTT and employees and also take into account the fears of the great majority of Tunisian actors, pull strings to help its 'friends', focus on social stability and security, and intervene directly. It also suggests that, while it is significant and widespread, state intervention is anything but rigid: it can adapt itself to relations of force and to conflicts between actors, and even take part in the violation of rules defined by the state bureaucracy itself.

The widespread state control is also evident from the establishment of an environment simultaneously favourable to privatizations and to the pursuit of political interventionism: the circular from the BCT of 23 November 1997 authorizes the banks to grant directly to those concerned medium-term credits to finance the purchase of a controlling shareholding or of elements of assets; the SICAR (*Société d'investissement en capital à risque* – Society for Investment in Venture Capital) are encouraged to participate in privatizations; the acquirers can benefit from tax relief for revenues or profits reinvested, or from a five-year exemption from the tax on the profits of newly privatized companies. All these measures need to be understood within the framework of the ambiguous relations between the central power and the economic world. From a reading of the buyers of privatized enterprises between 1998 and 2004, it becomes clear that the privatizations are integrated into the strategy of 'dispersal' that I mentioned above. Only once do we find the same buyer involved in two operations – which in fact turn out to be liquidations rather than privatizations, with all the other enterprises being transferred to different buyers for each operation. Of course, prudence must remain the order of the day in this interpretation, given the importance of 'gaps' in the data, and the use of nominee companies. According to the sparse information I have managed to pick up from interviews, it seems that, for every operation, the central power chooses the entrepreneur to whom the privatized company will be transferred. But these chosen entrepreneurs are almost never the same, and usually they already belong to the economic community, to the traditional economic elite that developed under Bourguiba in the shadow of the state. Political distrust towards the establishing of big groups thus appears confirmed by the privatizations that did not favour operations of concentration or vertical specialization.

This strategy of dispersal is not, however, systematic. In this well-trained and 'docile' Tunisia, alert to considerations on the critical size necessary for enterprises to be competitive, and perhaps even attentive to more political considerations, privatization and 'upgrading' have made it possible for the restructuring and consolidation of certain businesses to be achieved. This seems to be the case with certain well-established entrepreneurs, but also with several of those 'close' to the President who, by means of various practices (associations, intermediary financing, bank loans, advantageous prices and conditions of purchase . . .) have built up a real empire for themselves. These wheeler-dealers do not, however, constitute consolidated and structured groups, insofar as they prefer to prosper as middlemen and financiers rather than as entrepreneurs properly speaking.

In the absence of information, in a climate of censorship and pressure, rumour reigns unchallenged. But everyone, including donors, agrees that privatizations have often been grabbed by those 'close to the regime', that they have been the object (as indeed in many other countries) of widespread corruption and substantial commissions, either by a more or less forced alliance with potential buyers, or by a well-rewarded intervention in favour of one of the buyers.[28] It now seems that the presidential entourage intervenes not only in activities of predation on the big contracts, but also as intermediaries, or even shareholders in operations of privatization and concession. This hypothesis seems to be corroborated by the fact that even donors have not been able to gain access to certain sensitive information. These businessmen are also active in land and property speculation. In fact, the operations of privatization have made it possible for certain people to get rich quick by a system of reduced-price purchase and high-price resale. This mode of intervention could explain the low level of the sums brought in by privatizations on behalf of national companies, especially during the first years of the process.

Privatization must not be interpreted merely as a formal process of capital transfer from the public to the private sectors. As elsewhere, more flexible and non-institutionalized formulae are used – 'creeping' privatization, or 'unregulated', 'informal', or 'criminal' privatization. They concern agricultural land, the development of parallel markets or the inveiglement of markets. In spite of the reschedulings of finance, the *Office national des huiles* (ONH), for example, experiences serious difficulties as a result mainly of unregulated liberalization and the establishment of parallel private trading circuits which, it is said, are controlled by those close to Cartage.[29] Also worth mentioning is the double process of privatization of profits and the nationalization of losses, illustrated by what happens in air transports, where the public enterprise, Tunisair, experiences losses while Karthago, which belongs to private parties close to the President, is prospering thanks to the flight authorizations, one-sided maintenance contracts with Tunisair, and a whole series of advantages that mean that its costs are carried over to the public enterprise,[30] and thanks, as well, to the administration's tolerance of concrete modes of operation and the non-respect of European norms.[31]

Without underestimating these phenomena, which are by nature impossible to quantify, the fact remains that this tendency is doubtless less clearly marked here than in many other countries: Tunisia is still a country of state control, and the favoured techniques of government are still mainly regulation and direct control. Corruption is now integrated into the modes of government, but it does not comprise its main instrument: far from it.

Rejection of outside vantage points, adoption of a global lexicon

The rejection of any external gaze needs to be understood in the very particular context of national-liberalism and the defence of Tunisian-ness. The failure of the programme of technical assistance from the European Union and the early departure from Tunisia of the team of aid workers sent to implement it are a perfect illustration of this almost paranoid behaviour.[32] From the middle of the 1990s, the European Union negotiated with Tunisia to send a team of experts to speed up and improve the process of privatization, at the heart of the liberal reforms that it supported. An agreement was finally signed between the two parties in 1998, but the consortium chosen, ICEA/GOPA/COMETE, was unable to fulfil its mission before 2001. After a whole series of conflicts, as demonstrated in particular by the stopping of the consortium's payment in May 2003, the Tunisian party demanded the early departure of the experts. In fact, the cell providing aid for privatizations, financed within the framework of the MEDA funds, never managed to integrate itself into the country's structures. The political authorities did not want any part of it and, in these circumstances, the administration did nothing to receive a technical assistance for which it was, in any case, not prepared.

This failure can certainly be explained by mutual rigidity and incompatibilities between personalities, or indeed errors in targeting: the cell's mission and the composition of its members were in fact turned towards aid in the methodology and techniques of privatization, its monitoring, follow-up and major operations, whereas in Tunisia transfers concern only small enterprises, and the authorities never envisaged any modification of their modes of privatization. The cell was the object of a misunderstanding that hampered things severely: the Europeans thought they could improve the current process while gaining access to information; in this way they thought they could contribute to the perpetuation (within an entirely bureaucratic logic) of a success story that was all the more useful to them in that the Euro-Mediterranean Partnership was severely criticized. The Tunisians saw this project as a means of satisfying the Europeans easily, and thus of improving relations with them, of obtaining material and, secondarily, 'de luxe secretaries' to manage an important proportion of European aid.[33] In fact, the cell was allocated to the *Direction générale de la privatisation*, a non-sovereign entity acting first and foremost as a registration body, and not to the only entities able to take decisions, namely the CAREPP, the Presidency (core cabinet meetings) or the enterprises to be privatized. Contrary to what had been programmed, the members of the cell never had any Tunisian counterparts assigned to them; they were never able to take part in any decisions or even to discuss matters with the CAREPP, the technical committee or the state secretariat; they never managed to contact directly the enterprises to be privatized . . .

But in this game of hide-and-seek, the part played by the donors should not be underestimated. The failure of European technical assistance can also be explained by bureaucratic considerations and by power struggles within and between international institutions. There are many tensions between the Commission in Brussels and the European Delegation in Tunis and, within the Delegation, between European experts and civil servants or between political considerations and considerations of a technical order. The Commission and the management of the Delegation consider the MEDA funds as a political question, which leads them to instrumentalize the civil servants and, even more, the experts, and to reject their recommendations if political interests come into play or if they have the illusion that they can benefit from pulling strings. In spite of all the rhetoric on complementarity and the coordination of aid, the competition between bureaucratic organizations is, in any case, something that belongs merely to the past.[34]

Be that as it may, the advice on privatization was never accepted and the rejection of technical assistance was indisputably the rejection of an external gaze on the 'black box' of relations between various Tunisian actors. Thus, privatizations need to be analysed less in terms of the modernization of the productive apparatus and entrepreneurial government, and more in terms of modes of government, control and surveillance. The national preference needs to be understood as the new form of expression of Tunisian-ness and, in consequence, as the new mode of management of extraversion. Without passing any judgement of value on this expression of nationalism, we can simply highlight the primacy of this dimension over all the others, in particular over the desire for modernization. We can doubtless explain the significance of these sentiments by reference to the retrospective interpretation of the penetration of French capitalism as an instrument of the political domination of the colonizer. Even these days, this interpretation of a causal relation between reformism and imperialism, which dominates Tunisian historiography, imbues the whole Tunisian *imaginaire*.

Indisputably, nineteenth-century reformism went hand in hand with European imperialism; the colonization of Tunisia was not the result merely of debt and a failure to pay,[35] it was also and perhaps above all the result of the penetration of French economic and financial capitalism, including through concessions.[36] That of the Dakhlet-Jendouba railway line is still interpreted in those terms: 'The "Bône-Guelma" [i.e. the railway company of that name] was merely a means of opening the colonial frontier, and its network would accelerate the process of French colonization in Tunisia. Right from the start, the concession and the construction of the Medjerba line were conceived and considered by the "Bône-Guelma" not merely as an affair that concerned the company but an affair that concerned France. The penetration of the company was exactly the same as the penetration of France and its interests into that new country of Tunisia. The task of the "Bône-Guelma" into Tunisia was often deemed by its administrators to be a "patriotic task"'.[37] In the same way, the Gafsa Company was never considered as a private colonial enterprise. It depended on charter companies which, in agreement with the colonial state, developed new socio-economic activities and relations that were not without influence in the development of the Protectorate.[38]

Current privatizations and concessions should also be understood in the light of this episode, or rather of the way it persists in the reformist *imaginaire*. The Tunisian authorities these days are ready to deprive themselves of the acquisition of modern knowledge, technologies and materials, of a more dynamic currency and exports, if they deem it more important to protect the pre-existing national fabric of production, to favour national companies, to maintain supervision of national economic activities, and to keep control of the political and social domains. For financial reasons and, more marginally, under pressure from donors, the total eviction of foreign entrepreneurs is, however, impossible. So the obligatory openness is conceived on the basis of a strategy of the national diversification of foreign partners. Thus, only one privatization – admittedly strategic and certainly symbolic, since it concerns a bank – benefited the French, even though they were and are present in vast numbers in Tunisia and the country's first economic partners; this privatization was, in addition, merely partial and gave rise to many vicissitudes. The other main partners met with the same treatment: three small businesses were transferred to the Italians and none to the Belgians, British or (especially) the Germans, even though the latter provided the country with most of its tourists. On the other hand, the Portuguese – considered as coming from a 'little' country and thus 'controllable' – found themselves being awarded three important operations (two cement factories and a company for processing cork), the Swiss and the Libyans were given two each (in commerce and tourism respectively), and the Egyptians benefited from an important concession (the second GSM licence).

This latter example is a perfect illustration of the principally political dimension of the privatizations. ORASCOM, whose financial difficulties and technical mediocrity were known to everyone, was given preference over Telefonica, even though the latter had put in a financial offer comparable to that of the Egyptian operator. The Tunisian operators deliberately chose to manage without technical competence and any real modernization of the telecommunications sector; and they knowingly decided to go without supplementary currency inflow since Tunisian participation in the consortium led by the Spanish was marginal when compared with the solution chosen by the Egyptians. The choice of ORASCOM is thus explained mainly by the desire for control – a control dictated by security considerations (facilitating the work of the Ministry of the Interior), by financial and political considerations (favouring those close to the Presidency through the Karthago company, tolerating political interference) and by nationalist considerations (avoiding an over-distant and over-critical external gaze). The desire for control is more imperious than any external pressure when it is a question of defending, not Tunisian society in the abstract, but a highly specific order, which enables the exercise of surveillance and domination with a minimum of repression. In the concession of the second GSM licence, the Tunisian authorities were perfectly aware that the donors would envisage not paying part of the financing previously arranged. Indeed, the European Union refused to pay out the last tranche of the part devoted to 'Technology of information and communication'.[39] This firmness is rare enough for it to be pointed out. But it is mainly explained by the rancour of the Spanish.[40]

Between the Tunisians and their foreign partners, a subtle game developed, one made up of concessions, rapprochements, pressures, advances and retreats, pretences and misunderstandings. Rough-and-ready arrangements are obviously not encountered in Tunisia alone, but characterize the strategies of resistance and adaptation of those 'small dependent countries' that are in permanent negotiation with donors.[41] However, they do find a particularly favourable echo in the strong tradition of formalism, as described above. In March 1996, for instance, President Ben Ali decided to create a state secretariat for privatizations after a visit from J. Wolfensohn during which the latter had, in private, expressed regret over the slowness of the process.[42] Nonetheless, the rhythm of the reforms was not significantly modified, as is proved by the memoranda of the IMF which followed this interview. Donors are not always taken in by this formalist window-dressing. On the contrary: they are often complicit with it. Thus, one of the conditionalities imposed by the institutions of Bretton Woods and the European Commission was, in 1996, the effective transfer, on 31 December 1996, of 20 per cent of the two hundred and twelve privatizable enterprises, meant to bring in 1.4 billion $ to the budget. The government, in urgent need of new financing and taking advantage of the bureaucratic limitations on donors, resorted to one of the oldest tricks of 'dependent economies': to play along while respecting the forms. To make the pay-out possible, it initiated the necessary steps, in particular by publishing invitations to tender. But, at the limit date, no proposal had been deemed sufficient. However, the European Commission did pay out everything, asking in return that the government make a gesture: the sale of the two cement works, in two operations, meant that it was possible to respect the conditionalities . . . with the exception of two details. In the first place, this respect was honoured at the cost of a shift in criteria: whereas the outward payment was initially demanded on the basis of the number of enterprises and the amount of capital transferred, it was eventually realized on the basis of the number of operations engaged in, and the amount obtained by a single operation. And, secondly, there was a shift in dates: whereas the initial conditionality was fixed for December 1996, it gradually shifted to 1998, the date on which the transfer of the cement factories was to be decided, and even to 1999 and 2000, since the income foreseen was actually paid to the Tunisian government only at that period.[43]

The Tunisian authorities realized that the conditionalities were often fictive and that the important thing was not to liberalize or to privatize in due form, but to show goodwill, to make a gesture, to use a certain number of little 'arrangements', even if they were anti-liberal, with the donors not being very particular with the way in which the privatizations were carried out. It is true that donors only glance at the concrete implementations and, consequently, the reality of privatization, being more sensitive to overall results and good relations with a recipient country than to the means by which these results are obtained.[44] Even though they create tensions with the donors, opacity, corruption, and slowness in operations do not nullify the situation.[45] Conditionalities may not be fulfilled: indeed, they may be toned down by the very same people who first imposed them. As the extent of aid demonstrates, this rule is a general one, and gives concrete form to another involuntary contribution on the part of donors to the reformist myth.

What is the socio-political meaning of privatizations? In spite of their slowness, the low level of revenue generated, and the marginality of transformations of the productive fabric, the process cannot be described as a failure or analysed in terms of subterfuge. Privatization is also a technique of government, as, in their time, nationalization or the collectivization of land had been. It is indeed striking to see that a follow-up analysis of privatized enterprises arouses no interest on the part of the authorities. This follow-up exists, but it is neither developed nor used with any rigour. In the final analysis, it cannot be used: from one year to the next, the sample of enterprises investigated is not the same; information is difficult to obtain; the economic impact, the participation of privatized enterprises in wealth, recuperation by the state, and the social balance sheet, have not been studied.[46] How are we to analyse this lack of interest in a technique of control? How are we to explain that no sanction is imposed when the enterprise does not reply to the questionnaire? How are we to understand the absence of any follow-up or any penalties, when the terms and conditions – mainly investment and employment – are not fulfilled?[47]

Unquestionably, the main function of privatizations lies elsewhere. What counts most is the defence of the existing Tunisian social order, in its multiple dimensions, the defence of normalizing discipline and the security pact. The priority given to employment explains the prudence with which privatizations are carried out and, more generally, the fact that it is laid down in the terms and conditions that the staff of the privatized enterprise must be kept identical for at least five years. The Tunisian authorities proclaim it loud and clear: 'the first principle concerns the preservation of the general interest. Indeed, privatization is not limited to a mere transfer of property from the public sector to the private, nor to the quest for a maximum transfer. In fact, *the state is, first and foremost, concerned for the permanence of the enterprise in question*; it then grants a particular importance to the *preservation of the greatest number of jobs* compatible with the criteria of efficiency and profitability of the enterprise'.[48] This social preoccupation is also demonstrated by territorial conditions, by a focus on regional development and a desire to lessen inequalities between regions. Maintaining enterprises in poor regions where unemployment is endemic, regions considered to be social and political hotspots, is part of the policy of national integration, and expresses a security pact that is not simply the rhetoric of unanimity. The fact that the Tunisian authorities focus on the social dimension must not be considered merely as a desire to control the world of the working classes or the middle classes, the business world, or the world of sensitive regions, zones or places, even if this dimension cannot be underestimated. The presence of the Minister of the Interior is systematic when it comes to taking decisions, sometimes officially since this latter benefits from a representative in the CAREPP and the party is also represented by senior civil servants who feel obliged to watch over the perpetuation of the allegiance of buyers to the central power. However, this obsession with control is made possible only by the way the primacy of the social pervades the whole of society.

Likewise, the national preference is not merely a decision taken from 'on high' to favour or, on the contrary, cause problems for this or that entrepreneur, to impose one strategy rather than another or to forestall any external gaze. It is intimately experienced by the members of Tunisian society as the exercise of national sovereignty, and as the defence of Tunisian identity and of a certain mode of existence able to safeguard certain types of social relations. Of course, these interventions, which are simultaneously training techniques, make it possible for individuals in society to be controlled. These social relations favour the surveillance of the actors and of economic and financial interests; they normalize their behaviour. Disciplinary power is thus legitimatized. So privatizations make it possible to carry out an activity of classification, observation, and individualization of entrepreneurs; they guide their activities in such a way that the process deemed to symbolize the emancipation of the private sphere is transformed into firmly directed planning, freedom under surveillance, and continuous control.

The panoptic ideal of the industrial *mise à niveau* (upgrading)

The ambiguity of economic reformism is also illustrated by the programme of 'upgrading', a symbol of state voluntarism, of modernization, and of economic openness. The programme was meant to end officially in 2001, but it is carrying on, turning itself more towards SMEs. Its results are far from being disgraceful and Tunisia is still, in the region, a relatively dynamic economy. The donors underline the government's voluntarism and determination, while Tunisians point to the extent of investments and the industrial modernization realized within this framework. It is still very surprising that this programme should be considered a success. It is erroneous to speak of modifications in entrepreneurial behaviour, modernization of modes of financing or improvement in industrial performances in 2004. Ever since the programme began, the Tunisian economy has not basically risen in the international hierarchy of specializations: the main activities generating currency remain tourism, the textile industry, and the machine industry. The country has not managed to break through into modern technologies, into current consumer goods or into the communications economy. The textile and garment industry is in great difficulties these days even though the enterprises in this sector represent the biggest battalion of upgraded enterprises. All the reports emphasize the absence of any significant development in the model of production since 1997: in spite of the programme, the sector has not diversified, and there has been no qualitative improvement of the industry, nor any intensification of capital, while the niches that were picked out as promising – top-of-the-range, short chain of order – have not been explored much.[49]

In these conditions, it seems that we need to seek elsewhere for the foundations of this positive evaluation and the apparent paradox: the upgrading is less an economic policy, or a strategy of adaptation to free trade, and more a technique of discipline, a procedure that is deemed to be able to inspect, register, and evaluate permanently – a sort of 'panopticon' (Bentham's term) of industrial and entrepreneurial regulation. In the next section, I hope to show that the strength of reformism resides in this capacity to synthesize things and bring them under its control: it is a myth, but it is also a language of the political, a mode of government that integrates the majority, if not the totality, of the population. It is indisputably from here that it draws its strength.

The economic rationality of the mise à niveau

However, according to the economic discourse of the Tunisian authorities and donors, 'upgrading' is an industrial policy aimed at helping enterprises to face up to international competition.[50] With this in mind, the government has set in place a highly structured system at the Ministry of Industry: the *Bureau de la mise à niveau* (BMN – Office for Upgrading) thinks out and coordinates actions in favour of enterprises, while the *Agence de promotion de l'industrie* (API – Agency for Promoting Industry) concretely sets up the structures of modernization, in particular adaptation to the new European norms. After the establishment of a diagnostic that checks off their weaknesses, enterprises are now approved by an authority, the *Comité de pilotage* (Copil – piloting committee). The diagnostics are carried out by Tunisian research consultancies, either alone or in association with European consultancies. Between 1996 and 2001, the object of the arrangement was to train up 2,000 enterprises so they could upgrade, i.e. an annual rhythm of 400 per year: the state subsidized 70 per cent of the cost of the diagnostics and 10 per cent (or 20 per cent for the enterprises installed in the interior of the country) of that of material investments.[51] The modes of financing evolved over time: in 1996, enterprises had to advance the totality of the consultancy costs and wait to be reimbursed by the state. From 1998, however, given the reluctance of entrepreneurs to commit to the programme, they managed to reach an agreement whereby they paid out only their due, i.e. the 30 per cent of the sum of the diagnostic, whereas the 70 per cent subsidized by the state was directly paid into the selected research consultancy. Between 1996 and 2001, 1,062 enterprises of the 2,000 anticipated were 'upgraded', i.e. a rate of realization of 53 per cent According to the follow-up investigations, these enterprises invested massively for a total sum of 2 billion DT, which represents a significant sum, thanks to subsidies that were also significant, representing 275 MDT – some 13.5 per cent of the investments undertaken. The latter represent, on average for the years 1996–2000, 40 per cent of the private manufactured investment, according to a broad definition of the 'private' sector, which, here, includes the public enterprises of the competing sectors. In March 2004, the date of the latest statistical publication which I have managed to see, 2,906 enterprises had joined the programme and 1,729 of them had obtained approval for their applications for a total projected – and not realized – investment of 2,693 MDT and subsidies of 384 MDT.

This policy has produced positive economic results because these investments have contributed to growth and enabled employment to increase, as well as exports and economic performances in general. On the other hand, it is more difficult to evaluate the efficiency of the allocation of subsidized resources, especially in the absence of comparative studies. As its reorientation to SMEs in 2001 indicates, the upgrading programme had initially favoured big enterprises and those with public holdings, doubtless because from an administrative point of view the task was easier, but certainly also because (a point to which I shall return) these enterprises are easier to keep under surveillance. Be this as it may, the upgrading programme created new needs for the majority of enterprises. Before, the ISO norms (for example) were unknown to them, like the quality guarantee; even though they are not really integrated into the operation of enterprises, these days everyone talks about them.

The relative failure of politics in favour of immaterial investments suggests, however, that modernization – if it exists – is still in its early stages. As the government itself admits, this part is disappointing in spite of higher subsidies for intangible investments.[52] The delicate situation in which bankers and entrepreneurs find themselves, as revealed by the slump in profitability of enterprises and by the necessity to pass a bill on struggling enterprises, indubitably explains this lack of enthusiasm – which the dynamism of public organizations has not managed to temper. In spite of the mobilization of the API and investment by donors in it, the upgrading programme was unable to modify a situation characterized – to use the very terms of the Ministry of Industry – by bad management, a low level of technical supervision, and by the aggravation of financial problems (excessive debt, a lack of their own resources, inadequate funds for circulation, an excessive resorting to short-term credit). Another problem was the lack of preparation for openings abroad (due less to the suppression of protection than to the development of the informal sector) and the increase in the rate of interest and the policy of devaluation.[53] So upgrading seems not to be of any help in evaluating the process of modernization of the Tunisian industrial fabric. The inventory of the criticism and the praise poured on this programme, on the other hand, *does* make it possible to evaluate the modes of the exercise of power in the economic field.

The mise à niveau *as 'affair of state'*

The upgrading programme is an almost caricatural expression of Tunisian state voluntarism – a point that has often been emphasized by those it has let down, its detractors, its promoters and its partisans, as well as by external and independent analysts.[54] I would here like to underline one important aspect of this: pernickety interventionism is at the same time a more or less forced mobilization, a more or less real support, a more or less effective surveillance. When donors praise Tunisian voluntarism and contribute to the financing (even the partial financing) of this kind of policy, they are at the same time granting carte blanche to techniques of control and modes of the exercise of power that do not necessarily fit the rules that (in other respects) they are trying to promote – for example, those of the rule of law and good governance. Whether or not they are aware of this matters little in the final analysis, insofar as their support amounts to an external legitimatization that is conscientiously exploited by the Tunisian authorities. On the other hand, it is obvious that, for entrepreneurs, upgrading is first and foremost an 'affair of state',[55] in the logic of a liberal and authoritarian interventionism.[56]

It is an 'affair of state', in the first place, because the programme is the direct contrary of liberalism and an apprenticeship in market mechanisms, and instead perpetuates a tradition of interventionism. The discourse that surrounds upgrading maintains the illusion that subsidized investments will protect the personnel and the enterprise. This interpretation is particularly credible because it fits previous practices and the level of effective protection has indeed risen since the first stages of openness: the protection of locally produced goods has not (or has hardly) fallen, while non-locally produced input and equipment have seen their import tax diminish. In addition, subsidies constitute another mode of protection and are interpreted as an aid for investment – often already planned-for – and not necessarily as an incitement to modernization. The quantitative evaluations published with the aim of mobilizing economic actors, in fact, do not highlight the liberal argument. They draw, rather, on shock data such as the well-known rule of the three thirds – a third of enterprises will survive, a third will die, and a third will have difficulty putting up any resistance – that does not rest on any serious study. They also play on the effects of legitimatization by scientificity, as is proved by the recurrent mention of the positive results of the models of calculable general equilibrium.[57] What is forgotten is both the complexity of the factors that influence the results of liberalization – external investment, the enterprises' capacity for modernization, the orientation of economic policies, exterior financing, flexibility and adaptability of the workforce, foreign demand[58] – and the requirement of virtuous series that, however, are not self-evident: for instance, the positive way that openness drives the productive systems and the activities of national and foreign economic actors.[59] This administrative mobilization shows a misunderstanding of market mechanisms and, furthermore, transmits a very state-controlled vision of competitive international integration. The paternalist rhetoric of the central power also reinforces the idea that the ultimate ambition of aid is to benefit the whole population – in other words, that upgrading is part of the complex arrangement that I analysed above in terms of the security pact.

It is an affair of state, in the second place, because the public authorities seem to be much more concerned by the success of the programme than are the entrepreneurs, who participate only half-heartedly in the dynamics of upgrading. The bureaucratic logic is expressed by the desire to 'produce good figures': the regular presentation of the advances in the process emphasize, for instance, the number of dossiers approved by the Bureau and not the number of enterprises concerned – which would be more relevant in a purely economic logic. Now, these figures are respectively 1,885 and 245, i.e. an average of 8 dossiers per enterprise.[60] The presentation thus provided has the evident object of showing, by quantification, that there is a dynamic at work, as well as demonstrating the efficacy of state voluntarism. If we follow the concrete procedures that the 'upgraded' enterprises need to respect, we understand the terms used to describe this administrative process ('a sort of gosplan', according to one donor, or 'a Soviet conception of public intervention' according to one entrepreneur).[61]

The ways in which businessmen are mobilized often increase this impression of counter-productivity. In the press, on television, in the headquarters of the party and the employers' unions, in association meetings and at conferences, the proliferation of interventions ends up being tiresome. The expression 'upgrading' is repeated ad nauseam and applied so systematically to such very heterogeneous situations that it becomes empty for entrepreneurs used to 'campaigns', to magic formulae, to the inevitable gaps between discourse and reality. During my interviews with bankers and businessmen, the latter did not hesitate to tell me, off the record, that 'the authorities go in for them too much', that they are 'not credible' as a result, and that upgrading 'is gradually starting to turn in on itself',[62] unable to get beyond its procedural and bureaucratic dimension. Studies are carried out because studies need to be carried out; enterprises find their hand forced to enter the programme, to publicize it, to take part in delegations abroad and to vaunt the merits of Tunisia, and so on.[63]

As a result, this progressive shift from encouragement to pressures that can rapidly intensify so as to become practically an obligation constitutes the other face of state voluntarism.[64] Upgrading definitely no longer has anything to do with liberalization. It is part of the disciplinary arrangement of the Tunisian authorities. With the approach of the final date of 2001, this dimension appeared more nakedly: the object of preparation for competition was eclipsed by the administrative and political necessity of fulfilling the contract – 2,000 enterprises updated – to show a success that could be obtained only with the clientelist and *rentier* mobilization of the networks of power. This does not mean that upgrading is pure fiction and that it has no administrative consistency. Quite the contrary, as is shown by the institutionalization of the bureaucratic mechanisms by way of funds such as the *Fonds de promotion et de maîtrise de la technologie*, the FOPOMAT (Fund for the promotion and control of technology), managed by the API, or by financial procedures, such as the bonus for investments in research and development. The very low level of investment of these institutions by the actors concerned does however suggest the main dimension of upgrading: 'The institutional and financial impulse given by the state [. . .] follows a circular path that brings it back to the starting point', since upgrading is 'led by and for the state.'[65] As a disciplinary bureaucratic process, it thus enables the administration to throw out its own adjustments that might undermine the mechanisms of control. The objective of shaping a competitive industrial fabric thus appears, in the final analysis, as marginal – and it is in any case understood as such by the main foreign partners of the Tunisian state. For the World Bank, for example, upgrading is a 'safety net'.[66]

The mise à niveau, *an integrated discipline*

This kind of authoritarian state intervention obviously runs into resistances on the part of entrepreneurs who are often reluctant to open the accounts of their company and to become increasingly involved with state bureaucracy. But it is no less obvious that, in the Tunisian political economy, these tensions and resistances lead very rarely to any real confrontations. As often as not, they are transformed into negotiations and compromises all the more easily because the interests of entrepreneurs, and of the state, are interlinked and interwoven. Admittedly, in this area as in others, fear is never absent: the enterprises interpret the upgrading programme as a process of domestication. The low profile of entrepreneurs right at the start of the programme needs to be understood in this historically constructed context of the apprehension of the political, a context re-actualized by the proliferation of official discourse, by the mobilization of bureaucratic and party apparatuses, and by the invasion of the public space of repetitive slogans. As I heard time and again in the course of my research, official language often arouses fear and leads people to withdraw into themselves.

But fear alone cannot explain the entrance of an after all significant number of enterprises into the upgrading programme; there is a certain kind of support, if not for the concrete shape of state control, at least for the types of relations of power made manifest by these programmes. Many entrepreneurs doubt the success of liberalization and the real openness of the Tunisian economy, but they support it for financial reasons, for political reasons in particular, so as to 'look good' or, to use the official term, 'as a gesture of citizenship'. Others criticize the ways in which aid is provided, the delays in payment or the administrative difficulties, but emphasize that the authorities are willing to listen and are anxious to preserve the Tunisian industrial fabric. Both groups consider upgrading as the new expression of relations between enterprises and central power, formalized in administrative and financial terms. In this way, the programme seems to materialize a new stage in the reinforcing of links between state and entrepreneurs, the latter being rewarded by the granting to them of 'titles of nobility', by social recognition, or by a certain high profile in the media.[67]

The vocabulary here is significant: people 'look good' in the eyes of the central power if they 'go along with' upgrading and if they 'support' the programme, not if they modernize the enterprise by their own means. The political dimension is illustrated by the ups and downs that accompanied the choice of the enterprises that first entered the programme in 1996 and 1997.[68] Like entering the Stock Exchange, or the quality of relations with the Inland Revenue, this sort of co-option has played a role as a barometer of relations with the authorities and has constituted a place of negotiation with them. Certain enterprises, it appears, were 'chosen' and others not; certain entrepreneurs were, on this occasion, given a high profile and others not; the central power did or did not guarantee the success of the operation. The degree of overinterpretation is perhaps significant, but the fact remains that entrepreneurs, well-informed observers of the business world and a large majority of Tunisians understand upgrading first and foremost in political terms.

The programme's ambition is to condition enterprises for international competition. Even though the Tunisian enterprises have continued to be protected since their creation, the market mechanisms have not been explicitly revealed. As in the past, the way the programme proceeds and the control of activities seem more important than its pedagogical dimension.[69] Few questions are asked about the ultimate economic rationality of upgrading, or its cost in resources. The authorities do not really seem bothered by changes that are, not to put too fine a point on it, unexpected, such as the development of re-exportation, a certain specialization in commercial intermediation and warehousing, the pursuit of strategies aimed at splitting up enterprises, with one part producing and the other marketing the products imported, the realizing of false investments in intangibles, the inadequacy and under-use of training, and even the perpetuation of an increased level of specialization in services.[70] On the other hand, the authorities enumerate the qualities of the ideal enterprise: the aim of upgrading is not the really existing enterprise, but the normative enterprise, which says what the enterprise should be, the norms it needs to respect, the steps it should follow, and the aims it should meet.[71]

Upgrading is an attempt, perhaps unconscious, to put into practice the panoptic ideal of the central power, a continuous surveillance of entrepreneurs, the symbolic illustration of a 'technical *imaginaire* of social discipline'.[72] When the central power defines the 'good' (or 'bad') entrepreneur, it is probably less interested in bringing out the ethical and moral dimension of the economic sphere[73] than in seeing a disciplinary technique being exercised. What Foucault says about the mechanisms of disciplinary normalization can be applied perfectly well to upgrading: this 'consists in first setting up a model, an optimal model that is constructed with a certain result in mind, and the operation consists in trying to make people, gestures and acts fit this model; the normal here is, precisely, what is able to fit this norm, and the abnormal is what is unable to do so. In other words, there is an originally prescriptive character of the discipline'.[74]

Entrepreneurs are not taken in. Those who 'support' the programme do so, as we have seen, to 'look good', which is to be in the norm. Others 'avoid' the programme since it is deemed to be inappropriate and because 'confidentiality is not respected', which comes down to saying that they refuse the process of normalization whereby, too, things are brought out into the light and all the 'dark shadows' eliminated. And others, who have supported the programme, 'get out' once the diagnostic phase has been completed, since 'the process is extremely bureaucratically complicated' or 'because we already know what we have to do and the subsidies aren't worth it': they deem the 'price to be paid' in terms of control and surveillance to be too high.[75] Upgrading is thus an efficient mechanism of surveillance and normalization: anyone is 'good' if they can be registered in the process, added to the list of upgraded enterprises, or classified as an exporter. . . . The obsession with surveillance and order is rather reminiscent of the obsession of the inspectors and different technical bodies of Colbert's administration which Philippe Minard has magnificently analysed.

Even if upgrading is developed and implemented in a rational way, with objectives by sectors and regions, with a real desire for modernization and adaptation to international competition, and also out of a desire to respond to the anxieties of the economic world, the programme is naturally integrated into the diffuse ethos of reformism. Entrepreneurs understand the programme in terms of relations of force, of administrative and political control of the world of enterprise, in a direct line from previous policies whose foundations were the precise opposite of current policies. As a result, upgrading is not interpreted as an apprenticeship in free trade, but as a protective subsidy and, at the same time, as a benevolent and yet inquisitorial surveillance. Quite unlike liberalism itself, 'upgrading' is an additional opportunity to obtain aid, the pursuit, in new forms, of a public policy, economically interventionist and politically clientelist. Subsidies emerge from their economic framework to become an honorary bonus, an importunate gaze, a reassuring and simultaneously dangerous protection.[76] The lack of economic credibility for upgrading also stems from this alliance between a liberal discourse and interventionist practices, of a discourse of openness and protectionist and political interpretations of this discourse.[77]

This technique of surveillance, then, is legitimized by entrepreneurs once upgrading is integrated into Tunisian modes of government and the reformist ethos. But it is also legitimized by foreign partners, who see in it both state voluntarism and a mobilization of national capacities. Donors appreciate a country in which decisions in the domain of public policies 'make a noise'.[78] It does not really matter whether the programme is effective or not, so long as this way of looking at things exists and fits international canons: 'Here, they know what they want, they have a plan, which is by and large positive' – this was the conclusion of an international civil servant, in spite of the demurrals he had himself contributed during a conversation devoted to the results (which he judged to be middling) of the 'upgrading'. And the European Union underlines how much Tunisia is 'reacting well' and is 'imaginative', proposing 'fluid and diversified programmes' that the country 'has itself adopted', emphasizing that upgrading is a Tunisian initiative.[79] Unlike in many other African or Middle Eastern countries, the Tunisian discourse is technocratic, articulated, and constructed round the dominant themes of the international community. As a result, donors do not view themselves as being in a *terra incognita*, even if implementation does not follow on.

Reformism: an ambiguous and interiorized domination

The fact that the reforms are perpetual is not a distinguishing feature of contemporary 'liberalism', as we can see from the succession of reforms over the interventionist and socialist periods. This recurrence has been analysed in terms of cycles, following a simplified interpretation of the theses of Ibn Khaldun, the great Arab thinker of the fourteenth century,[80] or, following a historicizing interpretation, in terms of the 'fabrication of ruin',[81] with each prince striving to destroy the reforming work of his predecessor. These readings adopt an over-utilitarian conception of the reforms, without leaving any place for ambiguities and misunderstandings, involuntary appropriations and processes.

On the contrary, I myself have tried to show that in the final analysis it matters very little whether the reforms do or do not fulfil their avowed objectives, since their interest lies elsewhere – in the way they form an integral part of relations of power. In this sense, one might almost say that these successive failures make it possible for techniques of surveillance to perpetuate themselves; thus, in the terms used by Michel Foucault in his analysis of prisons, they authorize the expression of 'tactics that shift according to how closely they reach their target'.[82] These failures or these imperfections are not necessarily thought out, conceived of and brought into being by a dominant central power, but it is certainly true that this latter finds new (and ever-renewed) spaces to occupy in them. In a totalitarian system where any expression of dissent is impossible, failure is unmentionable. But the permanent improvement of the reforms, their extension or their consolidation express this same imperfection, this same inability to fill their 'terms and conditions'.[83] They are part of the very operation of the reformist political economy. By perpetuating themselves endlessly, the reforms succeed because the domains to be reformed are always more numerous, since the instruments, the procedures and the mechanisms of discipline are forever extending themselves.

The incompleteness of reform thus also acts as an instrument of domination. These reforms become an integral part both of the logics of inclusion and of exclusion, necessarily unfinished and often mutually incompatible: the irreducible simultaneity of these two types of practices leads to a nuanced reading of the mechanisms of domination in which the degree of support is fundamental. Reformism, as a series of endless reforms, requires this incomplete and imperfect character.[84] The incompleteness and the impossibility of the reforms ever dying form part of the Tunisian *imaginaire*, of the history of the construction of the state in Tunisia. So these days it is less a matter of elucidating the enigma of the durability of the 'Ben Ali regime' in the face of the reforms, and more a matter of understanding the current reforms in their historical context:[85] how they are understood, interpreted, and appropriated with regard to this reformist ethos, why they are endlessly renewed, reshaped and redeployed, the rationalities that dictate their development, and the ways in which they form part of the modes of government and the processes of subjection.[86]

The problematization of the exercise of power in terms of reformism means that individuals can be subjected – by the soothing discourse on national unity and consensus, by a state control which sees the administration as the instrument of a rational and active management, by the voluntarist illusion, and by a rejection of the real, which says what is good and what is bad, which orders, prescribes, and formulates reforms that are 'artificial' in relation to any reality.[87] But it also makes recognition and support possible. So reformism constitutes a form of ambiguous and interiorized domination which makes everyday life normal, conceivable, and even desirable. Such a life, in which the element of control, of coercion, or even repression cannot be denied, is accepted as a success because the appearance of peace and tranquillity prevails. Order and social stability are an effective result as much as a discourse, and a representation as much as a preoccupation: they refer directly to reformism and Tunisian-ness, and this reference is explicit and has become a matter of routine. Reforms and reformism benefited from positive connotations in the nineteenth century as they do these days – but in reality, these connotations conceal the multiplicity of modes of the exercise of power, and the simultaneity of repression and support, of pressure and accommodation, of servitude and belonging. Tunisian reformism is a 'good government' which masks the impossibility of any frank expression of freedom.

Now, as this chapter comes to its end, I would like to come back to the very terms 'reform' and 'reformism'. Like 'liberalism', 'protectionism', 'state intervention', or 'collectivism' in the economic field, or 'democracy', 'authoritarianism', 'governance', or the 'rule of law' in the political field,[88] they screen out any more nuanced understanding of political and social practices.[89] All of them refer to such heterogeneous and sometimes such contradictory experiences, they assume such different meanings, and these differences themselves are so irreducible, that in the end they lose any meaning. The fact that reform and reformism are part of the global lexicon, of the imposed readings of the transformations of the contemporary world, of the legitimate problematizations of life under current globalization, contributes to obscuring their sense. It is difficult to say whether the misunderstanding thereby created is working or not, since such a conclusion depends so much on value judgements. But it is certain that the misunderstanding of the very meaning of reformism is, in Tunisia, an important element in the transformation of the latter into myth and *imaginaire*.

Tunisian reformism synthesizes at least two sets of norms, two sets of interpretations and ways of being that are not necessarily compatible. The former emphasize openness, the rule of law, and emancipation, whereas the latter insist on social integration and protection. The former correspond to the adoption of a dominant lexicon, and thus to the attempt at integration into the hierarchized structure of the globalized world, while the latter express a desire for integration and thus an attempt at safeguarding specifically Tunisian features. The translation of *islah* by 'reformism' is also a process whereby a dominant western discourse is appropriated – one that is particularly easy to assimilate because *islah* transmits the same ideas of openness to the Other. The misunderstanding thus also stems from the articulation, in a recognized language that is taken to be transparent, of concepts of understanding the world that are inherent in contemporary Tunisian situation and practices.[90] The language of reformism, like that of liberalism or nationalism, makes it possible to face the globalized version of the world, just as it had previously made it possible to understand its colonial version. Tunisian reformism appears, in these conditions, more banal than specific, since the political sphere is ambiguous by nature and this ambiguity cannot be reduced to Tunisian-ness. Also, in most Muslim countries, reformism is also understood in the complex sense in which the religious reference is implicit, but diffuse and pregnant with meaning; and most populist regimes instrumentalize reformist rhetoric. As the experiments in reform carried out without any reformist myth suggest,[91] the Tunisian trajectory is specific only in the way it links the rhetoric of reforms to particular feelings, problematizations and ideas, and in the *imaginaire* that it conveys.

Conclusion

Is the 'Ben Ali' regime authoritarian, neo-authoritarian, or a police state? Is it a dictatorship or a contemporary illustration of sultanism? In the final analysis, this debate does not add much to our understanding of the political. The exercise of power appears, as we reach the end of our investigation, ambiguous to say the least. On the one hand, it is impossible to deny the all-powerful role of the President, the extreme centralization of the political and administrative organization of the country, the arbitrary nature of decisions handed down 'from on high', the intensive use of police techniques, the desire for control and the intrusion into people's private lives. But, on the other hand, the analysis of everyday life, in particular in its economic dimension, has brought out the tangible nature of negotiations, a certain ability to listen to the worries of the populace, and the existence of a pact of security. Starting from this apparent contradiction, I would now like to refine the way one can understand this 'authoritarian regime', perhaps less singular than it appears, and attempt to sketch an outline of the Tunisian modes of government.

Personal power and extreme centralization: the reality behind 'absolute control'

The cult of personality and the personalization of power cannot be doubted. You need simply go for a stroll through a big city or a small village and you will be crushed by the physical presence of the President. Everywhere his portrait is displayed above users, consumers, schoolchildren, citizens, employees, television spectators, entrepreneurs and the administered. Radio and television unwearyingly relate his 'beneficent' and 'avant-garde' actions, remind people of his 'high-mindedness' and his 'far-sightedness'. One of the essential functions of the apparatuses of state and party is precisely to keep this permanent celebration of the Leader going, from one day to the next.[1] Not a single public space is free of symbols glorifying the admirable exercise of his power: 'Places du 7 Novembre', 'boulevards de l'Environnement' as you go into every town and village, decorated with little statues depicting pet animals, monuments of every kind (clocks, fountains, aircraft, gates, sculptures) to the glory of the number 7 (the Head of State's fetish number), and to the glory of mauve (said to be his favourite colour . . .). Not a day goes by without the newspapers publishing his photo, top left on the first page, showing him receiving a minister, an opposite number from abroad, or a delegation. There is something almost grotesque about the systematic way all this is done. And this is indeed, perhaps, what is being unconsciously sought: when it is made fun of, power cannot be circumvented.[2] Such an omnipresence pervades even such personal areas as religion: in a way verging on caricature, on 11 November 2003, Zine El Abidine Ben Ali opened the great mosque of Carthage located between two Roman sites and, in all modesty, proclaimed its name: 'El Abidine' (the adorers)! And as people are their own best friends, the President never misses a chance to salute his own perspicacity (for example in his fight against terrorism), his sense of initiative and his ability to listen to ordinary people (in his fight against poverty), his modernizing and reforming vision (in the politics of promotion of women's rights), and his balanced but bold conception of the 'Change' (in the progressive establishment of democracy and the choice of reforms).

This omnipresence is, of course, not limited to discourse or to the theatricality of the exercise of power. In reality, it spreads out into public action. Ben Ali is at the origin of every decision, from an international negotiation to a municipal building site by way of a lowering of prices (that of electricity, for instance), or the concrete setting up of a social programme.[3] He guides the laws, modifies them, applies them or suspends them, governs by decree and, even more, decides whether or not the law should be respected. He himself awards prizes and hands out gifts. He is the one who frames every policy. The poor, the needy, and women are his, and his alone. This appropriation is not merely rhetorical, as is illustrated by his very modes of action. When a woman without income or a roof over her head divorces, it is the President in person who intervenes as a matter of urgency to help her, and not some institution.[4] The good works of the 26.26 are personally carried out by the President, who comes in person to offer them to the poor or has them given out by his personal representatives. He is endlessly broadcasting the fact that he is in advance of society, and even of his most faithful allies. So he is the personal and unique protector of women, whose status would be in danger if he should die, as a result, ironically enough, of the 'retrograde character of the majority of members' of his own party.[5] Every function of mediation can be legitimatized only by its link with the President: the intermediary can sometimes take advantage of this, either directly – as a councillor, member of the family, or close associate – or else indirectly, through a chain of relations that necessarily lead, via more or less tortuous routes, to the President or, as is more common, by referring to the Presidential discourse. Allegiance to the Head of State and his blessing are indispensable in the exercise of power. The most anodyne of collective actions necessitates the personal approval of this man, the first among all. In the choice of his men as well as of his actions, the President is omniscient. As a result, this extreme personalization is a central element in the construction of the Tunisian fiction.

Decisions are highly centralized. Nothing significant or symbolic is decided outside 'Carthage'. Ministers are non-existent, unless they have some personal link to the President. The real political decision-making bodies are not the cabinet meetings but, on the one hand, the *conseils ministériels restreints* (CMR – core cabinet meetings) which are attended only by the ministers concerned and the President's personal advisers – the latter being, in reality, the only people whose ideas can prevail; and, on the other hand, 'an elusive informal network, constituted by cooptation, in which there mingle business milieus, personal, family and regional relations, senior figures in the running of the state apparatus, all of them linked by bonds of "disloyal loyalty" (Zweig)'.[6] So the government does not actually govern, since everything is decided in the presidential palace and passed on through the party.[7] In fact, the omnipresence of the RCD in the administration favours bureaucratic centralization and, conversely, makes it impossible for anything to be undertaken without the approval of the Head of State.

This extreme centralization has even spread to the National Assembly since the 'Change'. Now, the President's power to legislate is immense. The constitutional revision has meant that all executive power is concentrated in his hands. Nine amendments in particular have transferred to the President certain regulatory powers that had hitherto been held by the Prime Minister.[8] In addition, presidential bills take precedence over those put forward by members of parliament. The latter are also given their orders during the week preceding the vote on each bill.[9] Everything is organized in advance: the members of the RCD are watched, and members of the official opposition authorized only to utter bromides: no debate is possible.

Decisions are taken only after they have been rubber-stamped by the President – including those taken as a matter of urgency, since the state services, central as well as local, and even the ministers too, have not acquired the adequate margins for manoeuvre, or capacity for taking the initiative, that would enable them to deploy their means of action autonomously. A good example of bureaucratic paralysis resulting directly from the extreme centralization of power can be found in the reform of health insurance: negotiations with the administrators and the trade union appear to be mainly just alibis; in reality, the discussions are faked in the sense that nothing is decided during them, even when the CEOs of the two departments, the private (CNSS) and the public (CNPRS), the managing director, the minister and even the general secretary for Social Affairs attend; the only reply to proposals from trade union workers and professionals is a promise to 'transmit' the information, that is to pass it back for the Palace to scrutinize and decide on it. It is interesting to note in this respect that, in these negotiations, no documents are distributed, and oral discussion takes precedence.[10] I will be returning shortly to this important mode of action, but the main thing here is to underline its role in the process of centralization: nothing can exist that might go against the decision of the supreme authority.

Centralization and pyramid organization go together with the intensive use of intermediaries. The massive presence of the latter contradicts the idea of the existence of any single and direct relation of subordination between the individual and the supreme power. There are several of these intermediaries, and their number is actually increasing as centralism intensifies. This does not mean that a process of delegation is at work – quite the opposite. Even administrative decentralization is de facto transformed into centralization and does not lead to delegation: the municipal level is, these days, essentially an extra cog in the wheel of presidential power.[11] These intermediaries forward information, grievances, and, more rarely, proposals. They do not take any decisions. They should rather be understood as indispensable elements in the exercise of a hierarchical gaze, of a mechanism of surveillance supported by a permanent recording system, from the lowest level of the administration right up to its higher strata. Everyone has a fixed place; the least decision is controlled; all events are recorded; and there is uninterrupted activity between the centre (i.e. Carthage) and the periphery (i.e. the administration, the ministers, the offices, the party and its cells). Only those closest to the Head of State are qualified to act as his personal representatives, self-proclaimed or officially invested. Within the limits of their proximity to the all-powerful, they then arrogate every right to themselves. So centralization and pyramid organization do not actually mean that public policies or overall vision are actually consistent. They are inevitably associated with the arbitrariness characteristic of authoritarian, security, centralized, and personal powers. Thus the 'clans' close to the President often exert pressure for decisions to be taken, without any account being taken of a general policy, nor of the pyramid organization of the administration and the party, nor even of the work done by all the intermediaries circulating between the centre and the periphery. They act not only within the Palace, but also by controlling administrations – a control implemented by means of networks of clients and businessmen.

Historically, this personalization is not found in the current Head of State alone. As one sociologist suggests, 'the Ben Ali regime is distinguished by the extreme reproduction of the personalization of power – but without the charisma and the enlightened side of the "*Zaïm* of the Nation" [Bourguiba]'.[12] And academics point out the importance of the centralizing tradition of the state under Hussein, the foundational character of the first years of independence, with the establishment of the cult of personality of the 'Supreme Fighter', to suggest the historicity and significance of this mode of government.[13] Now as before, personal power fosters arbitrary actions and subjects Tunisians to its whims. The Prince attributes all rights to himself, mainly that of not respecting the law and of calling it into question whenever he sees fit. Every law needs his consent.

We need to come back to this image of the Leader.[14] If we over-interpret this cult of power and become over-focused on the personalization and excessive power of the Head of State, we run the risk of falling into the 'institutionalized egotism' stigmatized by Peter Brown.[15] On the one hand, the role of qualified intermediaries and the interweaving of different interests (of clients, family, region and friends) suggest that the President is never alone, and that power is neither indivisible nor unconditioned. The personal power of Ben Ali – and of Bourguiba or Hussein Bin Ali before him – is made effective only because its representatives are aware of the limits of a power which, admittedly, strives to be absolute, but which necessarily has to work through intermediaries. On the other hand, if the analysis focuses on the Prince alone, on his personal power, on his whims, on his survival, it will fail to take into account both the modes of government (i.e., the mutual dependencies, relations of domination, power plays and social relations without which power cannot pervade society and exert its influence in it),[16] and the set of mechanisms that lead to servitude, however voluntary.

Furthermore, can we endorse this culturalist vision that turns the cult of the leader into an eternal given in Tunisia? It is stated that, 'already, at bottom, family and social structures are preparing to reproduce the tyrannical power of the Father to which Tunisians accommodate themselves really rather well. Hence the current absolute power of the Head of State is hardly an innovation, but rather the *mere renewal* of an old political structure that, in order the better to maintain itself, abolishes the political realm as such and replaces it with the President's enlightened and incomparable action'.[17] But is not the real exercise of power here being confused with the political *imaginaire*?[18] Are the historical situations comparable?[19] And if there is indeed reproduction, what does it mean, and how is it carried out? Does not this love of the Leader rather reflect a 'lack of precise historical analysis', in Foucault's terms, a 'floating signifier whose functions come down to denunciation'?[20] Or a 'trivialization of the problem of the Leader',[21] in Gentile's words? A sceptical eye should also be turned on the academic versions of the love of the Leader, such as interpretations in terms of sultanism or of praetorian regimes or the more sophisticated interpretations of cultural leadership.[22] The first group of these studies bases its arguments on the fact that the state cannot reach into society and that, in the absence of any broader social base, loyalty to the Leader rests on fear and reward. Even if they distance themselves from the popular imagery of the omnipotent Leader, the second group is still marked by a historical vision of the 'strong man', a gap between the elite and the people, and an interpretation of the exercise of power based on the political personnel.[23] However, the analysis of the arrangements, negotiations and mechanisms of voluntary servitude suggests that we should not take the love of the Leader, the personalization of power and the culturalist vision of an infantilized people at face value; their significance in discourse and in representation does however suggest that they act as a functional myth, certainly useful and widely instrumentalized by those who govern.

The question then arises: what are the reasons behind this myth? If we follow Hannah Arendt's argument, analyses in terms of the strong man reflect two complementary ways of understanding the political: either as a sort of superstition, and the illusion that people can do something in the domain of human affairs, or as a sort of discouragement of all action, albeit associated with the hope that it is possible to treat men as raw materials.[24] It might be said that, in Tunisia, the former corresponds to the vision of those who govern, a vision which reveals the concept of an omniscient state, while the latter is put into circulation by the opposition. But the two interpretations express the same concept of the Tunisian state as a state which knows society and can act upon it, and more specifically upon its population. In short, a 'policing state', as I aim to show in the following pages. It is probably this convergence which partly explains how the myth has spread throughout society.

But only partly. For the fact that the need for the Leader is rationalized by the – undisciplined – nature of the population suggests a second line of analysis: the cult of the strong man and the need for the leader are, first and foremost, techniques of power, and more precisely techniques of surveillance and normalization. Timothy Mitchell has shown, in the case of the Arab world, that this intellectual tradition, which emerged from nineteenth-century orientalism and the civilizing endeavours of colonization, had partly been integrated by the 'Orientals' themselves, precisely because the conception of power that these endeavours transmitted fulfilled a definite function for them: the reversal of the colonizers' methods rapidly ensured that those who governed the new independent states could rely on particularly efficient instruments of control and discipline, especially when faced with nascent opposition.[25] In Tunisia, as Mohamed Kerrou suggests, the figure of the *Zaîm* is a recent historical phenomenon that directly emerged from the national movement and the construction of the nation-state.[26] The reinvention of the concept of the *Zaîm* has been interpreted by Mohamed Tozy as the expression of a 'theology of servitude'.[27] This expression needs to be understood not in the sense of a relation from master to disciple, of a servility imposed by the Prince on the people, but in that of the voluntary servitude analysed by E. de la Boétie. The latter emphasized in his *Discourse* that servitude did not spring from a basic and original fear; the Prince was not the origin and principle of servitude, and it was even dangerous to locate evil within the Prince, insofar as this blindness stopped people seeing how this subjection really took place. His answer was indeed that 'the tyrant enslaves his subjects by means of each other'.[28] In other words, analyses in terms of Father, *Zaîm* and single individual betray a perception of political practices as a relation between an owner and his belongings. If we centre everything on the Leader and the personalization of power, we are unable to analyse the many different forms of domination.

The image of the Leader and the strong man is generally associated with a vision of the state as being external to society. Historians have shown how, under Hussein, the state was foreign to local society, and taxation often provided the only link between the two.[29] Sociologists and political theorists these days frequently take up the idea of the permanence of this longstanding history of the exteriority of the state to society. The significance of this model is ceaselessly emphasized. According to some writers, political participation cannot be anything other than mere allegiance, or a source of incomprehension and repression; others claim that Tunisians cannot exercise their citizenship; people are convinced that the aim of power is to maintain itself, and that this configuration makes it possible to transcend any tensions arising from modernity.[30] Our analysis of the security pact, and of the never-ending negotiations, has shown, however, that power was exercised within society. It has also brought out the impossibility of any gap between forms of power (economic, political, social, or cultural) and the place – the central place – of the economy in modes of government. It has underlined the fact that the latter drew on prohibitions, on repression and discipline, but also on encouragements, regulations and arrangements. The myth of exteriority and duality – interior/exterior, present/absent, conquering institution/negotiating institution, discretion/power, secrecy/display – then appears as a disciplinary power: now as before, the reality of its exercise is much more bureaucratized than people's representations of it might suggest.[31]

In these conditions, the idea of an 'absolute control' needs to be qualified. It would be wrong to understand the excess of centralism only in terms of a supposedly totalitarian power imposing itself. The latter is deployed within a network of relations and in a social organization that authorizes it to exercise itself that way, and not vice versa. The structuring and the operation of society do indeed favour a pyramid organization, a permanent political control, and the centralization of decisions. Total discipline is an illusion. It is an objective, a myth representing domination in its most convenient mode of action.[32] So the role of the Prince and his all-powerful action must not be exaggerated.

But, likewise, it would be a mistake to underestimate this role. The Head of State remains a sort of 'guarantor and model in the exercise of all power'.[33] Even if this image of a supreme power is largely a construction, it is with this image in mind that notables, entrepreneurs, qualified intermediaries, and individuals who occupy a position in the hierarchy exercise their own authority and a certain domination over those around them. We have seen how significant the discourse on the need for a Leader was in the business world. The importance of this representation also comes across in the analyses that highlight the 'fatalism' of the Tunisians or underline the absence of parliamentary activity and public debate. People contribute to the process of centralization by their expectations and their demands for efficiency. They act in such a way as to gain access to the bodies which, in their view, are truly authoritative. These bodies constitute the supreme power.

'Corruption', 'illegalities', and nepotism: one mode of government among others

Our analysis of how the economy operates has shown the importance of arrangements, negotiations, and practices of allegiance, of clientelism and 'networking'. In this area, Tunisian modes of government are characterized by the general and growing involvement of individuals and groups in a system of relations that 'keeps a hold' on people and prevents them from speaking out, from criticizing, and opposing. Does this mean, as the majority of opponents (and also, to an increasing extent, foreign actors) imply, that corruption constitutes one of the main means of control – if not *the* main one – and that corruption is knowingly and politically organized?

The very concept of 'corruption' is problematic, thanks to the plurality of practices that it covers, and its vagueness.[34] In particular, 'corruption' cannot be understood outside a given social context. Generally, there is no active organization of corruption, but, because corruption is consubstantial with social practices, the political domain invades it and relations of power are deployed within it – thereby reinforcing this very corruption.[35] In the Tunisian case, we can understand the significance of corruption and illegality within political regulations only if we take into account the modes of action of control and repression: less by means of fear, physical violence and direct intimidation than via buying, arranging, exchanging and negotiating. So it would probably be more accurate to speak of generally economic, and sometimes social, delinquencies that are so many forms of 'checked illegalities'.[36] I would here like to suggest, by drawing on my previous analyses of the modes of 'voluntary servitude', that corruption is created less by the Head of State in an attempt to exercise fully his power of control, and produced rather by the whole set of actors, and penetrated by the apparatuses of discipline and the mechanisms of surveillance.

In fact, interventions are a permanent feature: you can appeal to an old acquaintance to swing a judicial decision and win a case, or you can activate a network within the party to disregard a rule, you can give a little extra something to a civil servant to speed up a procedure...The rules are constantly being violated, including the most elementary rules of law. The protective dimension of corruption is indissociable from its disciplinary dimension. In this system of permanent control by party and police, corruption is the daily bread of active people, those who wish to try their hand at business and succeed, who wish to become ever more integrated into the fabric of social relations, who wish to climb the ladder of the social hierarchy. These practices (which are universally condemned) need to be understood within a specific context, which comprises the fake attributions of the public markets, distorted privatizations attributed to nominee companies in obscure conditions, and the pressure from 'clans' to influence decisions, or to create a forced association with an entrepreneur or an importer, or to impose oneself as a necessary business intermediary. While certain excesses are criticized and their systematic nature intensely resented, these practices are generally considered to be commonplace, and are experienced as such since they are part and parcel of everyday life in Tunisia. The importer who finds himself being offered the services of the member of a 'clan' to import the product that he markets traditionally is in the best cases merely annoyed by this offer. He might feel constrained to accept it, for fear of tax or property reprisals but, more often than not, he will accept without regret, knowing that his merchandise will get through customs and other administrative checks very quickly and without any hassle. The consumers do not lose out, since they will pay the same price for the product, with the 'clan' commission more or less compensating for the non-payment of customs duties. As for the administration, it will go along without batting an eyelid, insofar as clan members are personal representatives of the President. But if the importer were so obtuse as to refuse such an offer, his working conditions would rapidly get worse, his products could rot away in the customs sheds, the Inland revenue officials could launch an investigation, the CNSS could ask for his arrears, and the bank could refuse to grant him a final loan. Likewise, a research consultancy which refuses to accept certain of these practices finds that the administrative obstacles will increase in number, preventing it from keeping to the deadlines issued for the competition; and an entrepreneur who refuses to sell a significant proportion of his shares to those close to the clans risks finding that his 'business environment' will deteriorate, as the police can exert pressure on suppliers or service providers to refuse to work with the rebel.

On the other hand, misappropriation of funds in due and proper form, in other words pure and simple theft from the enterprises' coffers, from the company, or from the party, is severely repressed, precisely because it does do not activate the same mechanisms. Those who commit such misdemeanours may be members of the party, but they are still brought before the courts, unless they are extremely powerful. This is probably why Tunisia is classified by international organizations, in particular by Transparency International, as a country in which the level of corruption is particularly low.[37] The biases in these studies are now well known and documented. But their analysis is interesting precisely because of the characteristics of the opinion surveys on which the country's classification rests. The interviewees are foreign entrepreneurs who are not integrated – or not well integrated – into the tangled fabric of economic and social relations, who are not involved – or not to any great extent – in the relations of force and the exercise of power in Tunisia, especially if they are established in offshore zones. They generally invest in sectors deemed to be high priority by the central power, which then does everything it can to respect the rules and may even, in compensation for various intermediations, distort or even violate some of these rules in favour of foreigners. Finally, given the current situation, direct foreign investments (the increasing of which is considered to lie within the President's domain) benefit from the privilege that goes with this status: once they have passed the entrance gate into Tunisia, they are protected from the predatory activities of greedy intermediaries.

National or 'Tunisified' economic actors, who, by nature, are not rebellious, are on the other hand subjected to these practices, which they consider as something they cannot get round. Most of these actors even consider these practices as the day-to-day reality of their environment, the normal run of economic practices. Few and far between are cases of rebellion against 'rackets', or rejections of the corruption and illegality that go with them. Those who run a business are used to receiving requests from the party and satellite associations for aid; they are used to appealing to the cell or to an acquaintance in the routine operation of their activity. The person who applies for a 'gift' – for example, the credit manager of a bank, a tax inspector, a registrar – can at the same time possess an administrative authority that he thus exploits. The entrepreneur who passes by way of an intermediary merely pays him back by giving him a percentage, offering him shares, proposing a job for one of his clients. And by doing so he makes his future secure.

This system of pressures and anticipations is particularly efficient in that, historically speaking, entrepreneurs depend on the state authority. Intermediaries are mere cogs in the relations of power that extend from the centre to the periphery. However, cases of refusal, or of the adoption of evasive strategies, are more frequent than is believed. Nothing serious happens to them, apart from the fact that certain contracts and access to certain markets are then barred to them. In particular, extortions and illegal practices are not the preserve of certain 'clans'. On the contrary, if we pay attention to the economic practices and juridical disputes, we soon see how commonplace are rivalries, illegal competition, swindles and extortions.[38] The majority of foreign investors, especially in the offshore domain, are small and medium European enterprises which rarely attract the predatory eyes of those close to power.[39] However, it is not rare to hear them complaining about their Tunisian partners, who, apparently, are hellbent on swindling them and taking advantage of a windfall from abroad. Foreign chambers of commerce and aid organizations, indeed, advise SMEs endeavouring to establish themselves on the territory not to operate any association of capital. In their view, the apparent advantages in terms of knowing the milieu, and of contacts in the administration and in influential milieus, turn out to be illusory – mere sources of problems and inconveniences.[40]

It may be retorted – and, in the course of my interviews, many people have intimated as much to me – that the 'immoralism' of the powerful has encouraged, permitted and intensified this 'degeneration', this 'loss of moral principles and reflexes', this 'disappearance of the general interest'; their behaviour, it is said, demonstrates the 'benefits' of illegality and the fact that they go unpunished.[41] There is no doubt that this illegality, known or half-glimpsed, real or supposed, estimated or over-estimated – it is of little importance here – operates as a mechanism that suppresses all inhibition and any sense of guilt. On the contrary, it provides the population with a facile self-justification for such practices. But can we not turn the argument round and ask ourselves why the latter have taken root in Tunisian society? Why have they been accepted and why have they become so very widespread? We inevitably come back to the operations of the Tunisian political economy as described above, with its conflicts, its negotiations, its arrangements, its accepted constraints and its imposed consensus: corruption, just like the informal sphere, is fully part of the process. Because any debate is banned, because information circulates as rumour, because it is easier to throw the blame onto the corruption of the powerful than on the activities of all, the problem of corruption has become, in Tunisia, a central feature in the denunciations of the authoritarianism of the 'Ben Ali regime'. In the process, we forget the insidious mechanisms at work in it, those which are more difficult to condemn, because they are ambiguous and because they simultaneously explain and permit the accommodations made and the consensus reached.[42]

In the day-to-day reality of social practices, corruption and the practice of illegality produce a subtle effect of normalization in the shape of obligatory participation in a system of exchange, or of privileges, of special favours – and thus, gradually, lead to its legitimization. The central power reinforces its supervisory capacity by involving the whole population in it. The latter thereby becomes the best defender of a set of relations that at once includes it and protects it. In this, certainly, corruption is crucial and plays a full part in modes of government; increased perception of it is certainly revelatory of the ongoing transformations. This, too, is perfectly commonplace. Gilles Favarel-Garrigues, for example, has shown how the denunciation of corruption in Russia was also the expression of a certain nostalgia (for socialism and its familiar rules) and of a difficulty in adapting to new norms, which are, to crown it all, unstable.[43] Research on China brings out how capitalism is fundamentally perceived as bad, and a vector of corruption of people's activities and minds.[44] In Tunisia, there is no doubt that liberalization, in spite of all the restrictions that it faces, also feeds into an awareness of corruption by transforming rules and reference marks. The modes of creating and managing wealth are modified and de facto compromise the centrality of the central power, a power that was shaped by previous activities; the overlaps between public and private, between legal and illegal, and more generally the widespread illegality, do however offer it new opportunities to reposition itself, thanks to alliances, participations, privileges, and barriers. In Tunisian-style liberalism as in many other situations, wheeling and dealing does not turn out to be merely a way towards self-enrichment. It also illustrates the overlap between the power of control and the development of resources from rents.[45] As a result, the transformations are not merely in the economic realm. The perception of an increased corruption also reveals a transformation in the modes of government and the rules of social life. Corruption has no doubt increased quantitatively less than one thinks; rather, its role and meaning have changed: today it is much more intrusive, more political too, and operates as an important aspect of voluntary servitude.

Opposition circles often stigmatize the centrality of corruption in Ben Ali's exercise of power ('Ben Ali keeps his grip on power through corruption', 'Ben Ali's power is corrupt'), and even the criminalization of that power. Moncef Marzouki denounces the 'possession of absolute power with all its corollaries, the most important of which is corruption',[46] while Sihem Bensedrine and Omar Mestiri hammer home the point that 'the despot walks on two feet: repression and corruption. He uses the repressive arsenal to reduce resistance and bring society under control; he uses corruption to ensure the loyalty of groups which ensure the permanence of his power'.[47] Academics who analyse the Tunisian 'regime' in terms of neo-patrimonialism also place this confusion between public and private, between legal and illegal, at the source of the corruption and the degeneration of the idea of the common weal.[48] Corruption is a reality, there is no doubt about that, but, being partly imaginary, it encourages a problematic shortcut. By falling into the trap of 'institutionalized egotism', it isolates the Head of State from society, and covers over the way everyone takes part in practices that comprise Tunisian social being. Most analyses of 'corruption' are distorted: by centring everything on the 'clans', they forget the day-to-day activities of 'ordinary Tunisians'. They reproduce the myth of the personalization of power and the supreme Leader and go too far in the direction of a certain elitism, as if it were more important for the power in place to cajole the elites than to focus on managing its dear old middle class and its poor. As Michel Foucault put it, paraphrasing Bacon on the raison d'État: 'it is also possible to get round the great men and the nobles. Either you bribe them, or you execute them. A noble can be decapitated, a noble can betray – so a noble is always on the side of power, and not a problem for it.'[49] More than corruption, the mechanisms of security that concern the population as a whole form the basis of the modes of government.

The mechanism of 'corruption', like the mechanism of the police force, is definitely spiralling out of control. It is impossible to stop the chain of reciprocity and dependency, and it is even becoming increasingly difficult not to intensify the use of exchange, financial exploitation, and clientelism. This consolidation simultaneously produces fault lines, opening up gaps for denunciation and criticism. Increasingly, people keep silent while feeling disapproval. Aversion for these practices cannot be transformed into opposition, but silence and cover-ups are the expression of an increasing sense of unease and a gradual delegitimatization of the main techniques of government.

The hypothesis of the Tunisian state as a 'policing state'

The notion of a 'policing state' seems in my view able to transcend these largely imaginary visions of the exercise of power. The idea of mobilizing such a concept came to me from my analysis of the security pact and the intense desire of the Tunisian authorities to forestall any possibility of uncertainty and instability, in the areas of politics and police, of course, but also – and above all – in everyday life, in economic and social practices. Personal involvement does not stop people either exercising continuous actions and negotiating with everyone, nor being concerned with the well-being and security of the population, both of which are indispensable for the maintenance of the social order.

The policing state is not a police state in the accepted sense of the term, but a system and modes of regulation that make it possible for people's behaviour to be controlled. It is the 'set of mechanisms through which order, the channelled growth of wealth, and the conditions of maintenance [of the well-being of the population] can be ensured'.[50] The idea of a policing state emerged in western Europe at the end of the sixteenth century and spread until the eighteenth century, being linked to the new art of governing, which sought above all to increase a country's wealth and power by managing its population. Michel Foucault exhumed this notion in the 1960s, and considers that this problematization of the exercise of power marks the threshold of political modernity.

I decided that the concept of the policing state was useful if we were to gain a better understanding of the way the Tunisian state operated, since it enables us to get beyond the myth of the Leader as well as the image of the exteriority of state to society. The policing state, indeed, is characterized by a certain number of practices and conceptions that are not foreign to Tunisian modes of government: seventeenth-century texts all emphasize how the police must preserve 'the good order of society';[51] that it must contribute to the 'splendour of the entire state' and maintain 'the set of means by which the state's forces can be increased while preserving the state in good order'[52] that it deems itself in possession of an adequate and detailed understanding of what must be governed, and of knowledge itself;[53] that it thinks itself able to 'create a system of regulation of the general conduct of individuals whereby everything would be controlled to the point of self-sustenance, without the need for intervention';[54] that it can act on the population in such a way that reality will fit its own interests.[55] What concerns the policing state is what men do, their activity, their 'occupation'. The aim of the police is thus the control and supervision of men's activity insofar as this activity can constitute a differential element in the development of the state's forces.[56]

Since it has 'man as its real subject',[57] the policing state considers the population as a vast family and endeavours to enhance its power by using the tools of political economy, by investments, taxation, social protection, etc. In short, it is a question of governing rationally.[58] By so doing, it needs to pay attention to the 'fine grain of materiality', to 'details' and to 'little things', to act 'promptly and immediately':[59] 'police regulations are quite different in kind from other civil laws. police matters affect every moment, while legal matters are definitive and permanent things. The police focuses on little things, whereas the laws focus on important things. The police is forever focusing on details.'[60] So the policing state fits into a world of regulation – a regulation that is permanent and perpetually being renewed, becoming increasingly detailed so as endlessly to increase the state's power: 'the police needs regulations more than it needs laws'.[61]

So, in a more modern language, we might say that the policing state is an engineering state.[62] It is a direct organizer of the economy and implicitly hostile to liberalism, on nationalist bases. Hence its technical conception of the economy, and the fundamental role of planning. The production and circulation of goods and services are at the heart of its preoccupations, and it deems itself to be, 'as it were directly responsible for the satisfaction of needs in the same way as the technical director of a business concerns himself with the supplies necessary to his production'.[63] It is within this context that we need to understand the daily announcement of technical measures, each one more derisory than the rest, by Ben Ali in person. It is a matter of showing the state's solicitude, a solicitude all the stronger because it is expressed by the President. The 'voluntarism' characteristic of the Tunisian modes of government here takes on its full meaning: the Tunisian policing state is a state which knows that it can act on reality, knows that it can act so that reality will fit its own interests. It can say what is good and what is bad, and hence prescribe measures, and set up for itself definite limits without any strict relation to a reality: it can order and hierarchize. Voluntarism presupposes a population transparent to state action since it simultaneously prescribes and interprets the results obtained in terms of obedience or refusal.

The exteriority of liberal thinking which is characteristic of the policing state and of its obsession with rules and regulations[64] is one of the main features of Tunisian modes of government. As we have seen, disciplinary normalization mainly passed through regulatory modes, and the role of the state in the Tunisian economy was anything but liberal. Liberalization has changed none of this, since it always proceeds by direct interventions: the state only very rarely envisages acting indirectly in the economy, relying on mechanisms and variables that are apparently far removed from its aims and objectives, but which might turn out to be effective; it seeks first and foremost obedience and the respect for 'good order'. In other words, in Tunisia we do not find any scepticism as to the effectiveness of state actions, or the concrete capacities and possibilities of being thoroughly acquainted with what the state must govern, or its modes of intervention – a scepticism characteristic of liberalism.[65] In this sense, the current processes of liberalization and privatization are not liberal. The 'neoliberal conversion of the elites'[66] is doubtless rather ethereal, and liberal philosophy seems not to have penetrated either people's minds or their understanding of the real:[67] at best, there is a discourse on liberalism, with people putting forward liberal recipes, but not thinking outside regulation and incessant intervention; at worst, liberalization is imposed by injunction, by imperatives and prohibitions. Liberalization is understood in terms of an ethos of planning and intervention. Criticism from the left denounces the abandonment of the redistributive and protective role of the state. However, this means ignoring the appearance of other modes of regulation, for instance credit, consumption, redistribution through enforced solidarity . . .

However, none of this is really coherent and these reference points are not the only ones. The Tunisian state is obviously not a 'pure' policing state (has there ever been such a thing?) and the regulation associated with a certain dose of liberalism does of course exist. As our analysis of the measures of security and laissez faire in certain areas has suggested, regulatory intervention is not always the norm. There is also regulation, which encourages, facilitates and then lets people get on with it.[68] The concrete aspect of modes of government, in Tunisia as elsewhere, swings between these two modes. The interrelations between the latter are many and varied, even if resistance to including freedom in individual rights, as well as in modes of government (especially in economic activity), is particularly intense here. In Tunisia, it is unquestionably difficult to assume a 'self-limiting of governmental reason' and to 'govern less, out of a desire for maximum efficiency'.[69] By suggesting that the Tunisian state is a policing state, I did not wish to describe it but simply to show the significance of this utopia that shapes the vision of the state, the conception of modes of government and the ethos of power.

The randomness of the rule of law

Even if the approach I have adopted is an attempt to apprehend power in its totality, beyond institutions and any relation to the law, the juridical aspect of power remains a major cog in its exercise. In Tunisia, this appears very clearly: in the reforming line of the nineteenth century, central power aims to present itself as constitutionalist. This is shown in concrete form in the way that, ever since 1994, the expression 'rule of law' appears on 10-dinar banknotes.[70]

The rule of law is not merely part of the façade of democracy. The leitmotiv of the international community finds a favourable echo in the Tunisian tradition of juridical formalism. Donors and national authorities place more stress on procedures, rules and law than on the substance of public action, the modes of action, and the concrete side of practices. They also share the same apolitical conception of power: it is well known that international organizations have adopted the language of governance and of the rule of law precisely so as to evade the political 'problem', thereby following a certain interpretation of the rule of law in the social sciences, one that claimed that law was hegemonic in social regulation.[71] In Tunisia, the rule of law is seen as the 'reign of consensus, of security and reason', as opposed to the political, 'the reign of division, uncertainty, acts of force'.[72]

In spite of the vagueness and the normative character of the concept,[73] international organizations have turned it into a central instrument of their recommendations, with the rule of law being placed at the service of economic development, the application of market rules, and the flourishing of the private sector, thanks to fixed, irreversible, and foreseeable rules.[74] For the Tunisian authorities, the rule of law makes possible a certain conformity to the catechism of its main donors, but it is above all a political resource authorizing the legalization of disciplinary or even repressive practices. One of the consequences is that the adoption of this discourse by the Tunisian central power has dispossessed the opposition of one of its main themes. The national Pact reflects this enforced convergence, and Rafâa Ben Achour has said that, 'in this way, the notion of the rule of law has become transformed into a programme that is common to the government in power and to the opposition'.[75]

In spite of appearances, the rule of law is an excessively normative concept which reveals a certain conception of power, describing the legitimate modes of government, and fostering a normative vision of the state.[76] Now this conception is that of the policing state, that of 'the increase of the strength of the state *in good order*'. The rule of law needs to deliver the prosperity and the material progress promised by the security pact. This explains why this demand is presented as a constant feature of the Tunisian state, even if, in the nineteenth century, the terms used were not those which have now been translated, for reasons of legitimatization, as rule of law.[77] In the conception of the Tunisian central power, law is functional and meant to serve this precise order of state.[78] Rejection by the State Security Council, then by the Constitutional Council, of the control of laws on associations makes it possible to circumscribe democratic pressures and to supervise the associative movement strictly.[79] In the name of the rule of law, the administrative tribunal accepts recourse for excessive use of power, but the tribunal's decisions are not applied. Here we see the other face of political functionality: behind the 'interiorization of the code of constitutionality'[80] we can glimpse the formalist conception of the rule of law. The latter is easy to demand . . . on the explicit condition that the exercise of power is not limited. 'A law, in its real effects, is much more closely linked to attitudes, to schemas of behaviour than to legal formulations' as Michel Foucault reminded us.[81]

The rule of law appears as a technique that is 'less neutral than neutralizing of social relations'.[82] Generally speaking, the law is a privileged instrument of the reproduction and preservation of the social and relational capital of the governing milieus,[83] a 'privilege of the powerful'.[84] It can be understood, in particular, as a *dispositif* that masks domination, and which marks out the legal obligation of obedience. This is precisely what explains the importance of law in what are called authoritarian or totalitarian regimes. Sub-Saharan Africa since independence, the Portugal of Salazar, the Vichy regime, Fascist Italy, and even Nazi Germany, all demanded respect for law and the rule of law.[85] In the case of Italy, for instance, Emilio Gentile uses the term 'legal revolution' to analyse the approval by Parliament of a set of authoritarian laws and to show how Fascism was able to destroy the parliamentary regime while apparently keeping intact the façade of the constitutional monarchy; all political innovations were introduced by formal laws.[86] Juridical instruments were among the most important techniques of domination of the Fascist regime. Bernardo Sordi emphasizes how jurists were not repressed when they disagreed with the Fascist authorities and that one of the country's major jurists, who had no party affiliation, was appointed as head of the Council of State precisely to show the importance granted by Fascism to the law and its independence.[87] What did change, of course, was the political style, the style of government, those attitudes and activities that transformed, or rather gave a different meaning to, legality. But all the jurists who have defined the Fascist state as a totalitarian state also defined it as a rule of law.

Indeed, it was this fact – a very disturbing fact in the aftermath of the Second World War – which impelled jurists to develop a substantialist vision of the rule of law.[88] In these conditions, it is clear how impossible it is to ignore the question of the relation between violence and law. Walter Benjamin provides us with a useful way of looking at the issue: he showed that the law principally protected itself[89] and thereby protected the law in the order of state, for example, in Tunisia, in the order of the policing state. Sana Ben Achour has brought out the element of 'foundational violence' – to use Benjamin's term – that goes to make up modern Tunisian law, in particular through the interplay between different juridical orders during colonization.[90] This order endures because it forms the basis of current law.

'What is most remarkable in our country is the fact that every political decision can at any moment revise the laws it lays down. Thus, independence appears as a brief and special moment, in which national life massively produced its fundamental legislation, but almost immediately left behind the reality of that legislation':[91] the author of *National Disenchantment* here highlights what many jurists show in their technical work.[92] What dominates in Tunisia is the non-respect for laws and the way they are violated, the reversibility of regulations and their application, the absence of practical mechanisms for the implementation of laws, the frequent overturning of the hierarchy between laws, decrees, circulars and speeches, the application of laws to individuals, their relations, their connections and the degree of their social integration, their lifestyle, too, and the way they think, and the arbitrary decisions made possible by redundant, superfluous and sometimes contradictory laws. These practices can be found in every area, in connection with a building permit or the constitutional control of law, in connection with the right to import or the right of association. They bring out the strength of the policing state: it is not the institutionalized political life which is at the heart of control and surveillance, but the detail of day-to-day practices.

This juridical disorder and the extensive use of oral rather than written media favour this random exercise of the law and the rule of law. It often happens that decisions are made without any legal basis, like those announced during a presidential speech, which come into effect without ever giving rise to the publication of laws or decrees, or else those decrees that take precedence over the law, as is shown by the case of regulations concerning foreign investments.[93] What in Tunisia are called *talimet* are non-written instructions or orders that have the force of law, and sometimes even more force than the law; what must be done but cannot be written, and is applied most frequently in situations where there is an unexplained rejection, precisely to avoid having to give any explanation.[94] The administration rarely writes down the reasons for its rejection of a decision, and does not even supply a document notifying the rejection. The civil servant will use word of mouth to give a negative reply in the case of non-deliverance of a document, of rejection during a recruitment process, or when an association is being set up or a public event organized, precisely so as to prevent anyone from resorting to the law. As with torture, no trace must be left. And the civil servant in contact with the citizen will not in all honesty be able to do more than repeat that he is 'applying the *talimet*' when he announces to the opponent that his passport is still not available or that he has been handed down some sentence of which he is unaware, when he tells the villager that he cannot fence off his field or construct a shed on his land, and to the town dweller that he cannot sort out or even just obtain his property deed.

Uncertainty about the rule of law is increased, too, by an administrative organization characterized by the absence of any sense of responsibility and the impossibility of localizing the source of authority. No agent can take the initiative for applying the law. Even when the law is clear, a civil servant always needs to ask for an authorization at the higher level of his hierarchy for a recruitment or for the provision of an administrative document, the unblocking of a sum of money or the implementation of a policy, because the norm can be in force but it can just as well be suspended as the effect of a presidential decision, an intercession from a party member, or an injunction from the President's family. This uncertainty increases the stagnation, since survival is more important than action. To protect oneself from the hierarchical gaze and its effects of power, it is preferable to shake off any decisions. But, at the same time, the way in which things have in general to be straightened out, and the reign of the *talimet*, constitute a mode of the exercise of arbitrary power. The non-application of the law, or rather its intermittent and discretionary application (made possible by this specific way the administration operates), are both instruments of control, of punishment, of reward and repression, like the exploitation of gaps in the law. The confusion between public and private is echoed by the confusion between juridical orders: insofar as they are produced in a juridical vacuum, acts – such as oral instructions within the administration or presidential decisions – cannot be juridically determined. 'Fact and law seem to become indiscernible',[95] and as a result the decisions cannot be refuted, criticized or questioned. All of this reinforces and strengthens the central myth of consensus.

According to Hannah Arendt, the replacement of laws by decrees and juridical uncertainties are 'characteristic of every bureaucratic form of tyranny in which government and the normal operation of the laws are replaced by the administration and by anonymous decisions'.[96] What jurists describe as vagueness, reversibility and intermittence, exemption and laxity, can be read in terms of temporary suspensions of the juridical system, in other words as the recurrence of 'states of exception'.[97] In Tunisia, the latter are never formalized. There is no formal decision, and above all no general measures; rather, there is a whole series of microdecisions that foster this meshing of logics characteristic of Tunisian modes of government. It might be said, paraphrasing Étienne Balibar, that the exercise of power in Tunisia is a 'rule of law but also a policing state; a state in which individuals and groups are integrated into the "community of citizens", but also a state which excludes rebels, the abnormal, the deviant and foreigners; a "social" state, but a class state too'.[98] Which in the final analysis leads to a sort of diffuse state of exception intimately linked to the rule of law to which people become accustomed. Like the 'insidious leniencies' of the economic sphere, '*little by little people get used to* seeing [the law] leaving itself behind, or resting on criteria that it constantly pushes towards into nonsense: it becomes a fiction to the nth degree'.[99] In addition, Tunisian jurists emphasize the importance of the exorbitant character of the laws, measures, decisions and rules, and of the recurrence of states of exception in administrative or economic law.[100] As everywhere else, this suspension of order is justified and even demanded by the maintenance of order when this is threatened.[101] In Tunisia, this is what explains the set of exorbitant legal measures, those little exceptional measures, which have made it possible for political Islamism to be criminalized and the order of the Tunisian state protected.

The individual and the intimate sphere at the heart of relations of power

The different techniques of power analysed in my study all confirm that disciplines produce a process of individualization, as had been claimed by Foucault and, before him, Tocqueville. Power individualizes those on whom it is brought to bear – by control, by surveillance, by normalization, but also by negotiation and arrangements. I have tried to demonstrate this with regard to the grid and economic and social mechanisms. All these *dispositifs* make it possible for everyone's individual situation to be improved, whether they be policemen, informers, grasses, active cell members, executive directors, ministers, or else entrepreneurs, Stock Exchange operators, employees, civil servants, trade unionists, tax payers, consumers, debtors, tradesmen, importers, constituents, opponents . . .

The fine mesh of society and even more the set of mutual dependencies make the individual control and surveillance of everyone possible and, individually, they make reward and punishment possible. RCD cells are places for sociability and the development of social relations which simultaneously strengthen the position and the personal power of each of their members, in political, economic and social terms. The party operates as an efficient and high-performance administration, as we have seen, but it is an administration that knows everyone individually, in particular through the different structures that are linked to it and the different mechanisms of supervision. This knowledge is effective, as we have already mentioned, with real consequences for a person's career, social recognition, and standard of living; but it is also widely presupposed. All, or almost all, individuals have integrated this dimension: the awareness of the omnipresence of individual mechanisms of control and supervision functions as a process of intimidation, of spreading fear, and thus of normalization. Individuals, even when objectively they do not have much to fear, feel individually integrated into this hierarchical gaze, into this disciplinary whole; they imagine all the possible situations of repression, which exist de facto but are not permanently active (far from it). It is not uncommon to hear people stating that they are 'taking risks for their jobs', 'that they wish to protect their children', 'that they don't want any problems' in completely innocuous situations; they invent, by themselves, all sorts of mechanisms and techniques by which they might, individually, be affected by power, by which they might, individually, be repressed.

The *imaginaire* of fear is an individualizing *imaginaire*. The force of the central power is precisely to do everything to allow fear and the imagination of fear to inveigle its way into each individual, starting with those who, ultimately, risk little with regard to their life style and their docile integration into society. This policy of branding people, whether real or phantasmatic, is particularly effective because, in parallel with the many mechanisms of supervision, social relations are deployed in a space that is, in the last analysis, narrow – and because (in spite of fierce competition) clientele networks intersect, and qualified intermediaries know each other and need to live and work together. Diffuse control, fear and intimidation, the multiple pressures, the innumerable mechanisms of inclusion and the procedures of subjection neutralize the majority of Tunisians. But they thereby individualize the same Tunisians by letting the sword of Damocles hover over their heads – the sword that could, in the case of rebellion or ostentatious passivity, stigmatize them and even attack them in their flesh, individually.

Because it 'watches over the living',[102] the policing state extends the various processes of individualization to private life, to the most intimate depths of every individual, to the right of death and power over life. What Michel Foucault described in terms of biopower to characterize the Christian West from the seventeenth and eighteenth centuries onwards is found, in other forms and in other configurations, elsewhere – for example in Singapore since the 1960s and these days in Malaysia,[103] or, as it happens, in Tunisia. Disciplinary power, after all, is largely focused on the body. Its most violent form is indubitably death: the real, physical death of certain militants, assassinated, tortured, or forced out of despair to choose suicide; but also the social death of opponents who are restricted, shut away, and find it impossible to live in society – a fate that marks them physically, for life. What Michel Foucault called the 'political anatomy' of the human body[104] takes several other forms, for example police checks and round-ups, or hunger strikes.

The former take place at regular intervals, intermittently and in a haphazard fashion, but they are repeated often enough in the lives of Tunisians to remain present in their memories. Memory passes essentially through the body which 'thus preserves traces of power, directly, in a person's flesh'.[105] By bringing together the public and the private, police checks and round-ups form part of the mechanisms whereby discipline is interiorized, and thereby contribute to shaping voluntary servitude.[106] As for hunger strikes, while they express a form of social despair, while they are an attempt to denounce the inhumanity of prison or of repressive techniques, while they have the function of alerting people to certain – intolerable – modes of the exercise of power, they also say (and perhaps say first and foremost) that the only freedom for the ostracized individual, the only action at his disposal, is to turn against himself, against the only thing that he still possesses: his body.[107] By this gesture, the individual constitutes himself as a subject acting through self-mutilation, a self-mutilation which brings with it the hope of a rebirth, a death foretold that portends, finally, the possibility of life. In an environment that prohibits the political, the expression of freedom alone, the expression of the political, passes through what the individual in an ultimate sense possesses: 'naked life', that 'subject that needs to be at once turned into the exception and included in the city'.[108] This gesture constitutes an usurpation of the right of death which the sovereign alone should possess, in this totalitarian conception of power.

However, more often than not, this power over life and these actions of subjection are less dramatic, and pass through material mediations that not only are dependent on technology and logistics, but are modes of subjection.[109] In this connection, we cannot avoid talking about that specific form of the power of regulation of the population, wearing the headscarf. Throughout the 1960s and 1970s, Bourguiba, with characteristic ambiguity, aimed to use his power to administer Islam, to use it for public order and political competition, exercising a tight control over the exercise of worship, over religious personages, places and messages.[110] Among the latter, he had endeavoured, through symbolic gestures, to focus on transformations in the clothes people wore, in particular by giving its full political significance to the use of the scarf, which was sometimes tolerated or ignored, but more often decried and repressed. Conversely, at a time when the central power was tensing up in its fight against political Islamism, President Ben Ali accentuated the tendency of the state to appropriate religion by legislating on, nationalizing, and bureaucratizing Islam, turning the imams into state functionaries and rigorously controlling places of worship; at the same time, he ordered a merciless repression of women who wore headscarves, especially between 1989 and 1992. As a result of this, in the 1990s, the headscarf had practically vanished. However, since around 2000, more and more women (in particular the younger generation) have again started to wear it. This movement was for a while ignored; since the middle of 2003, it has been subjected to a new campaign of repression: in public spaces, these young girls are arrested, taken to the local police headquarters and ordered to remove their scarves; they are subject to blackmail as they try to pursue their profession or their studies, and are physically threatened, just to drive the lesson home. There is no point in going over the disciplinary dimension of these practices which take the form of punishing the body by means of the headscarf. Conversely, wearing the headscarf suggests another political dimension, that of subjectivation. As Fariba Adelkhah has shown in a different context (that of Iran),[111] these veiled women thereby constitute themselves as modern subjects, fully integrated into society. They certainly do not take part in political action in its classical form – participating in party political movements. They do however contribute to the emergence of the debate (which, like all debate in Tunisia, is prohibited) on secularism and religious commitment;[112] they take part in relations of force within society, spurning laws and rules, but also practices of intimidation and of fear;[113] certain of them endeavour to exhibit an alternative form of modernity and feminine emancipation, while others blatantly reject it; they express a desire for differentiation and recognition; they construct themselves as self-possessed, serious, desirable women, women worth marrying – as well as being individuals in search of a certain form of religiosity.[114]

But there is more than just the veil. In 1967, just as he was fighting against the wearing of the veil, Habib Bourguiba created a *Conseil national d'habillement* (CNH – National Council on Dress) whose task was 'to draw up a programme to foster people's access to decent clothing and a raising of the level of dress worn by the population, to determine the needs in this area and to propose the means and all the measures likely to contribute to the realization of this programme'.[115] This control was openly taken over by the Supreme Fighter, as is suggested by the title of one of his speeches: 'Educating body and mind'.[116] It was for this reason that sport was and still is important in supervision and disciplining.[117] Under the cover of respect for Islamic precepts, moral and political censorship persists.[118] In the 1970s, as we have seen, the heads of young people who frequented the night clubs and hung out with tourists were shaved during raids or moral campaigns. These days, the sale of alcohol to Muslims is made extremely difficult and Tunisians are still banned from clubs and tourist complexes. The law which makes it possible for offences against public decency to be repressed is often brought back into force, following campaigns and in parallel with the way that Tunisians are 'privatizing' themselves, in other words withdrawing from the public scene.[119] But, at the same time, spaces of 'freedom' are organized, places 'appointed' for public intimacy. At the Berges du Lac, you can see couples holding each other's hands in perfect tranquillity . . .

This moralization, indeed, was reaffirmed as soon as Ben Ali came to power. He aimed to 'establish a moral and religious climate'[120] thanks to an unprecedented reinforcing of controls over public places and public transport. As Ilhem Marzouki points out, 'the individual found himself governed right down to the slightest details of his relation to his body and his intimate life' and the state started to codify 'modes of dress, food, family planning, control over sexuality, with – even today – "campaigns for the safeguarding of morality"'.[121] The return to a certain religiosity, as brought about by the Change, needs to be understood in this sense:[122] admittedly, it makes disciplining possible, but it also makes possible a subjection that affects the individual on the deepest level, by affecting his body. Physical bodies are subjected to police raids, but moral campaigns can also be less dramatic. In December 2003, for example, a campaign for the 'rationalization of consumption' was aimed at 'implanting *healthy behaviour into the minds of young people* in particular'.[123]

In this register, sexuality is a weapon that is particularly highly appreciated by the policing state, and one that is relatively effective. Young couples are, from time to time, the object of campaigns aimed at the 'safeguard of morality', such as the one which took place in February and March 2004.[124] They are arrested for offences to morality outside high schools, cafes and in public places on the pretext that they are wearing figure-hugging jeans or tops that are cut too low.[125] The technique is also used, very frequently, to attack in the Arabic-language newspapers the private lives of human rights activists, political opponents or former 'friends' who need to be punished. Newspapers throw dirt at them, making up stories about their homosexuality or adultery, and rumours circulate about the loose lives of some and the immorality of others. This is the case with Sihem Bensédrine, the victim of several campaigns of denigration by a press that does not hesitate to stoop to obscenity through pornographic photomontages and insulting descriptions. This female journalist and spokesperson for the CNLT is described as a 'devil creature' who goes round debauching teenagers and as a 'crazy machine for any man who draws near her enclosure or tries to knock on the door of her prostitution'. She is accused of 'renting out her back to foreigners in general and to Zionists in particular' – a tortuous way of accusing her of sodomy.[126]

Islamists are the most affected by this attack on private life, as by the other techniques of control and repression. The story of Ali Laaridh mentioned above is emblematic of this. He found himself being accused of homosexuality while he was in jail, and a faked video was broadcast by the Tunisian services (and with the participation of anti-Islamist opponents) suggesting that he kept feeling up the man sharing his cell, a voice offstage adding that he had forced the latter to give him a massage and had attempted to sodomize him. In the introductory sequence of the video, this same voice utters the following accusation: 'These Islamists, in their intimate lives, forget their prayers and their fasts and abandon themselves to their passions and their diabolical instincts. Then they sow corruption, setting up places for debauchery and organizing "orgies" '.[127] Many more examples could be cited of those people who find the most ridiculous words being put into their mouths, thanks to IT techniques that allow intrusion into e-mail,[128] or of those others who are shown in fake videos in disreputable company.[129]

The power of regulation of the population is also implemented by taking away something from the individual who is forced into a posture of withdrawal. This dimension, which deprives people of their privacy, their intimacy, has been brought out by Hannah Arendt in *The Human Condition*: as she puts it, 'the privative trait of privacy [is] the consciousness of being deprived of something essential in a life spent exclusively in the restricted sphere of the household'.[130] To be deprived of an objective relation with others is to be deprived of the things essential to social life. Being forced back into the family, the private, the intimate sphere also constitutes a loss, a loss in particular of any recognition of the social value of actions, forms of thought, or lives themselves. Even if they continue to use the rhetoric of Islamist danger, those who govern deem that Tunisian Islamists no longer exist in the country as a political force. In any case, 'Islamist opponents' have never existed; they were 'extremists', 'terrorists', 'religious fanatics'. The vast majority of members of the secular opposition, human rights activists and foreign partners consider them, at best, to be victims. And the few people who see them as political actors are marginalized. Islamists sense this when they claim that 'we are being forced into social death'; this is their way of saying that they are left with nothing but 'bare life', that social recognition is denied them as dissidents, political actors, democrats 'of course', but also, quite simply, as social actors, citizens, men or women.

In the same way, hunger strikers are sometimes the object of compassion, and often arouse irritation, but, generally speaking, the political and social dimension of the struggles on which they have embarked is not recognized. These days, 'everyone' goes on hunger strike:[131] the female lawyer Radhia Nasraoui, her supporters, political prisoners in pretty much every jail, the supporters of those political prisoners, militants subjected to harassment, the families of Internet users who have been sentenced and jailed, students and former Islamist student trade union members prevented from pursuing their studies, and unemployed workers male and female – for example at Sidi Bouzid and Moknine. This form of struggle and protest develops by default, out of despair, because – more than direct repression – diffuse techniques of control and discipline are effective. In these conditions, the sole margin of manoeuvre, the sole liberty, is to deprive oneself of the 'first of liberties',[132] the liberty to eat.

This dimension of privacy and deprivation is not, however, reserved to identified 'enemies' alone; it concerns the population as a whole, a population which is forced to withdraw into the intimate sphere.[133] People who, for one reason or another, have had to undergo victimization, intimidation, or disciplinary action, interiorize these constraints, and suffer in silence the mechanisms of discipline, supervision and even repression; they 'keep these problems to themselves' and are even forced by this silence to feel guilty, to turn against themselves, as they turn a critical eye on their behaviour, on any possible errors or failings they may have committed, and wonder whether they have not 'misbehaved'.[134] Intellectuals have, so to speak, 'padlocked their intellects'.[135] They flee into an 'inner exile'[136] in the intimacy of their lives with family and friends. The absence of watertight boundaries between public and private, and the practices of the policing state, lead Tunisians to 'privatize' themselves, as they withdraw from circulation any expressive signs of their social being, and reduce and limit entire swathes of their activity and social existence.

Notes

Preface to the English Edition

1 *Compétitivité et croissance. Le défi de l'emploi aux multiples dimensions*, Consultation nationale sur l'emploi, Tunisia 2008, Intermediary report, version 2, September 2008 (produced by the World Bank and the Tunisian authorities). More precisely, it appears that there are 70,000 graduates each year, 40,000 of whom emerge from professional training and 30,000 without such training.

2 H. Meddeb, 'Tunisie, pays émergent?', *Sociétés politiques comparées*, 29, November 2010 (accessible or the website www.fasopo.org/reasopo/n29/article.pdf).

3 On the deconstruction of the 'economic miracle', see B. Hibou, 'Les marges de manoeuvre d'un "bon élève" économique: la Tunisie de Ben Ali', *Les Etudes du CERI*, no. 60, December 1999 (accessible at http://www.ceri-sciences-po.org/publica/etsude/etude60.pdf) and *Surveiller et réformer. Economie politique de la servitude volontaire en Tunisie*, habilitation thesis for directing research, Paris, SciencesPo, 7 November 2005, ch. 2.

4 I have shown this, including for the case of Tunisia, in my *Anatomie politique de la domination. Une économie politique comparée des régimes autoritaires* (Paris: La Découverte, 2011). It is also emphasized by P. Ramos Pinto (2009) on Salazar's Portugal in 'Housing and citizenship: building social rights in twentieth-century Portugal', *Contemporary European History*, 18 (2) 2009, pp. 199–215.

5 Michel de Certeau, *The Practice of Everyday Life*, trans. Steven Rendall (Berkeley; London: University of California Press, 1984), p. 105.

6 H. Meddeb, 'L'ambivalence de la course à *el thobza*. obéir et se révolter en Tunisie', *Politique africaine*, no. 121, March 2011 on this sense of *hogra* (humiliation).

7 A. Allal, 'Réformes néoliberales, clientélismes et protestations en situation autoritaire. Les mouvements contestataires dans le basin minier de Gafsa', *Politique africaine*, no. 117, March 2010, pp. 107–26; see too the film devoted to these events, produced by the Tunisian Committee for Support for the population of the mining area of Gafsa, *Redeyef: le combat de la dignité*.

8 See the thesis being written by H. Meddeb on young people and the insertion of mechanisms of power in their make-do economy.

9 Michel Foucault, 'Nietzsche, genealogy, history', in *Essential Works of Foucault 1954–1984*, series editor Paul Rabinow, vol. 2, *Aesthetics*, ed. by James D. Faubion, trans. Robert Hurley et al. (London: Penguin, 1994), pp. 369–91, p. 381.

10 See P. Veyne, *Le Quotidien et l'intéressant. Entretiens avec Catherine Darbo-Peschanski* (Paris: Hachette Littérature, 1995), where the author speaks of the 'dangerous disorder of action' and develops the idea that men and women make history but cannot know what history will be; M. de Certeau, Luce Giard and Pierre Mayol, *The Practice of Everyday Life*, vol. 2, *Living and Cooking*, trans. Timothy J. Tomasik, revised and enlarged edn (Minneapolis: University of Minnesota Press, 1998), which underlines the importance of 'indefinite' things, of eventful periods and, in *La Faiblesse de croire* (Paris: Le Seuil, 1987) speaks of the 'insolence of facts'. See also the texts by Max Weber that emphasize contingency, the unexpected and the lack of completion that opens up possibilities, especially in his *Political Writings*, ed. Peter Lassman and Ronald Speirs (Cambridge: Cambridge University Press, 1994).

11 Michel de Certeau, *La Faiblesse de croire* (Paris: Le Seuil, 1987); B. Hibou, *Anatomie politique de la domination*.

12 This has been well analysed by Alexei Yurchak in *Everything Was Forever Until It Was No More. The Last Soviet Generation* (Princeton: Princeton University Press, 2006).

13 B. Hibou, '"Nous ne prendrons jamais le maquis": entrepreneurs et politique en Tunisie', *Politix*, 21 (84), 2008, pp. 115–41.

14 S. Elbaz, 'Quand le régime du "Changement" prône la "stabilité". Mots et trajectoire du développement en Tunisie', *Revue Tiers Monde*, no. 200, October–December 2009, pp. 821–36 and H. Meddeb, '"Une jeunesse capable de relever les défis"'.

15 H. Medeles, 'Tunisie, pays émergent?'

16 B. Hibou, *Anatomie politique de la domination*.

Introduction

1 Michel Foucault, *Discipline and Punish: The Birth of the Prison*, trans. Alan Sheridan, 2nd edn (New York: Vintage Books, 1995), p. 139.

2 These are the words used by Paul Veyne in *Le Quotidien et l'intéressant. Entretiens avec Catherine Darbo-Peschanski* (Paris: Hachette Littérature, 1995).

3 It is difficult to give the exact number of 'political prisoners', as the authorities reject this term and the reality that it designates. However, the penitentiary administration reserves a particular treatment for those detained because of political 'affiliation' or those 'of special character'. See especially CNLT, *Rapport sur la situation dans les prisons en Tunisie* (Tunis, 20 October 1999); LTDH, *Rapports annuels 2001 et 2002* (Tunis, mimeograph); LTDH, *Les Murs du silence. Rapport sur les prisons* (Tunis, 2004), and the various annual reports of human rights organizations, especially the communiqués of the Association internationale de soutien aux prisonniers politiques (AISPP – International Association for the Support of Political Prisoners). For an account based on personal experience, see A. Manaï, *Supplice tunisien, le jardin secret du général Ben Ali* (Paris: La Découverte, 1995). For a historical analysis, S. Belhassen, 'Les legs bourguibiens de la répression' (pp. 391–404), in M. Camau and V. Geisser (eds), *Habib Bourguiba. La Trace et l'héritage* (Paris: Karthala; Aix-en-Provence: Institut d'études politiques, 2004).

4 This paragraph is mainly based on a series of interviews I did with ex-political prisoners, members of the families of detainees, lawyers, and human rights activists in Tunis, especially in November 2001, December 2002 and December 2003, as well as in Paris, especially in November 2001 and January 2002. See also the descriptions in the collective work published by the 'Reporters sans frontières' group, *Tunisie, le livre noir* (Paris: La Découverte, 2002): this reprints the main reports of the CNLT, LTDH, Human Rights Watch, Amnesty International, etc.; and more especially in LTDH, *Rapport annuel 2001*, and the third part of the Amnesty International report, *Le Cycle de l'injustice*, MDE 30/001/2003 (London, June 2003).

5 Giorgio Agamben, 'Form of life', *Means Without End: Notes on Politics*, trans. Vincenzo Binetti and Cesare Casarino (Minneapolis; London: University of Minneapolis Press, 2000), p. 5.

6 The LTDH reports, for instance, the case of Ali Ben Mohamed Chortani, who, for six whole years, every day had to go to four different places: the special services brigade, the district intelligence brigade, the search brigade of the national guard of Gafsa, and the police station. Mentioned in LTDH, *Rapport annuel 2001*, p. 20.

7 The term '*stratégie du pourtour*' comes from Michel Foucault. He forged it in connection with the events at Longwy [the town in Lorraine where, at the start of the 1980s, there were mass demonstrations against unemployment in the iron industry – Tr.]. Here, unlike the workers themselves, the students, high school children and young unemployed who had come to support those workers were severely punished by the courts, to set an example. Michel Foucault, 'La stratégie du pourtour', in *Dits et écrits, III, 1976–1979*, eds Daniel Defert and François Ewald (Paris: Gallimard, 1994), pp. 794–7.

8 The 'B3' is the document attesting that one has a police record with a sentence of more than 2 months in jail. The 'B2', which includes all sentences, is not explicitly asked for, but the administration gets hold of it, in critical cases.

9 The reports quoted previously mention this briefly, but one document is dedicated entirely to this question: CRLDHT, *Familles, victimes et otages, rapport 2002* (Paris, 24 January 2002).

10 I heard about this case frequently during my interviews. It is also mentioned in the report of the LTDH and in M. Marzouki, *Le Mal arabe. Entre dictatures et intégrismes: la démocratie interdite* (Paris: L'Harmattan, 2004).

11 It is, by definition, difficult to quote an exact number here. During the period of greatest repression (1991–4), police raids in local districts appear to have sent between 20,000 and 25,000 people to prison; 3,000 of them, it is claimed, spent several years there.

12 H. E. Chehabi and J. Linz (eds), *Sultanic Regimes* (Baltimore; London: The Johns Hopkins University Press, 1998).

13 C. M. Henry and R. Springborg, *Globalization and the Politics of Development in the Middle East* (Cambridge: Cambridge University Press, 2001).

14 E. Bellin, *Stalled Democracy. Capital, Labor and the Paradox of State-Sponsored Development* (Ithaca; London: Cornell University Press, 2002); E. Murphy, *Economic and Political Change in Tunisia. From Bourguiba to Ben Ali* (New York; London: St Martin's Press; MacMillan Press, 1999); L. Anderson, 'The

prospects for democracy in the Arab world', *Middle Eastern Lectures*, no. 1, 1995, pp. 59–71.
15 C. M. Henry, *The Mediterranean Debt Crescent. Money and Power in Algeria, Egypt, Morocco, Tunisia and Turkey* (Gainesville: University Press of Florida, 1996); C. H. Moore, 'Tunisian banking: politics of adjustment and the adjustment of politics' (pp. 67–97), in I. W. Zartman (ed.), *Tunisia: The Political Economy of Reform* (Boulder: Lynne Rienner, 1991).
16 J. J. Linz and A. Stepan, *Problems of Democratic Transition and Consolidation. Southern Europe, South America and Post-Communist Europe* (Baltimore; London: Johns Hopkins University Press, 1996). They define economic society as the 'institutionalization of a socially and politically regulated market', p. 13.
17 Hannah Arendt, *The Origins of Totalitarianism* (London: Deutsch, 1986).
18 G. Aly, *Comment Hitler a acheté les Allemands* (Paris: Flammarion, 2005); English version: *Hitler's Beneficiaries. Plunder, Racial War, and the Nazi Welfare State* (New York; London: Verso, 2007).
19 These are works on authoritarian situations (Guy Hermet, Alain Rouquié) and democratic situations (Guy Hermet), and research groups on 'popular modes of political action' (Jean-François Bayart) and the 'Trajepo' (i.e. trajectories of the political, directed by Jean-François Bayart).
20 This research, like that of Guy Hermet on Spain or Latin America, concentrates mainly on the mechanisms and concrete functioning of the apparatuses of power. Jean Leca's work was a pioneering attempt to propose a political, and non-orientalist, analysis of societies too often presented as specific (because Muslim), and to analyse concrete situations on the basis of the interplay between empiricism and theorization. As for Jean-François Bayart, he has drawn inspiration from the works of Foucault, always linking discipline to subjection, and thus to a certain form of consent. His work has inspired me to follow similar paths. I have been particularly influenced by his political procedure, which puts great emphasis on the 'banalisation' of historical trajectories; by the importance he gives to details, to little things – in short, to whatever does not constitute the 'nobility' of the political; by his multi-disciplinary method, and more particularly his ability to draw on anthropology and history so as better to understand contemporary authoritarian situations; and by his sensitivity to all that is paradoxical and ambiguous.
21 P. Minard, *La Fortune du colbertisme. État et industrie dans la France des Lumières* (Paris: Fayard, 1998), p. 13. A 'secular' history is, in the view of this author, a history freed of dogma, rhetoric and abstract notions, centred on the analysis of concrete practices.
22 Critique is immediately understood as normative, as the judgement that 'things aren't good the way they are', without any understanding of the interest that resides in 'seeing on what type of assumptions, of familiar notions, of established, unexamined ways of thinking the accepted practices are based': Michel Foucault, 'So is it important to think?' in Michel Foucault, *Essential Works of Foucault 1954–1984*, vol. 3, *Power*, ed. James D. Faubion, trans. Robert Hurley and others (London: Penguin, 2002), pp. 454–8; p. 456.
23 I have been influenced by two very different lines of research. Firstly, that of Étienne Balibar on fictive ethnicity and the imaginary social community: see in particular E. Balibar and I. Wallerstein, *Race, Nation, Class: Ambiguous*

Identities, trans. (of Balibar) Christ Turner (London: Verso, 1991). Secondly, that of Françoise Mengin on a very specific situation: Taiwan and the fiction of a non-state which does not lead to the 'non-recognition' of a state, but to the recognition of a 'non-state' (see *Les Relations entre la France et Taiwan de 1964 à 1994. Contribution à une étude des relations extérieures d'un non-État*, doctoral thesis in political science (Institut d'études politiques de Paris: Paris, 1994), and 'Une privatisation fictive: le cas des relations avec Taiwan', in B. Hibou (ed.), *La Privatisation des États* (Paris: Karthala, 1999), pp. 197–223 (English version: F. Mengin, 'A Pretence of Privatisation. Taiwan's External Relations' in B. Hibou (ed.), *Privatising the State*, trans. Jonathan Derrick (London: Hurst; New York: Columbia University Press, 2004), pp. 147–67.

24 The quotation is from M. Foucault, 'Introduction', in *Dits et écrits, I, 1954–1969*, ed. Daniel Defert and François Ewald (Paris: Gallimard, 1994), no. 7, p. 186. See also the works of Foucault's early years, reproduced in this volume (no. 17, 'Distance, aspect, origine' and no. 36, 'L'arrière-fable'); Roland Barthes, *Mythologies*, selected and trans. Annette Lavers (London: Vintage, 1993) and *Writing Degree Zero*, trans. Annette Lavers and Colin Smith (London: Cape, 1967); Herbert Marcuse, *One-Dimensional Man: Studies in the Ideology of Advanced Industrial Society*, with a new introduction by Douglas Kellner; 2nd edn (London: Routledge, 2002; originally published in 1964).

25 Gilles Deleuze, *Negotiations 1972–1990*, trans. Martin Joughin (New York; Chichester: Columbia University Press, 1995), and J.-F. Bayart, *L'Illusion identitaire* (Paris: Fayard, 1996) (English version, J.-F. Bayart, *The Illusion of Cultural Identity*, trans. Steven Rendall (London: Hurst, 2005).

26 D. Dessert, *Argent, pouvoir et société au Grand Siècle* (Paris: Fayard, 1984).

27 Béatrice Hibou, *Les Fables du développement* (forthcoming).

28 I used this expression in the article I wrote with M. Tozy, 'De la friture sur la ligne des réformes. La libéralisation des télécommunications au Maroc', *Critique internationale*, no. 14, January 2002, pp. 91–118.

29 It should be remembered that Max Weber developed his general theories on the basis of highly specialized research into the structures of property, tax legislation, the organizational forms of the craft industry and industrial corporations, and the relations between juridical forms and political practices – and not vice versa.

30 Michel de Certeau, *L'Invention du quotidien. 1. Arts de faire* (Paris: Gallimard, new edn 1990) (English version M. de Certeau, *The Practice of Everyday Life*, trans. Steven Rendall (University of California Press, 1984); A. Desrosières, *The Politics of Large Numbers: A History of Statistical Reasoning*, trans. Camille Naish (Cambridge, Mass; London: Harvard University Press, 1998); P. Minard, *La Fortune du colbertisme*; and various texts by Foucault, especially the lecture of 18 January 1978 in *Security, Territory, Population: Lectures at the Collège de France 1977–78*, ed. Michel Senellart; general editors François Ewald and Alessandro Fontana, trans. Graham Burchell (Basingstoke: Palgrave Macmillan, 2007), pp. 29–53.

31 See the works by M. Callon, B. Latour, P. Rabinow and A. Barry. On the economy, see the works by J. Coussy, especially 'L'avantage comparatif, cet inconnu', *Économies et sociétés*, series 'Relations économiques internationales', P, no. 32, September 1993 (pp. 5–40); and on finance, see O. Vallée, 'La dette

publique est-elle privée? Traites, traitement, traite: modes de la dette africaine', *Politique africaine*, 73, March 1999, pp. 50–67.

32 According to Max Weber, the object of the economy is 'the knowledge of relationships that prove to be *valuable* in the causal imputation of concrete historical events' ('The "objectivity" of knowledge in social science and social policy' (1904)), in Sam Whimster (ed.) *The Essential Weber. A Reader* (London: Routledge, 2003), pp. 359–404 (pp. 373–4). He adds, 'the social science that we wish to pursue is a *science of reality*. Our aim is an understanding of the *uniqueness* of the lived reality within which we are placed. We wish to understand on the one hand the context and cultural *significance* of individual phenomena in this lived reality; and on the other, the reasons for their being historically so and not otherwise' (p. 374).

33 References are to the French original: Paul Veyne, *Le Pain et le cirque. Sociologie historique d'un pluralisme politique* (Paris: Seuil, 1976), p. 38. There is an abridged translation in English: P. Veyne, *Bread and Circuses: Historical Sociology and Political Pluralism*, with an introduction by Oswyn Murray; trans. Brian Pearce (London: Allen Lane, 1990).

34 Ibid., p. 39.

Part I   Power by Credit

1 M. L. Gharbi, *Le Capital français à la traîne. Ébauche d'un réseau bancaire au Maghreb colonial (1847–1914)*, Faculté des Lettres Manouba, University of Manouba, Tunis, 2003.

2 J. Ganiage, *Les Origines du Protectorat français en Tunisie (1861–1881)* (Paris: PUF, 1959); M. H. Cherif, 'Fermage (*lizma*) et fermiers d'impôts (*lazzam*) dans la Tunisie des XVII et XVIIIe siècles', in 'États et pouvoirs en Méditerranée', *Les Cahiers de la Méditerranée*, University of Nice, Nice, 1989, pp. 19–29, and *Pouvoir et société dans la Tunisie de H'usayn bin 'Ali (1705–1740)*, vol. 2 (Tunis: Publications de l'Université de Tunis, 1986).

1   Bad Debts

1 For the following analysis, I have focused in particular on these reports, to which it is easier to gain access: IMF, 'IMF concludes Article IV consultation with Tunisia', *IMF Public Information Notice, no.* 01/13, External Relations Department, Washington DC, 13 February 2001; IMF, 'Tunisia: financial system stability assessment', *IMF Country Report*, no. 02/119, June 2002; IMF, 'Tunisia – preliminary findings of the 2004 Article IV consultation mission', IMF, Washington DC, 20 July 2004; IMF, 'Tunisia-Articles IV' 1999, 2001, 2003 and 2004; World Bank, *Stratégie de coopération République tunisienne-Banque mondiale, 2005–2004*, December 2004; World Bank Operation Evaluation Department, *Republic of Tunisia. Country Assistance Evaluation, Advance Copy*, The World Bank, Washington DC, 2004; *Financial Digest. La Revue d'analyse financière*, no. 8, AFC-Axis, Tunis, December 2004; and confidential documents based on unpublished data from the Central Bank. See too the annual reports of the BCT and the main banks, and data issued by the

Commission de suivi des entreprises économiques, the Cour des Comptes, the Centrale des risques and the Chambre des députés.

2   According to *Tunisie Valeurs*, in 2003, the ratio of bad debts to bank commitments was 2 per cent in Spain, 6 per cent in France, 8 per cent in Italy, 18 per cent in Morocco, and 20 per cent in Egypt, as opposed to 24 per cent in Tunisia.

3   The figures are published with some difficulty, and after long delays. These recent data, especially those for 2002–4, are taken from interviews with professionals. I have ventured to quote them only when I have managed to confirm them from several sources, in particular from confidential documents of the BCT, European cooperations and the IMF. This removes none of their uncertain, hit-and-miss character.

4   IMF, 'IMF concludes Article IV consultation with Tunisia', *IMF Public Information Notice*, no. 01/13, External Relations Department, Washington DC, 13 February 2001, p. 2.

5   IMF, 'Tunisia: 2000 Article IV Consultation – Staff Report', *IMF Country Report*, no. 01/36, IMF, Washington DC, February 2001, p. 41.

6   Figures drawn from the *Centrale des risques*, concerning solely the bad debts incurred by enterprises with banks, quoted by S. Kolsi, 'Les contrats passés par les sociétés de recouvrement de créances avec leurs clients', *Mélanges en l'honneur de Habib Ayadi*, Centre de publication universitaire, Tunis, 2000, pp. 567–94.

7   'Tunisia: 2000 Article IV', p. 41.

8   According to the BCT and the IMF, bad debts have passed from being 15.9 per cent of all debts in 1989 to 35 per cent in 1994, then dropping regularly, but reaching 26 per cent in 1999 and 24 per cent in 2003. As a percentage of GDP, debts went from around 29 per cent in 1994 to 21 per cent in 2003.

9   Interviews, Tunis, between 1997 and 2005.

10   In 1996, according to the *Institute National de la Statistique*, independents represented 81.8 per cent of enterprises; companies with fewer than six employees, 15.2 per cent; and companies with between six and nine employees, 0.9 per cent.

11   C. M. Henry, *The Mediterranean Debt Crescent*, p. 208.

12   Interviews, Tunis, between 1997 and 2005. Without quoting any figures, the IMF mentions the concentration of bad debts in the hands of a few persons or groups (see IMF, 'Staff report for Article IV consultation', *IMF Staff Country Report*, no. 99/104, Washington DC, September 1999).

13   All this information is taken from interviews, Tunis, 1997–2002. For more detail on the facilities offered to the beneficiaries of privatizations, see chapter 9.

14   On this phenomenon of 'heroization', see J.-P. Cassarino, *Tunisian New Entrepreneurs and Their Past Experiences of Migration in Europe: Resource Mobilisation, Networks, and Hidden Disaffection* (Ashgate Publishing: Aldershot, 2000).

15   Interviews, Tunis, January 1999, July 2000 and December 2002.

16   Interviews, Tunis, December 2002 and December 2003; Paris, November 2003. See also World Bank, *Stratégie de développement touristique en Tunisie. Rapport de phase 1*, UP'Management, KPMG THL, Consulting, JC Consultants, KA02R20, 13 July 2002; Fich Ratings, *L'Industrie touristique tunisienne*, Fich Ratings-Corporate Finance, New York and Tunis, 24 June 2004, and French

Embassy in Tunisia (summary report of the economic mission to the Embassy), *Le Secteur du tourisme en Tunisie*, 13 December 2004.

17 Interviews, January–March 2005, and Fich Ratings, *L'industrie touristique tunisienne*.

18 Interviews, Tunis, May 1997 and January 1999.

19 *Le Secteur du tourisme en Tunisie*.

20 Ibid., and Fich Ratings, *L'Industrie touristique tunisienne*, and interviews, December 2003 and January–March 2005.

21 IMF, 'Banking System Issues and Statistical Appendix', *IMF Staff Country Report*, no. 98/129, Washington DC, December 1998.

22 Interviews, Tunis, July 1999 and January 2000.

23 In relation to the total number of bank commitments, the level fell from 34.8 per cent to 29.9 per cent; in relation to GDP, the level went from 29.3 per cent to 23.9 per cent. Source: *Article IV pour l'année 2000*.

24 IMF, 'Banking System Issues'.

25 This is a very frequently used technique in the financial world, widely employed by the CCF or Crédit Lyonnais in handling their losses.

26 According to the IMF, the level of provisioning of bad debts is low but it has continued to improve, officially, from an overall level of 31 per cent in 1994 to 53 per cent in 1999. The development banks have always experienced better levels in this regard (35.5 per cent in 1994 and 56 per cent in 2001) than commercial banks (29.5 per cent in 1994, 43 per cent in 2003).

27 Interviews, Tunis, January 1999, July 2000, December 2001 and December 2003. The IMF's figure was being mentioned throughout the world of cooperation in 2003.

28 Interviews, Tunis, January 1999 and July 2000. See also ch. 4 below.

29 Parliamentary debates of February 1998 on the creation of debt collection companies, quoted by S. Kolsi, 'Les contrats passés par les sociétés de recouvrement'.

30 Interviews, Tunis, December 2001 and Brussels, May 2002.

31 C. M. Henry, *The Mediterranean Debt Crescent*, p. 71.

32 This remark comes from discussions with banking professionals and donors, Tunis, December 2003.

33 See the annual reports of the BCT and the APBT. A Karoui ('Risque systémique et vulnérabilité bancaire: quels indicateurs prédictifs pour la Tunisie?', *Économie et finance internationale*, University of Tunis El Manar, Faculté des sciences économiques et de gestion de Tunis, academic year 2002–3) shows that the economic profitability of the banks is developing in a positive way and that their productivity is improving. On the other hand, S. Mouley (in 'Enjeux et impératifs des politiques de libéralisation des comptes externes en Tunisie face à la nouvelle architecture financière internationale', *CEFI Working Paper*, 2004, p. 6) emphasizes 'the worrying drop in profitability as demonstrated by the relatively low level of commissions in the net banking product, which barely went above an average of 38 per cent in 2001, while general costs have continued to swell'. In this connection, see the IMF reports and those of the World Bank quoted in note 1 of this chapter.

34 See the successive *Rapports annuels* of the BCT and the APBT, and 'Les défis de la banque tunisienne', *Réalités*, Supplement, February 1992; interview with

Governor Daouas: M. Daouas, 'La santé de notre monnaie nous met à l'abri de toutes les rumeurs injustifiées', *L'Économiste maghrébin*, no. 296, 12–26 September 2001, pp. 8–14, or IMF, 'Financial System Stability Assessment', *IMF Country Report*, no. 02/119, June 2002.

35 According to the IMF and BCT, the development banks have never had any problem in respecting the Cook ratio. On the other hand, the public commercial banks had to travel a long road before reaching the acceptable norm of a ratio superior to eight per cent (passing from –5.3 per cent in 1993 to 2.1 per cent in 1994, 5.9 per cent in 1997, 8.8 per cent in 1998 and 11.5 per cent in 2001). After some difficulties in the 1980s, the private commercial banks respected the ratio from the mid-1990s onwards.

36 Interviews, Tunis, Paris, and Brussels, in particular with donors (which, indeed, suggests that the latter are far from being dupes, and knowingly accept the element of fiction contained in these reforms).

37 See C. M. Henry, *The Mediterranean Debt Crescent*, pp. 177–211. The author for his part notes that this liberalization began at the end of the 1970s with the permission granted to the first offshore banks. This interpretation strikes me as exaggerated – the Tunisian offshore is more closely akin to a tax haven than to a measure of liberalization.

38 J.-P. Cassarino, *Tunisian New Entrepreneurs*; C. H. Moore, 'Tunisian banking: politics of adjustment and the adjustment of politics', in I. W. Zartman (ed.), *Tunisia: The Political Economy of Reform* (Boulder: Lynne Rienner, 1991), pp. 67–97; B. Hibou and L. Martinez, 'Le Partenariat euro-maghrébin, un mariage blanc?', *Les Études du CERI*, no. 47, November 1997. For more details, see ch. 3.

39 Interview, Tunis, December 2001.

40 Interview, Tunis, December 2002.

41 This expression comes from Carentin, a cashier at the Franco-Tunisienne bank, and is quoted by M.L. Gharbi, *Le Capital français*, p. 241, n. 6.

42 See http://www.bvmt.com.tn, the site of the Tunis Stock Exchange.

43 Interviews, Tunis, December 2001 and December 2003 and IMF, *Article IV de l'année 2000*, p. 24.

44 Interviews, Tunis, 1999–2005.

45 G. Gherairi, 'Réflexions sur la nature juridique du conseil du marché financier', *Mélanges en l'honneur de Habib Ayadi*, Centre de publication universitaire, Tunis, 2000, pp. 499–516.

46 Interviews, Tunis, December 2001, December 2002 and December 2003.

47 For Tunisia, E. Saïdane, 'La Bourse de Tunis: une naissance difficile', *Revue Techniques financières et développement*, nos. 44–5, September–December 1996, pp. 45–56; for example Morocco, see G. Corm, 'Maroc: ajustements structurels, privatisations et marchés émergents', *Revue d'économie financière*, no. 29, Summer 1994, pp. 183–90; and for the region, C. de Boissieu, 'Une vue perspective' (pp. 3–13) and G. Corm, 'La Méditerranée, un marché émergent?' (pp. 14–21), *Revue Techniques financières et développement*, nos. 44–5, September–December 1996. For China, D. L. Wank, *Commodifying Communism. Business, Trust, and Politics in a Chinese City* (Cambridge; New York: Cambridge University Press, 1999), and D. L.Wank, 'The making of China's rentier entrepreneur élite: state, clientelism, and power conversion, 1978–1995', in F.

Mengin and J.-L. Rocca (eds), *Politics in China. Moving Frontiers* (New York: Palgrave Macmillan, 2002), pp. 118–39.

48   A. Abdelkefi, 'Le marché financier tunisien: présent et avenir', *Tunisie valeurs*, no. 16, 2002, p. 11.

49   Interviews, Tunis, December 2001 and December 2003.

50   C. M. Henry, *The Mediterranean Debt Crescent*, p. 64.

51   M. Weber, 'L'éthique économique des religions mondiales (1915–1920)', in *Sociologie des religions* (Paris: Gallimard, 1996), pp. 329–486. This is a French translation of Weber's 'Die Wirtschaftsethik der Weltreligionen: Konfuzianismus and Taoismus' ('The Economic Ethics of World Religions: Confucianism and Taoism'; translated and published in English as *The Religion of China: Confucianism and Taoism*, trans. and ed. H.H. Gerth (New York: Macmillan, 1964).

52   J.-P. Cassarino, *Tunisian Entrepreneurs*, pp. 138–41.

53   Interviews, January 1999 and July 2000. See also A. Mamlouk, 'Commentaire de l'arrêt no. 69197 du 6 octobre 2000 de la Cour d'appel de Tunis', *Revue tunisienne de droit*, Centre de publication universitaire, Tunis, 2000, pp. 463–75.

54   Interviews, Tunis, January 2005.

55   Interviews, Tunis, December 2002 and December 2003: Paris, November 2003.

56   The UIB represents eight per cent of the market, while the purchase of the 52 per cent cost the *Société Générale* merely 75 M$. Source: interviews, Tunis, December 2002.

57   This is true of countries other than Tunisia. In China, for example, bad debts have been made visible by restructuring and stabilization projects for public enterprises. Only after this date did the authorities demonstrate the general nature of the phenomenon. See A. Kernen, *La Chine vers l'économie du marché. Les Privatisations à Shenyang* (Paris: Karthala, 2004).

58   Interviews, Tunis, July 1999, January 2000 and December 2001.

59   P. D. Pelletreau, 'Private sector development through public sector restructuring? The cases of the Gafsa Phosphate Company and the Chemical Group', in W.I. Zartman (ed.), *Tunisia: Political Economy of Reform*, pp. 129–41, and R. Zghal, 'Le développement participatoire, participation et monde du travail en Tunisie', in D. Guerraoui and X. Richet (eds), *Stratégies de privatisation. Comparaison Maghreb-Europe* (Paris; Casablanca: L'Harmattan, Toubkal, 1995), pp. 205–29.

60   C. M. Henry, *The Mediterranean Debt Crescent*, p. 50.

61   On this process of the privatization of debt, see O. Vallée, 'La dette publique est-elle privée?' On practices in Tunisia, C. H. Moore, 'Tunisian banking'.

62   H. Dimassi and H. Zaïem, 'L'industrie: mythe et stratégies', in M. Camau (ed.), *Tunisie au présent, une modernité au-dessus de tout soupçon?* (Paris: CNRS, 1987), pp. 161–79; E. Bellin, *Stalled Democracy*; E. Murphy, *Economic and Political Change in Tunisia*; M. Bechri, T. Najah and J.-B. Nugent, 'Tunisia's lending programme to SME's: anatomy of an institutional failure', *World Bank Working Paper*, 6 February, World Bank, Washington DC, 2000.

63   See J.-P. Cassarino, 'The EU-Tunisian association agreement and Tunisia's structural reform program', *Middle East Journal*, vol. 53, no. 1, Winter 1999, pp. 59–74; and ch. 9 below.

64   H. Sethom, 'L'action des pouvoirs publics sur les paysages agraires et l'économie rurale dans la Tunisie indépendante', pp. 307–22, and H. Attia, 'L'étatisation de

l'eau dans les oasis du Jerid tunisien: lecture d'une dépossession', pp. 361–85, in R. Baduel (ed.), *États, territoires et terroirs au Maghreb* (Paris: Éditions du CNRS, 1985) and J.-P. Gachet, 'L'agriculture: discours et stratégies', in M. Camau (ed.) *Tunisie au présent*, pp. 181–228.

65   A. Abaab and M. Elloumi, 'L'agriculture tunisienne: de l'ajustement au défi de la mondialisation', in M. Elloumi (ed.), *Politiques agricoles et stratégies paysannes au Maghreb et en Méditerranée occidentale* (Tunis: Alif and IRMC, 1996), pp. 114–45; H. Sethom, *Pouvoir urbain et paysannerie en Tunisie* (Tunis: Cérès Productions et Fondation nationale de la recherche scientifique, 1992), pp. 139–44; P. Signoles, 'Industrialisation, urbanisation et mutations de l'espace tunisien' (pp. 277–306), in R. Baduel (ed.), *États, territoires et terroirs au Maghreb*.

66   B. Hibou, 'Les marges de manoeuvre d'un "bon élève" économique: la Tunisie de Ben Ali', *Les Études du CERI*, no. 60, December 1999.

67   H. Sethom, *Pouvoir urbain et paysannerie en Tunisie*, pp. 145–54. 'The farmers who benefit from agricultural credit every year are a small minority: in the most favourable hypothesis, they represent 20 per cent of farmers', p. 150. A. Abaab and M. Elloumi, 'L'agriculture tunisienne', mention (p. 127) that 'only 15 per cent of farmers benefit' from bank credit.

68   The terms used by a banker, Tunis, December 2002.

69   B. Hibou, 'Les marges de manoeuvre', pp. 20–2.

70   Interviews, Tunis, December 2001. For a more detailed discussion, see ch. 7 below.

71   C. M. Henry, *The Mediterranean Debt Crescent*.

72   World Bank, *Actualisation de l'évaluation du secteur privé*, 2 vols, The World Bank, Washington DC, May 2000; P.A. Casero and A. Varoudakis, *Growth, Private Investment, and the Cost of Doing Business in Tunisia: A Comparative Perspective*, World Bank Discussion Paper, January 2004; World Bank, *Republic of Tunisia. Country Assistance Evaluation, Advance Copy*, The World Bank, Washington DC, 2004.

73   P. Signoles, 'Industrialisation, urbanisation et mutations de l'espace tunisien', shows how the strategy of renouncing tax was aimed at developing the national economy.

74   I have attempted in vain to find data on these inter-company credits. My remarks are thus based solely on interviews – that have, however, all confirmed this tendency, Tunis, December 2001 and, in particular, December 2002 and December 2003.

75   S. Kolsi, 'Les contrats passés', p. 567.

76   Interviews, Tunis and governorates of Tunis and Nabeul, January–March 2005. Employers can act as guarantors vis-à-vis the banks or, as is more usual, they themselves lend to employees in the form of wages paid in advance. See also J.-P. Bras, 'Tunisie: Ben Ali et sa classe moyenne', *Pôles*, no. 1, April–June 1996, pp. 174–5, and H. Yousfi, E. Filipiak and H. Bougault, 'Poulina, un management tunisien', *Notes et documents*, no. 17, AFD, Paris, May 2005.

77   On the juridical aspects of consumer credit, see Y. Knani, 'La vente avec facilités de paiement', *Mélanges en l'honneur de Habib Ayadi*, pp. 545–66.

78   Interviews, Tunis, July 2000.

79   Here too it has not been possible for me to confirm these figures by official publications. They were given to me during interviews.

80 IMF, *Article IV de l'année 2000*, p. 23.
81 According to the BCT and the IMF, the rate of irrecoverable debts in development banks as a percentage of banking commitments was 52.2 per cent in 1992 and continued to increase until 1997, when it reached 67 per cent. Thanks to discharge of debts, it has been sinking since that date and by 2001 had reached the level of the early 1990s (52.5 per cent).
82 The rate of irrecoverable debts of public banks improved noticeably in the 1990s and in 2000 almost reached the level of that of the private banks: 33.4 per cent in 1992; 40.7 per cent in 1993, followed by a continuous decrease and 19.5 per cent in 2001, 20.7 per cent in 2002.
83 The rate of irrecoverable debts of private banks passed from 24.4 per cent in 1992 to 15.9 per cent in 2001 and 18 per cent in 2002.
84 For a denunciation, see for example the brochure 'Les 7 familles qui pillent la Tunisie'. For a critical analysis, B. Hibou, 'Tunisie: le coût d'un "miracle"', *Critique internationale*, no. 4, Summer, 1999, pp. 48–56.
85 All of this information is drawn from the press and, in particular, from interviews, Tunis, December 2001, December 2002 and December 2003.
86 Interview, Paris, May 2004.

2 Dependence through Debt

1 Interview, Tunis, July 2000.
2 A. Karoui, *Risque systémique et vulnérabilité bancaire*.
3 On belief in economy, see F. Lordon, 'Croyances économiques et pouvoir symbolique', *L'Année de la regulation*, no. 3, 1999, pp. 169–212, and 'La force des idées simples. Misère épistémique des comportements économiques', *Politix*, vol.13, no. 52, pp. 183–209. See also P.-N. Giraud (*Le Commerce des promesses. Petit traité sur la finance moderne* (Paris: Seuil, 2001)), which centres the system of belief on the idea that it is possible to transfer wealth in time securely, and J.-M. Rey, 'Qu'est-ce que faire crédit? Entre littérature et économie', *Esprit*, March–April 2005, pp. 87–100, for whom belief rests on the fact that credit is forever betting 'on what is most indeterminate and most uncertain, namely the future' (p. 89).
4 The expression comes from Herbert Marcuse, *One-Dimensional Man*.
5 J.-M. Rey, 'Qu'est-ce que faire crédit?', p. 100. In his work, Jean-Michel Rey also emphasizes the role of fiction, which he calls – using the literary language of the eighteenth century, the 'fiduciary' element.
6 Interviews, Tunis, December 2001 and December 2002.
7 C. M. Henry, *The Mediterranean Debt Crescent*, p. 187.
8 All this information is taken from interviews, Tunis, January 1999, July 2000, December 2001 and December 2002. The expressions in inverted commas are those used by my interviewees.
9 K. Polanyi, *Origins of Our Time: The Great Transformation*, revised edn (London: Victor Gollancz, 1945); C. Kindleberger, *Manias, Panics and Crashes: A History of Financial Crises*, 4th edn (Basingstoke: Palgrave, 2002).
10 D. de Blic, 'Le scandale financier du siècle, ça ne vous intéresse pas? Difficiles mobilisations autour du Crédit Lyonnais', *Politix*, vol. 13, no. 52, 2000, pp. 157–81.

11   A. Karoui, *Risque systémique et vulnérabilité bancaire.*

12   External debt represented 60 per cent of GDP in the 1990s, and is tending to decrease.

13   According to the IMF, currency reserves were maintained in the 1990s for about 3 months, with recurrent drops below that norm (1995, 1998, 2002 and 2003). The ratio of external debt is heavy (61 per cent in 2002) if we consider the investment ambitions of the Tunisian authorities measured by the yardstick of different plans, and if we compare Tunisia with other countries classed as triple-B by the rating agencies, which, on average and for the same year 2002, experienced debt at 48 per cent.

14   B. Hibou, 'Les marges de manoeuvre'.

15   David Landes, in *Bankers and Pashas. International Finance and Economic Imperialism in Egypt* (Cambridge, MA: Harvard University Press, 1958) has brought this out very clearly with respect to Egypt during the financial imperialism of the nineteenth century and the beginning of the twentieth.

16   Y. Guessoum, 'Évaluation du risque pays par les agences de rating: transparence et convergence des méthodes', CEFI seminar, mimeograph, February 2004, and J. Cernès, 'Les instruments de mesure du risque pays sont-ils fiables?', *Atelier de recherche ESG*, 23 March 2004.

17   A. Karoui, *Risque systémique et vulnérabilité bancaire*, p. 140, notes that 'for Tunisia, the rating of its banking system happens to be among the most fragile systems, given the importance of the compromised portfolio and the inadequacies of the provisions [. . .] the individual ratings of banks are low. For example, the STB following its merger with the BNDT and the BDET has been downgraded since its rating has moved from D- to E+1'.

18   IMF, *IMF Concludes Article IV*, p. 1: the 2000 loan in euros was obtained on much better conditions (130 base points) than that of the previous year (280 base points). In March 2004, as Tunisia was seeking 300 M € to finance its current deficit and the repayment of its debt, it raised 450 M and could have obtained considerably more.

19   In 'Le scandale financier du siècle', Damien de Blic raises this hypothesis in connection with Crédit Lyonnais.

20   Interview, Tunis, January 1999 and Sfax, April 1998. Agency bosses can spend their whole careers in the same subsidiary or the same branch.

21   Interviews, Tunis, December 2003, with donors who told me about certain refusals coming from national or international institutions.

22   Interviews, Tunis, January–March 2005.

23   Interviews, Tunis, December 2003.

24   IMF, *Article IV de l'année 2000*, p. 22.

25   It needs to be remembered that only 15 per cent to 20 per cent of farmers had access to bank credit in the 1970s and 1980s. With the stabilization and restructuring of the banks, their proportion is now even lower.

26   J.-P. Cassarino, *Tunisian New Entrepreneurs*, pp. 128–30; R. Zghal, 'Le développement participatoire'.

27   National press (especially *Le Quotidien*, 11 December 2001), and M.H. Lakhoua, 'L'encombrement de la justice pénale', *Revue tunisienne de droit 2000*, pp. 287–98. According to the texts, the least overdraft is illegal and actionable, which leaves room for any arbitrary interpretation and the meting out of unequal treatment depending on the personality of the debtors.

28 This reading has drawn on the analysis of debt in the north of Cameroon by Janet Roitman: J. Roitman, 'Unsanctioned wealth; or the productivity of debt in Northern Cameroon', *Public Culture*, 15 (2), 2003, pp. 211–37.
29 In the words of Herbert Marcuse: cf. the title of ch. 4 of *One-Dimensional Man*, 'The Closing of the Universe of Discourse' (p. 87).
30 A. Abdelkafi, 'Le marché tunisien', pp. 11–12 (my emphasis).
31 Cf J.-M. Rey's analysis of John Law's bankruptcy in 'Qu'est-ce que faire crédit?', quotations respectively from p. 100 and pp. 101–2.
32 Michel Foucault, 'La stratégie du pourtour', p. 796.
33 This episode is now very well documented: apart from the interviews I carried out between 1997 and 2003, see C.H. Moore, 'Tunisian banking', pp. 84–5; C. M. Henry, *The Mediterranean Debt Crescent*, pp. 199–202 and pp. 210–11; J.-P. Cassarino, *Tunisian New Entrepreneurs*.
34 This episode, however, is much less well known, mainly because it has still not been brought to a close. Apart from my interviews with A. Bouden and Tunis bankers, and the different decisions of the International Chamber of Commerce in Paris and the International Court of Arbitration in London (provided to me by A. Bouden), see C. M. Henry, *The Mediterranean Debt Crescent*, pp. 189–99.
35 J.-Y. Grenier, *L'Économie d'Ancien Régime. Un monde de l'échange et de l'incertitude* (Paris: Albin Michel, 1996), p. 89.
36 C.H. Moore, 'Tunisian banking'.
37 M. Galloux, *Finance islamique et pouvoir politique* (Paris: PUF, 1997).
38 M. Kraïem, *Pouvoir colonial et mouvement national. La Tunisie des années 30*, vol. 1 (Tunis: Alif, 1990).
39 M. L. Gharbi, *Le Capital français*, and P. Sebag, *La Tunisie: essai de monographie* (Paris: Éditions sociales, 1951).
40 Interviews, Tunis, December 2001.
41 R. Bistolfi, *Structure économique et indépendance monétaire* (Paris: Éditions Cujas, 1967), pp. 235ff; C. M. Henry, *The Mediterranean Debt Crescent*.
42 Interviews, Tunis, December 2001 and December 2002.
43 Interviews, Tunis, January 1999 and July 2000.
44 C.H. Moore, 'Tunisian banking', and B. Hibou, 'Les marges de manoeuvres'.
45 I heard this systematically repeated to me in interviews. See also J.-P. Cassarino, *Tunisian New Entrepreneurs*.
46 Interviews, Sfax, December 2002 and Tunis, December 2003.
47 This technique is found in countries other than Tunisia. Gilles Favarel-Garrigues mentions it being used in Russia, in an international context (G. Favarel-Garrigues, 'La bureaucratie policière et la chute du regime soviétique', *Sociétés contemporaines*, no. 57, 2005, pp. 63–82). Thierry Godefroy and Pierre Lascoumes likewise analyse the blacklists published by organizations involved in the struggle against money laundering in T. Godefroy and P. Lascoumes, *Le Capitalisme clandestin. L'illusoire régulation des places offshore* (Paris: La Découverte, 2004).
48 D. Dessert, *Argent, pouvoir et société*, p. 319.
49 J.-F. Bayart, *L'État au Cameroun* (Paris: Presses de la Fondation des sciences politiques, 1985).
50 Interviews, Tunis, January 1999, July 2000, December 2001, December 2002.
51 This configuration is found in many other situations. On the French Ancien Régime, see D. Dessert, *Argent, pouvoir et société*, and P. Minard, *La Fortune*

du colbertisme; on Morocco, B. Hibou and M. Tozy, 'Une lecture d'anthropologie politique de la corruption au Maroc: fondement historique d'une prise de liberté avec le droit', *Revue Tiers Monde*, January–March 2000, pp. 23–47.

52 J.-G. Ymbert, *L'Art de faire des dettes* (Paris: Rivages, 1996 (1824)), p. 45.

53 See in particular J.-Y. Grenier's analysis in *L'Économie d'Ancien Régime*. For contemporary situations in Africa, see O. Vallée, *Le Prix de l'argent CFA: heurs et malheurs de la zone franc* (Paris: Karthala, 1989) and J.-F. Bayart, *The State in Africa. The politics of the belly*, trans. Mary Harper, Christopher and Elizabeth Harrison, 1st edn (London: Longman, 1993); 2nd edn (Cambridge: Polity Press, 2009).

54 J.-Y. Grenier, *L'Économie d'Ancien Régime*, p. 89.

55 This mechanism was suggested to me by a reading of P. Brown, *Power and Persuasion in Late Antiquity: Towards a Christian Empire* (Madison, Wis.: University of Wisconsin Press, 1992).

56 All the data below were obtained on my successive field trips in Tunisia, in particular in December 2001, December 2002 and December 2003. Various articles (the information in which is strictly controlled, of course) have been published in the press, in particular in the weekly *Réalités*.

57 Interviews, Tunis, December 2003.

58 J.-M. Rey, 'Qu'est-ce que faire crédit?', p. 105.

59 Interviews, December 2003 and local press 2003.

60 Interviews, Tunis, December 2002 and 2003; Paris, November 2003 and February 2004. This can also be read in the communiqués of RAID/Attac-Tunisie. See also J.-P. Bras, 'Croissance économique et autoritarisme politique en Tunisie: le dilemme', *Naqd*, no. 19/20, Autumn–Winter 2004, pp. 157–66.

61 P. Veyne, *Le Pain et le cirque*, pp. 93–4.

62 Ibid., p. 660.

Part II　Constriction and Adhesion

1 The *zaîm* is the man who commands.

2 This is the phrase used by M. Kerrou, 'La *zaîm* comme individu unique', in *L'individu au Maghreb*, Éditions TS, Tunis, 1993, pp. 235–48 (Actes du colloque international de Beit el-Hikma, Carthage, 31 October–2 November 1991). He begins his article with these words: 'The hypothesis of the present work could be formulated in the following way: in the Arab world, the emergence of the *zaîms* is inseparable from the existence of the myth of the undifferentiated and subordinate mass, and not of the society of free and autonomous individuals. By imposing himself as a unique individual, the *Zaîm* rejoins the old symbolic order centred on the figure of the father ("patriarchy"). Now, this order is these days unable to resolve the tensions of modernity' (p. 235).

3　A Meticulous Grid

1 H. Arendt, 'On violence', in *Crises of the Republic* (Harmondsworth: Penguin, 1973), p. 50.

2 The figures quoted are those that are systematically heard in Tunisia – though their reliability cannot be deduced from this. The comparative data have come from M. Camau and V. Geisser, *Le Syndrome autoritaire*, pp. 203–5.

3 Interviews, Tunis, December 2001. See too the various reports of human rights organizations, in particular CNLT, *Deuxième rapport sur l'état des libertés en Tunisie*, and LTDH, *Rapport annuel 2002*.

4 Reprinted in the foreign press, especially *Libération* (Paris), 10 January 2004, and in the reports of human rights organizations previously quoted.

5 S. Khiari, *Tunisie, le délitement de la cité*, p. 102.

6 During my field trips, the taxi I took would often act as a relay for the police agents tailing me. To prevent the circulation of dissidents in a manner less visible than a direct police intervention, the '*louages*' [literally = 'rentings', Tr.] – in other words the collective taxis between the different cities in the country – can be used either to prevent an undesirable from getting into the car, or to intercept him at the toll. In March 2005, opponents were in this way prevented from participating in the demonstration in support of the students repressed during the anti-Sharon demonstration. See the LTDH communiqués of mid-March 2005.

7 Interviews, Tunis, December 2003, and O. Lamloun, 'Janvier 1984 en Tunisie ou le symbole d'une transition', in D. LeSaout and M. Rollinde (eds), *Émeutes et mouvements sociaux au Maghreb* (Paris: Karthala-IME, 1999), pp. 231–42 (especially pp. 236–8). On Algeria, see L. Martinez, *The Algerian Civil War 1990–1998*, trans. Jonathan Derrick (London, Paris: Hurst; Le Centre d'Études et de Recherches internationales, 2000), and, on Morocco, interviews, September 1999 and October 2000, and M. Tozy, *Monarchie et islam politique au Maroc* (Paris: Presses de Sciences Po, 1999).

8 On these heritages and differences, see M. Kilani, 'Sur-pouvoir personnel et évanescence du politique', *La Tunisie sous Ben Ali*, December 2000, on the website www.ceri-sciences-po.org/kiosque/archives/déc.2000; M. Camau and V. Geisser, *Le Syndrome autoritaire*; S. Khiari, *Tunisie, le délitement de la cité*; S. Belhassen, 'Les legs bourguibiens de la répression'. An interesting account is provided by Mohamed Talbi in his interview-book: M. Talbi and G. Jarczyk, *Penseur libre en islam* (Paris: Albin Michel, 2002).

9 A. Zghal, 'L'islam, les janissaires et le Destour', in M. Camau (ed.), *Tunisie au présent*, pp. 375–402; A. Tlili, *Lettre ouverte*, quoted by H. Béji, *Désenchantement national*.

10 M. Foucault, *Discipline and Punish: The Birth of the Prison*, trans. Alan Sheridan (Harmondsworth: Penguin, 1999), p. 235.

11 M. Kerrou, 'Le *mezwâr* ou le censeur des moeurs au Maghreb'.

12 S. Khiari, *Tunisie, le délitement de la cité*. He writes, for instance: 'The Ben Ali system aims to isolate individuals in such a way that the only bonds linking them will be formed in the interweaving of its own mesh' (p. 104).

13 G. Agamben, *Means without End: Notes on Politics*, trans. Vincenzo Binetti and Cesare Casarino (Minneapolis; London: University of Minneapolis Press, 2000), 'Sovereign police', pp. 103–8 (p. 104).

14 W. Benjamin, 'Critique of Violence', in *One Way Street and Other Writings*, trans. Edmund Jephcott (London: Verso, 1997), pp. 132–54 (p. 141).

15 S. Khiari, *Tunisie, le délitement de la cité*, p. 104.

16 The Zitounians were educated at the Zitouna, the great mosque in Tunis; in the *imaginaire* prevalent under Bourguiba, they were then identified with the supporters of conservatism, the adversaries of a secular modernization of Tunisia.

17 M. Camau and V. Geisser, *Le Syndrome autoritaire*, ch. III; S. Bessis and S. Belhassen, *Bourguiba. À la conquête d'un destin, 1901–1957* (Paris: Jeune Afrique Livres, 1988) and *Bourguiba. Un si long règne, 1957–1989* (Paris: Jeune Afrique Livres, Paris, 1989); M. Kraïem, 'État, syndicats et mouvement social lors des événements du 26 janvier 1978', in 'Les mouvements sociaux en Tunisie et dans l'immigration', *Cahiers du CERES*, série Histoire no. 6, Tunis, 1996, pp. 197–249.

18 On colonial violence, C.-A. Julien, *L'Afrique du Nord en marche* (Paris: Julliard, 1972) (Tunisian edn: CERES editions, 2001, 2 vols, Tunis); M. Kraïem, *Pouvoir colonial et mouvement national. La Tunisie des années trente* (Tunis: Alif, 1990), vol. 1, *Crise et renouveau*; E. Mouilleau, *Fonctionnaires de la République et artisans de l'Empire. Le Cas des contrôleurs civils en Tunisie (1881–1956)* (Paris: L'Harmattan, 2000), pp. 36 and 82–93; O. le Cour Grandmaison, *Coloniser, exterminer. Sur la Guerre et l'État colonial* (Fayard: Paris, 2005, especially ch. IV).

19 N. Dougui, *Histoire d'une grande entrprise coloniale: la compagnie des phosphates et du chemin de fer de Gafsa, 1897–1930*, Faculté des lettres de la Manouba, Tunis, 1995; M.L. Gharbi, *Impérialisme et réformisme au Maghreb. Histoire d'un chemin de fer algéro-tunisien* (Tunis: Cérès, 1994) and *Le Capital français à la traîne*; A. Mahjoubi, 'Économie et société: la formation du "sous-développement", l'évolution socio-économique de la Tunisie pré-coloniale et coloniale', in M. Camau (ed.), *Tunisie au présent*, pp. 97–117; A. Mahjoubi, *L'Établissement du protectorat français en Tunisie*, University of Tunis, Tunis, 1977.

20 S. Ben Achour, 'Aux sources du droit moderne tunisien', *Correspondances*, no. 42, IRMC, Tunis, which develops the main argument of her PhD thesis: *Aux sources du droit moderne tunisien: la législation tunisienne en période coloniale*, Tunis, 24 January 1996. Quotations, p. 8 (my emphasis).

21 W. Benjamin, 'Critique of violence', p. 141.

22 In the last pages of her article 'On violence', Hannah Arendt develops this idea, criticizing the recurrent confusions between violence and power and demonstrating in particular that 'violence appears where power is in jeopardy, but left to its own course it ends in power's disappearance' (p. 56).

23 Precise information on the RCD cells is hard to obtain and this paragraph is based mainly on interviews. However, see the website (www.rcd.tn) and the documents of the RCD; M. Camau and V. Geisser, *Le Syndrome autoritaire*, pp. 158–64 and 214–20; for the symbolic (and architectural!) dimension, M. Kilani 'Sur-pouvoir personnel et évanescence du politique'. Olivier Feneyrol's article, based on the very specific and circumscribed case of the renovation of a traditional district of the capital, the article by Mouldi Lahmar and Abdelkader Zghal on that of the village of Al-Mabrouka during the revolt over bread in 1984 and the work of Ali Rebhi on local power in the periphery of Kairouan are indisputably the most interesting pieces I know of for an understanding of the ambivalence and complexity of Destourian cells in modes of government: O. Feneyrol, 'L'État à l'épreuve du local. Le réaménagement du quartier "Bab Souiqa-Halfaouine" in Tunis (1983–1992)', *Monde arabe, Maghreb-Machrek*, no. 157, July–September 1997, pp. 58–68; M. Lahmar and A. Zghal, ' "La Révolte du pain" et la crise du modèle du parti unique', in M. Ben Romdhane (ed.),

Tunisie: mouvements sociaux et modernité, CODESRIA, Dakar, 1997, pp. 151–92; A. Rebhi, 'Pouvoirs locaux et réhabilitation urbaine. L'exemple du quartier Menchia à Kairouan', paper presented at the seminar on *Governance and Local Collectivities*, Faculté des sciences économiques et de gestion de Tunis, Tunis, 2–3 October 2003.

24   It is worth consulting the website of the party, www.rcd.tn: comments on the directions to be followed by the party are few and far between; on the other hand, the site is filled with statistics on the number of cells, the relative proportions of the sexes, age groups, socio-professional categories, etc.

25   This is a thesis often defended. See for example V. Geisser, 'Tunisie, des élections pour quoi faire? Enjeux et "sens" du fait électoral de Bourguiba à Ben Ali', *Monde arabe, Maghreb, Machrek*, no. 168, April–June 2000, pp. 14–28, where it is stated that the RCD emptied of all ideological contents is, first and foremost, a security apparatus.

26   M. Lahmar and A. Zghal, ' "La révolte du pain" et la crise du parti unique', p. 186.

27   M. Kilani, 'Sur-pouvoir personnel et évanescence du politique'; M. Camau, 'D'une République à l'autre. Refondation politique et aléas de la transition libérale'.

28   All the following information is taken from interviews, Tunis, 1997–2003.

29   Interviews, December 2002.

30   Apart from the references mentioned in note 23 of this chapter, D. Chamekh, *État et pauvreté en Tunisie: assistance et/ou insertion*, DEA dissertation in political sciences, University of Tunis III, Tunis, academic year 1998–99; K. Zamiti, 'Exploitation du travail paysan en situation de dépendance et mutation d'un parti de masse en parti de cadres', *Les Temps modernes*, special number, 'Maghreb', October 1977, pp. 312–33.

31   Interviews, December 2003.

32   In the expression used by an interviewee, December 2002.

33   Interview, Tunis, January 2005.

34   M. Camau and V. Geisser, *Le Syndrome autoritaire*.

35   M. Lahmar and A. Zghal, ' "Le révolte du pain" ', p. 188.

36   Ali Rebhi, for example, shows how the selection of a particular district to host an urban rehabilitation project is directly linked to the desire on the part of RCD officials 'to reply, at least in part, to the aspirations of the population which has showed its discontent on various occasions because of the lack of provision of decent water and roads' (A. Rebhi, 'Pouvoirs locaux et réhabilitation urbaine', p. 350).

37   M. Lahmar has magnificently brought this out for the rural world, in connection with the policy of land collectivization – see M. Lahmar, *Du mouton à l'olivier. Essai sur les mutations de la vie rurale maghrébine* (Tunis: Cérès, 1994) and M. Lahmar and A. Zghal in the case of the village of Al-Malbrouka in M. Lahmar and A. Zghal, ' "Le révolte du pain" ', pp. 151–92. K. Zamiti analyses the phenomenon in the framework of social policies (K. Zamiti, 'Le Fonds de solidarité nationale: pour une approche sociologique du politique', *Annuaire de l'Afrique du Nord*, vol. 35, 1996, pp. 705–12). For the urban environment, see O. Feneyrol, 'L'État à l'épreuve du local'.

38   M. Ben Romdhane, although known for his opposition, says of the Destourian cells that they are not 'an empty shell', that 'the people can project its history

onto them as against the colonial occupation and the construction of the state'; they have 'allowed Tunisia to realize remarkable economic and social advances and to contain the contradictions of society within "certain limits"' and the party 'has shown itself able to renew itself and to attract massive support following 7 November 1987'. See M. Ben Romdhane, 'Les groupements de l'opposition séculière en Tunisie', in M. Ben Romdhane (ed.), *Tunisie: mouvements sociaux et modernité*, pp. 63–150 (p. 144).

39   M. Lahmar and A. Zghal, ' "La révolte du pain" ', p. 187. The authors continue: 'The local members of the party are indeed no longer political militants in the precise sense of the term. Their passivity during the bread revolt shows the limits of their political commitment. The local elites do not confuse state with party. But the party's force of attraction is mainly derived from its close link with the decision-making institutions of state. So it is probable that, for as long as this liaison is maintained, the party's local structures will always be predisposed to play the role of a "machine" for getting people to vote for the official Destour candidate'.

40   Interviews, Tunis, December, 2003.

41   S. Khiari, 'De Wassila à Leïla, premières dames et pouvoir en Tunisie', *Politique africaine*, 95, October 2004, pp. 55–70.

42   O. Feneyrol, 'L'État à l'épreuve du local', p. 67.

43   M. Foucault, *History of Sexuality, 1. The Will to Knowledge*, trans. Robert Hurley (London: Penguin, 1990).

44   On the UTSS, *Brochure d'activités générales* (Tunis: Cité el Khadra, n.d.), and www.utss.org.tn. The other national organizations, created at the start of the 1960s, are the UNFT (women's movement), the UGTT (employees' union), the UTICA (employers' union), the UNAT (agricultural union) and the UGET (students' union).

45   R. Ben Amor, 'Politiques sociales, ajustement structurel et pauvreté en Tunisie', *Les Cahiers du CERES,* sociological series no. 24, 1995, and D. Chakerli, 'Lutte contre la pauvreté et solidarité nationale', file on *La Tunisie sous Ben Ali*, December 2000 on the website www.ceri-sciences-po.org/kiosque/archives/déc2000.

46   R. Ben Amor, p. 303.

47   D. Chakerli, 'Lutte contre la pauvreté', p. 10.

48   Ibid.

49   For the district committees ('comités de quartier'), I have mainly drawn on interviews in Tunisia, in December 2002 and December 2003, and Paris in November 2003, as well as on the detailed text by Hafidah Chekir, 'La gestion des affaires locales par les citoyens: une certaine forme de gouvernance' in *Mélanges en l'honneur de M. Belaïd*, CPU, Tunis, 2005, pp., 323–34. See also G. Denoeux, 'La Tunisie de Ben Ali et ses paradoxes', *Monde arabe, Maghreb-Machrek*, no. 166, October–December 1999, pp. 32–52.

50   It is revealing that members of this union were behind this experience; the union of the Régie des tabacs et des allumettes in fact embarked on sustained strike action and played an essential role in the struggles of the 1980s for the independence of the UGTT. It was finally broken up. Source: interviews, Tunis, December 2002 and December 2003.

51   Figures provided by S. Khiari, *Tunisie, le délitement de la cité*, p. 108.

52   H. Chekir, 'La gestion des affaires locales par les citoyens' mentions the different decrees, mainly issued in 1991 and 1992.

53   Article in *Le Renouveau*, 15 March 1996, quoted by H. Chekir, p. 9.

54   Interviews, Tunis, December 2001.

55   These figures were provided for the parliamentary debate on the budget in 2004 and published by the Tunisian press, in particular in *Chourouk* (Arabic daily published in Tunis) on 17 December 2003. See also the official site: www. association.org.tn.

56   On the difficulties of gaining access to this information, see E. Bellin, 'Civil society in formation: Tunisia', in A.R. Norton (ed.), *Civil Society in the Middle East* (Leiden; New York: Brill, 1995), and O. Lamloun and S. Khiari, 'Tunisie: des élections en trompe-l'oeil', *Politique africaine*, no. 76, December 1999, pp. 106–15.

57   Interview carried out by M. Desmères, 'La société civile tunisienne prise en otage?', file *La Tunisie sous Ben Ali*, December 2000 on the website www.ceri-sciences-po.org/kiosque/archives/déc2000, p. 22.

58   A. Narâghi, *Les Contours de l'entente politique: étude de cas à partir du mileu associatif tunisien*, DEA dissertation, Institut d'études politiques d'Aix-en-Provence, 1999. The author shows how the 'Islamist peril' and the risk of a loss of control were contrasted with the creation of a local NGO specialized in that activity, just as the authorities rejected the request for a waiver made by a French NGO associated with a Tunisian NGO even though the latter had already been approved. For more details, see ch. 7.

59   Interview carried out by M. Desmères, 'La société civile prise en otage?', p. 24.

60   Quoted by J.-P. Cassarino, *Tunisian New Entrepreneurs*.

61   For Tunisia, M. Camau and V. Geisser, *Le Syndrome autoritaire*, p. 218. For the World Bank, B. Hibou, 'Économie politique de la Banque mondiale en Afrique. Du catéchisme économique au fait (et méfait) missionnaire', *Les Études du CERI*, 39, March 1998 (English version: B. Hibou, 'The Political Economy of the World Bank's Discourse. From Economic Catechism to Missionary Deeds and Misdeeds', *Les Etudes du CERI*, no. 39, January 2000 (trans. Janet Roitman).

62   A. Hermassi, 'Les associations à l'heure de la mise à niveau intégrale', *Études internationales*, no. 60, 3rd trimester, 1996, p. 7.

63   J.-P. Cassarino, *Tunisian New Entrepreneurs*. He quotes a speech made by Ben Ali that perfectly illustrates this interpretation of associations – an interpretation at once functional and disciplinary. 'An association is a social school, it illustrates another domain in which benefits are materialized so well that they become complements of government action and make the role of civil society sufficiently tangible to attain its objectives' (*Le Renouveau*, 23 April 1995).

64   For the contemporary period, M. Camau and V. Geisser, *Le Syndrome autoritaire*, talk of government rhetoric on associations as a 'repressive discourse' (p. 111). For the colonial period, H. Belaïd, 'État et associations en Tunisie à l'époque coloniale', paper given at the colloquium on 'State Reform in the Mediterranean Muslim World, Starting With the Example of Maghreb', IRMC, Tunis, 3–5 April 2003. For the period of Bourguiba's rule, H. Belaïd, 'Bourguiba et la vie associative pendant la période coloniale et après l'indépendance', in M. Camau and V. Geisser (eds), *Habib Bourguiba*, pp. 325–39.

65   R. Ben Achour, 'L'État de droit en Tunisie', *Annuaire de l'Afrique du Nord*, vol. 34, 1995, pp. 245–56; J.-P. Cassarino, *Tunisian New Entrepreneurs*, pp. 100ff; S. Ben Achour, *La Liberté d'association entre droit et société*, LTDH, Tunis, 10 December 2004. The classification goes as follows: women's associations, sports associations, scientific associations, cultural and artistic associations, benevolent, aid, and social associations, development associations, friendly associations, general associations.

66   Until 1991, ad hoc committees were able to survive repression. But, very quickly, there was a complete crack-down. The symptomatic event of this period of great repression was the arrest, on the very same day it was created, of all the constitutive members of the Comité pour la libération des prisonniers d'opinion [Committee for the Liberation of Political Prisoners], in 1993: Salah Hamzaoui had been its coordinator. The harshness of the reaction had the objective (and the actual effect) of stopping any other initiative of such scope. Only with the establishment of the CNLT in December 1998 did the Tunisian authorities draw back for the first time. Source: interviews, Tunis, December 2002; Paris, May 2004.

67   For an exhaustive and very interesting analysis of the different laws on associations, see the internal LTDH document prepared by Sana Ben Achour (S. Ben Achour, *La Liberté d'association entre droit et société*), and the various reports of the LTDH, in particular 2001 and 2002. See too M. Desmères, 'La société civile tunisienne prise en otage?'

68   Article 24 of the law of 2 August 1988.

69   Organic law no. 92–25, 2 April 1992, article 2.

70   As well as the *Rapports annuels 2001 et 2002* of the LTDH, see R. Ben Achour, 'L'État de droit en Tunisie'; S. Ben Achour, *La Liberté d'association entre droit et société*, and the FIDH *Rapport de la Commission des droits de l'homme des Nations Unies*, 58th session, 18 March–26 April 2002, point 11, and the Human Rights Watch reports on 2001 and 2003 (*Tunisia: Country Reports on Human Rights Practices*), in particular pp. 35–6 of that of 2003.

71   Interviews, Tunis, December 2002 and Paris, March 2003: information gathered from associations that have been refused financing, but also from the administrations of foreign countries or international organizations that have received, from the Tunisian authorities, the text of the beylical law issued, if any reminder is needed, under the French Protectorate.

72   On all these techniques and procedures, N. Beau and J.-P. Tuquoi, *Notre ami Ben Ali. L'envers du miracle tunisien* (Paris: La Découverte, 2002); M. Camau and V. Geisser, *Le Syndrome autoritaire*, ch. VI and, in particular, R. Ben Achour, 'L'État de droit en Tunisie', and S. Ben Achour, *La Liberté d'association.*

73   For sub-Saharan Africa, see J.-F. Bayart, *The State in Africa*; for Fascist Italy, see E. Gentile, *Qu'est-ce que le fascisme?* (Paris: Gallimard, 2005); for a theoretical overview, H. Arendt, *The Origins of Totalitarianism.*

74   Press communiqué of the LTDH, 'Le gouvernement prive la LTDH de financement européen', 2 November 2003.

75   Interviews, Tunis, January–March 2005: in the case of European funds, blocked since April 2004, the sums were returned to Brussels – evidence of the EU's lucidity about the operations of justice, but also of its nervousness; in the case of the World Human Rights Fund, American funds have been blocked since January 2005.

76 Interviews, Tunis, December 2002, December 2003, January–March 2005.

77 J.-F. Bayart, in *Global Subjects: A Political Critique of Globalization*, trans. Andrew Brown (Cambridge: Polity Press, 2007) devotes several pages to the ambiguous nature of international civil society, suggesting how it makes an often indirect contribution to the formation of the nation-state – a contribution that often goes against the effects proclaimed and expected (see his ch. 2, 'The State, a product of globalisation', pp. 30–125).

78 O. Lamloun, 'L'indéfectible soutien français à l'exclusion de l'islamisme tunisien', in O. Lamloun and B. Ravenel (eds), *La Tunisie de Ben Ali*, pp. 103–21; B. Hibou and L. Martinez, 'Le Partenariat euro-maghrébin, un mariage blanc?', and the contributions by O. Lamloun, B. Hibou and E. Ritaine, in *Critique internationale*, special number, no. 18, January 2003. See also the file 'L'Europe des camps. La mise à l'écart des étrangers', in *Cultures et conflits*, no. 57, Spring 2005, pp. 5–250, in particular the articles by A. Belguendouz, C. Rodier and C. Teule, and the LTDH communiqué of 9 January 2004 concerning law 2003–1975 of 10 December 2003 on terrorism, which suggests how international constraints can be tacitly supported by international civil society and help to support the established power and fight against opponents.

79 The justifiable despair of Mohamed Talbi still seems excessively optimistic: the annual reports of the CNLT and the LTDH 2001 and 2002 still relate cases of deaths in prisons following violence and torture.

80 M. Talbi, interview with Beat Stauffer, *Kalima*, nos 16–17, September 2003, p. 24.

81 Interviews, Tunis, December 2001 and December 2002; Paris, October 2002; Brussels, April–May 2002. See also, for the French cooperation, J.-F. Bayart, *Le Dispositif français en matière de promotion de la démocratie et des droits de l'homme, rapport au ministre des Affaires étrangères*, multigrade, Paris, Januray 2002.

82 But the same applies to France (cooperation via the DGCID of the Ministry of Foreign Affairs) or Germany, including for its private financing, which in theory is not limited by diplomatic considerations (Ebert and Adenauer Foundations).

83 This was the case with the blocking of the second tranche of the European Initiative for Democracy and Human Rights: the authorities justified the blockage by the existence of a case brought against the League and an unfavourable judgement against the management committee. Even if the motivation behind this, and the way it developed, can be matter for dispute, the fact of the matter is true enough; however, the outgoing management has the official mandate of preparing the next congress and European financing was aimed at helping the League to restructure in preparation for the congress. Interviews, Tunis, March 2005.

84 J.-F. Bayart, *Global Subjects*, p. 59.

85 This can also be seen in the awkward position of certain human rights activists and politicians committed to the democratization of the country, and financed by the European Union. This is the case, for example, with K. Chammari, one of the founders of the Réseau Euromed pour la défense des droits de l'homme (REMDH – Euromed Network for the Defence of Human Rights) and the Euro-Mediterranean Foundation for the Support of the Defenders of Human Rights. For example, K. Chammari's paper ('L'impact de l'engagement de

l'Union européenne sur les structures des sociétés euro-méditerranéennes', given at the Rabat colloquium, 4–5 December 2004) remains at the formal level, and describes all the procedures undertaken by the European Union in favour of respect for human rights, without criticizing them, hiding behind other criticisms to refer to dysfunctions that he himself cannot mention directly. These interventions, furthermore, are aimed at a European public and not at Tunisians.

86   What follows stems from indirect conversations on the subject, Tunis, December 2001, December 2002 and December 2003. I tried 'on the off chance' to argue with the people tailing me, but I was never able to address a single word to them!

87   Interviews, Tunis, December 2003.

88   As far as the *omda* is concerned, I have drawn mainly on interviews in Tunisia (December 2002 and December 2003) and the historical work of Béchir Tekari: B. Tekari, *Du cheik à l'omda. Institution locale traditionnelle et intégration partisane* (Tunis: Imprimerie officielle de la République tunisienne, 1981).

89   A law passed in 1962 had already stripped them of their tax functions.

4   The Normalizing Activity of the Bureaucratic Apparatus

1   For these evaluations, see the notes of donors, especially those of the European Union, which draws up a comparative evaluation by distributing MEDA funds in proportion with the performances of different countries, which are given marks mainly in terms of bureaucratic criteria. For an analysis, see B. Hibou, 'Les marges de manoeuvre d'un "bon élève" économique'.

2   Interview, January–March 2005. See also the texts of international organizations that highlight the efficiency of the administration for the offshore sector: for example, World Bank, *Republic of Tunisia. Development Policy Review. Making Deeper Trade Integration Work for Growth and Jobs*, Report no. 29847-TN, Washington DC, October 2004.

3   The World Bank echoes this situation, by launching inquiries among entrepreneurs: World Bank, *Actualisation de l'évaluation du secteur privé*, 2 vols (Washington, DC: The World Bank, May 2000); P.-A. Casero and A. Varoudakis, *Growth, Private Investment, and the Cost of Doing Business in Tunisia*; World Bank Operation Evaluation Department, *Republic of Tunisia. Country Assistance Evaluation, Advance Copy*, The World Bank, Washington, DC, 2004.

4   Max Weber, 'Parliament and government in Germany under a new political order', in *Political Writings*, ed. Peter Lassman and Ronald Speirs (Cambridge: Cambridge University Press, 1994), pp. 130–271, p. 225.

5   Ibid.

6   As well as my interviews, see J.-P. Cassarino, *Tunisian New Entrepreneurs*.

7   Interviews, Tunis, July 2000, December 2002 and Paris, June 2001.

8   Quoted by M. Weber, p. 240.

9   On the centrality of the Plan, see E. Murphy, *Economic and Political Change in Tunisia*.

10   F. Siino, *Science et pouvoir dans la Tunisie contemporaine* (Paris: Karthala-IREMAM, 2004).

11   S. Ben Achour, 'Permis de bâtir et régulation urbaine', in *Mélanges en l'honneur d'Habib Ayadi*, pp. 173–92 (especially pp. 179–83). She states that an 'overwhelming majority of households own their accommodation' in those districts dominated by informal lodging, and that it is in no way a case of squatters (p. 181). M. Ben Letaïef, 'Institutions, modes de gestion et devenir: la politique tunisienne de la ville', *Revue tunisienne de droit*, Centre de publication universitaire, Tunis, 2000, pp. 159–93. See also P. Signoles, 'Acteurs publics et acteurs privés dans le développement des villes du monde arabe', in P. Signoles, G. El Kadi and R. Sidi Boumedine (eds), *L'Urbain dans le monde arabe. Politiques, instruments et acteurs* (Paris: Éditions du CNRS, 1999), pp. 19–53.

12   This example was given me by Adel Arfaoui – my thanks to him. He teaches at Jendouba and is a member of the LTDH, and he gave me information and documentation, especially press articles, on this example and several others.

13   Sanitary caravans are convoys composed of doctors who travel through poor regions where a certain number of specialist medical treatments are not found, and where surgery is not performed: www.rcd.tn.

14   M. Kerrou (ed.), *Public et privé en Islam* (Paris: Maisonneuve et Larose, 2002); B. Hibou, 'Tunisie: le coût d'un "miracle"'.

15   A. Bédoui, 'Limites, contraintes et perspectives de croissance et de développement en Tunisie', *Horizons maghrébins*, no. 46, 2002, pp. 61–76, and 'La question de l'État et la gouvernance en Tunisie', *La Lettre de dilapidation économique et budgétaire en Tunisie*, no. 5, November 2003; S. Khiari, *Tunisie, le délitement de la cité*, ch. III on desocialization and ch. IV on the state's loss of meaning.

16   See the different contributions by A. Barry, T. Osborne, and N. Rose (eds), *Foucault and Political Reason, Liberalism, Neo-Liberalism and Rationalities of Government* (Chicago, University of Chicago Press, 1996), and B. Hibou, 'From privatising the economy to privatising the state' in B. Hibou (ed.), *Privatising the State*, pp. 1–46.

17   C. Gaddès emphasizes how the abuse of IT is frequent in the administration: there are no laws that protect private life in Tunisia: C. Gaddès, 'Nouvelles technologies de l'information et mise à niveau de l'administration en Tunisie', in *Mélanges en l'honneur d'Habib Ayadi*, pp. 490ff.

18   M. Weber, 'Parliament and government in Germany', p. 237.

19   All these and the following data come from the Conseil de l'ordre et du barreau de Tunis (the Tunis Order and Bar Council), on the basis of interviews that I undertook with a significant number of their members. Tunis, December 2001, December 2002 and December 2003.

20   Interviews, Tunis, January–March 2005.

21   An argument inspired by work on China: I. Thireau, 'The moral universe of aggrieved Chinese workers: workers' appeals to arbitration committees and letters and visits to offices', *China Journal*, vol. 7, no. 50, 2003, pp. 83–103; J.-L. Rocca, *La Condition chinoise. Capitalisme, mise au travail et résistances dans la Chine des réformes* (Paris: Karthala, 2006).

22   For the interventions of the political and the political use of justice, interviews, Tunis, December 2001 and December 2002, in particular. For the period 1956–1988, see also S. Belaïd, 'La justice politique en Tunisie', *Revue tunisienne de droit*, 2000, pp. 361–404. For the recent period, see the reports of the LTDH, the CNLT and the Centre pour l'indépendance de la justice, in particular:

Commission internationale des juristes, *Rapport sur la Tunisie*, Human Rights Watch, 12 March 2003; *Avocats et défenseurs des droits humains sous forte pression en Tunisie*, 17 March 2003.

23   S. Belaïd, 'La justice politique en Tunisie', mentions the code on the press, the code on the postal services, the law on associations and the law on public gatherings.

24   A detail published by the newspaper on 12 December 2001, and again in *Le Quotidien*, 13 December 2001.

25   M.-H. Lakhoua, 'L'encombrement de la justice pénale', *Revue tunisienne de droit* (Tunis: Centre de publication universitaire, 2000), pp. 287–98. Rubber cheques do not constitute the sole infraction concerned; also affected are prostitution, vagrancy, suicide, drug abuse and juvenile delinquency.

26   Interview, Tunis, December 2002.

27   For a significant commentary by Amel Mamlouk, see A. Mamlouk, 'Commentaire de l'arrêt no. 69197 du 6 octobre 2000 de la cour d'appel de Tunis', *Revue tunsienne de droit* (Tunis: Centre de publication universitaire, 2000), pp. 463–75.

28   Interviews, Tunis, mainly December 2001 and December 2002.

29   Interview in Tunis, December 2002 and December 2003, and FNUJA, *Rapport de la commission des droits de l'homme et des libertés de la Fédération nationale des unions de jeunes avocats*, mission to Tunis, 10–14 July 2003, mimeograph, Paris.

30   All the following information was gathered during interviews in Tunis, mainly in July 2000, December 2001, December 2002 and December 2003.

31   This development corresponded to the Bab Souikha affair in February 1991: in the framework of the systematic fight against the Islamists, it was a question of preventing the judicial machine from defending dissidents fairly.

32   This was the case for the barristers Ayadi and Jmour at the meeting of the Union des avocats africains in Ghana, and in the participation of the barrister Ben Amor at conferences of human rights organizations in Geneva: interviews, December 2003.

33   Whereas the judge of the canton had previously been able to take over from the lawyer's ministry for sums less than 3,000 DT, the limit is now raised to 7,000 DT. In accordance with the 2002 code, the tax council suffices for tax affairs, and tax-payers are discouraged by the administration from taking a lawyer. However, no law has taken this novelty into account, and according to the Tunisian code of civil procedure, only the lawyer can advise a client on tax affairs.

34   Interviews, Tunis, December 2002.

35   See the works of R. Zghal, in particular 'Hiérarchie et processus du pouvoir dans les organisations', in *Élites et pouvoir dans le monde arabe pendant la période moderne et contemporaine*, CERES, série Histoire no. 5, Tunis, 1992, pp. 237–50, and R. Zghal, 'Nouvelles orientations du syndicalisme tunisien', *Monde arabe, Maghreb-Machrek*, no. 162, October–December 1998, pp. 6–17; various contributions in the *Actes du séminaire Syndicat et société*, 1 December 1987, Tunis, CERES, série sociologique no. 14, 1989; S. Zeghidi, 'L'UGTT, pôle central de la contestation sociale et politique', in M. Ben Romdhane (ed.), *Tunisie: mouvements sociaux et modernité*, pp. 13–61; S. Hamzaoui, 'Champ politique et syndicalisme', *Annuaire de l'Afrique du Nord*, vol. 27, 1999,

pp. 369–80; S. Khiari, *Tunisie, le délitement de la cité* and 'Reclassement et recompositions au sein de la bureaucratie syndicale depuis l'Indépendance. La place de l'UGTT dans le système politique tunisien', *La Tunisie sous Ben Ali*, CERI website, www.ceri-sciences-po.org/kiosque/archives/déc2000; K. Zamiti, 'De l'insurrection syndicale à la révolte du pain: janvier 1978–janvier 1984', *Revue tunisienne de sciences sociales*, vol. 28, nos. 104–105, 1991, pp. 41–68; M. Camau and V. Geisser, *Le Syndrome autoritaire*.

36 S. Zghidi, 'Les mutations du mouvement syndical tunisien au cours des quinze dernières années', in *Actes du séminaire Syndicat et société*, pp. 275–94.

37 S. Khiari, *Tunisie, le délitement de la cité*, pp. 33–4.

38 Interviews, Sfax, December 2002 and Tunis, December 2003.

39 Source: interviews, Tunis, December 2003. The case of Dr Ezzaoui, who was unable to stand at the elections to the union of hospital and university doctors.

40 For example, a general secretary of the union for secondary education, who works in a private school. Interviews, Tunis, December 2002.

41 Source: interviews, Tunis, December 2002 and December 2003.

42 Interview, Tunis, December 2003.

43 R. Zghal, 'Nouvelles orientations du syndicalisme tunisien', p. 6.

44 S. Zghidi, 'UGTT, pôle central de la contestation', p. 52.

45 The case for higher education since 2004. Interviews, Tunis, December 2003 and January 2005.

46 Interviews, Tunis and Monastir, January–March 2005.

47 Information provided on several occasions during interviews (Tunis, January–March 2005) – but that I have never been able to confirm. R. Zghal, 'Nouvelles orientations du syndicalisme tunisien' also mentions it without quoting any figures.

48 E. Bellin, *Stalled Democracy*, pp. 61–6.

49 Interviews, Tunis, December 2002. We should note that, in agriculture, it is the UTAP (Union tunisienne pour l'agriculture et la pêche – the Tunisian Union for Agriculture and Fishing) that performs this role.

50 J.-P. Cassarino, *Tunisian New Entrepreneurs*.

51 M. Porter, 'Clusters and the New Economics of Competition', *Harvard Business Review*, vol. 76, no. 6, 1998, pp. 77–90.

52 M. Cammett, 'The Politics of Constructing "industrial clusters": Comparative Insights from Morocco and Tunisia', paper presented to the Fifth Mediterranean Social and Political Research Meeting, European University Institute, Florence and Montecatini Terme, 24–28 March 2004; K. Dammak-Chebbi, 'Situation et perspectives de l'industrie textile tunisienne'; Cettex-Gherzi, *Mise à jour de l'étude stratégique du secteur textile-habillement*; Fich Ratings, *L'Industrie touristique tunisienne*, and R. Meddeb, *L'Industrie du textile-habillement en Tunisie*.

53 M. Catusse, *L'Entrée en politique des entrepreneurs au Maroc. Libéralisation économique et réforme de l'ordre politique*, doctoral thesis in political science, IEP of Aix-en-Provence, Aix-en-Provence, 1999.

54 J.-P. Cassarino, *Tunisian New Entrepreneurs*.

55 M. Cammett, 'The Politics of Constructing "industrial clusters"'.

56 This significance can be explained by the high number of businessmen who come from the ordinary public, and by a generational effect: educated in the

1960s and 1970s, they were influenced by this intellectual tradition and experienced these statist practices as the only legitimate ones; they profited from liberalization to go into the private realm, but this mutation was conceived as a supplementary opportunity, a new mode of state action, not as a new political philosophy. See J.-P. Cassarino, *Tunisian New Entrepreneurs*.

57 The persistence of Third-World-centred and anti-liberal thought is doubtless what appears most clearly from interviews with entrepreneurs, but also with politicians and senior civil servants. See also H.-R. Hamza, 'Rôle et centralité des enseignants et du syndicalisme enseignant dans le processus de formation du nationalisme et de l'État national tunisien', in *Élites et pouvoir dans le monde arabe*, pp. 221–37, which suggests that dirigisme and state control can be historically explained by the unshakeable link between nationalism, the struggle for independence, and the construction of the national state on the one hand and, on the other, by access to the civil service, both in terms of jobs (the civil servant) and in terms of the political and economic *imaginaire* (he uses the term *paradis administratifs*, 'administrative havens', p. 22). Short biographies of influential entrepreneurs or businessmen show that the current apologists for liberalism and free trade with Europe have, at other periods, played an active part in the definition of economic policies in the period of nationalizations and the collectivization of the 1960s or in the period of 'liberal' state interventionism of the years 1970–80. This is the case, for example, of Ahmed Abdelkefi, the current president of the first venture capital company, who was a cabinet director during the period of nationalizations and the experience of cooperatives (source: interviews, Tunis, April 1998, January 1999 and December 2003).

58 Interviews, Tunis, April 1997, May 1998, January–March 2005.

59 These are the words used by M. Gasmi, 'L'espace industriel à Sfax', p. 83. On the marginal quality of councils and commissions in Tunisia, see H. Roussillon, 'Administration consultative et représentation des intérêts professionnels en Tunisie', *Revue franco-maghrébine de droit*, no. 2, 1994, pp. 181–97. For purposes of comparison, for Egypt, see F. Clément, 'Libéralisation économique et nouvelles configurations de l'emploi en Égypte', *Revue tiers-monde*, no. 163, July–September 2000, pp. 669–91; for Mexico, R. Camp, *Entrepreneurs and Politics in Twentieth-Century Mexico* (New York: Oxford University Press, 1989); and, for Portugal, F. Rosas, *O Estado Novo nos Anas Trinta, 1928–1938* (Lisbon: Editorial Estampa, 1986).

60 M. Kilani, 'Sur-pouvoir personnel et évanescence du politique en Tunisie', p. 2.

61 See for example R. Chennoufi, 'Sujet ou citoyen', *Revue tunisienne de droit* (Tunis: Centre de publication universitaire, 2000), pp. 205–20; I. Marzouki, 'L'individu au mépris du citoyen', *Bulletin de l'AISLF*, no. 21, 2005, pp. 169–82.

Part III Negotiations and Consensus: The Force of 'Insidious Leniencies '

1 The notion of 'power of disposition' comes from M. Weber, in *Economy and Society*. The quotation is taken from C. Colliot-Thélène, *Études wébériennes* (Paris: PUF, 2001), p. 290.

2 J. J. Linz and A. Stepan, *Problems of Democratic Transition and Consolidation*.

3 For Tunisia, see E. Bellin, *Stalled Democracy*, and E. Murphy, *Economic and Political Change in Tunisia*. In other countries of the Arab world, see R. Springborg, *Mubarak's Egypt: Fragmentation of a Political Order* (Boulder: Westview, 1989); C. M. Henry and R. Springborg, *Globalization and the Politics of Development in the Middle East*; S. Heydemann, 'The political logic of economic rationality: selective stabilization in Syria', in J. Barkey (ed.), *The Politics of Economic Reform in the Middle East* (New York: St Martin Press, 1992), and *Authoritarianism in Syria. Institutions and Social Conflict, 1946–1970* (Ithaca: Cornell University Press, 1999); M. Hachemaoui, *Clientélisme et corruption dans le système politique algérien (1999–2004)*, doctoral thesis in political science, IEP de Paris, Paris, mimeograph, December 2004.

4 All these expressions are taken from interviews, Tunis, various places.

5 Between Hidden Conflictuality and the Permanent Search for Compromise

1 For the 1970s, see H. Ayadi, 'Les tendances générales de la politique fiscale de la Tunisie depuis l'indépendance', *Revue tunisienne de droit*, CPU, Tunis, 1980, pp. 17–75. For the 1980s, L. Chikhaoui concludes: 'The whole difficulty, this came from the implementation of the reform, and not its conception, and this implementation came up against an incoherent set of political desires when it came to tax, marked by hesitations, and in particular by a constant increase in rates, together with a legal erosion of the taxable income by the increased number of regimes of favour, exemptions, non-taxable allowances . . .' (L. Chikhaoui, *Pour une stratégie de la réforme fiscale*, p. 95). For the 1990s, see N. Baccouche, 'Les implications de l'accord d'association sur le droit fiscal et douanier', in *Mélanges en l'honneur d'Habib Ayadi*, pp. 5–27).

2 The public sector fund (CNRPS: *Caisse nationale de retraite et de prévoyance sociale* – The National Pension and Provident Fund), for its part, 'conforms' much more closely to the sector's international canons and is now showing a chronic deficit.

3 Various interviews, Tunis, 1997–2005, and A. Bédoui, 'Spécificités et limites du modèle de développement tunisien', a paper presented at the colloquium *Démocratie, développement et dialogue social*, organized by the UGTT in Tunis, November 2004.

4 Interviews, Tunis, December 2003 and January–March 2005 in particular. In order to be reimbursed or to take advantage of free health care, you need to go to the public hospitals or dispensaries whose opening hours are very limited, generally just in the morning between 8 am and 2 pm, closed on Saturdays and Sundays; the CNSS does not reimburse absences until the fourth day of absence, even though most stoppages last no more than two or three days; the 'free' nature of medicine is real only when the patient asks the pharmacies in hospitals and the latter stock the medicine required . . . which is not often the case. And so on.

5 A. Bédoui, 'La question de l'État et la gouvernance en Tunisie', *La Lettre de la dilapidation économique et budgétaire en Tunisie*, no. 5, November 2003. The author reminds us that resources for borrowing rose from 5.7 per cent of the GDP in 1987 to 14.5 per cent in 1996 and then fell to 13 per cent in 2001. By

way of comparison, we need to remember that European countries are experiencing a fiscal pressure of 40 per cent on average.

6   G. Luciani, 'Allocation vs production states: a theoretical framework', in H. Beblawi and G. Luciani (eds), *The Rentier State* (London: Croom Helm, 1987), and 'The Oil Rent, Fiscal Crisis of the State and Democratization' in G. Salamé (ed.), *Democracy without Democrats? The Renewal of Politics in the Muslim World* (New York; London: Tauris, 1994), pp. 130–55; L. Anderson, 'The state in the Middle East and North Africa', *Comparative Politics*, no. 20, October 1987; A. Richards and J. Waterbury, *A Political Economy in the Middle East* (Boulder: Westview Press, 1996). This thesis has spread across many states, including non-*rentier* states. For China, see T.P. Bernstein and X. Lu, *Taxation Without Representation in Contemporary China* (Cambridge: Cambridge University Press, 2003).

7   A. Bédoui, 'La question de l'État et la gouvernance en Tunisie', pp. 2 and 5.

8   Interviews, Tunis, April–May 1997 and April 1998; also quoted by *Marchés tropicaux et méditerranéens*, 17 January 1997.

9   IMF data for 1985, quoted by L. Chikhaoui, *Pour une stratégie de la réforme fiscale*, p. 84.

10   For the case of Morocco, see B. Hibou, 'Les enjeux de l'ouverture au Maroc: dissidence économique et contrôle politique', *Les Études du CERI*, no. 15, April 1996; B. Hibou, 'Fiscal trajectories in Morocco and Tunisia', in S. Heydemann (ed.), *Networks of Privilege in the Middle East. The Politics of Economic Reform Revisited* (New York: Palgrave MacMillan, 2004), pp. 201–22; B. Hibou, 'Greece and Portugal: convergent or divergent Europeanization?', in S. Bulmer and C. Lequesne (eds), *The Member States of the European Union* (Oxford: Oxford University Press, 2005), pp. 229–53.

11   L. Chikhaoui demonstrates that 'the Tunisian tax administration suffers from an inadequacy that is at once quantitative and qualitative concerning its human means'; she adds that 'the material means of the fiscal administration do not always offer ideal working conditions' and points to 'the decrepit and delapidated state of several tax offices' (L. Chikhaoui, *Pour une stratégie de la réforme fiscale*, pp. 124 and 127).

12   Interviews, Sfax, April 1998; Tunis, July 2000.

13   Source: IMF and Mission économique de l'Ambassade de France. See, for example, IMF: *Tunisia: 2004 Article IV Consultation – Staff Report*, IMF Country Report, no. 04/359, November 2004.

14   Interviews, Tunis, April 1998 and January 1999.

15   During several interviews (Tunis and Sfax, July 2000, December 2002, December 2003 and January 2005), I was told the same story: the reimbursement of VAT credits is very slow (up to five or six years); there is a recurrence of tax inspections whenever a demand is made for the laws to be respected; reimbursement by tapering tranches, for example 20 per cent the first year, 15 per cent the second, five per cent the third, and so on.

16   P. Signoles, 'Industrialisation, urbanisation et mutations de l'espace tunisien' refers to the speech given by Hédi Nouira explaining that the fiscal advantages 'are a renunciation on the part of the state to the benefit of certain investors, against the help given by these enterprises towards the solution of problems that arise in the country' (declaration of Hédi Nouira to *La Presse*, quoted by

Signoles, p. 290). See also H. Dimassi and H. Zaïem, 'L'industrie: mythe et stratégies'.

17 Interviews, Tunis and Sfax, April–May 1997, April 1998 and January 1999.

18 M. Affes and A. Yaich, 'Les difficultés pratiques de la nouvelle imposition des revenus', *Études juridiques*, no. 2, 1992, Faculty of Law, Sfax, pp. 151–68 (pp. 168 and 165).

19 Ibid., p. 168.

20 See A. Yaich and M. Affes, 'Les difficultés pratiques d'application de la TVA', *Études juridiques*, no. 1, 1991, Faculty of Law, Sfax, pp. 101–5, and L. Chikhaoui, *Pour une stratégie de la réforme fiscale*, pp. 103–6 and pp. 111–13. These texts are a little old, but, through my interviews (in Tunis and Sfax, 1997–8), in particular with some of their authors, their continuing validity has been confirmed.

21 The gross figures are those of 1997 quoted by S. Zakraoui, 'Le régime forfaitaire d'imposition, quoi de neuf?', *Revue tunisienne de droit*, CPU, 2000, pp. 389–400; the proportion of enterprises paying at the fixed rate is drawn from UGTT, *Rapport économique et social 2002*, mimeograph, Tunis, December 2001. The comparison with a base-line civil servant (in this case a primary school teacher) was given me during an interview in Tunis, April 1998.

22 S. Zakraoui, 'Le régime forfaitaire d'imposition, quoi de neuf?', p. 391.

23 Ibid., and L. Chikhaoui, *Pour une stratégie de la réforme fiscale*.

24 Out of 253,398 tax-payers paying at the fixed rate, only 146,614 had handed in their tax returns.

25 A. Bédoui, 'Spécificités et limites du modèle de développement tunisien': the author also mentions the significant inequality within this very system, since 66 per cent of tax-payers subject to the the fixed rate apparently pay only 15 DT per year.

26 Interviews, Tunis, various field trips between 1997 and 2000.

27 This is noted by practically all tax consultants, chartered accountants, lawyers and entrepreneurs interviewed on the tax system. See also S. Zakraoui, 'Le régime forfaitaire, quoi de neuf?'; L. Chikhaoui, *Pour une stratégie de la réforme fiscale*, and, in particular, N. Baccouche, 'Regard sur le code d'incitations aux investissements de 1993 et ses démembrements', *Revue tunisienne de droit*, Centre de publication universitaire, Tunis, 2000, pp. 1–47.

28 Interviews, Sfax, April 1998.

29 Interviews, Tunis and Hammamet, January–March 2005.

30 As well as the interviews in Tunis and Sfax (various field trips between 1988 and 2001), M. Affes, 'Projet de loi relatif aux droits fiscaux', mimeograph, Sfax, 1997.

31 On the conciliation commissions and the special rate of taxation (and the complexity of the legal problems they raise), see L. Chikhaoui, *Pour une stratégie de la réforme fiscale*, and S. Zakraoui, 'Le régime forfaitaire d'imposition, quoi de neuf?', which in particular notes the barely legal character of these regional commissions of consultation and the possibilities of interpretation opened by the laws that govern the special rate of taxation.

32 M. Affes, 'Projet de loi relatif aux droits fiscaux', p. 3, notes the existence of 'legal or administrative arrangements that lead to back payment of excessive taxes', as well as the excessively long character of inspections and their recurrence, often for one and the same business, the retrospectiveness of the laws, the

unavailability of the taxpayer's charter (with the result that he does not know his rights in any detail), the fact that providing proof is incumbent on the tax-payer, etc.

33   Interviews, Tunis, December 2002. See L. Chikhaoui, *Pour une stratégie de la réforme fiscale*, p. 148, n. 43. The author mentions that, 'out of 386 tax appeals, only 28 rulings were overturned in favour of the petitioning tax-payer, 6 were overturned in favour of the administration, 113 applications were rejected, 225 were declared inadmissible, and there were 15 withdrawals'.

34   Interviews, Tunis, 2000–3. All this information is tentative, since there is no definite evidence available to a foreign researcher. However, it seems to me important to mention this information, for at least two reasons. On the one hand, there is a high probability that these facts are valid, given the diversity of the sources from which they come, including sources hostile to the idea that criminal practices are widespread in the spheres of power. On the other hand, even if all we have are rumours, the significance of the latter shapes people's behaviour and actions and also fuels an *imaginaire* that turns the tax system into the supreme weapon of the central power.

35   See Y. Matsunaga, 'L'État rentier est-il réfractaire à la démocratie?', *Critique internationale*, no. 8, July 2000, pp. 46–58. See too J. Leca, 'Democratization in the Arab world. Uncertainty, vulnerability and legitimacy. A tentative conceptualization and some hypothesis' in particular (pp. 48–83) and J. Waterbury, 'Democracy without democrats? The potential for political liberalization in the Middle East', in particular (pp. 23–47) in G. Salamé (ed.), *Democracy without Democrats?* These texts emphasize how the tax system is not the only condition for the citizens' demand for political rights; the political autonomy of the state, symbolized by the absence of taxes, is not the same as its immunity from democratic demands; between the state and the actors in a society there are other bargaining mechanisms than tax; and coercion and discipline exist and exercise a fundamental influence.

36   B. Hibou, 'L'intégration européenne du Portugal et de la Grèce: le rôle des marges', in S. Mappa (ed.), *La Coopération fondamentale face au libéralisme* (Paris: Karthala, 2003), pp. 87–134.

37   The *mehalla*, literally 'camps' or 'locations', were the pacific movements of the Bey's troops as they moved around the country, in particular for tax purposes.

38   M.-H. Chérif, *Pouvoir et société dans la Tunisie de H'usayn Bin Ali (1705–1740)*, vol. 2 (Tunis: University of Tunis, 1986); J. Ganiage, *Les Origines du Protectorat français en Tunisie (1861–1881)* (Paris: PUF, 1959); L. C. Brown, *The Tunisia of Ahmad Bey (1837–1855)* (Princeton: Princeton University Press, 1974); T. Bachrouch, *Formation sociale barbaresque et pouvoir à Tunis au XVIIe siècle* (Tunis: Publications universitaires de Tunis, 1977); A. Hénia, *Le Grîd, ses rapports avec le Beylik de Tunis (1676–1840)* (Tunis: Publications de l'Université de Tunis, 1980); J. Dakhlia, *L'Oubli de la cité. La Mémoire collective à l'épreuve du lignage dans le Jérid tunisien* (Paris: La Découverte, 1990); K. Chater, *Dépendance et mutations précoloniales. La Régence de Tunis de 1815 à 1857* (Tunis: Publications de l'Université de Tunis, Faculté des lettres et sciences humaines, série Histoire no. 28, 1984); L. Valensi, *Fellahs tunisiens. L'économie rurale et la vie des campagnes aux XVIIIe et XIXe siècles* (Paris: Mouton and

EHESS, 1977). See also J. Dakhlia, *Le Divan des rois. Le Politique et le religieux dans l'islam* (Paris: Aubier, 1998); in this work, the author casts doubt on the idea that the absence of a tax system is a sign of liberty.

39 See for example L. Chikhaoui, *Pour une stratégie de la réforme fiscale.*

40 A few days after 7 November 1987 (more precisely, on 26 November), a fiscal amnesty was proclaimed, with the intention of symbolizing a new political era and not, as more technicist interpretations claimed, the start of fiscal reforms: N. Baccouche, 'L'amnistie fiscale de 1987', *Revue tunisienne de droit*, CPU, 1988, pp. 13–35, and L. Chikhaoui, *Pour une stratégie de la réforme fiscale.*

41 Interview, Tunis, December 2003.

42 Interview, Tunis, December 2001. The details of this fiscal dimension of the Yahyahoui affair are described in LTDH, *Rapport annuel 2003*, Tunis.

43 These two 'nuisance factors' were mentioned to me in interviews I carried out between 1997 and 2005. Over time, the thesis of the investment strike has assumed some importance. These themes are also taken up by various dissidents: see the wesbites of TuneZine or Kalima, or the publication of the wheeler-dealer dissident Khémaïs Toumi, *La Lettre de la dilapidation économique et budgétaire en Tunisie*. See also M. Marzouki, *Le Mal arabe*, pp. 97–100; M. Marzouki, 'Entretien avec Ben Jaafar', in O. Lamloum and B. Ravenel (eds), *La Tunisie de Ben Ali*, pp. 216–17; S. Bensedrine and O. Mestiri, *L'Europe et ses despotes*, ch. V. All focus their criticisms on the absence or inadequacies of the rule of law and the corruption of those near the seat of power.

44 Interviews, Tunis, July 2000 and December 2001. See also World Bank Operation Evaluation Department, *Republic of Tunisia. Country Assistance Evaluation*, Advance Copy, and the statistics of the INS. In 1996, big businesses – with over 100 employees – represented 0.4 per cent of the total number of businesses; medium-sized businesses – over 50 employees – 0.3 per cent of the total or 1.7 per cent if the number of their employees is brought down to over 10; some 82 per cent of businesses are run independently and the majority of businesses have fewer than 6 employees (15.2 per cent).

45 H. Youfsi, E. Filipiak and H. Bougault, *Poulina, un management tunisien*: the law on holding companies dates from only 2001 and is still not really being applied. Previously they were independent companies: they have gradually become reorganized into subsidiaries and a 'head office which is akin to a holding company' (ibid., p. 31).

46 S. Radwan and J.-L. Reiffers, *Le Partenariat euro-méditerranéen, 10 ans après Barcelone. Acquis et perspectives*, BCT and FEMISE, February 2005. English version: *The Euro-Mediterranean Partnership. 10 Years after Barcelona. Achievements and Perspectives*, FEMISE Report, February 2005.

47 P.-A. Casero and A. Varoudakis, *Growth, Private Investment, and the Cost of Doing Business in Tunisia.*

48 Fich Ratings, *L'Industrie touristique tunisienne.*

49 See A. Bédoui, 'Le désarroi et le comportement de repli du secteur privé tunisien'.

50 Privatizations have clearly brought out how public enterprises and the state had adopted the same technique of dispersing their property: R. Zghal, 'Le développement participatoire, participation et monde du travail en Tunisie'; A. Grissa, 'The Tunisian state enterprises and privatization policy', pp. 109–27, in

W.-I. Zartman (ed.), *Tunisia: Political Econmy of Reform*, and P.-D. Pelletreau, 'Private sector development through public sector restructuring?'. For the textile industry, Mission Économique et financière de l'Ambassade de France à Tunis, *Le Secteur textile-habillement*, résumé, September 2004; J.-R. Chaponnière and S. Perrin, *Le Textile-habillement tunisien et le défi de la libéralisation. Quel rôle pour l'investissement direct étranger?* (Paris: AFD, March 2005).

51　This last option is not legal, but it is made possible by the size of the émigré community: H. Boubakri, 'Les entrepreneurs migrants d'Europe: dispositifs communautaires et économie éthique. Le cas des entrepreneurs tunisiens en France', in J. Cesari (ed.), *Les Anonymes de la mondialisation, Cultures and Conflits*, nos. 33–34, Spring–Summer 1999, pp. 69–88; J.-P. Cassarino, *Tunisian New Entrepreneurs*, and S. Bava and S. Mazzella, 'Samir en voyage d'affaires. Le business entre plusieurs mondes', in M. Peraldi (ed.), *Cabas et containers. Activités marchandes informelles et réseaux migrants transfrontaliers* (Paris: Maisonneuve et Larose, 2001), pp. 269–77.

52　The following enumeration is a synthesis of interviews (1997–2005) and research on business strategies: M. Bouchrara, *7 millions d'entrepreneurs. Études sur l'esprit d'entreprise, l'innovation et la création d'emplois en Tunisie, 1984–1987*, mimeograph, Tunis, June 1996, and *L'économie tunisienne entre sa légalité et son identité. 12 propositions pour ramener la confiance économique*, mimeograph, Tunis, 1995; P.-N. Denieul, *Les Entrepreneurs du développement. L'ethno-industrialisation en Tunisie. La Dynamique de Sfax* (Paris: L'Harmattan, 1992); R. Zghal, 'Postface', in P.-N. Denieul, *Les Entrepreneurs du développement*; P.-N Denieul and A. B'Chir, 'La PME tunisienne', in A. Sid Ahmet (ed.), *Économies du Maghreb. L'impératif de Barcelone* (Paris: Éditions du CNRS, 1998), pp. 181–93; H. Yousfi, E. Filipiak and H. Bougault, *Poulina, un management tunisien*.

53　This myth rests on exemplary cases or on re-readings that consist of creating such cases. We can here mention the BIAT affair mentioned in ch. 2, or the difficulties that seem to have been experienced by the Poulina group over the last few years, with pressures facilitating the entry of 'intruders' into the capital of certain of those companies, the obligation to enter the Stock Exchange, and tax blackmailings. Interviews, Tunis, 1997–2005.

54　J.-P. Cassarino, 'Participatory development and liberal reforms in Tunisia: the gradual incorporation of some economic networks', in S. Heydemann (ed.), *Networks of Privilege in the Middle East*, pp. 223–42 (especially pp. 232–3).

55　For the rumours, *Les Familles qui pillent la Tunisie* or the different tracts and pamphlets in circulation on opposition websites. For political interpretations, S. Bensedrine and O. Mestiri, *L'Europe et ses despotes*; M. Markouzi, *Le Mal arabe*. For an academic critique, N. Baccouche, 'Regards sur le code d'incitations aux investissements'; M. Camau and V. Geisser, *Le Syndrome autoritaire*, pp. 197–8; E. Murphy, *Economic and Political Change in Tunisia*.

56　Interviews, Tunis, January and February 2005; starting with its activity representing Neckerman in Tunisia, the group then specialized in tourist services and in air transport. The only diversification, into the dairy industry, was motivated by political considerations, more precisely – in the view of M. Aziz

Miled himself – 'in response to the requests of the President, who had enjoined entrepreneurs to participate in the objective of becoming self-sufficient in this domain', in a 'nationalist act' (interview, Tunis, January 2005). It is interesting to note that instead of congratulating itself on this, the group's CEO regrets this strategy of integration for economic reasons, in particular because it concentrates risks. Admittedly, the tourist sector is currently experiencing a serious crisis.

57 J.-P. Cassarino, *Tunisian New Entrepreneurs*, pp. 125–6.

58 These are the words of H. Fehri and M. Soussi, 'Politiques d'investissement et chômage en Tunisie', mimeograph, Tunis, 2003 – and they ironically reprise the analyses of the World Bank. For all the figures in this paragraph: World Bank, *Tunisia. Economic Monitoring Update*, The World Bank, MENA Region, September 2003; World Bank Operation Evaluation Department, *Republic of Tunisia. Country Assistance Evaluation*, Advance Copy.

59 World Bank, ibid., UGTT, *Rapport économique et social 2002*, and A. Bédoui, 'Le désarroi et le comportement de repli du secteur privé tunisien', and H. Fehri and M. Soussi, 'Politique d'investissement et chômage en Tunisie'.

60 For the case of the organization of the Tunisian pilgrimage to Mecca, on the pretext of security norms and the organization of the Israeli pilgrimage to the synagogue of La Ghriba, in Djerba, see J.-P. Bras, 'L'islam administré: illustrations tunisiennes', in M. Kerrou (ed.), *Public et privé en islam*, pp. 227–46; N. Baccouche, 'Les implications de l'accord d'association sur le droit fiscal et douanier'.

61 For the case of private broadcasting at the end of 2003: interviews, December 2003. See also the national press at the end of 2003. More generally, see N. Baccouche, 'Les implications de l'accord d'association' and 'Regard sur le code d'incitations'.

62 M. Foucault, *Discipline and Punish*, p. 198.

63 This happens in countries other than Tunisia. See A. Ong, *Flexible Citizenship. The Cultural Logics of Transnationality* (Durham; London: Duke University Press, 1999). The author emphasizes this with regard to South East Asia, and David Wank highlights the same thing in the case of China (D. Wank, *Commodifying Communism*).

64 Interview, Tunis, January 2005.

65 N. Baccouche, 'Les implications de l'accord d'association', and 'Regard sur le code d'incitations'; S. Ben Achour, 'L'administration et son droit, quelles mutations?', introduction to the conference *Les Mutations de l'administration et de son droit*, Association tunisienne pour les sciences administratives, Faculté des sciences juridiques de Tunis, Tunis, 17 April 2002.

66 L. Chikhaoui, *Pour une stratégie de la réforme fiscale*; A. Larif-Beatrix, *Édification étatique et environnement culturel. Le Personnel politico-administratif dans la Tunisie contemporaine* (Publisud-OPU, 1988); S. Ben Achour, 'L'administration et son droit, quelles mutations?' C. Gaddes mentions 'dozens of national commissions' which have given rise to 'successive reforms': see C. Gaddes, 'NTI et mise à niveau de l'administration en Tunisie', in *Mélanges en l'honneur de Habib Ayadi*, pp. 453–97 (p. 469).

67 Interviews, Tunis, April 1998 and January 1999 and Sfax, April 1998.

68 C. Gaddes, 'NTI et mise à niveau de l'administration en Tunisie', p. 490.

69 For a theoretical and general discussion of this thesis, see B. Hibou, 'From privatising the economy to privatising the state'; for Tunisia, see S. Ben Achour, 'L'administration et son droit, quelles mutations?' B. Müller observes the same phenomenon in the reunified East Germany, see B. Müller, 'Pouvoir et discipline, du monde du plan à celui du marché', *Cahiers internationaux de sociologie*, vol. 95, 1993, pp. 333–53.

70 H. Béji, *Désenchantement national*, p. 66.

71 Interviews, Tunis, January 1999, July 2000 and December 2003, and Y. Ben Achour, 'Le pouvoir réglementaire général et la Constitution', *Mélanges Habib Ayadi*, pp. 193–214.

72 On the importance of these networks during the interventionist period, see J. Leca and Y. Schemeil, 'Clientélisme et néo-patrimonialisme dans le monde arabe', *Revue internationale de science politique*, vol. 4, no. 4, 1983; for the liberal period, see J. Leca, 'Democratization in the Arab world'.

73 Interviews, Tunis, December 2002 and December 2003.

74 Interviews, Tunis, December 2003.

75 These remarks have often been made to me in the course of interviews with dissidents or critics.

76 R. Delorme and C. André, *L'État et l'économie. Un essai d'explication de l'évolution des dépenses publiques en France, 1870–1980* (Paris: Seuil, 1983).

77 M. Foucault, *Discipline and Punish*, p. 308.

78 All these quotations and the following ones are taken from interviews, January, February and March 2005, governorates of Tunis and Nabeul.

79 A. Bédoui, 'Analyse critique des fondements du PAS et propositions pour un projet alternatif', *Revue tunisienne d'économie*, no. 3/4, 1993, pp. 340–65; S. Khiari, *Tunisie, le délitement de la cité*, pp. 96–7.

80 For the first name, see A. Bédoui, 'Analyse critique des fondements du PAS', and S. Khiari, *Tunisie, le délitement de la cité*, and, for the second, E. Bellin, 'Tunisian industrialists and the state', in W.-I. Zartman, *Tunisia. The Political Economy of Reform*, pp. 45–65.

81 Interview, February 2005, Tunis.

82 Interview, Tunis, January 2005.

83 The event takes place on 17 January of each year: J.-P. Cassarino, *Tunisian New Entrepreneurs*, underlines the way the Tunisian press echoes, on a day-by-day basis, the speeches on the 'responsibility' of entrepreneurs. For the 1970s, R. Zghal, 'Postface'.

84 The paragraph on 'Appartenance' ('Belonging') in the document 'Politique générale de Poulina' is available on www.poulina.gnet.tn and in H. Yousfi, E. Filipiak and H. Bougault, *Poulina, un management tunisien*, p. 97.

85 On the couple submission/sedition, see M. Camau, 'Politique dans le passé, politique aujourd'hui au Maghreb', in J.-F. Bayart (ed.), *La Greffe de l'État* (Paris: Karthala, 1996), pp. 63–93; for the 'exit option' strategies, L. C. Brown, *The Tunisia of Ahmad Bey*; S. Waltz, 'Clientelism and reform in Ben Ali's Tunisia', in W.-I. Zartman (ed.), *Tunisia: The Political Economy of Reform*, pp. 29–44, and J.-P. Cassarino, *Tunisian New Entrepreneurs*.

86 This thesis was originally developed with respect to the entreneurs of Sfax, and then extended: M. Bouchrara, *7 millions d'entrepreneurs*; P.-N. Denieul, *Les Entrepreneurs du développement*.

87 Interviews, Tunis, December 2001 and December 2003; Brussels, May 2002; Paris, November 2003. The classical American theses on liberal political economy are very widespread among the international community. E. Murphy develops this thesis in *Economic and Political Change in Tunisia*.

88 M. Bouchrara, *7 millions d'entrepreneurs* and *L'Économie tunisienne*; B. Hibou, 'Les marges de manoeuvre'.

89 These were the phrases I heard in interviews, Tunis, January 1999 and July 2000; Tunis and Hammamet, January–March 2005. See also M. Gasmi, 'L'espace industriel à Sfax: un système productif local', *Maghreb-Machrek*, no. 181, Autumn 2004, pp. 69–92, and L.-M. El Hédi, 'The business environment in Tunisia', paper presented at the workshop on *Public-Private Partnership in the MENA Region*, Marrakesh, 3–6 September 1998. For an illustration of the 'Young Promotors' financing programme, see J.-P. Cassarino, *Tunisian New Entrepreneurs*, and for the failure of the FOPRODI, P.-A. Casero and A. Varoudakis, *Growth, Private Investment and the Cost of Doing Business in Tunisia*.

90 H. Fehri, 'Économie politique de la réforme: de la tyrannie du statu quo à l'ajustement structurel', *Annales d'économie et de gestion*, vol. 5, no. 10, March 1998, p. 104.

91 A. Bédoui, 'Les relations sociales dans l'entreprise', *L'Entreprise et l'environnement social* (Tunis: IACE, 1990), pp. 159–223 (p. 201).

92 C. Colliot-Thélène, 'Introduction aux textes politiques de Max Weber', p. 96. In the wake of Max Weber, this article questions this ahistorical and naive vision of democracy.

93 Interviews, Paris, Brussels, Washington, 1997–2003; see also the texts on the good governance of these international institutions and, for example, The World Bank, *Governance and Development* (Washington, DC: The World Bank, 1992).

94 Various texts in the *Political Writings* of Max Weber, and the reading of these by C. Colliot-Thélène, *Études wébériennes*, and 'Introduction'.

95 This is typical of authoritarian situations. On China, see J.-L. Rocca, *La Condition chinoise*.

96 F. Mengin, forthcoming, and 'A contingent outcome of the unfinished Chinese civil war: state-formation in Taiwan by transnational actors', paper presented at the Franco-British conference *Économies morales et formation de l'État dans le monde extra-européen* (CERI, Paris, FASOPO, Paris and Trinity College, Cambridge, 27 May 2005).

97 A. Sen, *Development as Freedom* (Oxford: Oxford University Press, 1999).

98 J. Leca, 'Democratization in the Arab World'.

99 All these expressions come from interviews based on the question of how far the political dimension intrudes into business, Tunis, 1997–2005.

100 Interview, Paris, January 2005; Tunis, January and March 2005. It is worth noting that these judgements are shared by Tunisian and foreign entrepreneurs.

101 This is the thesis developed, for example, by E. Bellin, *Stalled Democracy*.

102 Interview, Tunis, May 2005.

103 This is obviously true of countries other than Tunisia. In China too, it has been shown that bosses preferred prosperity to political change: D. L. Wank, *Commodifying Communism*.

6   Negotiated Accommodation

1   A. Bédoui, 'La question de l'État'; H. Fehri, 'Économie politique de la réforme'; certain analyses carried out by RAID/Attac Tunisie published in its bulletin *Raid-Niouz*.

2   On this reconcilation of the two founding fathers of historical sociology, see J. Lonsdale, 'States and social processes: a historical survey', *African Studies Review*, vol. 24, nos. 2–3, June–September 1981, p. 140; J.-F. Bayart, 'L'invention paradoxale de la modernité économique', in J.-F. Bayart (ed.), *La Réinvention du capitalisme*, pp. 9–43; C. Colliot-Thélène, *Etudes wébériennes*.

3   M. Weber, *Political Writings*, in particular 'On the situation of constitutional democracy in Russia', from which the following excerpt is particularly relevant: 'If the *only* things that mattered were "material" conditions and the constellations of interest directly or indirectly "created" by them, any sober observer would be bound to conclude that all *economic* auguries point in the direction of a growing *loss* of freedom. It is quite ridiculous to attribute to today's high capitalism, as it exists in America and is being imported into Russia, to this "inevitability" of our economic development, any "elective affinity" with "democracy" or indeed "freedom" (in *any* sense of the word), when the only question one can ask is how all these things can "possibly" survive at all in the long run under the rule of capitalism. They are in fact only possible if they are supported by the permanent, determined *will* of a nation not to be governed like a flock of sheep' (p. 69).

4   These figures are averages over the period 1997–2002. Source: Mission économique et financière de l'Ambassade de France à Tunis.

5   This again is found outside Tunisia – it happens in China, for instance. This is the main argument of the book by Y. S. Huang, who interprets the importance of FDIs in China as a sign of the weakness of the Chinese economy, see Y. S. Huang, *Selling China: Direct Investment During the Reform Era* (New York: Cambridge University Press, 2003).

6   H. Dimassi and H. Zaïem, 'L'industrie: mythe et stratégies', and P. Signoles, 'Industrialisation, urbanisation et mutations', and the agencies of cooperation (interviews, Tunis, 1997–2005, and IMF, *Article IV 2003*, p. 20).

7   Interviews, Tunis, January–March 2005.

8   Interviews, Tunis, July 1999, January 2000, January–March 2005, and A. Bédoui, *Spécificités et limites du modèle de développement tunisien*; World Bank, *Republic of Tunisia. Development Policy Review. Making Deeper Trade Integration Work for Growth and Jobs*, Washington, DC, Report no. 29847-TN, October 2004; P.-A. Casero and A. Varoudakis, *Growth, Private Investment, and the Cost of Doing Business in Tunisia*, and World Bank, *Stratégie de coopération, République tunisienne*.

9   Mission Économique et financière de l'Ambassade de France à Tunis, *Les Investissements directs étrangers en Tunisie*, summary report, November 2004.

10 We should cite: physical, linguistic, and cultural proximity to Europe; relatively low wages; tax and customs facilities; the efficiency of the single window; the help of the FIPA in purchasing land and the accessibility of the regulations in force; the flexibility of the workforce; state aid for young jobseekers and training; the pleasant environment for expatriates; the availability of the

workforce, etc. Source: interviews, Tunis, January–March 2005; B. Bellon and R. Gouia (eds), *Investissements directs étrangers et développement industriel méditerranéen* (Paris: Economica, 1998); *Livre blanc sur l'environnement industriel en Tunisie*, Les Cahiers du CEPI, final report, no. 1, December 1999; J.-P. Barbier and J.-B. Véron, *Les Zones franches industrielles d'exportation (Haïti, Maurice, Sénégal, Tunisie)* (Paris: Karthala, 1991); see also sites such as www.offshore-development.com; www.tunisie.com/économie/douanes; www.industrie.web-tunisie.com.

11 C.-A. Michalet, 'Investissements étrangers: les économies du sud de la Méditerranée sont-elles attractives?', *Monde arabe, Maghreb-Machrek*, December 1992, pp. 3–82; J.-P. Barbier and J.-P. Véron, *Les Zones franches*; A. Ferguene and E. Ben Hamida, 'Les implantations d'entreprises off shore en Tunisie: quelles retombées sur l'économie?', *Monde arabe, Maghreb-Machrek*, no. 160, April–June 1998, pp. 50–68; P. Signoles, *L'Espace tunisien: capitale et État-région*, 2 vols (Tours: URBAMA, 1985).

12 J.-P. Cassarino, *Tunisian New Entrepreneurs*.

13 Interviews and factory visits, governorate of Tunis and Nabeul, January–March 2005.

14 World Bank, *Stratégie de développement touristique*, and Fich Ratings, *L'industrie touristique tunisienne*; interviews, Paris, December 2004 and February 2005, and governorates of Tunis and Nabeul, January–March 2005.

15 J.-M. Miossec, 'Le tourisme en Tunisie: acteurs et enjeux', *Bulletin de l'Association des géographes français*, no. 1, March 1997, pp. 56–69; M. Sahli, 'Tourisme et développement en Tunisie', *Bulletin du groupe de recherche et d'étude en économie du développement*, no. 15, December 1990, pp. 37–50; R. Meddeb, *Le Tourisme en Tunisie*, paper given on 10 January 2003, Club Bochra El Khair. In general, on the perverse effects of tourist 'zones', see O. Dehoorne, 'Tourisme, travail et migration: interrelations et logique mobilitaires', *Revue européenne des migrations internationales*, vol. 18, no. 1, 2002, pp. 7–36.

16 Interviews and visit of complexes, Tunis and Hammamet, January–March 2005. M. Kerrou, 'Le *mezwâr*'.

17 World Bank, *Stratégie de développement touristique en Tunisie*.

18 J. Roitman and G. Roso, 'Guinée équatoriale: être "offshore" pour rester national', *Politique africaine*, no. 81, March 2001, pp. 121–42.

19 Interns are paid around 80–100 DT per month, but sometimes much less (sometimes only 20 DT per month); the length of the internship can be up to three or four years. The contracts known as 'internships for integration into professional life' do not cost the employer much, since the state finances these jobs and entrepreneurs add no more than a minimal sum. The personnel may be partly moonlighting, with their overtime not being carried forward, and part of their wages not being declared to the Inland Revenue and the CNSS. Interviews, Tunis, December 2003, January–March 2005.

20 P.-A. Casero and A. Varoudakis, *Growth, Private Investment and the Cost of Doing Business in Tunisia*; World Bank, *Tunisia. Economic Monitoring Update*.

21 DREE, *Le Textile-habillement dans les pays méditerranéens et d'Europe centrale: l'enjeu de la compétitivité* (Paris: Ministère de l'Économie, des Finances et de l'Industrie, 2002).

22   Interviews, Tunis, January–March 2005.
23   T. Coutrot, *L'Entreprise néo-libérale, nouvelle utopie capitaliste* (Paris: La Découverte, 1998), and 'Néolibération du travail et autogestion', *La Pensée*, no. 330, April–June 2002, pp. 5–20; L. Boltanski and E. Chiapello, *The New Spirit of Capitalism* (London; New York: Verso, 2005).
24   J.-P. Durand, *La Chaîne invisible. Travailler aujourd'hui: flux tendu et servitude volontaire* (Paris: Seuil, 2004), pp. 78–9.
25   This has been shown in Marx's *Capital* or the work of E. P. Thompson (especially 'Time, Work-Discipline, and Industrial Capitalism', available at http://www.chass.utoronto.ca/~salaff/Thompson.pdf), and Foucault's analyses of liberalism, especially 'The eye of power' in C. Gordon (ed.,), *Power/Knowledge* (Hemel Hempstead: Harvester, 1980). More recently, and on Malaysia, A. Ong, *Spirits of Resistance and Capitalist Discipline* (New York: State University of New York, 1987). One expatriate summed up the situation for me in the following terms: 'In Tunisia, it's the model of the workshop that operates: there are no executives, no transfer of power within the enterprise, there are merely "warders"', interview, governorate of Tunis, January 2005.
26   Interviews, governorates of Tunis, Nabeul and Monastir, December 1999, January and March 2005.
27   This title refers, of course, to J.-L. Rocca's work on China: 'La "mise au travail" capitaliste des Chinois', in J.-F. Bayart (ed.), *La Réinvention du capitalisme* (Paris: Karthala, 1994), pp. 47–72, and in particular J.-L. Rocca, *La Condition chinoise*. For these techniques in Tunisia, interviews, governorates of Tunis, Nabeul, Sfax and Monastir, 1997–2005, and H. Yousfi, E. Filipiak and H. Bougault, *Poulina, un management tunisien*.
28   Interviews, governorates of Tunis, Nabeul and Monastir, January and March 2005.
29   Several interviews, between 1999 and 2005.
30   All these expressions and quotations are taken from interviews, governorates of Tunis and Nabeul, January–March 2005.
31   E. P. Thompson, 'Time, Work-Discipline and Industrial Capitalism', p. 93 (my emphasis).
32   This reading draws on Aiwha Ong, *Spirits of Resistance*, which analyses the acts of possession of female workers in the Malaysian textile industry as attempts at conciliation between their 'traditional' world and the modernity of the enterprise.
33   Entrepreneurs often justify the rigour of checks and discipline by the fact that employees steal (or might do so). Various interviews. H. Yousfi, E. Filipak and H. Bougault state: 'The word "misdemeanour" is always cropping up, and our interlocutors mean by this word the set of fraudulent or clientelist practices that may tempt the Poulina employees if there are no checks. The initial premise is that the worker will always try to find some "trick" or other to steal, or to avoid doing his work' (H. Yousfi, E. Filipiak and H. Bougault, *Poulina, un management tunisien*, p. 39, n. 18).
34   Ben Ali, respectively in his speech of 3 February 1988, Carthage; 7 November 1988, Le Bardo; and 31 July 1988, Tunis.
35   E. Gentile, *Qu'est-ce que le fascisme?*; J.-C. Valente, *Estado Novo e Alegria no Trabalho. Uma Historia Politica da FNAT (1935–1958)* (Lisbon: Edições Colibri, 1999), and A. Ong, *Spirits of Resistance*.

36 The reader will recognize the argument put forward by Max Weber, for instance in *The Protestant Ethic and the Spirit of Capitalism*, ed. and trans. Stephen Kalberg (Chicago; London: Fitzroy, Dearborn, 2001). See also the preface by A. Maillard, 'E. P. Thompson. La quête d'une autre expérience des temps', to the French edn of E. P. Thompson's *Time, Work-Discipline and Industrial Capitalism* (*Temps, discipline de travail et capitalisme industriel*, trans. Isabelle Taudière (Paris: La Fabrique, 2004)).

37 As is stated by a senior executive of Poulina, quoted by H. Yousfi, E. Filipiak and H. Bougault, *Poulina. Un management tunisien*, p. 65.

38 www.poulina.gnet.tn, quoted in ibid., p. 31.

39 All these quotations are from ibid., pp. 55 and 65.

40 Interviews, governorates of Tunis and Nabeul, January–March 2005. This may be compared with Taiwan (G. Guiheux, *Les Grands Entrepreneurs privés à Taiwan. La Main visible de la prospérité* (Paris: Éditions du CNRS, 2002)) or with South China where paternalism is even more in evidence (C. K. Lee, 'Factory regimes of China capitalism: different cultural logics in labor control', in A. Ong and D. Nonini (eds), *Underground Empires: The Cultural Politics of Modern Chinese Transnationalism* (New York: Routledge, 1997), pp. 115–42, and *Gender and the South China Miracle: Two Worlds of Factory Women* (Berkeley, Los Angeles; London: University of California Press, 1998).

41 All these examples are taken from interviews, governorates of Tunis, Nabeul and Monastir, January–March 2005 and December 2000, December 2001 and December 2003. This system does not concern merely female textile workers, of course. Companies in the tourist sector can do likewise with their employees (mainly the male employees).

42 Interviews, governorates of Tunis and Nabeul, January and March 2005; I. Ruiz, 'Du rural à l'urbain. Travail féminin et mutations sociales dans une petite ville du Sahel tunisien', *Correspondances*, no. 25, IRMC, Tunis, and M. Peraldi (with H. Bettaïeb and C. Lainati), 'Affranchissement et protection: les petits mondes de la confection en Tunisie', paper presented at the Sousse conference, Tunisia, 2003.

43 I. Melliti, 'Observatoire de la condition de la femme en Tunisie', *Correspondances*, IRMC, no. 26, Tunis.

44 All these expressions and comments are taken from interviews, January–March 2005.

45 This ideology of the 'chief' in the entrepreneurial world imbues the whole of society, including many intellectuals, under the theme of the 'culture of allegiance' (see H. Redissi, *L'Exception islamique* (Paris: Seuil, 2004)) or the theme of the 'domination of a servile culture' (see R. Chenouffi, 'Sujet ou citoyen', *Revue tunisienne de droit*, 2000, Centre de publication universitaire, Tunis, pp. 205–550). For the image of the state as foreign to society, see J. Leca, 'Democratization in the Arab world'. For the culture of sedition and riot, see M. Camau, 'Politique dans le passé'.

46 S. Khiari, *Tunisie, le délitement de la cité*; D. Le Saout and M. Rolline (eds), *Émeutes et mouvements sociaux au Maghreb* (Paris: Karthala, 1999).

47 Interviews, governorate of Nabeul and Tunis (January–March 2005).

48 Speech given by Ben Ali, 1 May 1990, Carthage (my emphasis).

49 Interviews, Tunis, January 2005 and March 2005.

50 Interviews, governorate of Tunis and Nabeul, January–March 2005, and I. Ruiz, 'Du rural à l'urbain'. This practice is found in countries other than Tunisia, even if the modes of control differ. For China, see C.K. Lee, *Gender and the South China Miracle*, and A. Chan, *China's Workers under Assault: the Exploitation of Labor in a Globalizing Economy* (Armonk: M.E. Sharpe, 2001). For Malysia, Aiwha Ong shows how industrial discipline is relayed by family control: see A. Ong, *Spirits of Resistance*; apart from the practices described for Tunisia, parents are invited by the entreprise to come and see the work of their daughters and to become involved in the system of surveillance.

51 J. Maalej, quoted by P.-N. Denieul, *Les Entrepreneurs du développement*, p. 69; R. Zghal, 'Postface'; H. Yousfi, E. Filipiak and H. Bougault, *Poulina, un management tunisien*.

52 Interview, Tunis, March 2005.

53 Interviews, Paris, December 2004 and Tunis, January 2005.

54 The position of the customs official who can work in enterprise is extremely highly prized, since the work is very easy and the perks are significant. Corruption in this sector is commonplace, and widely denounced by entrepreneurs. Interviews, January–March 2005.

55 All these examples are taken from interviews, governorate of Tunis and Hammamet, January and March 2005.

56 This is certainly to be explained by the relatively unattractive nature of the whole region. However, one cannot but notice the regressive tendency that has been active over the past ten years or so: whereas Tunisia possesed almost half the stock of FDI in Central Maghreb until 1997, it now attracts only a quarter of the flows. In particular, official statistics never mention outgoings from the FDI; but these are in fact almost equal to the incomings (some 650 M DT per year for outgoings, as opposed to 700–750 M DT for incomings), which means that in net terms the FDIs are really very few and far between. Source: FEMISE 2005, *Le Partenariat euro-méditerranéen, 10 ans après Barcelone* (English version: S. Radwan and J.-L. Reiffers, *The Euro-Mediterranean Partnership*); *Les Investissements directs étrangers en Tunisie*, summary report of the Mission économique et financière de l'Ambassade de France à Tunis, December 2003; C.-A. Michalet, 'Investissements étrangers'.

57 This was the original result of studies carried out jointly by the AFD and the DREE of the French Ministry of the Economy; J.-R. Chaponnière and S. Perrin, *Le Textile-habillement tunisien*, and J.-R. Chaponnière, J.-P. Cling and M.-A. Marouani, *Les Conséquences pour les pays en développement de la suppression des quotas dans le textile-habillement: le cas de la Tunisie*, Document de travail, DIAL, Paris, DT/2004/16. For Italy, see C. Lainati, *Le Imprese straniere in Tunisia. Nascita e sviluppo dei circuiti produttivi: gli italiani nel tessile-abbigliamento*, research report, mimeograph, October–December 2001; M. Peraldi (with the collaboration of H. Bettaïeb and C. Lainati), 'Affranchissement et protection'. The cases of France and Italy are revelatory, since they represent the two nationalities that are most deeply implanted in Tunisia.

58 See the work of Marx and his followers, for example, I. Wallerstein, *The Capitalist World-Economy* (Cambridge: Cambridge University Press, 1979), and *The Modern World System II. Mercantilism and the Consolidation of the European World-Economy, 1600–1750* (New York: Academic Press, 1980), and

E. P. Thompson, *The Making of the English Working Class* (New York: Vintage Books, 1963). But see also Weber (the reinterpretation put forward by C. Colliot-Thélène also emphasizes this dimension), Polanyi or Braudel. For a contemporary political re-reading, see various contributions by J-F. Bayart (ed.), *La Réinvention du capitalisme.*

59　Interview, January 2005, governorate of Nabeul.

60　On the basis of highly specific cases, these situations were narrated to me by entrepreneurs, employees and unionists: fieldwork, January–March 2005. P.-A. Casero and A. Varoudakis show that administrative measures regulating the operation of the entreprise have been implemented, but that those relating to dismissals and the closure of businesses have turned out to be much more difficult to apply, see P.-A. Casero and A. Varoudakis, *Growth, Private Investment and the Cost of Doing Business in Tunisia.*

61　Interviews, January–March 2005; S. Khiari, *Tunisie, le délitement de la cité*, and communiqués from the LTDH, which is becoming increasingly involved in the topic, and of RAID/Attac-Tunisie, where it is a major preoccupation.

62　Employers who do not experience any serious conflicts in fact often accuse their counterparts of 'lacking tact', or not 'playing by the rules', or wanting to 'muscle in', or quite simply of 'being dishonest'. Interviews, January–March 2005.

63　This argument was inspired by the work of F. Mengin on the plasticity of relational forms between state and entrepreneurial rationalities in Greater China: F. Mengin, *Trajectoires chinoises. Taiwan, Hong Kong, Pékin* (Paris: Karthala, 1998), and 'A contingent outcome'.

64　Interviews, January–March 2005. See also World Bank, *Stratégie de coopération République tunisienne – Banque mondiale, 2004–2005*, December 2004, and World Bank Operation Evaluation Department, *Republic of Tunisia. Country Assistance Evaluation*; International Confederation of Free Trade Unions, *Tunisia, Annual Survey of Violations of Trade Unions Rights*, for the years 2002, 2003 and 2004; World Bank, *Stratégie de développement touristique en Tunisie*; Fich Ratings, *L'Industrie touristique tunisienne*; L. Boltanski and E. Chiapello, *The New Spirit of Capitalism*; T. Coutrot, *L'entreprise néolibérale*; J.-P. Durand, *La Chaîne invisible.*

65　M. Lallement, *Temps, travail et modes de vie* (Paris: PUF, 2003).

66　S. Khiari, *Tunisie, le délitement de la cité.*

67　Interviews, January–February 2005, and the World Bank, *Stratégie de développement touristique*, and Fich Ratings, *L'Industrie touristique tunisienne.*

68　M. Foucault, 'Pouvoirs et stratégies'. By way of comparison, it is interesting to compare Emilio Gentile's critique of the idea that fascism is an instrument of big capital (*Qu'est-ce que le fascisme?*).

69　On the importance of interiorization, see Étienne de la Boétie, *On Voluntary Servitude*, in *Freedom Over Servitude*, ed. David Lewis Schaefer (Westport, Connecticut; London: Greenwood Press, 1998), or Bentham as read by Foucault.

70　It is worth remembering the words of Foucault: 'Nothing is political, everything can be politicized, everything may become political. Politics is no more or less than that which is born with resistance to governmentality, the first uprising, the first confrontation', manuscript on governmentality, quoted by M. Senellart, 'Course context', in M. Foucault, *Security, Territory, Population* (pp. 369–401; p. 390).

71 É. de la Boétie comments are clear: 'Let us then say that although all things to which man trains and accustoms himself are natural to him, that alone is innate in him to which his simple and unaltered nature calls him. Thus the first reason for voluntary servitude is custom' (*On Voluntary Servitude*, p. 205).

72 Interviews, governorates of Tunis and Nabeul, January–March 2005.

73 Here we find the same situation as that described by E. P. Thompson for the beginning of the nineteenth century (E. P. Thompson, *Time, Work-Discipline and Industrial Capitalism*). The quotations are taken from interviews.

74 On the (renewed) permanence of the preoccupations with moralization or the maintaining of 'clean living', see M. Kerrou, 'Le *mezwâr*'; on the link between the moralization and islamization of society, see Y. Ben Achour, *Politique, religion et droit dans le monde arabe* (Tunis: Céres Production-CERP, 1992); F. Frégosi, 'Les rapports entre l'islam et l'État en Algérie et en Tunisie: de leur revalorisation à leur contestation', *Annuaire de l'Afrique du Nord*, vol. 34, 1995, pp. 103–23; J.-P. Bras, 'L'islam administré: illustrations tunisiennes', in M. Kerrou (ed.), *Public et privé en Islam*, pp. 227–46.

75 Interview, Tunis, March 2005.

76 Interviews, Monastir, January 2005 and Tunis, March 2005.

77 This analysis draws on N. Hatzfeld, 'La pause casse-croûte. Quand les chaînes s'arrêtent à Peugeot-Sochaux', *Terrain*, no. 39, September 2002, pp. 33–48, some of whose words I have used here.

78 J.-P. Durand, *La Chaîne invisible*, p. 373.

79 N. Flamand and M. Jeudy-Ballini, 'Le charme discret des entreprises', p. 9.

80 M. Foucault, 'Pouvoir et savoir', in *Dits et écrits, III, 1976–1979*, no. 219, p. 407.

81 E. de la Boétie, *On Voluntary Servitude*, p. 216.

82 J.-P. Durand, *La Chaîne invisible*, p. 311.

83 E. P. Thompson, *Time, Work-Discipline and Industrial Capitalism*, and A. Ong, *Spirits of Resistance*.

84 N. Flamand and M. Jeudy-Ballini, 'Le charme discret'; J.-P. Parry, 'Du bagne des champs aux riantes usines. Le travail dans une entreprise sidérurgique indienne', *Terrain*, no. 39, September 2002, pp. 121–40. On Cambodia, see R. Bottomley, 'Contested forests: an analysis of the Highlander response to logging, Rattanakiri Province, Northeast Cambodia', *Critical Asian Studies*, vol. 34, no. 4, 2002, pp. 587–606.

85 Interviews and I. Ruiz, 'Du rural à l'urbain'.

86 E. de la Boétie, *On Voluntary Servitude*.

87 M. Abensour and M. Gauchet, 'Présentation. Les leçons de la servitude et leur destin', in E. de la Boétie, *Le Discours de la servitude volontaire*, ed. Pierre Léonard (Paris: Payot, 1993), p. 21.

88 M. Foucault, 'Lives of Infamous Men', in *Essential Works of Foucault*, vol. 3, *Power*, pp. 157–75.

7 The Outline of the Tunisian Security Pact

1 Michel Foucault, *Security, Territory, Population*, in particular the lecture given on 25 January 1978.

2 M. Foucault, 'Méthodologie pour la connaissance du monde: comment se débarrasser du marxisme', interview with R. Yoshimoto in *Dits et écrits, III,*

1976–1979, no. 235, 25 April 1978. Here Foucault describes a 'sort of gigantic, irrepressible thirst that obliges people to turn to the state. We might speak of a desire for the state', p. 618. See also M. Foucault, 'Lecture of 7 March 1979', in *The Birth of Biopolitics: Lectures at the Collège de France, 1978–79*, ed. Michel Senellart, trans. Graham Burchell (New York: Palgrave Macmillan, 2008), pp. 185–207. This point was brought out by M. Senellart, 'Situation de cours', p. 398.

3 Jean Ganiage brings this point home: 'The Fundamental Pact, a real declaration of rights, proclaimed the *complete security of life* and of the property of the inhabitants of the Regency, equality before the law and before the tax system, freedom of religion, and a limitation on the length of military service', J. Ganiage, *Les Origines du Protectorat français en Tunisie*, p. 67 (my emphasis).

4 Ben Ali, interview for *Politique internationale*, no. 89, Autumn 2000, p. 390.

5 Following Pierre Rosanvallon, Ezzedine Bouslah speaks of a tutelary state, a kind of schoolteacher to the social realm – or, more simply, of a redistributive, clientelist and authoritarian state. He thus suggests that the number and significance of social policies, as well as an interest for 'the social' as such, did not for all that add up to a welfare state: E. Bouslah, 'Politiques de protection sociale et sociétés: quelques réflexions théorico-méthodologiques', *Revue tunisienne de droit 2000*, CPU, Tunis, 2001, pp. 195–204; see also D. Chamekh, *État et pauvreté en Tunisie*.

6 For countries in South East Asia, for instance, Aiwah Ong emphasizes how these material expectations are seen as much more important than political considerations: A. Ong, *Flexible Citizenship*.

7 All these descriptions come from interviews.

8 K. Polanyi, *The Great Transformation*.

9 This is the phrase used by Foucault, 'Michel Foucault: le sécurité et l'État', in *Dits et écrits, III, 1976–1978*, no. 213, pp. 383–8.

10 S. Khiari, *Tunisie, le délitement de la cité*, ch. IV; E. Murphy, *Economic and Political Change in Tunisia*; A. Bédoui, 'Limites, contraintes et perspectives de croissance et du développement en Tunisie', *Horizons maghrébins*, no. 46, 2002, pp. 61–76.

11 *La Réforme de l'assurance maladie*, Ministère des Affaires sociales, Tunis, November 2000; A. Bédoui, 'La question de l'État et de la gouvernance en Tunisie'; S. Khiari, *Tunisie, le délitement de la cité*; H. Fehri, 'Économie politique de la réforme'; D. Chamekh, *État et pauvreté en Tunisie*.

12 D. Chamekh, *État et pauvreté en Tunisie*; A. Guelmami, *La Politique sociale en Tunisie de 1881 à nos jours* (Paris: L'Harmattan, 1996); H. Fehri, 'Économie politique de la réforme'. In 2004, for example, a litre of diesel was still 30 euro centimes and unleaded was 50 euro centimes in spite of the leap in international prices. State subsidies thus rose to 580 MDT, i.e. 1.7 per cent of the GDP. Consumers paid only 20 per cent of the real price of petrol. Source: European cooperation agencies, and interviews, Tunis, January–March 2005.

13 E. Longuenesse, M. Catusse and B. Destremau, 'Le travail et la question sociale au Maghreb et au Moyen-Orient', *Revue des mondes musulmans et de la Méditerranée*, no. 105–106, put online on 1 March 2005 (http://remmm.revues.org/document2340.html).

14 The credit is awarded by specialized international institutions such as the ILO and the confederations of trade unions: annual reports of the International

Confederation of Free Trade Unions (see its *Tunisia, Annual Survey of Violations of Trade Unions Rights*). It is of course picked up by the Tunisian authorities, who are trying to create a label on the basis of the credit earned, and are thus attempting to save the industry. This good social image is relayed by donors (World bank, *Stratégie de coopération République tunisienne-Banque mondiale, 2005–2004*) and by industrialists (for example, the Gherzi report of 2004, *Mise à jour de l'étude textile-habillement*, for which good working conditions are one of the few strong points about the Tunisian textile industry).

15   J.P. Cling and G. Letilly, *Export Processing Zones.*

16   H. Fehri, 'Économie politique de la réforme'; A. Guelmami, *La Politique sociale en Tunisie*; D. Chamekh, *État et pauvreté en Tunisie*; D. Chakerli, 'Lutte contre la pauvreté et solidarité nationale'.

17   A. Bizberg, 'La transformation politique du Mexique: fin de l'ancien régime et apparition du nouveau?', *Critique internationale*, no. 19, April 2003, pp. 84–91; C. Messiant, 'La Fondation Eduardo dos Santos (FESA), À propos de "l'investissement" de la société civile par le pouvoir angolais', *Politique africaine*, no. 73, March 1999, pp. 82–102; B.-H. Chua, *Communitarian Ideology and Democracy in Singapore* (London; New York: Routledge, 1995); A. Carvalho and H. Mouro, *Serviço Social no Estado Novo* (Coimbra: Centhela, 1987), and F. Rosas, *O Estado Novo, 1926–1974*, Circula de Leitores, Historia de Portugal, vol. 7, Lisbon, 1994.

18   C. Lefort, 'Le nom d'Un', pp. 247–307, and P. Clastre, 'Liberté, malencontre, innommable', pp. 229–46, in E. de la Boétie, *Le Discours de la servitude volontaire.*

19   E. Balibar, especially in 'The Nation Form'.

20   E. Longuenesse, M. Catusse and B. Destremau, 'Le travail et la question sociale'.

21   M. Kraïem, *Pouvoir colonial et mouvement national. La Tunisie des années trente*, vol. 1 (Tunis: Alif, 1990); A. Mahjoubi, *Les Origines du mouvement national en Tunisie, 1904–1934* (Tunis: Publications de l'Université de Tunis, Faculté des Lettres, 1982); A. Larguèche, *Les Ombres de la ville. Pauvres, marginaux et minoritaires à Tunis (XVIII-XIXe siècles)* (Tunis: Centre de la publication universitaire, Faculté des lettres de Manouba, 1999); A. Guelmami, *La Politique sociale en Tunisie.*

22   E. Balibar, 'Insurrection et Constitution: la citoyenneté ambiguë', *Mouvements*, no. 1, November–December 1998, p. 113.

23   S. Chaabane, *Ben Ali et la voie pluraliste en Tunisie.*

24   Interviews, Tunis, July 2000, December 2001 and February 2005. See also P. Holmes-Eber, *Daughters of Tunis. Women, Family, and Networks in a Muslim City* (Boulder; Oxford: Westview Press, 2003), and *La Débrouille au féminin. Stratégie de débrouillardise des femmes de quartiers défavorisés en Tunisie* (Enda inter-arabe, 1997).

25   Interviews, Tunis, December 2003 and M. Ben Letaïef, 'Institutions, modes de gestion et devenir', and S. Ben Achour, 'Permis de bâtir'. Several buildings have been put up illegally on land without electricity, gas or water, and sold off cheaply.

26   L. Chouikha, 'Autoritarisme étatique'; A. Larif-Beatrix, *Édification étatique et environnement culturel*, and forthcoming work by Medhi Mabrouk on illegal emigration.

27 For the informal sector, see the abovementioned work by M. Bouchrara, P.-N. Denieul, J. Charmes. On fakes, see *La Contrefaçon et la piraterie* (Paris: Union des fabricants, 2003). See also the various contributions in M. Peraldi (ed.), *Cabas et containers*, in particular M. Peraldi et al., 'L'esprit de bazar. Mobilités transnationales maghrébines et société métropolitaines. Le comptoir démantelé', pp. 33–64; S. Bava and S. Mazella, 'Samir en voyage d'affaires'; S. Mazella, 'L'arrière-boutique du port de Marseille'; V. Manry, '"Être en affaire". Compétences relationnelles, éthique de la performance et ordre social au marché des Puces', pp. 279–314.

28 M. Peraldi (et al.), 'L'esprit de bazar . . . ', in M. Peraldi (ed.), *Cabas et containers*, pp. 329–61 (p. 360).

29 This is recognized by the Tunisian authorities. Ben Ali put it this way: 'If our determination to combat illegal immigration is obvious, we need, however, to acknowledge that our isolated efforts alone are not up to the task. [. . .] Human relations between the shore-dwelling peoples of the Mediterranean constitute a very ancient phenomenon, and a source of enrichment that cannot go in tandem with a closed-doors policy. *For our part, we do not have the sufficient means to stem this phenomenon in a lasting and effective way* [. . .]', *Le Figaro*, 3 December 2003 (my emphasis).

30 Interviews, Tunis, various field trips 1998–2005, and M. Peraldi et al., 'L'esprit de bazar', and S. Mazella, 'L'arrière-boutique du port de Marseille'.

31 In other configurations, see B. Hibou, *L'Afrique est-elle protectionniste?*; E. Grégoire and P. Labazée (eds), *Grands commerçants d'Afrique de l'Ouest: logiques et pratiques d'un groupe d'hommes d'affaires contemporains* (Paris: Karthala-ORSTOM, 1993); J. Roitman, 'Le pouvoir n'est pas souverain. Nouvelle autorités régulatrices et transformatrices de l'État dans le bassin du lac Tchad', in B. Hibou (ed.), *La Privatisation des États*, pp. 163–96 (English version: J. Roitman, 'Power is not sovereign. The pluralisation of economic regulatory authority in the Chad basin' in B. Hibou (ed.), *Privatising the State*, pp. 120–46), and 'The Garrison entrepôt', *Cahiers d'études africaines*, 38 (2–4), pp. 150–2, 1998, pp. 297–329.

32 M. Peraldi et al., 'L'esprit de bazar'.

33 This expression and the accompanying analysis come from a well-informed observer of the Tunisian scene, Paris, May 2005.

34 T. Mitchell shows that the state does not so much control the economic realm as designate it, thereby designating itself: see T. Mitchell, 'Nationalism, imperialism, economism: a comment on Habermas', *Public Culture*, vol. 10, no. 2, 1998, pp. 417–24.

35 On the myth of the marginality of the Tunisian state *vis-à-vis* society, see, for the historical background, M.-H. Chérif, *Pouvoir et société dans la Tunisie de H'usayn bin'Ali (1705–1740)*, vol. 2 (Tunis: Publications de l'Université de Tunis, 1986), and, for the contemporary period, J. Leca, 'Democratization in the Arab world' and M. Camau, 'Politique dans le passé'. On the other hand, the work of L. C. Brown, *The Tunisia of Ahmad Bey*, and L. Valensi, *Fellahs tunisiens*, have fed into this *imaginaire* for the beylical period – as also happens, these days, with works denouncing the authoritarianism of Ben Ali. The myth of the autonomy of entrepreneurs was first demonstrated with regard to the inhabitants of Sfax (by M. Bouchrara

and P.-N. Denieul), but it was then generalized to the whole Tunisian community.

36   K. Polanyi, *The Great Transformation.*

37   2004: 13.9 per cent unemployment; 14.3 per cent in 2003 and 14.9 per cent in 2002, 15.8 per cent in 1999. Source: INS. However, it is best to be cautious, as these figures are so frequently manipulated and negotiated.

38   The number of new entrants onto the labour market in the course of the Xth Plan is estimated at 80,000. Source: World Bank, *Stratégie de coopération.*

39   All this historical review is taken from A. Narâghi, *Les Contours de l'entente politique.*

40   For more institutional details on the 21.21 and the BTS, see the public documentation of the bank itself and the regular articles in the press on its benevolent actions, especially *La Presse*, 17 December 2003.

41   Interviews, Tunis, January 1999 and July 2000 and Paris, January 2001; for more detail, B. Hibou, 'Les marges de manoeuvre'. On the 'deviances' of the BTS and its non-respect of banking rules, see IMF, *Tunisia. Financial System Stability Assessment*, Washington, DC, 17 May 2002, p. 22.

42   *Le Nouvel Afrique Asie*, 115, April 1999, p. 50, which reports the official discourse (my emphasis).

43   According to the Tunisian Prime Minister, from September 1999, 17,000 projects have been financed since the operational opening of the BTS at the start of 1998; overall financing is at 25 MDT and has enabled the creation of 25,000 direct jobs. Quoted in *Marchés tropicaux et méditerranéens*, 8 October 1999.

44   A. Narâghi, *Les Contours de l'entente politique.*

45   S. Ben Achour, 'La liberté d'association entre droit et société', article for the LTDH, 10 December 2004.

46   More precisely, those under 29 represent 76 per cent of the unemployed. All these and the following figures come from the Banque mondiale, *Stratégie de coopération République tunisienne-Banque mondiale, 2005–2004*, on the basis of data suplied by the Tunisian ministries. These figures should be treated with caution since they are very unreliable, and the motives for manipulation and spin are sufficiently numerous to inspire a certain wariness.

47   TAP communiqué, January 2004.

48   For all these measures, see A. Bédoui, *Spécificité et limites*, and the press and the official websites.

49   The number of jobs on *chantiers de l'emploi* (employment schemes) has risen from 500,000 to 1,200,000 in 5 years. Source: MEF.

50   Interviews, Tunis, December 2003, January 2005 and Paris, September 2004. This figure is taken from the latest National Consultation of Young People.

51   Banque mondiale, *Stratégie de coopération République tunisienne-Banque mondiale, 2005–2004.*

52   Ibid., and P.-N. Denieul, *Les Entrepreneurs du développement.*

53   Survey of the Ministry of Culture, 2001: the results were published in 2003. Again, caution is required since the results of the survey were not made public – the press gave some inkling of them, but in a partial and unverifiable way.

54   On the 26.26, see S. Lombardo, *Un printemps tunisien*; *Les Cahiers de l'Orient*, no. 66, 2nd trimester 2002 (in particular the article by N. Hamza) and the Tunisian press for the official discourses and justifications, as well as for the

sums officially received and spent. For a critical analysis, see French and Belgian newspapers (*Le Monde, Libération, Croissance, La Croix, Le Soir, La Libre Belgique*). The best article is probably the one by C. Ayad, 'Le 26.26, c'est le président Ben Ali!', *Le Soir*, 2 August 1999. There are very few scholarly articles and books that go into detail about the mechanisms involved: it is worth mentioning K. Zamiti, 'Le Fonds de solidarité nationale: pour une approche sociologique du politique', *Annuaire de l'Afrique du Nord*, 35, 1996, pp. 705–12; B. Hibou, 'Les marges de manoeuvre'; D. Chamekh, *État et pauvreté en Tunisie*; D. Chakerli, 'Lutte contre la pauvreté'.

55 This was witnessed by one of my interviewees, Tunis, December 2003.

56 M. Ben Romdhane: personal interviews and quotation in C. Ayad, 'Le 26.26'.

57 Interviews and quotation in C. Simon, 'Les appétits d'un clan', *Le Monde*, 22 October 1999.

58 Confidential document drawn up by a consultancy for a cooperation agency.

59 S. Khiari and O. Lamloun, 'Le *Zaïm* et l'artisan'. The authors write: 'Solidarity funds, theoretically designed to deaden the shock of the suppression of the mechanisms of redistribution, in reality operate as instruments of clientelism and propaganda'. See also K. Zamiti, 'Le Fonds de solidarité nationale: pour une approche sociologique du politique'.

60 Interviews, Tunis, December 2001 and December 2002.

61 D. Chamekh, *État et pauvreté en Tunisie*.

62 S. Benedict, 'Tunisie, le mirage de l'État fort', *Esprit*, March 1997, pp. 27–42, and J.-P. Bras, 'Ben Ali et sa classe moyenne'.

63 It is edifying in this respect to read the Tunisian press: it is a question of 'eradicating zones of shadow' (FNS brochure), of moving out of the 'shadow' into the 'light' (*Le Renouveau*, 8 December 1996 – the religious terms are here repeated), of endeavouring to 'pick up the rejected' who were previously drawn to the Islamists (*Le Renouveau*, 11 December 1994), and of 'channelling contributions and gifts' (*Le Temps*, 22 March 1993).

64 B. Hibou, 'Tunisie: le coût d'un miracle'.

65 B. Hibou, 'From privatising the economy to privatising the state'.

66 M. Camau, 'D'une République à l'autre'.

67 M. Foucault, *Discipline and Punish*, pp. 184–95.

68 Exhibition of documents in the 'Archives nationales du 9 April' proving the existence of such mechanisms: January 2005.

69 *La Presse*, 18 October 1995, quoted by F. Siino, *Science et pouvoir*, p. 358 (my emphasis).

70 A. Mbembe, *La Naissance du maquis dans le Sud-Cameroun (1920–1960). Histoire des usages de la raison en colonie* (Paris: Karthala, 1996). C. Messiant, 'La Fondation Eduardo dos Santos'; F. Adelkah, *Being Modern in Iran*, trans. Jonathan Derrick (London: Hurst and Co., 1999).

71 C. Nicollet, *Censeurs et publicains. Économie et fiscalité dans la Rome antique* (Paris: Fayard, 2000); P. Veyne, *Bread and Circuses*; P. Brown, *Power and Persuasion*, in particular ch. II; D. Dessert, *Argent, pouvoir et société*; P. Minard, *La Fortune du colbertisme*.

72 J.-L. Rocca, *La Condition chinoise*.

73 E. de la Boétie, *On Voluntary Servitude*, p. 217.

74 M. Foucault, *'Society Must Be Defended': Lectures at the Collège de France 1975–76*, ed. Mauro Bertani and Alessandro Fontana. trans. David Macey (London: Allel Lane, 2003), p. 30.

75 A. Larguèche, *Les Ombres de la ville*, pp. 105–6.

76 On the history of the social policy, see A. Guelmami, *La Politique sociale en Tunisie*.

77 Interviews, Tunis, July 2000 and Paris, October 2000.

78 On the impossibility of making a 'charitable act' public, see the discussion in H. Arendt, *The Human Condition* (Chicago: University of Chicago Press, 1958), pp. 68–9.

79 *Le Temps*, 22 March 1993.

80 Speech of 1 June 1959 before the Constituent National Assembly, quoted by M. Camau, 'Leader and leadership in Tunisia', p. 174.

81 Evergetism is 'the ancient search for personal fame through well-publicized giving' (P. Brown, *Power and Persuasion*, p. 95). Paul Veyne also defines it in terms of civic patronage or sponsorship – 'the fact that collectivities expected the rich to contribute funds to public expenses, and their expectation was not in vain, since the rich contributed spontaneously and perfectly willingly' (P. Veyne, *Le Pain et le cirque*, p. 21). It is in this respect that evergetism is not the same as philanthropy: 'evergetic' sponsors and patrons contribute to public expenses and thus fulfill the duty of an entire class; it is not a gift as such, and the motivation of the evergetes is not charity, love of one's neighbour, or the respect of religious rules, but the recognition of a natural superiority and a subjective right to command.

82 Interview, Tunis, December 2003.

83 See *La Presse*, 18 November 1996, and *Tunisie Info* (ATCE), 20 December 1996, quoted by J.-P. Cassarino, *Tunisian New Entrepreneurs*, ch. IV, n. 46.

84 For an overview of these practices of resistance in the Maghreb and in the Arab world, see M. Bennani-Chraïbi and O. Fillieule (eds), *Résistances et protestations dans les sociétés musulmanes* (Paris: Presses de Sciences Po, 2003), which unfortunately does not deal with the case of Tunisia. For individual Tunisian examples, see J.-P. Bras, 'Les paradoxes de la parabole: images et identités au Maghreb', *Hermès*, no. 23–4, 1999, pp. 235–42; L. Chouikha, 'Autoritarisme étatique'; B. Hibou, 'Fiscal trajectories'.

85 B. Hibou, 'Tunisie: le coût d'un miracle économique'.

86 M. Foucault, 'Un système fini face à une demande infinie', in *Dits et écrits, IV*, no. 325, pp. 367–83.

87 A musical expression which a Tunisian intellectual 'presented' me with, during a rather desultory conversation.

88 I. Marzouki shows this convincingly on the basis of interviews with the ruling political elite and that of the opposition: I. Marzouki, 'Les alliances dangereuses'.

89 J.-P. Bras, 'Ben Ali et sa classe moyenne'. For a critique of the political use of the middle classes (in the 1970s – though the same is true today), see A. Zghal, 'Classes moyennes et développement au Maghreb', in A. Zghal et al., *Les Classes moyennes au Maghreb* (Paris: Éditions du CNRS, 1980).

90 Interviews, Tunis, March 2005.

91 E. Béji, *Désenchantement national*, pp. 51ff.

92   Interview, Paris, December 2003.
93   E. Gentile, *Qu'est-ce que le fascisme?*; B. Sordi, 'Le droit administratif sous le fascisme', paper presented at the seminar 'Administration et dictature', organized by M.O. Baruch and J.-Y. Dormagen, EHESS, 8 April 2005.
94   B.-H. Chua, *Communitarian Ideology*, especially pp. 9–39.
95   P. Brown, *Power and Persuasion*, p. 31.
96   Starting with a political history of the Jérid, Jocelyne Dakhlia brings this out in *L'Oubli de la cité*.
97   An analysis of these processes of negotiation, arrangements and arbitration as implemented by notables, as mediators of power, is given in A. Hénia, *Le Grîd*.
98   H. Bourguiba, speech of 19 June 1973 in Geneva, quoted by I. Marzouki, 'L'individu au mépris du citoyen', p. 171.
99   F. Siino, 'Une histoire de rechange, le nouveau temps bourguibien', in M. Camau and V. Geisser (eds), *Habib Bourguiba*, pp. 151–66.
100 In this construction of unity, the denunciation of past fluctuations but also of certain territories has been brought out in J.-P. Bras, 'L'autre Tunisie de Bourguiba: les ombres du Sud', in M. Camau and V. Geisser (eds), *Habib Bourguiba*, pp. 295–309.
101 F. Siino, 'Une histoire de rechange', p. 163.
102 These expressions are the ones used by M. Camau in 'Leader and leadership in Tunisia', in M. Camau and V. Geisser (eds), *Habib Bourguiba*, pp. 169–91 (p. 175).
103 Ben Ali, speech of 21 March 1989, Carthage.
104 S. Ben Achour, 'Les municipales de 2005', p. 4.
105 Ibid.; I. Marzouki, 'Alliances dangereuses'; M. Camau and V. Geisser, *Le Syndrome autoritaire*, ch. VI; J.-P. Bras, 'Élections et représentations au Maghreb', *Monde arabe, Maghreb-Macherk*, no. 168, April–June 2000, pp. 3–13.
106 Ben Ali, speech of 31 March 1989, Tunis.
107 W. Benjamin, 'Critique of violence'; the quotation from E. Unger, *Politik und Metaphysik*, is on p. 143.
108 E. Balibar, 'Vers une citoyenneté imparfaite', p. 97.
109 W. Benjamin, 'Critique of violence', p. 143.
110 Based on E. Balibar's reading in 'Le Hobbes de Schmitt, le Schmitt de Hobbes'.
111 S. Chaabane, *Ben Ali*, p. 141.
112 H. Bourguiba, speech of 3 December 1958, Ben Guardane, quoted by I. Marzouki, 'L'individu au mépris du citoyen'.
113 I. Marzouki, ibid.; R. Chennoufi, 'Sujet ou citoyen'.
114 E. Balibar, 'Vers une citoyenneté imparfaite'. In particular, he notes (p. 100) that citizenship is also the ability to 'fight against uniform, and uniformizing, majority "hegemonies"'.
115 M. Kerrou (ed.), *Public et privé en islam*.
116 All these expressions are taken from interviews, Tunis, March 2005.
117 C.J. Halperin, *Russia and the Golden Horde. The Mongol Impact on Russian History* (London: Tauris, 1985), p. 5, quoted by P. Brown, *Power and Persuasion*, ch. IV.
118 E. Balibar, 'Le Hobbes de Schmitt', where Schmitt's words are read as a self-justification of his position under Nazism. It is this very dimension that is interesting in the case of Tunisia: it suggests how much silence is neither

resistance, nor support, nor servitude, nor voluntary acceptance; but in the final analysis, in spite of everything, it *is* participation.
119   M. Foucault, *Discipline and Punish*, p. 308.

Part IV   Discipline and Reform

1   See E. Gentile, *Qu'est-ce que le fascisme?*, whose views I have here summarized.
2   This questioning in terms of 'problematization' is drawn from the work of Michel Foucault, in particular his *History of Sexuality*, trans. Robert Hurley, vol. 2, *The Use of Pleasure* (London: Viking, 1986), especially ch. I, introduction (pp. 14–24). See also M. Foucault, 'Polémique, politique et problématisations' in *Dits et écrits, IV, 1980–1988* (Paris: Gallimard, 1994), pp. 591–8.
3   Anyone who has read Max Weber's various political essays cannot fail to be astonished at the permanence of these debates, over a century after his brilliant analysis of the plasticity of social forms, on the importance of contingency, and on the exceptional nature of the experience of Enlightenment Europe, etc. See M. Weber, *Political Writings*.
4   S. Waltz emphasizes the incompatibility of liberal reforms and authoritarianism, the 'exit option' on the part of economic actors being the only possible solution for getting round the latter: see S. Waltz, 'Clientelism and reform in Ben Ali's Tunisia'. On the other hand, E. Bellin maintains that 'labour' and 'capital' favour authoritarianism, see E. Bellin, 'Tunisian industrialists and the state', and *Stalled Democracy*. C. M. Henry shows that economic opening and international pressure ought to oblige those in power to extend their basis of legitimacy to nourish a new social contract which, sooner or latter, should entail a democratization or at least an opening up of the regime. Likewise L. Anderson, 'Politics, pacts, liberalism and democracy' and 'The prospects for democracy in the Arab world', *Middle Eastern Lectures*, no. 1, 1995, pp. 59–71, sees in the National Pact a step –a fragile one, admittedly – towards pluralism. Conversely, E. Murphy, *Economic and Political Change in Tunisia*, shows that the economic reforms have tended to reinforce the single party and authoritarianism.
5   B. Moore, Jr, *Social Origins of Dictatorship and Democracy. Lord and Peasant in the Making of the Modern World* (Boston: Beacon Press, 1993); A. Krichen, 'La fracture de l'intelligentsia. Problèmes de la langue et de la culture nationales', in M. Camau (ed.), *Tunisie au present*, pp. 297–341; M. Camau, 'Tunisie au présent', and 'Le Maghreb'; C. Geertz, *The Interpretation of Cultures* (New York: Basic Books, 1973); A. Hermassi, 'Socio-economic change and political implications: the Maghreb' in G. Salamé (ed.), *Democracy without Democrats?*, pp. 227–42; , and C.H. Moore, *Politics in North Africa* (Boston: Little, Brown and Co., 1970), p. 108.
6   During my interviews, this was a judgement often expressed to me, in this form or in other, less explicit, ways, but all based on the same sense of certainty.
7   J. Leca, 'Democratization in the Arab world', p. 53. Jean Leca carries on: 'Such is the case when a concept (however vague and sometimes *because* it is vague) is taken for granted and is considered as expressing a conventional wisdom which it would be indecent to question'.

8 Reformism: The 'Correct Training'

1 To convince oneself of this, one need merely read the speeches of President Ben Ali, or simply the press. The National Pact refers explicitly to the reformers: 'The National Pact has lately appealed to our thinkers to follow the examples of the Renaissance and the Reformation that had managed to create a solid platform on which to base progress and social ascent and to build a civilized and advanced society, and to make their voices heard in support of the promotion of women', speech of 15 August 1989.

2 On the RCD site, the page devoted to the President bears the title, 'Zine El Abidine Ben Ali, reforming President of an innovative party'.

3 This analysis is based on interviews and informal discussions during my nine years of research, but also on the analysis of official speeches, especially those delivered by Ben Ali. For quotations, see B. Hibou, *Surveiller et réformer. Économie politique de la servitude volontaire en Tunisie*, habilitation thesis, IEP, Paris, 7 November 2005, ch. V.

4 Khayr ed-Din, a Mamelouk of Circassian origin, is considered as the great precolonial reformer. As a statesman, he was in particular president of the Financial Commission and then Prime Minister from 1873 to 1877. He also wrote essays, especially *Aqwam-al-masalik fi ma'rifat ahwal-al-mamalik*, published in 1867 – the French translation followed the next year, under the title *Essai sur les réformes nécessaires aux États musulmans* (*Essay on the Reforms Necessary for the Muslim States*), which had considerable influence during his lifetime, and up to the present day.

5 M. Camau, 'Le Maghreb'; S. Benedict, 'Tunisie, le mirage de l'État fort'.

6 M. Camau and V. Geisser, *Le Syndrome autoritaire*; I. Marzouki, 'L'individu au mépris du citoyen', *Bulletin de l'AISLF*, no. 21, 2005, pp. 169–82 (quotation p. 175). As with many other themes, this is also frequently found in Bourguiba, who stated: 'Only the strength of the State can guarantee the security and well-being of individuals', 1 June 1959, National Constituent Assembly, quoted in M. Camau, 'Leader and leadership in Tunisia'.

7 S. Mardin, *The Genesis of Young Ottoman Thought. A Study in the Modernization of Turkish Political Ideas* (Syracuse, New York: Syracuse University Press, 2000); B. Tlili, *Les Rapports culturels et idéologiques entre l'Orient et l'Occident en Tunisie au XXe siècle (1830–1880)* (Tunis: Publications de l'Université de Tunis, 1974); C. Kurzman, 'Introduction: the modernist Islamic movement', in C. Kurzman (ed.), *Modernist Islam, 1840–1940. A Sourcebook* (Oxford: Oxford University Press, 2002), pp. 3–27.

8 M. El Ayadi, 'Du fondamentalisme de l'État et de la Nasiha sultanienne: à propos d'un certain réformisme makhzénien', *Hespéris-Tamuda*, vol. 39, fasc. 2, 2001, pp. 85–107.

9 Khayr ed-Din, *Essai sur les réformes*; M. Morsy, 'Présentation de l'*Essai sur les réformes*'; A. Abdesselem, *Les Historiens tunisiens des XVII, XVIII et XIXe siècles. Essai d'histoire culturelle* (Paris: Librairie C. Klincksieck, 1973); M. Talbi and G. Jarczyk, *Penseur libre en Islam*. On the post-colonial period, A. Hermassi, 'Le mouvement islamiste en Tunisie et en Algérie'.

10   National Pact of 1988: 'The Tunisian state must strengthen this rational orientation which proceeds from *Ijtihad* and endeavour to ensure that *Ijtihad* and rationality have a clear impact on education, religious institutions, and means of information. [. . .] The Renaissance and Reformation movement in Tunisia is not limited to *Ijtihad* on the level of religion and has not merely advocated modernity, but has also opposed absolute power, and demanded a power that is governed by law'.

11   Y. Ben Achour, *Politique, religion et droit dans le monde arabe* (Tunis: Cérès-production, 1992), speaks of a 'burdensome bigotry'; F. Frégosi, 'Les rapports entre l'islam et l'État en Algérie et en Tunisie: de leur revalorisation à leur contestation', *Annuaire de l'Afrique du Nord*, vol. 34, 1995, pp. 103–23, writes that 'the 7 November marked a clear break in the symbolic order by consecrating the advent of a regime that would pay more attention to traditional religious values', p. 114; J.-P. Bras, 'L'Islam administré: illustrations tunisiennes'.

12   Thâalbi, a Muslim reformer and sheikh, was one of the most active political leaders under colonization: he was the co-author of *La Tunisie-martyre* (*Tunisia Martyred*), which provided Destour with its programme. He is one of the fathers of Tunisian nationalism. He opposed Bourguiba and, when the split happened, remained faithful to the old Destour and was for that very reason labelled a 'traditionalist'.

13   On the way history persists in social relations, see J.-F. Bayart, *Global Subjects*, especially ch. II, 'The state: a product of globalization'.

14   Thus the blessing of Khayr ed-Din and his *Essai sur les réformes* is forever being invoked, whereas Ibn Dhiaf, who plays the part of an intellectual more than a statesman, is much less frequently quoted, as are his *Chronicles*.

15   See the President's speeches and the exegetical texts of the organic intellectuals of the central power.

16   *La Presse*, 9 December 1996.

17   *Le Renouveau*, 11 December 1994.

18   *La Presse*, 12 December 1994.

19   R. Barthes, *Writing Degree Zero*, pp. 32–3.

20   C. Kurzman, 'Introduction: the modernist Islamic movement'.

21   Ibid., and S. Mardin, *The Genesis of Young Ottoman Thought*.

22   B. Tlili, *Les Rapports culturels et idéologiques entre l'Orient et l'Occident*.

23   I investigated this situation in B. Hibou, 'Tunisie: d'un réformisme à l'autre', in J.-F. Bayart, R. Bertrand, T. Gordadze, B. Hibou and F. Mengin, *Legs colonial et gouvernance contemporaine*, vol. 1 (Paris: FASOPO, December 2005), pp. 209–63 on the FASOPO website: www.fasopo.org/publications.htm.

24   For Morocco, see A. Kaddouri, 'Les réformes au Maroc: usages politiques, usages sociaux', *Hespéris-Tamuda*, vol. 39, fasc. 2, 2001, pp. 39–45. J. Baida, 'La pensée réformiste au Maroc à la veille du Protectorat', *Hespéris-Tamuda*, vol. 39, fasc. 2, 2001, pp. 49–69, details at least five reform projects, written and assembled on the eve of the Protectorate. For the Ottoman Empire, S. Mardin, *The Genesis of Young Ottoman Thought*, shows very precisely, via contrasted portraits, how diversified and plural reformism was, and how significant the divisions between the groups were. On the game of hide-and-seek between modernism and archaism, see F. Georgeon, *Abdülhamid II* (Paris: Fayard, 2004). For Tunisia, see L. C. Brown, *The Tunisia of Ahmad*

Bey. Here, the author shows that a display of modernity conceals the maintenance of traditional practices, especially those revealed by the place of the Palace. For the economic dimension of reformism, M.-L. Gharbi, *Impérialisme et réformisme au Maghreb.*

25 Under the Protectorate, Tahar Haddad was one of the leaders of the Destour, and close to Thâalbi; he got himself noticed thanks to his favourable attitude towards the emancipation of women and the proletariat. During the same period, Mohamed Ali was particularly aware of social questions. Bin Dhiaf, a fervent defender of administrative and state reforms, wrote the chronicle *Ithaf ahl az-zaman bi ahbar muluk Tunus wa 'ahd al 'aman* (*Chronicle of the Kings of Tunis and the Fundamental Pact*). He was one of the main authors of the 1861 Constitution. A sheikh and a poet, Mahmoud Qabadu can be considered as one of the main Tunisian thinkers of reformism: he was an associate of Ahmed Bey, and in 1844 he wrote an essay (*Diwan*) that theorized the reforms undertaken by the bey. He was an educationalist, a professor at the École Polytechnique of the Bardo, then mufti and professor at the great mosque at Zitouna; he suggested that Europeans be copied in two institutions, translation and education. The reformers who succeeded him developed in greater detail their thoughts on the power of the state and its organization.

26 E. Balibar, 'The nation form: history and ideology' in E. Balibar and Immanuel Wallerstein, *Race. Nation. Class. Ambiguous Identities*, trans. Chris Turner (New York; London: Verso, 1991), pp. 86–106.

27 Practically all contemporary authors consider this – implicitly – as an unquestionable given. For an explicit formulation, see N. Sraïeb, 'Élite et société: l'invention de la Tunisie'; M.-L. Gharbi, *Impérialisme et réformisme au Mahgreb*; R. Ben Achour, 'L'État de droit en Tunisie', writes very accurately that the legitimate state and constitutionalism have constituted 'a constant of the dominant political culture in Tunisia' since the nineteenth century, p. 247. Foreign scholars also promulgate this myth: see for example L. Anderson, *The State and Social Transformation*, or M. Morsy, 'Présentation de l'*Essai sur les réformes'*.

28 Even if her analysis is sometimes excessively culturalist, A. Larif-Beatrix provides an analysis that is more mediated and more sensitive to the break in Bourguiba's nation-state, sensitive in particular to the current social foundations of practices that might be described by some as reformist. See A. Larif-Beatrix, *Édification étatique et environnement culturel.* An author such as Michel Camau does not fail to emphasize the methodological problems posed by such a problematization in terms of continuities. See for example M. Camau, 'Politique dans le passé'. The fact remains that he sometimes fall prey to various errors, as the following quotation suggests.

29 E. Balibar, 'The nation form', p. 86.

30 M. Camau and V. Geisser, *Le Syndrome autoritaire*, p. 20.

31 B. Hibou, 'Tunisie: d'un réformisme à l'autre'.

32 Mustapha Khaznadar, Prime Minister of the bey from 1837 to 1873, was also the father-in-law of Khayr ed-Din: he gradually came to be considered as the figure *par excellence* of the ancien régime and the antireformist trend, even though he supported the Fundamental Pact. This bad reputation is linked to his role in the financial degradation of the beylicate, which ended up bankrupt and,

in the end, allowed French colonization to take place, partly as a result of this corruption.

33   E. Balibar, 'The nation form', p. 96.

34   J.-F. Bayart, *The Illusion of Cultural Identity*, title of ch. 3 and p. 145.

35   P. Bourdieu, *Distinction: A Social Critique of the Judgment of Taste*, trans. Richard Nice (London: Routledge and Kegan Paul, 1984).

36   All the problematization in terms of subjection comes from the work of Michel Foucault. For the quotation and the specific problematization of globalization, see J.-F. Bayart, *Global Subjects*.

37   N. Bhiri, a member of the Islamist movement, signed the Pact, officially in his own name, but all the actors in Tunisian political life had interpreted it and understood it as an expression of Nahdha's tacit commitment.

38   A. Zghal, 'Le retour du sacré' and 'The new strategy of the movement of the Islamic way'; M. Talbi, *Plaidoyer pour un islam moderne* (Tunis: Cérès, 1998). See also G. Krämer, 'L'intégration des intégristes: une étude comparative de l'Égypte, la Jordanie et la Tunisie', in G. Salamé (ed.), *Démocratie sans démocrates*, pp. 277–312 (English version: 'The integration of the integrists. A comparative study of Egypt, Jordan and Tunisia' in G. Salamé (ed.), *Democracy without Democrats?*, pp. 200–26); M. Camau and V. Geisser, *Le Syndrome autoritaire*.

39   See the interviews of Ghannouchi, for example: Ghannouchi, 'Déclarer l'échec de l'islamisme politique relève de la précipitation', pp. 255–69, in O. Lamloum and B. Ravenel (eds), *La Tunisie de Ben Ali*. For a sociological analysis of the positions defended by the Tunisian islamists, see E. Hermassi, 'La société tunisienne au miroir islamiste', and 'The Islamist movement and November 7'.

40   See for example the manifesto of 20 March 2001 (written by M. Charfi and H. Redissi): the presence of M. Charfi comes as no surprise, since he is the man who drew up the National Pact of 1988, and was minister under Ben Ali from 1987 to 1994. However, it is interesting to note that figures of a quite different opposition, such as Ben Jaafr or Marzouki (see for example M. Marzouki, *Le Mal arabe*) share this vision. See also M. Camau, 'Le discours politique de légitimité des élites tunisiennes'.

41   Intervention at the conference *Les Processus de démocratisation au Maghreb*, Faculty of legal and political sciences, Tunis, 12 March 2005.

42   'The RCD is the party of action in the field', speech by President Ben Ali delivered at the RCD Congress on 30 July 1993.

43   Declaration of Tunis, June 2003. My emphasis.

44   On the contemporary situation, S. Khiari, *Tunisie, le délitement de la cité*; M. Camau and V. Geisser, *Le Syndrome autoritaire*. On the colonial period, M. Kraïem, *Pouvoir colonial et mouvement national. La Tunisie des années trente* (Tunis: Alif, 1990).

45   P. Brown, *Power and Persuasion*, p. 41.

46   P. Bourdieu, *Distinction*, pp. 397–465.

47   See, among many others, for instance K. Dalacoura, who emphasizes the liberal and democratic potential of Tunisia on the basis of this reformist tradition (K. Dalacoura, *Islam, Liberalism, and Human Rights* (London; New York: Tauris, 1998)); N. Grimaud, *La Tunisie à la recherche de sa sécurité*

(Paris: PUF, 1995); including M. Morsy, 'Présentation de l'*Essai sur les réformes*'. The volunteers are generally showered with praise, in terms which reproduce the discourse on the benefits of reformism, voluntarism and openness to the West. Interviews, Tunis, 1997/2005; for the first years of independence, F. Decorsière and M. Lelong, 'L'expression tunisienne', *Esprit*, no. 7–8, July–August 1970, pp. 131–7.

48 O. Lamloun, *La Politique étrangère de la France*.

49 C. A. Bayly develops this argument with regard to liberalism in the India of the nineteenth century. See C.-A. Bayly, 'Liberalism and "moral economy" in nineteenth-century South and Southeast Asia', paper presented at the Franco-British conference *Économies morales et formation de l'État dans le monde extra-européen*, CERI, Paris; FASOPO, Paris and Trinity College, Cambridge, 27 May 2005.

50 M. Camau and V. Geisser, *Le Syndrome autoritaire* mention this in connection with the process of the autonomization of the reform of civil society. Conversely, S. Khiari implicitly rejects this gap and speaks in terms of elitism among the middle classes: see S. Khiari, 'De Wassila à Leïla, premières dames et pouvoir en Tunisie', *Politique africaine*, no. 95, October 2004, pp. 55–70.

51 A. Zghal, 'Le concept de société civile et la transition vers le multipartisme', in M. Camau (ed.), *Changements politiques au Maghreb, Annuaire de l'Afrique du Nord*, vol. 18 (CNRS, Paris, 1989), pp. 207–28, and 'Le concept de société civile et la crise du paradigme développementaliste', *Revue tunisienne de sciences sociales*, no. 115, 1993, pp. 67–94.

52 The main interest of the book by K.-J. Perkins, *A History of Modern Tunisia* (Cambridge: Cambridge University Press, 2004) is that he includes within his analysis literature, cinema and artistic creation in general. As regards our present concerns, see in particular pp. 197–201. See also Abdelaziz Belkhodia, *Le Retour de l'éléphant* (Tunis: Appolonia, 2004), one of the popular successes of recent years, which suggests the significance of beliefs in progress, rationalization, positivism and modernization, not to mention (of course) the importance of the myth of Hannibal and Carthage.

53 See M. Foucault, *History of Sexuality*, vol. 2, and J.-F. Bayart, *Global Subjects*. See also E. Balibar, who links Foucault's ideas with those of Lacan, Bataille and Althusser in E. Balibar, *Droit de cité* (Paris: PUF, 1997), and 'Insurrection et Constitution: la citoyenneté ambiguë', *Mouvements*, no. 1, November–December 1998, pp. 109–19.

54 See M. Tozy, 'Éléments pour une lecture de sociologie historique de la gouvernance au Maghreb', and in particular *Monarchie et islam politique*, which presents a very subtle analysis of the exercise of power on the basis of Muslim thinkers but also of Étienne de la Boétie.

55 M. Weber, 'Parliament and government in Germany', p. 153.

56 See J.-F. Bayart, *Global Subjects*, pp. 126–30.

57 S. Khiari, 'Les balbutiements du mouvement altermondialiste au Maghreb', *Annuaire de l'Afrique du Nord*, vol. 91, 2003, pp. 113–25.

58 Interviews, Tunis and Paris. This appears clearly from a reading of the documents published by the RAID/Attac Tunisie, *Raid-Niouz* (illegal bulletin of the RAID), for example, on privatizations, on the role of the trade union in support for strikes, etc.

59   R. Zghal, 'Nouvelles orientations', p. 7.

60   S. Khiari, *Tunisie, le délitement de la cité*, ch. III, 'Désengagement de l'État et désocialisation'.

61   Interviews, Tunis, Monastir, December 2003, January–March 2005 and Paris, August 2005. The term 'dignity' is the one used by the strikers themselves.

62   S. Ben Achour, 'L'administration et son droit, quelles mutations?'; A. Bédoui, 'La question de l'État et la gouvernance en Tunisie'; D. Chamekh, *État et pauvreté en Tunisie*; H. Fehri, 'Économie politique de la réforme', and S. Khiari, 'Les balbutiements du mouvement altermondialiste'.

63   Quoted by H. Yousfi, E. Filipiak and H. Bougault, *Poulina, un management tunisien*, p. 60.

64   E. Balibar, 'Insurrection et Constitution'.

65   In the sense given this word by C. Colliot-Thélène, *Études wébériennes* ('Thus, the vacancy of meaning [. . .] is one of the senses of the disenchantment of the world according to Weber', p. 7).

66   J.-F. Bayart, *The Illusion of Cultural Identity* and *Global Subjects*.

67   J.-F. Bayart, *The State in Africa*, and 'Africa in the world: a history of extraversion', *African Affairs*, vol. 99, no. 395, April 2000, pp. 217–67.

68   M. Morsy, 'Présentation', p. 46.

69   M. H. Chérif, *Pouvoir et société*; L. C. Brown, *The Tunisia of Ahmad Bey*.

70   This is the thesis held by certain reformers and its still has its supporters today, for example in the book by C. M. Henry, *The Mediterranean Debt Crescent* and in C. M. Henry and R. Springborg, *Globalization*.

71   See B. Tlili, *Les Rapports culturels et idéologiques*; T. Bachrouch, 'Le réformisme tunisien. Essai d'interprétation critique', *Cahiers de Tunisie*, no. 127–128, 1984, pp. 97–118; O. Moreau, 'La réforme de l'État dans le monde islamo-méditerranéen vu du Maghreb. XIX-XXe siècles', *Correspondance*, no. 66, May–June 2001, pp. 3–11.

72   E. Balibar, *Nous, citoyens d'Europe? Les Frontières, l'État, le peuple* (Paris: La Découverte, 2001) emphasizes that 'it is an antagonistic relation to the state that is experienced in an indirect way, and projected as a relation to an Other', p. 235.

73   See M. Camau and V. Geisser, *Le Syndrome autoritaire*, especially pp. 18–20 and pp. 95–112.

74   M. Camau, 'Leader et leadership en Tunisie', p. 175 (author's emphasis).

75   'These emblems that are *cultural identity*, *specificity*, and *national entity* have undergone a transformation that no longer makes it possible to equate them with forces of resistance', as Hélé Béji puts it in *Désenchantement national*, p. 16 (author's emphasis).

76   Interviews, Paris, January 2005 and Tunis, January–March 2005.

77   The abovementioned Declaration of Tunis of 17 June 2003 thus devotes two out of its twelve points to this question. After mentioning the specificity of Tunisian identity, the signataries ask for '4. respect for the identity of the people and its Arab-Muslim values, a guarantee of freedom of belief for all, and the political neutralisation of places of worship' and '5. the defence of the independence of the country and the sovereignty of the national decision'.

78   S. Chaabane, *Ben Ali et la voie pluraliste en Tunisie* thus states that secular opponents are linked by ideology to westerners and that Islamist opponents are linked to the Islamic internationale.

79 Interviews, Tunis, December 2001 and December 2003 and Paris, August 2004.
80 H. Béji, *Désenchantement national*, in particular chapters 9 and 10.
81 M. Brondino, 'Bourguiba, *policy maker* entre mondialisation et tunisianité: une approche systémique et interculturelle', in M. Camau and V. Geisser (eds), *Habib Bourguiba*, pp. 463–73.
82 Interview, Paris, August 2004.
83 J.-F. Bayart develops this argument in connection with colonization in *The Illusion of Cultural Identity*, pp. 163–4. For Tunisia, see I. Marzouki, 'Un compromis atypique'.
84 E. Balibar, 'The nation form'. The author gives the name of 'fictive ethnicity to the community instituted by the nation-state. This is an intentionally complex expression in which the term fiction [. . .] should not be taken in the sense of a pure and simple illusion without historical effects, but must, on the contrary, be understand by analogy with the *persona ficta* of the juridical tradition in the sense of an institutional effect, a "fabrication"' (p. 96).
85 S. Ben Achour, 'Aux sources du droit moderne tunisien': what Sana Ben Achour says here in legal and technical terms is here read in political terms.
86 H. Béji, *Désenchantement national*.
87 E. Balibar, 'Es gibt keinen Staat in Europa', in E. Balibar, *Nous, citoyens d'Europe*, pp. 221–41.
88 'Firstism' is the position that highlights the fact that Tunisia always comes first in everything: the first country in the Arab world to have a Constitution, the first to have a popular movement for the independence of the country, the first to sign an agreement on association with the European Union, the first to have created an organization for the defence of human rights, the first to have developed the Internet, etc.
89 On this well-worn rhetoric, see for example N. Grimaud, *La Tunisie*.
90 Médiamétrie study, December 2004. See also J. Garçon, 'La télé française en déclin au Maghreb', *Libération*, 20 June 2005.
91 All these examples are taken from interviews, Tunis, April 1998, January 1999, December 2001 and December 2002 and Paris, January 2005.
92 In other words, a position of passive partnership, interested solely in the sharing of financial benefits, not in the strategy of the enterprise. Interviews, Tunis, December 2003 and February 2005.
93 Decree 94–492 modified by decree 97–503 of 14 March 1997 published in the JORT, no. 24, 25 March 1997. The list of sectors is provided on the government's website.
94 A detailed analysis of these measures can be found in N. Baccouche, 'Les implications de l'accord d'association'.
95 Interviews, Tunis, April 1998 and January 1999.
96 Interviews, Tunis and Sfax, April 1998 and January 1999.
97 Interviews, Tunis, May 1997 and April 1998. For more detail, B. Hibou and L. Martinez, 'Le Partenariat euro-maghrébin: un mariage blanc?'
98 Interviews, Tunis, January 1999, July 2000 and December 2002; Sfax, April 1998 and December 2002.
99 This appears even more clearly if we compare the path taken by Tunisia with other situations, in Asia, for example: on Taiwan and China, F. Mengin, 'A contingent outcome', and *Trajectoires chinoises*; on Korea, A.-H. Amsden, *Asia's Next Giant: South Korea and Late Industrialization* (Oxford: Oxford University

Press, 1989); M. Lanzarotti, *La Corée du Sud: une sortie du sous-développement* (Paris: PUF, 1992).

100 Étienne Balibar underscores the difference between 'invisible' nationalisms, those of the dominant countries who express their domination, and 'too visible' nationalisms, those of the dominated countries who express a resistance: see E. Balibar, 'Internationalisme et barbarie'.

101 All the following examples are drawn from the national press and from interviews, Tunis, 1998–2003 and Paris, 2003–4.

102 Over 90 per cent of the operations of privatization have been carried out to the benefit of Tunisians. See my discussion of the political significance of privatizations in chapter 9.

103 Interviews, Tunis, December 2003.

104 Interviews, Tunis, December 2002.

105 All these expressions are taken from interviews.

106 E. Balibar, 'Internationalistes ou barbarie', p. 28.

107 This was clearly stated to me in interviews, Tunis, December 2001 and December 2002.

108 For a comparative overall analysis of these processes of appropriation, see J.-F. Bayart, *Global Subjects*. On the difference in perception between external gaze and internal perception, and an implicit and highly interesting critique of hybridity, see S. Abrevaya Stein, 'The permeable boundaries of Ottoman Jewry': she shows how the Ladino Jews of the Ottoman Empire did not experience their identity as plural; Jewishness was understood as an articulation of several allegiences, simultaneously to the Ottoman Empire, to Europe, to other millets, to modernity, etc.

109 See J. Clancy-Smith, *Rebel and Saint. Muslim Notables, Populist Protest, Colonial Encounters (Algeria and Tunisia, 1800–1904)* (Berkeley: University of California Press, 1997) and A. Hénia, *Le Grîd*, and in particular the work of Dalenda Larguèche, especially *Territoire sans frontières. La Contrebande et ses réseaux dans la Régence de Tunis au XIXe siècle* (Tunis: Centre de publication universitaire, 2002).

110 This name was for a long time reserved for the great informal markets situated on the border between Tunisia and Libya or supplied by products from Libya, but now extended and generalized to all informal markets.

111 Interviews, Tunis, December 2002, January–March 2005 and Sfax, December 2002.

112 C. Lainati, *Le Imprese stranieri in Tunisia*; M. Peraldi et al., 'Affranchissement et protection'.

113 Ibid., and the various contributions by M. Peraldi (ed.), *Cabas et containers*.

114 Interviews, Tunis, May 1997 and April–May 1998. In spite of the sensitive character of this activity, it is possible to obtain information on this sector in Tunisia, including within the UTICA, thanks to the discontent it arouses in many entrepreneurs.

115 According to the law, only 12 per cent of the 'production' of second-hand clothes by the sixteen recognized enterprises are authorized to enter Tunisian customs territory. In reality, fraud develops on the basis of false declarations and under-estimations of weight. In addition, associated industries (transformations of second-hand clothes into rags and nets) also lie at the origin of those

products smuggled in, by false declarations and under-estimation of the quality of the product. Interviews, May 1997 and April 1998.

116 M. Bouchrara, 'Comment dynamiser l'industrialisation rampante et l'innovation en Tunisie?', *Nouvelles de l'écodéveloppement*, MSH-EHESS, Paris, no. 32–3, March–June 1985; *7 millions d'entrepreneurs* and *L'économie tunisienne entre sa légalité et son identité;* J. Charmes, 'Secteur non structuré, politique économique, structuration sociale en Tunisie, 1970–1985', in M. Camau (ed.), *Tunisie au présent*, pp. 231–51; P.-N. Denieul, *Les Entrepreneurs du développement.*

117 The expression and the evaluation came from *La Contrefaçon et la piraterie*, p. 3, which notes a net increase in Tunisian fakes since 1995. I have also drawn on information gathered during interviews in Tunis with entrepreneurs, the Federation of Textile Workers, and the foreign services of cooperation, as well as in Paris and Brussels, with the OLAF, the European Anti-Fraid Office.

118 H. Boubakri, 'Échanges transfrontaliers et commerce parallèle aux frontières tuniso-libyennes' thus mentions that, in the south of Tunisia, crossborder commerce had made it possible to purchase tractors and heavy agricultural equipment, all impossible to acquire by other means.

119 Interviews, Tunis, Sfax, 1997–2005; H. Boubakri, 'Migrations, développements et réinsertion dans l'économie libérale. Cas de la Tunisie', in M. Berriane and H. Popp (eds), *Migrations internationales entre le Maghreb et l'Europe* (Verlag Passau, series Maghreb-Studien, 10, LIS, 1998) pp. 127–43; J. Charmes, 'L'apprentissage sur le tas dans le secteur non structuré en Tunisie', *Annuaire de l'Afrique du Nord*, 1981; P.-N. Denieul, *Les Entrepreneurs du développement*; L. Chouikha and K. Labidi, 'Dans l'attente de la démocratie … et des investissements étrangers. La Tunisie sans filet dans le grand jeu de la libéralisation économique', *Le Monde diplomatique*, July 1993, pp. 18–19.

120 M. Peraldi, 'L'esprit de bazar', and S. Mazzella, 'L'arrière-boutique du port de Marseille'.

121 P.-N. Denieul, *Les Entrepreneurs du développement.*

122 H. Boubakri, 'Échanges transfrontaliers'.

123 Interviews, Tunis, May 1997, April 1998, July 2000 and December 2002, and *La Contrefaçon et la piraterie.*

124 D. Larguèche, *Territoire sans frontières*, p. 9.

9 Reforms in Perpetuity: The Success of Reformism

1 M. Tozy, 'Représentation/intercessions: les enjeux de pouvoir dans les champs politiques désamorcés au Maroc', in M. Camau (ed.), *Changements politiques au Maghreb*, pp. 153–68.

2 As the reader will see, I have drawn on the problematization proposed by Michel Foucault for the reform of prisons (see the end of *Discipline and Punish*).

3 Ibid, p. 282.

4 See the decrees and the laws on the website or in the documentation of the privatization unit, especially law 98–9 of 1st February 1989 which fixes the legal foundations for public enterprises and profit-sharing. On this instability of definitions and data, see P.-D. Pelletreau, 'Private sector development'.

5   R. Zghal, 'Le développement participatoire', and A. Grissa, 'The Tunisian state enterprises and privatization policy', in W.-I. Zartman (ed.), *Tunisia: Political Economy of Reform*, pp. 109–27, which in particular mentions the objectives of job creation, income redistribution, town and country planning, and the control of the economy, among the aims and objectives of businesses (see especially p. 114).

6   On these two periods, see A. Grissa, 'The Tunisian state enterprises'.

7   Interviews, Tunis, December 2001 and December 2002. See also P.-D. Pelletreau, 'Private sector development'.

8   B. Hibou, 'Political economy of the World Bank's discourse', and *Les Fables du développement*.

9   Interview, Tunis, December 2003.

10 See the governments's website (www.tunisieinfo.com/privatisation) and the official brochures.

11 In nine years' research in Tunisia, I have never been able to obtain a single meeting at the Secretariat of State for Privatization or the Technical Committee for Privatization, in spite of repeated requests – as opposed to the Agency for the Promotion of Investments and, in particular, the Office for Upgrading.

12 All the quantitative data indicated in the following paragraphs are supplied, unless indicated to the contrary, by IMF, *Tunisia, Staff Report for 2000 Article IV Consultation*, IMF, Washington, DC, 19 January 2001, and in particular the official website (www.tunisieinfo.com/privatisation) and various evaluative reports of the unit supporting the privatization programme financed by the European Union in the framework of the MEDA.

13 176 enterprises privatized for a sum of 2,359 MDT for the whole of the period, and 97 enterprises privatized between 1998 and 2004 for a sum of 1,904 MDT.

14 On this first period, A. Grissa ('The Tunisian state enterprises') mentions the fact that the change in the percentage of state participation in the qualification of public enterprises, a percentage that rose from 10 per cent to 34 per cent in 1985 and to 50 per cent in 1989, made it possible to eliminate from the sector around a third of the businesses.

15 B. Hibou, 'Les enjeux de l'ouverture au Maroc', and C. Khosrowshashi, 'Privatisation in Morocco: politics of development', *Middle East Journal*, vol. 51, no. 2, Spring 1997, pp. 242–55.

16 Interviews, Tunis, January 1999 and July 2000; Paris, June 2000; Lisbon, January–February 2000 and March–April 2001.

17 The *Société de Ciment d'Enfidah* was sold to Uniland (Spain), the *Société de Ciment Jebel Ouest* to CIMPOR (Portugal), the *Société de Ciment de Gabès* to SECIL (Portugal) and *Ciment Artificiel Tunisien* to the Colacem Group (Italy).

18 Source: personal calculations based on a comparison between the different figures quoted above. It is worth noting that this information is not published as such, and that one needs to carry out a lot of work and to have considerable determination to reach this result. For example, the table on the division of the incomings from privatization by sectors of activity mentions the number of enterprises concerned, while the table on the proportion of foreign investments does not mention the incomings by sector, and hides the number of enterprises concerned. This unpublished information makes it possible to deduce the sensitivities of the Tunisian authorities, on this question as on others.

19 The Prime Minister's office – before 2002 the Ministry of Economic Development – and its overall management, the DGPV; the CAREPP, Comité d'assainissement et de restucturation des entreprises à participation publique (Committeee for the Improvement and Restructuring of Public Participation Enterprises); the Secretariat of State for Privatisation and the CTP, Comité technique de privatisation; the various restricted ministerial councils that meet for this purpose; the enterprises to be privatized; and the representatives of the ministries, departments and public organizations concerned.

20 For the 176 privatizations completed up until the end of 2005, 362 distinct operations have been necessary.

21 In particular the Direction Générale des Privatisations, 'Enquête de suivi des entreprises privatisées', *Manuel de procédures*, cahier no. 4, 2000–1.

22 See P.-D. Pelletreau, 'Private sector development'.

23 *Manuel de procédures*, cahier no. 4: the survey mentions that 50 per cent of the enterprises complained at this interference that was judged to be untimely and unfair. It is not possible to treat this proportion with any confidence, given the fact that the sample is too small to be statistically significant, but we can probably still deduce that this interventionism is neither marginal nor anodyne.

24 Quoted and analysed by P. Minard, *La Fortune du colbertisme*.

25 These alerts are transmitted by the traditional political channels and by more scientific publications. See for example UGTT, *Le Secteur textile-habillement en Tunisie*, and the ongoing UGTT study, 'Démocratie, développement et dialogue social'.

26 Interviews, Tunis, December 2002 and December 2003, and the follow-up study on privatized enterprises in 2000–1. See also S. Khiari, *Tunisie, le délitement de la cité*; H. Fehri, 'Économie politique de la réforme'; A. Bédoui, 'Spécificités et limites', and UGTT, *Le Secteur textile-habillement*.

27 B. Hibou, 'Tunisie: le coût d'un "miracle"', and 'From privatising the economy to privatising the state'.

28 On China, see A. Kernen, *La Chine vers l'économie du marché. Les Privatisations à Shenyang* (Paris: Karthala, 2004); J.-L. Rocca, 'La corruption en Chine: une construction du politique', *Mondes en développement*, vol. 26, no. 102, 1998, pp. 95–104. On sub-Saharan Africa, B. Hibou, 'The "social capital" of the state as an agent of deception, or the ruses of economic intelligence', in J.-F. Bayart, S. Ellis and B. Hibou, *The Criminalisation of the State in Africa* (Oxford: The International African Institute in Association with J. Currey, 1999); W. Reno, 'Old brigades, money bags, new breeds, or the ironies of reform in Nigeria', *Canadian Journal of African Studies*, vol. 27, no. 1, 1993, pp. 66–87, and 'Ironies of post-cold war structural adjustment in Sierra Leone', *Review of African Political Economy*, vol. 23, no. 67, March 1996, pp. 7–18.

29 Interviews, January 1999 and July 2000.

30 Interviews, Tunis, December 2002 and December 2003, and S. Bensedrine and O. Mestiri, *L'Europe et ses despotes*, pp. 100–2.

31 As is revealed by the disaster that befell Fly Air, one of whose planes had been chartered by Karthago in August 2005. See the press articles, in particular *Le Monde*, 24 and 25 August 2005; *Le Figaro*, 23, 25 and 31 August 2005.

32 Convention on financing no. TU/B7-4100/IB/96/0018, signed in April 1998 between the Tunisian government and the European Commission for a sum of

10 million euros. The ICEA/GOPA/COMETE consortium was in theory supposed to bring its mission to an end in March 2004, but an amendment to the contract, signed in May 2002, took into account the delays in its take-off and made it possible for the project to be completed. These arrangements ultimately had no impact, since the project was abandoned in anticipation of future difficulties. Source: interviews, Tunis, December 2003.

33   Interviews, Tunis, December 2003.

34   Interviews, Brussels, May 2002; Tunis, December 2003 and January 2005; Paris, August 2004.

35   The interpretation put forward by J. Ganiage, *Les Origines du Protectorat français*; C.-A. Julien, *L'Affaire tunisienne (1878–1881)* (Tunis: Dar el amal, 1981), A. Mahjoubi, *Établissement du protectorat français en Tunisie* (Tunis: Publications de l'Université de Tunis, 1977).

36   M.-L. Gharbi, *Impérialisme et réformisme au Maghreb*, and *Le Capital français*; N. Dougui, *Histoire d'une grande entreprise coloniale*; M. Kraïem, *Pouvoir colonial et mouvement national*; A. Mahjoub, 'Économie et société: la formation du "sous-développement", l'évolution socio-économique de la Tunisie précoloniale et coloniale', in M. Camau (ed.), *Tunisie au présent*, pp. 97–117.

37   M.-L. Gharbi, *Impérialisme et réformisme au Maghreb*, p. 111.

38   N. Dougui, *Histoire d'une grande entreprise coloniale*.

39   This whole narrative and its interpretation draw on press articles, and especially on interviews: Tunis, December 2002 and December 2003.

40   Madrid had done all in its power to favour the national telephone company and, after the rejection from the Tunisian authorities, it deployed all its ingenuity to 'punish' Tunis. Interview, Tunis, December 2003 and Paris, August 2004.

41   B. Hibou, *L'Afrique est-elle protectionniste?*, and 'Political economy of the World Bank's discourse'.

42   The number of *Nord/Sud Export*, 27 April 1996, relates this episode.

43   Interviews, Tunis and Brussels, between 1997 and 2000.

44   B. Hibou, 'Économie politique de la Banque mondiale'.

45   'Privatization and liberalization had proceeded at too slow a pace, relative to the existing potential' – which, in the veiled language of the IMF, is a harsh criticism. Source: IMF, *Tunisia, Staff Report for 2000 Article IV Consultation*, IMF, Washington, DC, 19 January, 2001, p. 25.

46   Interviews, Tunis, December 2002 and December 2003.

47   Follow-up of the privatizations: according to the survey of 2000–1, only 45 enterprises were selected by the administration and 39 of them replied; nearly two-thirds of companies did not fulfil the investment contract as laid out in the terms and conditions, but no action was taken against them.

48   From the official site, www.tunisieinfo.com/privatisation (my emphasis); according to this brochure, privatizations have three objectives – to consolidate public finance, to make the financial market more dynamic, and, above all, to guarantee the long-term survival of the business.

49   Cettex-Gherzi, *Mise à jour de l'étude stratégique du secteur textile-habillement*, summary report, May 2004; J.-R. Chaponnière, J.-P. Cling and M.-A. Marouani, *Les Conséquences pour les pays en développement*, and J.-R. Chaponnière and S. Perrin, *Le Textile-habillement tunisien*.

50   For the description and the operation of the upgrading process, I have drawn
     on interviews (Tunis, 1997–2000 in particular, and also Brussels, May 1997 and
     May 2002), and on a rather sizeable bureaucratic literature. See in particular S.
     Marniesee and E. Filipiak, *Compétitivité et mise à niveau des enterprises*, AFD,
     no. 1, Paris, November 2003, especially pp. 99–123; UTICA, *L'Accord de libre-
     échange Tunisie-Union européenne: impact sur l'entreprise tunisienne* (Tunis:
     Centre de formation des dirigeants des PME, 1995); Minister of Industry, Office
     for Upgrading, *Le Programme de mise à niveau* (Tunis, 1995), *Procédure de mise
     à niveau* (Tunis, 1995); and the *Bulletins du Bureau de la mise à niveau* published
     regularly since 1997.
51   All the quantitative data mentioned in this paragraph are, unless otherwise
     stated, taken from official sources, in particular the Bureau de la mise à niveau
     (available from its office in Tunis or on the net: www.pmn.nat.tn) between 1996
     and 2003 and the API (www.tunisieindustrie.nat.tn).
52   They now seem to represent no more than 10 per cent of the total number of
     investments and their rate of realization is only 29 per cent instead of 59 per
     cent for investments taken as a whole. These are the figures for 2001.
     Unfortunately, I have not had access to more recent data and the latest *Bulletin
     de la mise à niveau* does not give any quantitative data. However, everything
     seems to suggest that the problem is a persistent once, since the official
     publication of June 2004 mentions 'President Ben Ali's preoccupation' with this
     issue, asking businesses to devote 'more interest to immaterial investments,
     especially by endeavouring to improve the rate of surveillance, to promote
     quality systems and to consolidate the mechanisms of the enterprise' (*Bulletin
     de la mise à niveau*, Tunis, June 2004).
53   Report of the Ministry of Industry quoted and summarized in *Marchés tropicaux
     et méditerranéens*, 6 August 1999, and repeated in interviews of July 2000.
54   The most exhaustive and interesting analysis is that by J.-P. Cassarino, *Tunisian
     New Entrepreneurs*, and 'The EU-Tunisian association agreement'.
55   In the words of M. Camau, 'D'une république à l'autre'.
56   E. Bellin ('Tunisian industrialists and the state') shows that, whatever the
     discourse produced by, and the name given to, economic policy, this has found
     concrete and enduring expression both in a significant level of state
     interventionism and in a tendency favourable to the private sector.
57   For Tunisia, there are at least four applications of the model of calculable general
     equilibrium within the creation of the free trade zone: T. Rutherford, E. Ruström
     and D. Tarr, 'The free trade agreement between Tunisia and the European
     Union', The World Bank, Washington, DC, 1995; Comete Engineering, *Étude
     prospective de l'impact sur l'économie tunisienne de la mise en place d'une zone
     de libre-échange entre la Tunisie et l'Union européenne*, Ministry of National
     Economy, Tunis, November 1994; D. Brown, A. Deardorff and R. Stern, 'Some
     economic effects of the free trade agreement between Tunisia and the European
     Union', a paper given at the Egyptian Center for Economic Studies Conference,
     How can Egypt benefit from a free trade agreement with the EU, Cairo, 26 June
     1996; M.-A. Marouani, *Effets de l'Accord d'association avec l'Union européenne
     et du démantèlement de l'Accord multifibres sur l'emploi en Tunisie: une analyse
     en équilibre général intertemporel*, working document, DIAL, DT/2004/01.
     According to these judgements, the expected gains in well-being, obtained by

the rationalization of purchases, are more significant than the losses (the impossible reconversion of the entire capital due to its specificity or its obsolescence, and due to – at least short-term – labour). In consequence, free trade would be at best neutral or very slightly negative if not indeed positive in terms of growth (but not in terms of employment).

58   L. Jaidi, 'La zone de libre-échange Union européenne/Maroc: impact du projet sur l'économie marocaine', *Cahiers du GEMDEV*, no. 22, Paris, October 1995; B. Hamdouch, 'Perspectives d'une zone de libre-échange entre le Maroc et l'Union européenne: enjeux et impacts', *Reflets et perspectives de la vie économique*, vol. 35, no. 3, 3rd trimester 1996, pp. 273–96; A. Galal and B. Hoekman, 'Egypt and the partnership agreement with the EU: the road to maximum benefits', *The Egyptian Center for Economic Studies Working Paper*, no. 9603, June 1996.

59   For a detailed analysis of these necessary conditions, see B. Hibou and L. Martinez, *Le Partenariat euro-maghrébin*.

60   Interviews, Tunis, December 2002 and December 2003. The figures are those given orally by the Bureau de la mise à niveau, but also quoted in UGTT, *Le Secteur textile-habillement en Tunisie*.

61   These characteristics are not specific to the 'upgrading' process: the industrial zones created with town and country planning in view, in a highly bureaucratic way, are still empty. See the study of the Foreign Investment Advisory Service (an organization in the circle of the World Bank), quoted in *Marchés tropicaux et méditerranéens*, various numbers, in particular 28 June 1996; World Bank, *Actualisation de l'évaluation du secteur privé*, The World Bank, Washington, DC, May 2000.

62   Interviews, Tunis and Sfax, April–May 1997, April 1998 and January 1999.

63   Interviews, Tunis, 1997–2000. On the reluctance of businesses to get involved in the process, see also J.-P. Cassarino, *Tunisian New Entrepreneurs*. For their behaviour in recent years, UGTT, *Le Secteur textile-habillement en Tunisie*.

64   J.-P. Cassarino, 'The EU–Tunisian association agreement'.

65   F. Siino, *Science et pouvoir*, pp. 322–3.

66   Interview, Paris, July 2004.

67   J.-P. Cassarino, *Tunisian New Entrepreneurs*.

68   J.-P. Cassarino, 'The EU-Tunisian association agreement'.

69   See in particular P. Signoles, 'Industrialisation, urbanisation et mutations de l'espace tunisien', which draws a distinction between, on the one hand, state-led voluntarism and, on the other, the results, efficiency, and indeed effectiveness of the concrete measures.

70   Interviews, Tunis, 1997–2000. On the activities of warehousing and intermediation, Z. Daoud, 'Tunisie. Chronique intérieure', *Annuaire de l'Afrique du Nord*, vol. 33, 1994, pp. 713–45; on the strategy of splitting up businesses in the agribusiness and the textile industry, interviews, January 1999 and July 2000, and N. Baccouche, 'Les implications de l'accord d'association sur le droit fiscal et douanier'.

71   On normative enterprise, see J.-P. Durand, *La Chaîne invisible*, pp. 255–8.

72   P. Minard, *La Fortune du colbertisme*, p. 116, regarding the statistics of the inspectors of industry.

73   A thesis developed by J.-P. Cassarino, *Tunisian New Entrepreneurs*.

74   M. Foucault, *Security, Territory, Population*, lecture of 25 January 1978, p. 57.

75 All these expressions and details of strategies are taken from interviews, Tunis, July 2000, January–March 2005.

76 J.-Y. Grenier has clearly shown how the economic realm was transcended when the French state gave aid to eighteenth-century industrialists (J.-Y. Grenier, *L'Économie d'Ancien Régime*).

77 J.-P. Cassarino, 'The EU–Tunisian association agreement', and, in particular, *Tunisian New Entrepreneurs*.

78 Interview, Paris, July 2004, with my interviewee speaking of 'sound policies'.

79 There are no such procedures in the other developing countries of the Mediterranean. Morocco, for example, has adopted a much more 'liberal' approach, carrying out many studies (for example on competitive clusters), but without offering any particular financial or tax incentives. Interviews, Casablanca and Rabat, June 1998, February 1999, September–October 1999, October 2000.

80 See for example A. Larif-Beatrix, *Édification étatique et environnement culturel*.

81 L. Blili, 'Réformes et intendance. Cour beylicale, Tunis, XIXe siècle', paper given at the conference organized by O. Moreau, *La Réforme de l'État dans le monde musulman méditerranéen à partir de l'exemple du Maghreb*, Tunis, IRMC, 3–5 April 2003.

82 M. Foucault, *Discipline and Punish*, p. 285.

83 H. Arendt has shown the perpetual motion of political action that is inherent in totalitarian systems in her *The Origins of Totalitarianism*, especially ch. XII, 'Totalitarianism in power'.

84 In a quite different context, Adriana Kemp proposes an illuminating analysis of the simultaneity of such practices of inclusion and exclusion: see her 'Naissance d'une "minorité piégée". La Gestion de la population arabe dans les débuts de l'État d'Israel', *Critique internationale*, 15 April 2002, pp. 105–24 (English version: '"Dangerous population". State territoriality and the constitution of national minorities' in J. Migdal (ed.), *Boundaries and Belonging. States and Societies in the Struggle to Shape Identities and Local Practices* (Cambridge University Press, 2004), pp. 73–98)).

85 Y. Chevrier, 'De la Révolution à l'État par le communisme'.

86 This analysis is clearly akin to that carried out by Olivier Vallée on Africa – see his *Pouvoir et politique en Afrique* (Brussels: Desclée de Brouwer, 1999). In this book, he analyses the structural adjustments promoted by the World Bank in the light of the Protestant Reformation in Europe: the reaction of the African powers is here identified with the Counter-Reformation, which was never a head-on opposition but a permanent negotiation dropping the abandoned concessions and thereby renewing the appearance of procedures and methods.

87 M. Foucault, *Security, Territory, Population*, lecture of 18 January 1978.

88 This is shown by works such as P. Minard, *Les Fortunes du colbertisme* on Colbertist state intervention in France, or Polanyi, *The Great Transformation*, or J. Brewer, *The Sinews of Power. War and the English State, 1688–1783* (London: Unwin Hyman, 1989) on English 'liberalism'. On the way that the concept of 'collectivism' fails to analyse properly the changes in Russia, see O. Kharkhordin, *The Collective and the Individual in Russia. A Study of Practices* (Berkeley: University of California Press, 1999).

89   On democracy and authoritarianism, see G. Hermet, 'L'autoritarisme', in M. Grawitz and J. Leca (eds), *Traité de science politique* (Paris: PUF, 1985), vol. II, pp. 269–312; *Aux frontières de la démocratie* (Paris: PUF, 1983); G. Hermet (ed.), *Totalitarismes* (Paris: Economica, 1984); and J. Leca, 'Democratization in the Arab world'. On the rule of law, see M. Miaille, 'L'État de droit comme paradigme', and J. Ohnesorge, 'The rule of law, economic development and the developmental states of northeast Asia', in C. Antons (ed.), *Law and Development in East and South East Asia* (Richmond: Curzon Press, 2002) as well as 'État de droit et développement économique', *Critique internationale*, 18 January 2003, pp. 46–56. On governance, see G. Hermet, 'La gouvernance serait-elle le nom de l'après-démocracie? L'inlassable quête du pluralisme limité', in G. Hermet, A. Kazancigil and J.-F. Prud'homme (ed.), *La Gouvernance. Un concept et ses applications* (Paris: Kartala, 2005), pp. 17–47.

90   C. Bayly has analysed such processes of appropriation in connection with liberalism in India in the nineteenth century, in 'Liberalism and "moral economy"'.

91   I have already mentioned the case of Morocco in the Muslim world. China is another example, albeit in a quite different context.

Conclusion

1   This is characteristic of any authoritarian regime, as H. Arendt has shown, *The Origins of Totalitarianism*.

2   M. Foucault, *Discipline and Punish*.

3   For an uncritical analysis of the President's ways of governing, see the latest book to the glory of Ben Ali: F. Bécet, *Ben Ali et ses faux démocrates*, the third chapter of which is devoted to 'How Ben Ali governs'.

4   For all these examples relating to women, see H. Chekir, *Le Statut des femmes entre les textes et les résistances. Le Cas de la Tunisie* (Tunis: Chama, 2000).

5   Remarks made by a woman member of parliament, and member of the RCD.

6   S. Khiari, *Tunisie, le délitement de la cité*, p. 107.

7   For all this analysis, in particular the direct involvement of Ben Ali, see M. Camau and V. Geisser, *Le Syndrome autoritaire*. Starting from a very specific angle, namely that of scientific research, see also F. Siino, *Science et pouvoir*.

8   Y. Ben Achour, 'Le pouvoir réglementaire général'.

9   L. Chikhaoui, *Pour une stratégie de la réforme fiscale*.

10   Interviews, Tunis, December 2003 and January 2005.

11   S. Ben Achour, 'Les municipales de 2005', pp. 8–10, and N. Baccouche, 'Décentralisation et démocratie locale en Tunisie', in H. Ben Salah and H. Roussillon (eds), *Administration et changement: mutations structurelles et pénétration territoriale en Tunisie* (Tunis: Publications de la Faculté de droit et des sciences politiques de Tunis, 1991).

12   M. Kilani, 'Sur-pouvoir personnel et évanescence du politique', p. 2.

13   For the historical period, L. C. Brown, *The Tunisia of Ahmad Bey*. For historical continuity, L. Anderson, *The State and Social Transformation in Tunisia and Libya*. In a more nuanced version, M. Camau, 'Politique dans le passé'.

14   The opposition makes this a main theme in its critique of the 'Ben Ali régime': the Initiative Démocratique has thus justified its decision to put forward an

opposition candidate for an election, the results of which were known in advance. For this argument, see for example M. Ben Romdhane, 'Que l'étincelle reprenne', *Alternatives citoyennes*, no. 10, September 2004.

15 P. Brown, *Power and Persuasion*, ch. 1.

16 M. Foucault, *Security, Territory, Population*, pp. 243ff.

17 M. Kilani, 'Sur-pouvoir personnel', p. 3 (my emphasis).

18 On the *zaïm* as an *imaginaire*, see M. Kerrou, 'Le *Zaïm* comme individu unique'.

19 Although it commits the error of relapsing into neopatrimonial and culturalist analyses, Hamadi Redissi does bring out this problem of historical breaks and discontinuities in H. Redissi, 'Dynamique des moeurs'.

20 M. Foucault, 'Pouvoirs et stratégies', especially pp. 422ff.

21 E. Gentile, *Qu'est-ce que le fascisme?* In particular, he writes: 'The reduction of fascism to Mussolinism is a banalization of the problem of the leader in totalitarian regimes since, not content with neglecting the presence and the action of the mass organization, it ignores the fact that, without this organization, the very figure, function and myth of the duce, would have been historically incomprehensible' (pp. 262–3).

22 On sultanism, see J. Linz, 'Totalitarianism and authoritarian regimes', in N. Polsby and F. Greenstein (eds), *Handbook of Political Science* (Reading, Mass.: Addison-Wesley, 1975); J. Linz and A. Stepan, *Problems of Democratic Transition*, and H. E. Chehabi and J. Linz (eds), *Sultanistic Regimes* (Baltimore; London: The Johns Hopkins University Press, 1998), mainly for their introduction. For a use of the concept in the Tunisian case, H. Redissi, 'Dynamique des moeurs'. On praetorian regimes and their application to the Tunisian case, C. M. Henry and R. Springborg, *Globalization and the Politics of Development*. They class Tunisia as a 'bully praetorian regime'. On cultural leadership, M. Camau and V. Geisser, *Le Syndrome autoritaire*, ch. II, and M. Camau, 'Leader and leadership in Tunisia'.

23 M. Camau calls Bourguiba the 'keystone of an authoritarian formula' (C. Camau, 'Leader and leadership in Tunisia', p. 179), and views leadership as bringing into play 'a specialized elite, the political staff, its internal dynamics and its transactions both with other elites and with their followerrs' (p. 180).

24 H. Arendt, *The Human Condition*, pp. 167–70.

25 T. Mitchell, *Colonizing Egypt*, pp. 166ff.

26 M. Kerrou, 'Le *Zaïm*'.

27 M. Tozy, 'Éléments pour une lecture de sociologie historique'.

28 E. de la Boétie, *On Voluntary Servitude*, p. 216. See also the analyses of this text in C. Lefort, 'Le nom d'Un', and P. Clastre, 'Liberté, malencontre, innommable'.

29 L. C. Brown, *The Tunisia of Ahmad Bey*; L. Anderson, *The State and Social Transformation in Tunisia and Libya*.

30 S. Laghmani, 'La crise de la citoyenneté', *Attariq Aljadid*, September 2004; I. Marzouki, 'L'individu au mépris du citoyen'; H. Redissi, 'Dynamique des moeurs'; M. Kerrou, 'Le *Zaïm* comme individu unique'. For militant and political texts, see M. Marzouki, *Le Mal arabe*, or S. Bensedrine and O. Mestiri, *L'Europe et ses despotes*.

31 T. Mitchell, *Colonizing Egypt*; J. Dakhlia, *L'Oubli de la cité* shows that the collective memory of the *mehalla* transmits the image of a fluid and reversible

power, an ebb and flow of centralized power that stems from this very perception of the exteriority of the state and the neglect of the negotiations, collaborations and diversified relations with centralized power.

32   P. Veyne, *Le Pain et le cirque*. He writes: 'As often as not, iron-handed regimes are authoritarian less in order to impose respect for political or social interests than for the sole advantage of getting people to obey them *without any fuss and without arguing*; they do not imagine that authority can be exercised in any other way' (ibid., pp. 101–2, my emphasis).

33   P. Brown, *Power and Persuasion*.

34   For a presentation problematized in terms comparable to mine, P. Lascoumes, *Corruptions* (Paris: Presses de Sciences Po, 1999). For a somewhat different problematization, see D. Della Porta and Y. Mény, *Démocratie et corruption en Europe* (Paris: La Découverte, 1995).

35   J.-F. Bayart, *The State in Africa*; J.-F. Bayart, S. Ellis and B. Hibou, *The Criminalisation of the State in Africa*; J.-L. Rocca, 'La Confusion des devoirs: corruption et bureaucrates en Chine à la fin de l'Empire et dans les années 1980', *Revue française de sciences politiques*, vol. 44, no. 4, August 1994, pp. 647–65, and 'La corruption en Chine, une construction du politique', *Mondes en développement*, vol. 26, no. 102, 1998, pp. 95–104; G. Blundo (ed.), *Monnayer les pouvoirs. Espaces, mécanismes, representations de la corruption*, PUF, Nouveaux cahiers de l'IUED, no. 9, Paris, 2000; J-P. Olivier de Sardan, 'Économie morale de la corruption en Afrique', *Politique africaine*, no. 63, October 1996, pp. 97–116 (English version: 'A moral economy of corruption in Africa?', *The Journal of Modern African Studies*, 37 (1), pp. 25–52); special number of *Politique africaine*, 'La corruption au quotidien', no. 83, October 2001, pp. 5–114.

36   M. Foucault, *Discipline and Punish*, pp. 271–85.

37   See the biannual reports of Transparency International, the *Global Corruption Reports*, especially the number published in 2003. This classification is used in international meetings and by international bodies – see, for example, the *Global Competitiveness Report*, 2003.

38   Interviews, Tunis, January 1999 and December 2002; see also the discussion on Justice analysed in ch. 4, and M.-H. Lakhoua, 'L'encombrement de la justice pénale'.

39   J.-R. Chaponnière, J.-P. Cling and M.-A. Marouani, *Les Conséquences pour les pays*, and J.-R. Chaponnière and S. Perrin, *Le Textile-habillement tunisien*.

40   Interviews, Tunis, January 1999, December 2002 and January 2005; Paris, March 1999.

41   Interviews, governorates of Tunis, Nabeul and Monastir, December 2002, December 2003 and January–March 2005; all the expressions quoted are taken from these interviews. Generally speaking, the criminal activities of those close to the President are not mentioned openly, but my interviewees intimated them to me by using completely unambiguous expressions: 'high-up'; 'the people, you know', 'you know who I mean'.

42   The situation in other countries makes a critical analysis possible. Jean-Louis Rocca, for example, has shown how corruption in China (others have analysed Russia or East Europe) could not be considered as a dysfunctional, an unplanned practice, but that, on the contrary, it 'served as oil in the cogs of a complex

machine' (J.-L. Rocca, 'La corruption et la communuaté. Contre une analyse culturaliste de l'économie chinoise', *Revue Tiers Monde*, vol. 37, no. 147, July–September 1996, pp. 689–702), by encouraging overlaps between the public and the private – overlaps that explain the dynamism of China. For the countries of the East, G. Favarel-Garrigues, 'Privatisation and political change in Soviet and post-Soviet Russia', pp. 183–210 and F. Bafoil, 'From corruption to regulation. Post-Communist entreprises in Poland', pp. 48–76, in B. Hibou (ed.), *Privatising the State*; B. Müller, 'Pouvoir et discipline, du monde du plan à celui du marché'.

43 G. Favarel-Garrigues, 'Privatisation and political change', and G. Favarel-Garrigues and K. Rousselet, *La Société russe en quête d'ordre* (Paris: Autrement, 2004), pp. 72–5. See too, for the case of Bulgaria, N. Ragaru, 'La corruption en Bulgarie. Construction et usage d'un problème social', in G. Favarel-Garrigues (ed.), *Criminalité, police et gouvernement: trajectoires post-communistes* (Paris: L'Harmattan, 2003), pp. 41–82.

44 A. Kernen, *La Chine vers l'économie du marché*; J.-L. Rocca, *La Condition chinoise*.

45 O. Vallée, *Pouvoirs et politiques en Afrique*, and 'La dette publique est-elle privée? Traites, traitement, traite: modes de la dette africaine'.

46 M. Marzouki, *Le Mal arabe*, p. 97.

47 S. Bensedrine and O. Mestiri, *L'Europe et ses despotes*, p. 92.

48 A. Larif-Beatrix, 'L'État tutélaire', and *Édification étatique*; H. Redissi, 'Dynamique des moeurs'.

49 M. Foucault, *Security, Territory, Population*, p. 270.

50 Ibid, lectures of 29 March 1978 and 5 April 1978. The quotation is from *The History of Madness*, as cited in *Security, Territory, Population*, p. 329, n. 1. Translations from *Security, Territory, Population* have been slightly modified here.

51 Passage from the *Instructions of Catherine II*, quoted by M. Foucault, ibid., p. 329, note 2.

52 Ibid., p. 313.

53 Ibid. and G. Burchell, 'Liberal government and techniques of the self', in A. Barry, T. Osborne and N. Rose (eds), *Foucault and Political Reason*, pp. 19–36.

54 M. Foucault, 'Espace, savoir et pouvoir', in *Dits et écrits, IV*, no. 310, p. 272.

55 G. Burchell, 'Liberal government', p. 330.

56 M. Foucault, *Security, Territory, Population*, p. 322.

57 Ibid., p. 322.

58 Ibid., p. 367. M. Foucault describes the police as 'the rational art of government'; this emphasis on rationality is particularly significant in Tunisia, where the Plan is central and measures are always presented as a rationalization of previous practices.

59 Ibid., p. 340.

60 *Instructions of Catherine II*, quoted in ibid., p. 340.

61 *Supplement to the Instructions of Catherine II*, quoted in ibid, p. 340.

62 A. Desrosières, 'Historiciser l'action publique: l'État, le marché et les statistiques', in P. Laborier and D. Trom (eds), *Historicités de l'action publique* (Paris: PUF, 2003), pp. 207–21.

63   Ibid., p. 211.

64   M. Foucault, *Security, Territory, Population*, lecture of 5 April 1978.

65   See, on liberalism, M. Foucault, ibid., and *Naissance de la biopolitique*, lectures of 10, 17 and 24 January 1979.

66   O. Lamloun, *La Politique étrangère de la France*.

67   This, again, happens in other countries as well as Tunisia. This liberalization without liberalism can be found in many formerly socialist countries. For the case of East Germany after reunification, see B. Müller, 'Pouvoir et discipline'.

68   It is the entire distinction between regulation and control, between regulating and managing, that Michel Foucault analysed in his lectures at the Collège de France in 1978 and 1979 and more especially in the last lectures of *Security, Territory, Population* and the first lectures in *The Birth of Biopolitics*. 'The essential objective of this management will not be so much to prevent things as to ensure that the necessary and natural regulations work, or even to create regulations that enable natural regulations to work. Natural phenomena will have to be framed in such a way that they do not veer off course, or in such a way that clumsy, arbitrary, and blind intervention does not make them veer off course. That is to say, it will be necessary to set up mechanisms of security. The fundamental objective of governmentality will be mechanisms of security, or, let's say, it will be state intervention with the essential function of ensuring the security of the natural phenomena of economic processes or processes intrinsic to population' (*Security, Territory, Population*, p. 353).

69   An argument inspired by M. Senellart, 'Course context', pp. 369–401 (p. 400).

70   The complete inscription, in fact, reads: '7 November, Openness, Democracy, Rule of Law'.

71   B. Hibou, 'Political economy of the World Bank's discourse'; G. Hermet, 'La gouvernance'; M. Miaille, 'L'État de droit', which speaks of the 'repudiation of politics in the social sciences', p. 37.

72   M. Miaille, 'L'État de droit', p. 41.

73   J. Ohnesorge, 'The rule of law, economic development and the development states of northeast Asia', and 'État de droit'.

74   B. Hibou, 'Political economy of the World Bank's discourse', and B. Campbell, 'Governance, institutional reform and the state: international financial institutions and political transition in Africa', *Review of African Political Economy*, vol. 28, no. 88, June 2001, pp. 155–76.

75   R. Ben Achour, 'L'État de droit en Tunisie', *Annuaire de l'Afrique du Nord*, vol. 34, 1995, p. 246.

76   J. Ohnesorge, 'The rule of law, economic development and the developmental states of northeast Asia', and 'État de droit et développement économique'.

77   Khayr ed-Din, *Essai sur les réformes;* Ibn Abîl-Dhiaf, *Chronique des rois de Tunis et du Pacte fondamental*, ch. IV and V, critical edition and translation by André Raymond, vol. 1, text and translation, vol. 2, historical commentary (Tunis: IRMC-ISHMN, Alif, 1994); N. Sraïeb, 'Des droits de l'homme et de l'État de droit dans la pensée politique tunisienne du XIXe siècle', *Annuaire de l'Afrique du Nord*, vol. 34, 1995, pp. 93–9.

78   On this distinction between law and order, and the link with the policing state, see M. Foucault, 'La technologie politique des individus', in *Dits et écrits, IV*, no. 364, pp. 813–28.

79 The unconstitutional nature of the law is a recurrent theme of human rights activists. However, the 1959 law on associations, in its 1988 and 1992 versions, has always been refused a legal right of control of constitutionality. See H. Chekir, 'Quelques reflexions sur la cour de sûreté de l'État', *Revue tunisienne de droit*, 1980; R. Ben Achour, 'Le contrôle de la constitutionnalité des lois à la lumière de l'arrêt de la cour d'appel de Sousse en date du 11 avril 1988', *Revue tunisienne de droit*, 1989; S. Belaïd, 'De quelques problèmes posés par l'application de la norme constitutionnelle', *Revue tunisienne de droit*, 1983; S. Ben Achour, 'La liberté d'association'.

80 M. Camau, *Pouvoirs et institutions*.

81 M. Foucault, 'Le triomphe du plaisir sexuel', in *Dits et écrits, IV*, no. 313, p. 308.

82 M. Miaille, 'L'État de droit comme paradigme', p. 41.

83 Y. Dezalay and B.G. Garth, *The Internationalization of Palace Wars: Lawyers, Economists, and the Contest to Transform Latin American States* (Chicago; London: University of Chicago Press, 2002).

84 W. Benjamin, 'Critique of violence'.

85 This is borne out by the work of J.-F. Bayart, *The State in Africa*. For Portugal, see F. Rosas, *O Estado Novo, 1926–1974*, Historia de Portugal, vol. 7 (Lisbon: Circula de Leitores, 1994) and *O Estado Novo nos Anos Trinta, 1928–1938* (Lisbon: Editorial Estampa, 1986). For the Vichy regime, M.-O. Baruch, *Servir l'État français. L'administration en France de 1940 à 1944* (Paris: Fayard, 1997). For Mussolini's Italy, E. Gentile, *Qu'est-ce que le fascisme?*, and B. Sordi, 'Le droit administratif sous le fascisme'. For Nazism, C. Schmitt, *La Dictature* (Paris: Seuil, 2000). More generally, see H. Arendt, *The Origins of Totalitarianism*.

86 E. Gentile, *Qu'est ce que le fascisme?*

87 B. Sordi, 'Le droit administratif'.

88 M.-O. Baruch, *Servir l'État français*; M. Miaille, 'L'État de droit comme paradigme'.

89 W. Benjamin, 'Critique of violence'.

90 See in particular S. Ben Achour, 'Aux sources du droit moderne tunisien'.

91 H. Béji, *Désenchantement national*, p. 64.

92 See, inter alia, N. Baccouche, 'Les implications de l'accord d'association', and 'Regard sur le code d'incitations'; R. Ben Achour, 'L'État de droit en Tunisie'; S. Ben Achour, 'Permis de bâtir et régulation urbaine' and 'L'administration et son droit'; R. Ben Achour, for example, in 'La révision de la Constitution tunisienne du 25 juillet 1988', *Revue de science administrative de la Méditerrannée occidentale*, no. 26–27, 1989, pp. 117–27.

93 N. Baccouche, 'Regard sur le code d'incitations'.

94 This information, of which I have been unable to find any published analysis, was given me during interviews in Tunis, December 2003 and January–March 2005.

95 G. Agamben, *Homo Sacer: Sovereign Power and Bare Life*, trans. Daniel Heller-Roazen (Stanford, Calif.: Stanford University Press, 1998), p. 59.

96 H. Arendt, 'Autorité, tyrannie et totalitarisme', *Preuves*, no. 67 (1956).

97 This was brought out by Carl Schmitt and later by G. Agamben. See C. Schmitt, *The Leviathan in the State Theory of Thomas Hobbes: Meaning and Failure of a Political Symbol*, trans. George Schwab and Erna Hilfstein (Westport, Conn.; London: Greenwood Press, 1996) and E. Balibar, 'Le Hobbes de Schmitt, le

Schmitt de Hobbes' in the French translation, Carl Schmitt, *Le Léviathan dans la doctrine de l'État de Thomas Hobbes. Sens et échec d'un symbole politique*, trans. Denis Trierweiler (Paris: Seuil, 2002); and G. Agamben, *Home sacer.*

98   E. Balibar, 'Le Hobbes de Schmitt, le Schmitt de Hobbes', p. 11.

99   H. Béji, *Désenchantement national*, p. 82 (my emphasis).

100   S. Ben Achour, 'L'administration et son droit'; N. Baccouche, 'Les implications de l'accord d'association', and Y. Ben Achour, 'Le pouvoir réglementaire général'.

101   E. Balibar, 'Le Hobbes de Schmitt, le Schmitt de Hobbes'.

102   Lamarre, quoted by M. Foucault, 'The political technology of individuals', in *Essential Works of Foucault 1954–1984*, pp. 403–17 (p. 413).

103   For a presentation that justifies these practices, see the Memoirs (the limpidity of the remarks in them is enthralling) of the old strongman of Singapore, L. Kuan Yew, *From Third World to First. The Singapore Story, 1965–2000* (New York: Harper Collins Publishers, 2000). For a critical analysis, see B.H. Chua, *Communitarian Ideology and Democracy in Singapore*. For a Foucauldian analysis of these processes, see A. Ong, 'Urban assemblages: an ecological sense of the knowledge economy', in F. Mengin, *Cyber China. Reshaping National Identities in the Age of Information* (New York: Palgrave MacMillan, 2004), pp. 237–53.

104   M. Foucault, *Discipline and Punish*, p. 138.

105   S. Khiari, *Tunisie, le délitement de la cité*, p. 103.

106   M. Kerrou, 'Le *mezwâr*'.

107   On hunger strikes in Tunisia, there is a very good article by S. Khiari, 'Les dilemmes du jeûne militant', *Courrier international*, no. 627, 7 November 2002. This movement developed after 2001 and became visible after the much-reported hunger strike by Taoufik Ben Brik. Since then, hunger strikes have spread to social rather than political movements (the illegal or fraudulent closure of a factory, for example).

108   G. Agamben, 'Form of life', in *Means without End*, pp. 3–12 (p. 6).

109   As M. Foucault magisterially demonstrated in the three volumes of his *History of Sexuality*. For more detailed discussions on this dimension within the current context, see J.-F. Bayart and J.-P. Warnier (eds). *Matières à politique. Le Pouvoir, les corps et les choses* (Paris: Karthala, 2004), especially the introduction by J.-P. Warnier and the conclusion by J.-F. Bayart. See too J.-F. Bayart, *Global Subjects*, ch. VI, 'The global techniques of the body'.

110   See J.-P. Bras, 'L'islam administré: illustrations tunisiennes'; F. Frégosi, 'Les rapports entre l'islam et l'État'; Y. Ben Achour, *Politique, religion et droit dans le monde arabe* (Tunis: Cérès production-CERP, 1992); A. Larif-Beatrix, 'Habib Bourguiba, l'intelligibilité de l'histoire'.

111   F. Adelkhah, 'Logique étatique et pratiques populaires: la polysémie du *hejab* chez les femmes islamiques en Iran', *CEMOTI*, no. 10, 1989, pp. 69–85, and *La Révolution sous le voile* (Paris: Karthala, 1991), and *Being Modern in Iran*.

112   See the different communiqués of the ATFD and the LTDH, and the debate between the two institutions during the years 2003 and 2004.

113   Circular of 22 September 1981, renewed by the circulars of 6 December 1991 and 21 February 1992, which forbid Islamic dress to be worn by civil servants and in educational establishments, at any level.

114 See in particular the very illuminating article by Mohamed Kerrou: its advantage lies in the way it restores the historical dimension of this debate: M. Kerrou, 'Les débats autour de la visibilité de la femme et du voile dans l'espace public de la Tunisie contemporaine (milieu du XIXe –début du XXIe siècle)', *Chronos*, no. 12, 2005, pp. 37–77.

115 Extract from the decree of 13 July 1967 establishing the National Council on Dress.

116 Speech of 28 July 1962 in Tunis.

117 F. Moroy, 'L'Espérance sportive de Tunis: genèse d'un mythe bourguibien', *Monde arabe, Maghreb-Machrek*, no. 157, July–September 1997, pp. 69–77, and 'Football et politique à Tunis', *Correspondance*, IRMC, Tunis, no. 45.

118 M. Kerrou, 'Le *mezwâr*'.

119 I. Melliti, 'Seuils, passages et transitions. La liminarité dans la culture maghrébine', in M. Kerrou (ed.), *Public et privé en islam*, pp. 177–99.

120 Quoted and analysed by A. Larif-Beatrix, 'Chroniques tunisiennes', *Annuaire de l'Afrique du Nord*, 1988, p. 746.

121 I. Marzouki, 'La culture de la différence: une redéfinition des réformes démocratiques', paper given at the conference *La démocratie au Magreb*, March 2005 (quotation pp. 6–7), and I. Marzouki, 'La modernité, pour ou contre les femmes', in Ephesia, *La Place des femmes. Les Enjeux de l'identité et de l'égalité au regard des sciences sociales* (Paris: La Découverte, 1995).

122 F. Frégosi, 'Les rapports entre l'islam et l'État'; A. Larif-Beatrix, 'Chroniques tunisiennes'.

123 *La Presse*, 22 December 2003 (my emphasis).

124 But this is a recurring feature of the mode of government of the current President, who had begun his reign with a morality campaign, barely a fortnight after taking up office. Quoted by S. Khiari, *Tunisie, le délitement de la cité*.

125 On this episode, see the AFP telegram of 16 March and the communiqué of the ATFD the same day.

126 All these quotations are drawn from the Arabic-speaking press of Tunisia, respectively from *Al-Hadith* and *Al-Chourouk*, and also published in the French daily *Libération*, 7 June 2005.

127 This video cassette circulated from June 1991 onwards, among Tunis high society, and the information was disseminated generally by the malicious unofficial press and in particular by the weekly *Al Ialan*, but also by the official press (for example *La Presse*), by officials, and by the non-Islamist opposition. See O. Lamloun, *La Politique étrangère de la France*. Copies of the tape were offered to the French Embassy, for example, and the Minister of the Interior, M. Kallel, insisted on showing it to the foreigners he spoke with (interviews, Paris, January 2003).

128 Personal conversation.

129 E.g. Abdelfatah Mourou, considered as one of the most moderate leaders of *Nahda*, who froze his participation in the party in 1991 following the Bab Souika affair and now supports dialogue with the central power.

130 H. Arendt, *The Human Condition*, p. 55.

131 This is the word used by dissidents who are 'angered' (as they say) by the increasing number of hunger strikes and their 'facile' nature.

132   In reference to the speech given by Jacques Chirac during his last presidential visit to Tunisia – which caused a scandal: 'The first of human rights is that of being able to eat, to be looked after when ill, to receive an education and to have a place to live. From this point of view, it has to be acknowledged that Tunisia is far ahead of many countries'. These remarks were reported in the French press, see *Libération*, 5 December 2003, *Le Figaro* 5 December 2003, and *Le Monde* of 6 Decenber 2003.

133   I. Melitti, 'Seuils, passages et transitions'.

134   All these expressions are taken from interviews, Tunis, December 2001 and December 2002.

135   The words of a Moroccan senior civil servant, quoted by M. Tozy, *Monarchie et islam politique au Maroc*, p. 44.

136   The words of a Tunisian intellectual.

Index